THE ANZAC EXPERIENCE

Dr Christopher Pugsley is one of New Zealand's leading military historians. A former infantry officer in the New Zealand Army, he was Senior Lecturer in War Studies at the Royal Military Academy Sandhurst for 12 years before returning to New Zealand. His publications include: *Gallipoli: The New Zealand Story* (1984; fifth edition Libro International 2014); *On the Fringe of Hell: New Zealanders and Military Discipline in the First World War* (1991); *Te Hokowhitu A Tu: The Maori Pioneer Battalion in the First World War* (1995, third edition Libro International 2015); *From Emergency to Confrontation: The New Zealand Armed Forces in Malaya and Borneo 1949–1966* (2003); *Fighting for Empire: New Zealand and the Great War of 1914–1918* (2014); and *A Bloody Road Home: World War Two and New Zealand's Heroic Second Division* (2014). His most recent book, co-edited with Charles Ferrall, is *Remembering Gallipoli: Interviews with New Zealand Gallipoli Veterans* (2015).

Pugsley was Historical Director to the Gallipoli: The scale of our war exhibition at Te Papa Tongarewa – Museum of New Zealand. He is a consulting historian to The Great War Exhibition at Pukeahu – National War Memorial, Wellington. He was principal historian and narrator for the *Nga Tapuwae Heritage Trails* audio guides for Gallipoli and the Western Front released by the Ministry of Culture and Heritage in 2015.

Pugsley is a Fellow of the Royal Historical Society, an Adjunct Professor at the University of Canterbury, a Research Fellow of the University of Buckingham, a Distinguished Alumni of the University of Waikato and a Vice-President of the Western Front Association. He was made an Officer of the New Zealand Order of Merit (ONZM) for services as a military historian in the 2015 New Year Honours List.

THE ANZAC EXPERIENCE

New Zealand, Australia and Empire in the First World War

CHRISTOPHER PUGSLEY

Author of *Gallipoli*

Oratia
BOOKS

Front cover image: Detail from 'New Zealanders in the trenches in front of a captured commodious German dug out' (*G-13419-1/2, PAColl-5311, Alexander Turnbull Library, Wellington, NZ*); full image on page 10.

Back cover image: New Zealand troops in training behind the lines at an unidentified location during World War I. (*Photographer: Henry Armitage Sanders. G-12750-1/2, PAColl-5311, Alexander Turnbull Library, Wellington, NZ*)

Published by Oratia Books, Oratia Media Ltd,
783 West Coast Road, Oratia, Auckland 0604, New Zealand (www.oratia.co.nz).

ISBN 978-0-947506-00-1
Ebook ISBN 978-0-947506-01-8

First published by Reed Publishing (NZ) Ltd 2004
Reprinted 2006
This edition published 2016

Cover design by Cheryl Smith, Macarn Design

Printed in China

For Deanna, the other half of this Anzac experience,
and for our children, Joanna, Gareth, Susan, David,
and our grandson, Dylan;
and also for those originally responsible,
Olwen, Frank, Joan and Ray

'The past, which as always did not know the future, acted in ways that ask to be imagined before they are condemned, or even simplified.'

Paul Fussell, *Thank God for the Atomic Bomb*

'ANZAC — (1) Initial letters of Australian and New Zealand Army Corps used as contraction. (2) The area on the Gallipoli Peninsula occupied by the AIF and the NZEF. (3) A sarcastic name for a military policeman.'

W.H. Downing, *Digger Dialects*

CONTENTS

ABBREVIATIONS

AAG	Assistant Adjutant General
ADC	Aide-de-camp
AEF	American Expeditionary Force
AIF	Australian Imperial Force
AMR	Auckland Mounted Rifles
ANZAC	Australian and New Zealand Army Corps
AWOL	Absent Without Leave
BEF	British Expeditionary Force
BGGS	Brigadier-General General Staff
Bn	Battalion (800–1000 strong consisting of four rifle companies)
CEF	Canadian Expeditionary Force
CMR	Canterbury Mounted Rifles
CO	Commanding Officer (Battalion and Mounted Rifles Regiment)
Coy	Company (220 strong consisting of four rifle platoons)
CRA	Commander Royal Artillery
CSM	Company Sergeant Major
DMGO	Divisional Machine Gun Officer
EEF	Egyptian Expeditionary Force
En Zed	New Zealander
FGCM	Field General Court Martial
GHQ	General Headquarters
GOC	General Officer Commanding (Division)
GSO1	General Staff Officer Grade 1 (principal operations officer in the Division)
ICC	Imperial Camel Corps
LSI	Landing Ship Infantry
MEF	Mediterranean Expeditionary Force
MG	Machine Gun
MGGS	Major-General General Staff
NAMR	North Auckland Mounted Rifles
NCO	Non-commissioned officer

NZ&A Division	New Zealand and Australian Division
NZASC	New Zealand Army Service Corps
NZEF	New Zealand Expeditionary Force
NZFA	New Zealand Field Artillery
NZMR	New Zealand Mounted Rifles
NZPS	New Zealand Permanent Staff
NZSC	New Zealand Staff Corps
OC	Officer Commanding (Company/Squadron Commander)
OMR	Otago Mounted Rifles
Pl	Platoon (50 strong commanded by a 2Lt/Lt consisting of four sections, each 10–12 strong)
RHA	Royal Horse Artillery
RMO	Regimental Medical Officer
RSM	Regimental Sergeant Major
WMR	Wellington Mounted Rifles

Note to the 2016 edition

The *Anzac Experience* remains one of my favourite books, as it captures the evolution by trial and error of the New Zealand Division's military prowess alongside that of Australia and Canada in the First World War.

The research and writing involved walking every New Zealand battlefield on Gallipoli and the Western Front. It is a great pleasure to work with Peter Dowling (who published the original edition) and his marvellous team at Oratia Books and I thank them all.

Christopher Pugsley
Waikanae Beach, 2016

INTRODUCTION

The Anzac experience is inextricably interwoven into how New Zealand and Australia see themselves as nations. Anzac was a shared experience for a combined Australian and New Zealand force during the First World War, but the impact it had was different in each country. Indeed, working together in war confirmed how different we were as societies, with so much in common but moulded by two very different countries an ocean apart. What was similar was the need that war imposed to transform citizens into soldiers in both countries' armed forces, then to mould them into effective fighting machines. This is a path that is as old as war itself, and the principal theme of the book.

This book is a study both of war and of emerging nationality; how we came to see ourselves as citizen soldiers, as citizens of a country, and as members of a wider Empire. The Anzac experience is seen as something unique to Australia and New Zealand but by widening it to Empire, specifically the Canadian experience, the study shows that each country as a member of the British Empire groped its way down a parallel path in responding to the demands of war on an unprecedented scale. Britain itself is a silent partner in this story. No detailed comparisons of British divisions or British experience are attempted; they have been subject to extensive study and publication in the United Kingdom in recent years, and the bibliography provides the signposts for that journey. The emphasis here is on New Zealand, Australian and Canadian effectiveness in combat in an imperial context.

The book looks at various episodes encompassing the war in South Africa against the Boers in 1899–1902 and during the First World War of 1914–18. It assesses what the Anzac experience meant at the time to New Zealanders and Australians, and what it means today. Is it something shared between two nations or something uniquely national? This question is examined in a chronological survey covering the Boer War and its influence on peacetime citizen soldiering, and in turn the principal campaigns of the First World War: Gallipoli, Sinai and Palestine, and the Western Front. The study concludes with an examination of how the Anzac experience fits with the wider experience in war in the twentieth century by briefly comparing the major themes to the American experience in war.

The foundation of the Anzac experience in the First World War was strongly influenced by colonial participation in the war in South Africa against the Boers. I first looked at the New Zealand contribution to the Boer War while setting up and commanding the New Zealand Commissioning Course in the New Zealand Army in 1977–79. I was interested in this because key personalities such as Chaytor, Robin and Bauchop became permanent staff in the New Zealand Militia and were there at the foundation of the New Zealand Staff Corps (NZSC) and New Zealand Permanent Staff (NZPS), and in the 1970s it was still possible to talk to people who had a close working acquaintance with this generation. I returned to the Boer War again in my teaching in Australia and also examined it as one part of my research in Ottawa with the assistance of a Canadian Government Studies Grant. The Canadians were trailblazers in their response to the war in South Africa, being the first to appreciate and organise a national contingent that retained critical links for pay, welfare and reinforcements back to their government. The Australian colonies and New Zealand stumbled behind them in this, and had to evolve a system of national administration by trial and error during the course of the war.

This inevitably leads on to how that experience in South Africa influenced postwar citizen forces. Chapter three looks at how the need to raise an expeditionary force for imperial service formed the basis of Territorial planning in New Zealand, leading to peacetime compulsory military training, and a structure planned to sustain a force overseas for an indefinite period. This was triggered by the establishment of an Imperial General Staff in Britain, and grew out of a series of defence discussions linked to the Colonial and Imperial conferences in London. Australia and New Zealand both accepted a system of compulsory military training as the most efficient way of harnessing part-time soldiers, and adopted a standard Imperial model for their organisation and training. Canada, in contrast, retained its existing volunteer militia, which promised much but delivered little.

The conundrum that each society faced in marshalling its contribution to Empire for war in 1914 was how to balance national interest and citizen enthusiasm while at the same time providing a force capable of earning plaudits for its performance in battle. Sending the first contribution to a war that would be over by Christmas was comparatively easy — the hard part was maintaining the effectiveness of each dominion's contribution. This was determined by the country's ability to sustain a supply of trained reinforcements. New Zealand excelled at this; Canada eventually did so after it overcame the machinations and chaos left by its Minister for Defence, Sam Hughes, but Australia failed to sustain its flow of volunteers and this seriously impaired the performance of the Australian Corps in 1918. Sustainability of trained manpower was not appreciated initially by Australia or Canada and they suffered for it. How effectively they overcame the reinforcement problem influenced the performance of their national forces in combat, and became a means of measuring combat effectiveness. Indeed, sustaining manpower remains the key to understanding combat effectiveness in war to this day, and is also a major theme in this study.

The first major military involvement for Australia and New Zealand in the First World War was the invasion of Turkey during the Gallipoli or Canakkale Campaign of 1915. The landing by Lieutenant-General Birdwood's Australian and New Zealand Army Corps (ANZAC) gave us a day and an identity, the nature of which is examined in chapter one. The two chapters on the Gallipoli Campaign examine in turn the inevitability of a campaign of this type resulting from Britain's traditional maritime strategy, New Zealand's involvement in the campaign, then in closer detail the New Zealand Expeditionary Force's (NZEF) performance in the August offensive.

I see the attempt to force and then seize the Dardanelles Straits as part of the inevitable process of a democracy trying to learn the business of waging war by conducting what it saw as a maritime enterprise that took advantage of the traditional British strengths of naval power. Gallipoli was part of that learning experience. The overview of the New Zealanders on Gallipoli that follows provides a context to a study of the Gallipoli offensive of August 1915. This concentrates on the efforts of the ANZAC forces whose attempt to seize the high ground of the Sari Bair range was the primary purpose of the August offensive. The attacks at Helles in the south were feints, as was that of the landing of the much derided IX Corps under Lieutenant-General Stopford at Suvla Bay. This was also 'incidental' and very much secondary to the main effort out of the Anzac perimeter. It was Anzac success or failure that determined the outcome, rather than the failings of the Suvla fiasco. Indeed, it was New Zealand as the junior member of the Anzac partnership that had the primary role in this offensive, with the greater Australian numbers frittered away on a series of feints or, in the case of the 4th Australian Brigade, committed to the forlorn hope of taking Point 971.

The flawed nature of Birdwood's and Major-General Godley's planning hardly merited success, but was compensated for by the efforts of subordinate commanders such as Brigadier-General Andrew Russell of the New Zealand Mounted Rifles Brigade, who emerges as the outstanding New Zealand soldier to survive the Gallipoli Campaign. He was well served by Lieutenant-Colonel William Meldrum of the Wellington Mounted Rifles, who also survived, but central to the New Zealand story is the indomitable and difficult figure of Lieutenant-Colonel William George Malone of the

Wellington Battalion. Malone is the hero of my study *Gallipoli: The New Zealand Story*, first published in 1984 and now in its fourth printing.

I see the Battle of Chunuk Bair from 6 to 10 August as one of the defining moments in New Zealand history, where a handful of men were determined to hold on to what they had won and in doing so had the power to influence the course of a war. Chapter five reviews those critical days, and is based on detailed research into the notes and diaries of the Australian official historian, C.E.W. Bean. In particular it concentrates on the events of 9 August 1915, when the seaward slopes of Chunuk Bair were held by Meldrum's combined force of Wellington Mounted Rifles and Otago infantry. It was an epic day to rival that of the Wellington Infantry Battalion the day before, but it has been overshadowed in my writing by the events of 8 August. This was a chance to revisit it.

Before journeying to France with the New Zealand Division, the chapter on the New Zealand Mounted Rifles Brigade contains all the themes one finds with the evolution of the New Zealand Division but, one could argue, under even more arduous and trying circumstances. Once again it is a story of forgotten achievement involving perhaps the finest body of fighting men New Zealand has ever raised.

The chapter on discipline and morale in the New Zealand Expeditionary Force is but one means of tracing its journey from amateur to professional over the course of the First World War. It summarises the argument that I developed in my doctorate, published in 1991 as *On the Fringe of Hell: New Zealanders and Military Discipline in the First World War*. This is still one of the very few studies that place capital punishment in the context of discipline and morale within a national force, looking at the broad spectrum of offences. In asking what it tells us about New Zealanders at war, it speaks of universal truths in establishing patterns of behaviour that ring true for every country and every war. I place it in the context of the Canadian and Australian experiences, and here again it is one of the few works that provide such comparisons.

This chapter also emphasises the importance of Major-General Sir Andrew Hamilton Russell to New Zealand achievement and success on the Western Front. There has been criticism in New Zealand for my praise of Russell, in that I am seen to credit him with too much. However, my appreciation of his abilities has increased during my time at the Royal Military Academy Sandhurst, as I have learnt more about the Western Front and the armies of which his New Zealand Division formed a part. I believe there were few divisional commanders of his standing in any army and, as I argue, he stands superior to the Australian John Monash at that level. He exhibits the same strengths that underpin the outstanding corps commander on the Western Front, Lieutenant-General Sir Arthur Currie of the Canadian Corps, who also surpasses Monash in my estimation. I consider Russell to be the one figure of military genius that New Zealand produced in the twentieth century, and he remains central to any understanding of the outstanding performance of the New Zealand Division on the Western Front.

In the series of chapters that examine the New Zealanders on the Western Front I position the New Zealand performance in the context of the two ANZAC corps of which it formed an integral part. I also look at it in the context of Australian and Canadian performance in combat. The 'tyranny of distance' that divides New Zealand and Australia from scholarship in Europe and the US sometimes makes it difficult to see comparative performances in context. Monash and the performance of the Australian Corps stand centre-stage in Australian historiography of the war. However, as I argue in the chapter on the Canadian Corps on the Western Front, it was the Canadians who set the benchmark for tactical brilliance and who sustained this under their Canadian citizen commander, Lieutenant-General Sir Arthur Currie. The Canadians were at the forefront of the all-arms revolution that was built upon improvements in artillery techniques and technology combined with platoon-level infantry tactics, which are the keys to understanding the breaking of the trench deadlock on the Western Front.

The Australian Imperial Force (AIF) and the NZEF benefited from Canadian experience, but at corps level it was the Canadians who evolved a coherent tactical doctrine in 1918 that the exhausted Australian Corps was initially able to equal but not able to sustain. The Australian and Canadian Corps were the two outstanding corps in the British armies on the Western Front, but in measuring comparative performance I see Currie and his Canadians edging out Monash and his Australians for the position of premier corps.

In chapter nine I directly address the performance of Russell and Monash as divisional commanders on the Western Front. I remember the deafening silence that greeted my delivery of the paper on which this chapter is based at the Australian War Memorial History Conference in 1989. Finally General John Coates felt obliged to rise and say that it was not due to disbelief or any questioning of what I had said about Russell himself, but because I had produced this figure who was clearly an exceptional commander but one no Australians had ever heard of. Now here I was presenting him and comparing him to Monash, the Australian military icon. Russell is equally unknown in New Zealand. The Napoleonic adage that there are no good or bad battalions but only good or bad commanding officers is true at every level of command. The New Zealand Division was one of the finest fighting divisions on the Western Front; Russell was the divisional commander who made it so.

Chapter ten looks at the evolution of combat effectiveness in the AIF. I argue that the larrikin image of the irrepressible, irresponsible digger disguises the true nature of the AIF and the basis for its success. There were no intrinsic advantages in being an all-volunteer Australian force. The AIF had to go through the same learning process as the New Zealanders, Canadians and British Territorial and New Army divisions. It was a long, painful process involving many mistakes. It is customary to decry British generals of the First World War, but what this study shows is that they were an active and involved part of the evolutionary process of forming effective professional mass citizen armies of Empire. It is clear from my research that in 1917 Plumer's Second Army Headquarters provided a framework of planning and operating procedures in an atmosphere that allowed both ANZAC corps to develop into effective fighting formations. Initiative from Army level encouraged initiative within the New Zealand and Australian divisions of the two ANZAC corps.

The ANZAC Corps did not enjoy the experience of being a part of Gough's Fifth Army on the Somme in 1916 and in the battles before Bullecourt in 1917. Gough was a demanding general and although his army experimented with and encouraged the infantry and artillery revolution that was under way, it was in a more arbitrary fashion that brooked little criticism or advice from its subordinate formations. It was only when Birdwood's Australians were transferred to Plumer's Second Army in preparation for the Ypres offensive that they enjoyed the opportunity to address and solve the practical difficulties of defeating the German defensive system, which they then demonstrated so effectively in the battles before Passchendaele in September and on 4 October 1917.

I argue that it took until mid-1917 for Birdwood's I ANZAC Corps to become an effective formation. Gallipoli gave the ANZAC corps a reputation, but it was not until 1917 that this was matched by its combat performance. Lone Pine on Gallipoli, Fromelles, Pozières, Mouquet Farm and Bullecourt on the Western Front resound with tales of exceptional courage, endurance and sacrifice, but this should not be confused with effectiveness in battle; this had still to be developed, and it is not until September 1917 that we see a professional corps hitting its peak.

The larrikin image that is worn as a badge of honour by Australians today was the product of that learning process, a symptom of badly led, ill-disciplined battalions in 1914 that vanished as the AIF became more professional under commanders who knew their job, understood their men and were invariably 'strict disciplinarians' because that is what is needed in war. The resurgence of larrikinism in late 1917 and early 1918 was a symptom of a superb professional fighting formation — the Australian Corps — being pushed too hard and not receiving the reinforcements it needed to sustain its excellence. This was the result of an inefficient recruiting system based on volunteering and of a corps commander, John Monash, who had lost touch with the men he commanded. Exceptional in so many ways, Monash was as isolated as any British 'chateau general' and the Australian Corps paid in full for this remoteness in 1918 with the collapse of its combat effectiveness. It is for this reason that I place Monash second to Currie when assessing which of the two was the outstanding corps commander in the British armies in France.

The final chapter on the Western Front looks at the New Zealand Division in 1918. It is the story of a division that had to be restored to efficiency after its exertions before Passchendaele. One can see the parallels between its experience and those of the Australian and Canadian corps. In terms of preparation, planning and training the process is interchangeable; had the study been enlarged, one could have found a similar pattern in the better British divisions. However, it is the calibre of its leadership that makes the New Zealand Division stand out, and it is interesting to see how Russell commands his New Zealanders: confident in his subordinates, delegating tasks, giving guidelines and letting them fight their battles with the backing of divisional firepower. It is a picture of a professional division at its fighting peak, sustained by trained reinforcements, and in the hands of a consummate fighting commander — Major-General Sir Andrew Hamilton Russell.

In the epilogue I look at the parallels between the New Zealand, Australian and American experiences in war, and summarise the major themes that have been addressed in this book. Natural soldiers are rare individuals. The reality of war demands a sustained effort by professionals, and to achieve that in wartime with a citizen force is an expensive journey of trial and error involving enormous sacrifice. This is integral to the Anzac experience, and it is also the Empire story of the First World War.

This book grew out of a computer failure and a hurried audit of my files on themes that I had examined over the past 15 years. This presented me with the framework of a book that was all but written. My colleagues Drs Dan Todman and Paul Harris offered sound advice on the draft, as did my friends Dr Frank Glen, Ray Grover and Lieutenant-Colonel Kevin Arlidge. Ray Grover in particular interrogated me on my assertions and questioned the relevance of what I had written, forcing me to abandon comfortable clichés and think more closely about what I was trying to say. I also thank Dr Moreen Dee for her research on my behalf into the Monash papers both in the National Library of Australia and in the Australian War Memorial. Any mistakes and omissions are mine, but this is a far better book because of their contributions and I thank them.

I am fortunate to work on a common syllabus with 12 other military historians in the Department of War Studies, Royal Military Academy Sandhurst, under the benign encouragement of Dr Duncan Anderson. Each brings his own particular speciality to shared themes, providing an intensity of intellectual interchange that I have not experienced anywhere else. Like any department in any institution we have our differences, but underlying all is a shared passion for military history. This has been so stimulating. I have learnt so much in my brief time in the department, and while it is difficult to single out particular individuals I am grateful for the discussions I have had with fellow Western Front enthusiasts, particularly Dr Paul Harris and Lloyd Clark. My time here has given me the opportunity to walk battle ground in detail and argue through the whys and the wherefores with a wide-ranging audience of both academic and military professional. I have been very lucky and I thank them all.

I am grateful to Reed Publishing for keeping my books in print and for accepting this manuscript. Peter Dowling has been a perceptive editor with sage advice on the book's structure, and I thank him and all of Reed's staff, particularly Susan Brierley for working through my drafts and saving me from many errors, proofreader Eva Chan for her superb professionalism, Gillian Kootstra, designers Cheryl Rowe and Graeme Leather, and cover designer Sally Fullam. Early versions of three chapters have been published previously, and I thank the publishers for permission to include them here. I became sucked into a bibliography that grew and grew as I assessed my myriad sources, and I am conscious of what has been left out. I still consider, however, that with all its omissions it gives one a glimpse of the rich field in which one may search.

Also listed are the major archives and institutions from which I have drawn my research over the years. I acknowledge my debt to them and to all libraries and archives for their invaluable work, and I thank them for permission to publish the material listed in the notes and also the maps which are drawn from Sir Charles Lucas' *The Empire at War*.

As my dedication indicates, ours is a hybrid family drawing on Welsh, English, Irish, Australian and American roots, with a pinch of Swiss, German, Spanish and Italian thrown in for good measure. Combine this on one hand with a small-town New Zealand upbringing (Greymouth on the West Coast) and a Sydney girl from Leichhardt on the other and you have all the ingredients for a true Anzac experience.

Christopher Pugsley
Department of War Studies
Royal Military Academy Sandhurst
October 2003

ONE

New Zealand, Australia and ANZAC

I find the word 'ANZAC' a paradox that has a different meaning in Australia to that which it has in New Zealand. As is well known, it comes from the title of the Australian and New Zealand Army Corps that was formed in Egypt under the command of Lieutenant-General Sir William Birdwood in 1914. A New Zealander, Sergeant K.M. Little, who was working as a clerk on Birdwood's headquarters, coined the acronym 'ANZAC'. He had made a rubber stamp with the corps' initials on it to ink and register incoming mail, and C.E.W. Bean, the official Australian historian, records that he was the first to use the term by asking someone to pass him the 'ANZAC' stamp.[1]

Interestingly, the first title suggested for the corps was 'The Australasian Army Corps'. It was the New Zealanders who objected to this, knowing full well that it would be assumed that this was entirely made up of Australians. They preferred 'Australia and New Zealand Army Corps', with both countries' names being distinctly identified. In the same way, the mixed division of Australians and New Zealanders formed in Egypt and commanded by Major-General Sir Alexander Godley, who commanded the New Zealand Expeditionary Force (NZEF), was first called 'The New Zealand Division'. This time, and rightly, the Australians in the division objected. As Godley explained when he wrote to James Allen, the New Zealand Minister of Defence:

> We have hitherto called it the New Zealand Division, but now we have got two Australian Brigades in it … they naturally feel that they should be represented by name also, so I think the best way out … will be to call it the New Zealand and Australian Division, New Zealand coming first, as it is the nucleus on which the Division has been built, and as all the staff is New Zealand.[2]

'Anzac' as a name grew to encompass the corps to which they belonged, the cove where the Anzacs landed on 25 April 1915, the perimeter of the bridgehead they established and held on the Gallipoli Peninsula of Turkey, and most of all the soldiers who fought there — these were identified as the original Anzacs of legendary prowess, whose deeds and memory were originally the focus of the Anzac Day commemorations.[3]

Today it is a title enshrined in mythology, meaning something different in each case and to each of our two nations. In Australia the word 'Anzac' is used solely in national terms as a synonym for 'Australian'. Australians see themselves as 'Anzacs', and the spirit of Anzac as the national spirit of Australia unique to Australians alone. It represents everything that Australians believe about themselves and their country. It is the spirit of aggressive self-confidence that New Zealanders have never had. Australians go forth expecting to win in whatever they do. New Zealanders also want to win, especially against Australia, but never radiate that same certainty.[4]

Australia as a young nation, 13 years after Federation, anticipated that its sons would make their mark on the world stage when they went to war in 1914. The deeds of the Anzacs on that first morning on the Gallipoli Peninsula, which were reported by the British official war correspondent, Ellis Ashmead-Bartlett, were proof that this

New Zealanders and Australians of the New Zealand and Australian Division line the decks of the SS *Lutzow*, a captured German liner, en route to Gallipoli. *(Royal Military Academy Sandhurst Collection)*

confidence was justified. They confirmed the presence of a bold new nation on the world scene, exemplifying, in the words of an Australian editorial of 1918: 'That marvellous spirit and genius of the Australian and the immortal name of Anzac.'[5]

How Australians see the word explains why Patsy Adam-Smith's book *The ANZACs* makes only passing reference to New Zealanders, and then only in connection with the burning down of the brothels in the so-called battle of the Wazzir in Cairo on Good Friday 1915![6] The Australian television series of the same name told the story of the Australian Imperial Force (AIF) in the First World War. New Zealanders were occasionally mentioned, but not as 'Anzacs' — that accolade was for Australians alone.

In contrast, New Zealand has never seen the word 'Anzac' in national terms to mean simply a New Zealander — it has always meant 'Australia and New Zealand'. But this is the junior partner's perception, and from 1915 onwards there has always been a struggle to ensure that the 'and New Zealand' was noticed. There has always been something of a love-hate relationship between the two countries. This was evident in 1914 when the two national expeditionary forces — the NZEF commanded by the British Regular officer Major-General Sir Alexander Godley, and the AIF commanded by the Scots-born Major-General William Throsby Bridges — formed the Australian and New Zealand Army Corps under the command of Lieutenant-General Sir William Birdwood in Egypt.

> The Australian and more especially the town bred man is a skiting bumptious fool, who thinks nobody knows anything but himself. If we meet or see them in a restaurant or anywhere in town there is generally a row of some kind.[7]

This critical view was expressed by a trooper of the Canterbury Mounted Rifles in a letter diary sent home from Egypt. It is mirrored in the letters, diaries and recollections of all ranks from private to major-general in the NZEF for the period when the ANZAC Corps was establishing itself in Egypt before it set sail for the Gallipoli Campaign in early April 1915. It reflects similar criticism by New Zealanders of some Australian contingents in the Boer War.[8] One can trace such sentiments back even earlier to the New Zealand Wars of the 1860s, when the regiments of Waikato Militia recruited for service in Australia were referred to by New Zealand politicians as 'the scum and riff-raff of the streets of Melbourne and Sydney'. This led to the militia threatening to mutiny unless an apology was offered, which it was.[9]

As I mentioned, this is part of an ongoing love-hate, 'big brother' relationship that exists between our two countries. It is an expression of exasperation on New Zealand's part that Australia can so easily ignore New Zealand's interests and concerns and does so most of the time, and an equal exasperation on Australia's part when New Zealand takes a contrary view or has the temerity not to see things Australia's way.

For the 8417-strong Main Body of the NZEF in 1914, critical comments on Australians were the natural outcome of a growing *esprit de corps* as the soldiers moulded themselves into an identity that grew beyond the home town links and rivalries of the provincial regiments that made up the force. Having established individual unit identities, the force as a whole now compared itself with the soldiers of other countries, and the first obvious comparison was with the Australians. It started at the first port of call: Hobart, Tasmania. A soldier wrote:

> It seems great to be such a long way from home but we are all New Zealanders and now we are away from our own country we all stick together like glue ... We do not work and are fed and trained up to think that we are just it and fear nothing or nobody and the Tasmanians say that they have to admit that we are a better and smarter looking lot than their own.[10]

The Australian perspective of the time could be equally critical of New Zealanders. The diaries of the Australian war correspondent and later official historian C.E.W. Bean show his disapproval of New Zealand behaviour after an outbreak of drunkenness during leave in Colombo en route to Egypt in 1914: '... and we certainly saw numbers of them laid out in all directions on the landing stage. They have only dry canteens and they are liable to break out at every port they come to.'[11] Once in Egypt, Bean continued to assess and analyse the differences between the two nationalities that made up the ANZAC Corps. Naturally enough he came down in favour of his Australian countrymen. His description encapsulates the image of the Australian 'Anzac' that lives on in Bean's histories.

> I think we have to admit that our force contains more bad hats than the others, and I also think that the average Australian is certainly a harder liver. He does do bad things — at least things that the rest of the world considers as really bad; but it is also equally true that he has extraordinarily good points — more I should say than the English soldiers and than the New Zealanders. If he is unrestrained he is also extraordinarily generous and openhearted. He is not the least colourless or negative — you don't often meet an Australian who is without character.[12]

The different perceptions of the New Zealanders and Australians in Egypt reflected the levels of training and the degree to which the officers and non-commissioned officers (NCOs) in each force had got a grip of their men. Godley in the NZEF had got on top of this problem far more quickly than Bridges, his Australian counterpart. The image of drunken New Zealanders stretched out on the wharves in Colombo had been salutary enough, and Godley determined that this would not be repeated. It was not that the New Zealanders did not have their problems, but the Australians, with three infantry brigades drawn primarily from urban areas, had inherently greater problems in officer-men relationships. The officers, in the main, did not know their men, and the men in turn did not, as yet, trust and respect their officers. Cairo and the image of Australians suffered for it.[13]

The nature of the Australian fighting man was a primary theme in Bean's writings throughout the war, and the Gallipoli landings allowed him to assess both nationalities in battle. Once again he saw his Australian as superior to the New Zealander.

Three Australian soldiers stroll along Anzac Cove. (*Royal Military Academy Sandhurst Collection*)

And the truth is that there is no question [at least in operations such as we have had] that the Australian leaves the New Zealander behind. There is no doubt on this subject amongst those who have seen them fight here. The NZ man is a good trustworthy soldier; but he has not the devil of the Australians in him; the wild pastoral independent life of Australia, if it makes rather wild men, makes superb soldiers. The NZs are outspoken in their praise of the way the Australians fought. They are proud of any praise given them by the Australians …[14]

Bean would later add:

… the NZ man half consciously came to imitate the Australians, e.g. The Australian language was about 5 times as strong as that of the NZs — but the NZs began to adopt it. The Sydney men followed the Sydney custom of trying to get their backs and skins as brown as possible through sun-baking. The NZs followed them.[15]

Through Bean's eyes we see New Zealanders as pale imitations of their Australian counterparts, fortunate indeed to share in the reflected glory of Australian achievement — indeed, if Bean is any judge, we can blame a decline in moral tone and the increase in skin cancer in the twentieth century on the willingness of New Zealanders to copy the Australian example.

Certainly Bean records correctly the New Zealanders' admiration for what the Australians achieved in the initial landings on the first day of the invasion. He noted: 'The jealousy that existed between NZ and Australia vanished at one blow on the first day at Anzac — vanished utterly as far as the men were concerned …'[16] Anzac Day in terms of 25 April 1915 was recognised by the New Zealanders on Gallipoli as Australia's day and Australia's achievement. Indeed, any mention of New Zealanders in Ashmead-Bartlett's dispatches was the result of a fortuitous chance described by Godley in a letter to Colonel James Allen, the New Zealand Minister of Defence:

In Ashmead Bartlett's [sic] letter which you read with such interest the words 'New Zealand' and 'New Zealanders' was [sic] not used from start to finish by him. Fortunately before his letter was despatched, it fell into the hands of the Admiral's Chief of Staff, who is a friend of mine, and who inserted the words wherever necessary.[17]

In this way happenstance and an alert naval officer acting as censor on a war correspondent's dispatches wrote New Zealand into the Anzac legend. 'Anzac' as the name of a place refers to a small cove on the Gallipoli Peninsula on the Aegean coast of Turkey. The cove is formally known by that name today, and in 1915 it was also the name given to the 400 acres of ridges and gullies that formed the beachhead on a hostile coast held by Birdwood's ANZAC Corps. It also became the name for the experience shared by the soldiers within the beachhead. The word broadcast their reputation as fighting soldiers throughout the British Empire. Publicity about the Anzacs overshadowed the efforts of the British, French and other nationalities of Hamilton's Mediterranean Expeditionary Force (MEF), and more importantly the Anzac tradition came to symbolise the unique bond that exists between Australia and New Zealand.

This is how it is painted, but nothing is ever that clear-cut. The political strength of the Anzac relationship has always depended on national priorities, which have always come first. Indeed, Anzac as a relationship has in some ways meant the second-best solution, the one decided upon when it is impossible for Australia to do it alone. On numbers alone New Zealand has always been the junior partner, needing to establish its place within the working guidelines and organisation established by the larger partner, needing to make sure that its interests are heard and not just assumed to be the same as those of Australia. It was like this from the beginning.

In 1914, as the convoy carrying the two forces sailed from Prince George's Sound in Western Australia, news came of a revolt in South Africa that might see the convoy diverted away from its passage to Egypt. Major-General Bridges, commanding the AIF, was prepared to sacrifice the Australian Light Horse Brigade, which could go with the New Zealanders to put down the revolt, if it meant that the 1st Australian Division could continue on to Egypt and from there as he imagined to France.[18] The New Zealand linkage was expendable if Australian interests were at stake, and it has always been so. The crushing of the revolt in South Africa and the entry of Turkey into the war against the Entente powers dictated a different course of events, but from the beginning the Anzac association was always a marriage of convenience that took second place to the national interests of both countries. In Egypt and on Gallipoli the component parts of the ANZAC corps displayed different characteristics that were dictated by a number of factors, primarily discipline and training. The least important of these were some evident national traits:

> Now in the affairs of war there is also a difference between the New
> Zealander and the Australian. The Australian resembles the Irishman —

daring, desperate, and frequently reckless; the New Zealander resembles the Scot — equally daring, equally determined, but more canny and cautious. In brief, the New Zealander is more ready to weigh the issue and count the cost.[19]

Bean's image of the pre-eminent Australian soldier setting the standards of the Anzac soldier is myth. Size of force alone was the Australian advantage; both were largely amateur formations overmatched by the situation they found themselves facing. Indeed, one could argue that Australian command decisions by the first brigade commanders ashore on that first Anzac Day determined that the Australians would end up holding the right of the line and what was the southern flank within the Anzac perimeter — rather than the left on the more critical northern flank that faced the ascending ground towards the heights of Chunuk Bair.[20] This meant that the Australian role in any breakout would always be a secondary or minor one, because it was what happened on the northern flank, which was the New Zealand and Australia sector, that would determine success or failure. This is how it was in the August offensive of 1915. The seven Victoria Crosses and two thousand casualties in the Australian epic at Lone Pine were for a 'demonstration' that had questionable influence on the critical battle being fought for the heights of Chunuk Bair further to the north.[21]

However, the efforts of both were essential to holding the ANZAC corps' toehold on Turkey in those first fraught hours and days after the landing on 25 April. Although they were hampered by the Royal Navy blunder of landing the corps on the wrong beach, it was largely Anzac inexperience that frustrated success. The Anzacs greatly outnumbered the Turkish defenders on that stretch of coast, which was seen by the Turks as the least likely spot for a landing. However, changes in plan by the first Australian brigade commander ashore left the critical left flank facing the heights of Chunuk Bair unguarded. This, combined with the unwillingness of raw soldiers with but a thin veneer of military experience to dig in and consolidate after they believed the Turks had bolted, resulted in the leading Australian elements being surprised and disorganised by the Turkish counterattacks that began mid-morning on Anzac Day. Soldiers were killed as they sat on their packs in the scrub having a smoke. Anzac was a hard school where soldiers of both countries learnt war's realities. The pick and shovel became as important as the rifle and bayonet, and the best of the officers recognised that good men count for nothing and never fulfil their potential as soldiers if command is inept and officers and NCOs do not know their business.

It did not matter if he was Bean's image of a suntanned Sydneysider or a bushman from the New Zealand King Country — both showed equal potential as soldiers in displaying an adaptability and initiative that was not always evident in their British counterparts. What counted most was the calibre of their battalion and company commanders, and the soundness of divisional and corps planning. Battalions led by men such as Malone of the Wellingtons or Pope of the 16th Battalion would succeed while other Australian and New Zealand battalions would disintegrate because of too many officer casualties or indifferent leadership.[22]

This was equally true of divisional and corps staff. Competence was not the preserve of any single nationality. The litany of Gallipoli defeats for which the British are blamed, such as the charge of the Australian 3rd Light Horse Brigade at the Nek and the failure of the New Zealand Infantry Brigade to take Chunuk Bair on 7 August, are Australian and New Zealand blunders respectively. It was the British officer who took command of the Australian Division after Bridges' death, Major-General Harold 'Hooky' Walker, who was the outstanding commander on Gallipoli.[23] He reinvigorated the Australian Division and set standards that made it the benchmark division among the AIF for the war. He demanded and achieved a quality of staff planning for the Australian Division in the August feint on Lone Pine that was not matched by Godley's staff in the New Zealand and Australian Division in the assault on Chunuk Bair and the 971 feature. I believe that had Walker commanded the Chunuk Bair attack instead of Godley it may have resulted in one of the most brilliant victories of the First World War.

Anzac as a place and an experience caused a bitter sense of failure and an awareness of the enormous cost of poor planning and faulty administration. It saw the emergence of a high degree of professionalism in both forces that continues to be a defining characteristic to this day. Not at war to 'play the game', but rather waging war as New Zealand once played rugby — completely professional despite our amateur status.

The other reality of Anzac and the Anzac experience was a confirmation of difference. To administer a national force in war there has to be a national chain of command and communication that ensures that administrative needs are met; welfare facilities provided; casualties treated, repatriated and next of kin notified; mail delivered, pay received and trained reinforcements absorbed. Achieving this in adversity was also part of the Anzac experience. These needs could only be met by a national response. The Anzac experience on Gallipoli forced a better appreciation of the realities of war on the government of each country.

It cemented the identity of the New Zealand Expeditionary Force as a national body, which was confirmed by the formation of the New Zealand Division in February

1916. This was the 'national army' that General Sir Ian Hamilton had identified and spoken of during his inspection tour of New Zealand in May 1914, and which it had been New Zealand's intention to establish under Colonel R.H. Davies with the last three contingents to the war in South Africa against the Boers.

British authorities still lumped us together as 'Anzacs' and assumed that our interests were always the same. Gallipoli proved that they were not. In 1916 the Commander-in-Chief in Egypt considered merging the administration of the two countries' forces for greater efficiency. Godley objected:

> It would not be satisfactory to the New Zealand Government that any office should be established for the combined Australasian Forces. This was tried when we went to the Dardanelles last year and did not prove satisfactory with the result that last December the Australian and New Zealand [Administrative] headquarters were definitely separated, each under a Commandant, entirely independent of the other.[24]

Godley made quite clear both the question of the NZEF's identity and how he regarded his responsibility as the Commander NZEF. 'I was appointed to command the N.Z. Expeditionary Force on 1st September 1914, and, have commanded it since and am still commanding it. I am still paid by the N.Z. Government, and, as regards the N.Z. Expeditionary Force am the servant of that Government.'[25]

Independence and integrity became principles to be guarded by New Zealand and Australian commanders from that time forth. For New Zealand the formation of the New Zealand Division in February 1916, under the New Zealander Major-General Sir Andrew Hamilton Russell, confirmed this trend. This initiative was forced on the New Zealand Government by the Australian decision to expand its forces to five divisions. New Zealand had set in train the raising of one further infantry brigade in New Zealand, which, together with the existing brigade and Monash's 4th Australian Brigade, would provide the three-brigade structure needed for the standard British divisional organisation. Australian expansion meant that Monash's brigade was no longer available. Reluctantly the New Zealand Government accepted the need to find a third brigade, while worrying all the time that it may not be able to meet the ongoing manpower costs entailed.

On the Western Front in France and Flanders New Zealanders fought as part of the two ANZAC corps. Apart from a brief period in April–May 1916 when the New Zealand Division was part of it, I ANZAC was a *de facto* Australian corps, while II

Four New Zealand 'diggers' of the 9th Hawke's Bay Company of the Wellington Battalion, two wearing the 'lemon-squeezers' that distinguished New Zealand soldiers, enjoy a generous helping of rum while out of the front line in France. *(National Army Museum, Waiouru Collection)*

ANZAC had the New Zealand Division and Monash's 3rd Australian Division as its core with other Australian and British divisions rotated through. The New Zealanders also fought their first major battle in France — on the Somme from 15 September 1916 — not as part of II ANZAC but as part of the XV Corps. It would spend the last year of the war fighting as part of IV Corps, from March until the November Armistice in 1918. The New Zealand Division alone experienced the routine of most British divisions in being placed wherever need demanded, and it performed equally effectively either within II ANZAC Corps or as part of a British corps.

As their skills developed the New Zealand Division and the five Australian divisions became spearhead troops that in conjunction with the Canadian corps increasingly played a key role in the offensives of General, later Field Marshal, Sir Douglas Haig, the Commander-in-Chief of the British armies in France. Each national force strove to be best, with their respective governments living their success or failure, even though operational command was vested in Haig. Australian authorities and Australian commanders argued for the right to form an Australian corps and had ambitions to form an ANZAC Army. In fact they lacked the manpower resources to sustain these ambitions even had Haig been willing to contemplate such a formation, which he was not.

It was the New Zealand achievement on the Somme in 1916 that gave both forces a title that is used as a sobriquet for Australian soldiers to this day. The term 'digger' was given by British soldiers to the New Zealand Pioneer Battalion and New Zealand Engineers on the Somme as praise for their exploits as 'digging battalions', the term being used as an accolade to describe the skills needed in this new trench warfare. Field-Marshal Sir John French used it in a purely British context in June 1915 when he praised the men of the Pioneer Battalions for 'being of good physique and good diggers'.[26] It struck a chord among New Zealanders when they were spoken of in those terms on the Somme. By late 1916 'digger' had become the common term for New Zealand soldiers in the New Zealand Division, and it spread from there throughout the Australian divisions of the two ANZAC corps by mid-1917. Today it is thought that 'digger' was a term derived from the Australian goldfields or the New Zealand gumfields, and one that was in use from the creation of the force, which was not the case. C.E.W. Bean acknowledged its New Zealand origins:

> It was at this stage [1917] that Australian soldiers — in particular the infantry — came to be known, together with the New Zealanders, as the 'Diggers'. The term had occasionally been heard before, but hitherto had been general only among the New Zealanders, who are said to have inherited it from the gum-diggers in their country.[27]

As I have described, its origins were in fact much more immediate. They were captured at the time in a cartoon by Corporal W. Bell of the Rifle Brigade, who has a British General looking down at a New Zealand 'Digger' in a trench and asking him if he was an engineer or one of those 'Diggah fellows'. At the time, New Zealanders regarded themselves as the 'diggers', and the Australians were the 'Aussies' or 'Cornstalks'. The term was still used to describe New Zealand soldiers in the Second World War, but today the New Zealand connection has been lost. 'Digger' has been totally colonised by Australia, and it is now the generic term for an Australian soldier.[28]

In France and Flanders the New Zealanders and Australians shared a corps title and a common nickname, prided themselves on their ability to work together, and shared a healthy scepticism of high command, but the differences remained. Bean recorded

Tommy General: "Are you an engineoah or Are you one of those DIGGAH FELLOWS?" *(Corporal W. Bell, 3rd Battalion, NZ Rifle Brigade, pencil, charcoal and gouache sketch. National Army Museum, Waiouru Collection)*

the view of experienced Australian commanders on the differences evident between Australian and New Zealand soldiers.

> The New Zealander is much more like the Englishman ... more appreciative of appearances, he has a neater uniform, more brass and colour and cut about it — and less a child of nature than the Australian and more given to showing his respect for authority viz saluting. Therefore it is the custom of the British to contrast the New Zealanders' discipline and appearance to ours — and he honestly prefers him [the New Zealander] and no doubt believes he is right.[29]

In matters of discipline there were few differences in the Anzac approach, and I believe if one studies the film and photo records of the AIF on the Western Front it can be seen that Australian commanders were as particular about their soldiers' drill and dress as their New Zealand counterparts. As argued in later chapters, each borrowed from the Canadian experience on the Western Front and adopted a rigorous disciplinary policy. Commanders of both forces saw the death penalty as a necessary sanction. One hundred and seventeen Australians were sentenced to death in 1916–17 but a clause in the 1903 Australian Defence Act prevented Australian commanders carrying out executions. This remained the case despite a determined and prolonged campaign by Australian divisional commanders to have the AIF brought under the rules of the British Army Act in every respect.

The ferocity of the conscription referendum debate in Australia in 1916–17 ensured that this would never happen, but the Australian death sentences were awarded by Australian officers sitting in judgement of their own, in the firm belief that the sentence should be put into effect. This is something that contemporary Australia is reluctant to believe as it suggests that Australia had more in common with Britain than it likes to acknowledge. In 1914–18 both Australia and New Zealand saw Imperial Germany as a threat, believed that the Empire's cause was just, and saw this as a war that had to be fought and won. They saw no contradiction in being Australians or New Zealanders within the British Empire, as the title 'Australian Imperial Force' suggests.

Four soldiers of the New Zealand Division died by New Zealand firing squads in France and a fifth would die by British firing squad. Two of those executed by the New Zealand Division were Australian. Privates John Joseph Sweeney in 1916 and John King in 1917 were shot to death after being found guilty of desertion.[30] Today in hindsight we see them as two soldiers who, after prolonged combat experience — Sweeney as a tunneller on Gallipoli and King as an infantryman in the trenches — could no longer face the front line and its terrors. One notes that in endeavouring to escape the strains of combat they sought out the company of their own countrymen, not from knowledge that Australians had different disciplinary standards but for something I suspect was far more elemental — a longing for home. By the time they deserted they were both lonely men, outsiders among the new faces of reinforcement soldiers in their units, who sought solace in drink. Sweeney professed a wish to link up with the Australian tunnellers with whom he had served on Gallipoli. King defied repeated warnings and went absent without leave to knock about with Australians in the estaminets behind the lines on the Messines sector. One may ponder further, but indeed there is no answer to the question as to whether national traits such as those identified by Bean accentuated their isolation.

The two ANZAC corps built up the reputations of the soldiers of both nations. At

Messines and before Passchendaele in 1917 Australian divisions and the New Zealand Division fought side by side. This ceased with the formation of the Australian Corps, and the New Zealand Division became part of Godley's XXII Corps. Apart from Godley's position of Commander NZEF, it was like any British corps and indeed the New Zealanders did not fight any further major battles under Godley's command. They were thrown in with IV Corps to hold the German offensive in front of Amiens in late March 1918 and remained with that corps for the rest of the war. Australia put its priority on forming a national corps in the same manner as the Canadians, and got its wish at the end of 1917. The Anzac linkage had been superseded, demonstrating once again that Anzac in this sense had always a second-best option; important to New Zealand, not being big enough to go it alone, but less so to Australia, which found it convenient if the resources were available to form an association but soon discarded when not.

The ANZAC Mounted Division in Sinai and Palestine was the finest example of the Anzac connection working as we imagine it. First under the leadership of the Australian Light Horseman Major-General 'Harry' Chauvel, then under the command of the New Zealander Major-General E.W.C. 'Fiery Ted' Chaytor, the brigades of the Australian Light Horse and the single New Zealand Mounted Rifles Brigade worked together as one, detaching individual regiments in support of each other's brigades in a manner and to an extent rarely seen on Gallipoli and never in France.[31]

Yet even here small New Zealand elements forming part of units made up of a mix of nations, such as the companies of the Imperial Camel Corps or the New Zealand Mounted Machine Gun Squadron attached to the Australian Mounted Division, showed indications that there were perhaps command and administrative strains caused by this attachment that affected discipline and morale. Too much should not be made of this, however; 2049 New Zealanders are known to have served in the AIF, three of whom would be awarded the Victoria Cross, and in the same way, many Australians working in New Zealand joined the NZEF.

Anzac, then, in terms of our First World War experience showed both countries to be both increasingly aware of a sense of national identity uncomfortably linked by a single word, striving for a professionalism that each would achieve in France and on the scorched sands and stony hills of Sinai and Palestine. Fiercely competitive, especially against each other, the Anzac love-hate relationship continued away from the battlefield. This was seen in the fiercely fought Inter-Allied rugby competition for the King's Cup in 1919, where Australia defeated New Zealand. This was New Zealand's only loss in the round-robin competition before it went on to win the cup by defeating France in the grand final at Twickenham.

J. Ryan, captain of the NZEF All Blacks, receives the King's Cup from King George V after defeating France in the grand final at Twickenham on 19 April 1919. *(National Army Museum, Waiouru Collection)*

By 1919 Australia and New Zealand had through the First World War experience forged their own individual paths. In the words of Mary Boyd, they were 'autonomous communities within the British Commonwealth and separate members of the League of Nations — bent on going their own separate ways in the modern world. Federation and the First World War had destroyed the old sense of belonging to one or another of the seven colonies of Australasia.'[32] This difference was also seen in how both countries commemorated the enormous cost of this war. The Anzac Day commemoration is central to the Anzac tradition in each country. Once again, however, one is struck by the differences.

In Australia the focus is on those who went to war. William Morris Hughes' Government had been unable to persuade the country to accept conscription in two referenda. As a consequence the groundswell of public opinion that saw Anzac Day commemoration services held in almost every community in 1916 also led to their becoming a focus for volunteer recruiting to meet the voracious demands of the expanded AIF. In Australia you were a hero once you enlisted to go to war and this is still reflected in the Anzac Day parades, where the focus is on the veterans marching past on parade as their forefathers did in 1914–18. Most Australian war memorials list the names of all the men and women of the district who went to war, not just those who lost their lives. Their sacrifice is usually denoted by a symbol or cross beside the name, but each of the dead is simply one of the heroic volunteers. This march of heroes and heroines is still central to Australian commemoration, even if today it is the great-grandchildren who march proudly wearing a hero's medals on their chests, and are clapped and cheered by the crowds as they pass. The veterans are the 'Anzacs', but in this sense the term means 'Australian heroes' who still represent the fighting and national spirit of the Anzacs, those Australian men and women who fought in the wars since the Gallipoli Campaign of 1915. The Australian spirit of Anzac is alive and well, and it is something unique to Australia. This uniqueness became evident to me during a visit to Gallipoli, when a then serving New Zealand Army officer recounted how an Australian counterpart had bridled at the suggestion that the Anzac experience at Quinn's Post also had a New Zealand connection. I had a similar debate with my friend Bill Gammage, an Australian historian, during a visit on the 75th anniversary.

It is different in New Zealand. We have the same form of commemoration, particularly with the Dawn and Citizen Services, as John Moses has revealed in his important studies on the formalisation and spread of the Anzac Day ceremonies.[33] In New Zealand, however, the focus has always been on the cost of war and the names of the dead on the memorial; the parade has always been secondary to this. New Zealand memorials rarely list all those who went to war; they list the dead, and through the dead they illustrate the impact that war has had on New Zealand. Because of this difference there has been an easier transfer between generation to generation in New Zealand compared with the tensions that were evident in Australia in the last years of the twentieth century.

In the three years I spent in Australia at the end of the twentieth century it was evident that the dwindling numbers of Second World War veterans still saw Anzac Day as their day, and they worried about what would happen once they had gone. They had squatters' rights on the day and were reluctant to give these up, fearing that the next generation would not show the same respect and understanding. The fear was groundless. Those who served in the Gulf and East Timor have once again filled the Anzac ranks of Australian 'diggers', but these feelings reflect a stark difference to New Zealand.

In New Zealand the next generations had already taken over the day from the veterans. The flame had passed to those who had never served or known war, and were now prepared to ask questions about the people behind the names of the dead on the memorials. Who were they, why did they go, and what does this mean to New Zealand today? This has seen the regeneration of Anzac Day into a day of discovery, with crowds increasing year by year, driven by the young who do not carry the burdens and hang-ups of older generations scarred by Vietnam. It is they and their questions, which their parents cannot answer, that have triggered the rebirth and confirmed the day's centrality to our understanding of ourselves as New Zealanders.

The Anzac experience was a discovery of self, a growing awareness of what it means to be Australians or New Zealanders — one more step on the road to confirming a sense of national identity and national priorities. To each country the word 'Anzac' means something different. To Australians it is a synonym for 'Australian'. New Zealand as the junior partner has never been confident enough to use 'Anzac' in the same national terms. It has always been seen in terms of a partnership: 'Australia and New Zealand'. New Zealanders expect Australians to use the term in the same way, and are disconcerted when they do not. This struck me at the ceremonies on Anzac Cove on the 75th anniversary in 1990. The Australian Prime Minister, when speaking of the Anzacs, praised Australian heroes in national terms. New Zealand was represented by the Governor-General, Sir Paul Reeves, who spoke to the memory of the Anzacs in general,

With an escort of Scouts, New Zealand Returned Servicemen and war widows remember after an Anzac Day service in the 1930s at the Wellington Memorial with Parliament Buildings in the background. *(Robson & Boyer Photographers, F-75155-1/2, Alexander Turnbull Library, Wellington, NZ)*

and it was only later at the New Zealand ceremony at the New Zealand Memorial on Chunuk Bair that someone spoke for the New Zealand dead and their achievement.

Being heard is the traditional problem for the junior partner. It was a problem during the First World War, to the intense frustration of the New Zealand Prime Minister, William Massey, who wrote from London in January 1917:

> New Zealand soldiers have been given a good deal of publicity, but unfortunately the [British] public in many instances mix them up with Australians, and think they are one and the same. New Zealand itself is hardly ever mentioned, and the country suffers accordingly.[34]

One consequence of our shared experiences as Anzacs has been that given the involvement of a third party Australians and New Zealanders will happily forget the intense rivalry between them and gang up against the third. We do it today against the 'Poms' or 'Brits', Australia much more ferociously than New Zealanders. This anti-British element in Anzac also grew out of the Anzac experience in the First World War. To put petrol on the fire, however, I put its continuance down to Australia and the United Kingdom being too much alike. I see the two countries as much more similar in social institutions and, in Australia's case, unacknowledged class structures, than New Zealand. While New Zealanders are seen by Australians as being more British than the 'Brits', in reality they are anything but.[35]

Our national interests are not always similar, and history shows us that as a junior partner New Zealand has not relied and cannot rely on Australia to speak and act in New Zealand's interests. Nor should we accept Australian advice or policy as anything but an expression of the national point of view of a foreign government that has shared interests dictated by geography, history and culture. In any Anzac association, particularly the political act of waging war or the formulation of defence policy, our Anzac experience demonstrates that we must each pursue our own national interests within the partnership as vigorously as we do with other allies. This is the accumulated reality of the Anzac experience since 1915.

TWO

THE EMPIRE AT WAR IN SOUTH AFRICA, 1899–1902

> Whatever Tommy Cornstalk may be as a fighter, he owes little of his capacity
> for war to drill or instruction. He has known no riding-school, he has not
> studied the care of the horse in a little red book … He is feeble in the salute.
> He hardly ever knows when to turn out the guard.[1]

To understand New Zealand and Australian participation in the First World War, one
has to look at the colonial contribution to the war in South Africa from 1899 to 1902. The
journalist J.H.M. Abbott's description of 'Tommy Cornstalk' is the image of the colonial
soldier that has passed into legend, and one that Australians and New Zealanders have
been aping ever since. The reported performance of the colonial contingents from
the Australian colonies, Canada and New Zealand in South Africa confirmed on each
country's soldiers a reputation for being natural soldiers in the eyes of the public that
sent them. Unlike the Regular regiments and battalions of the British Army with which
they served, this achievement was not seen as the fruit of hard training and the discipline
of the drill square and parade ground. Rather it was, as Abbott described in *Tommy
Cornstalk*, daily life at the frontiers of Empire that made each citizen a natural 'highly
trained man of war'.[2]

> He has learned to ride through pine scrubs, down mountain sides, over
> rotten ground, about cattle camps. It has been his business to be a horseman.
> He has been more or less of a horseman from his babyhood. He has studied
> marching on the travelling stock routes; to endure thirst on the dry stages;
> to sleep in the mud or the saddle. Mother Earth is a familiar bed. His

> knowledge of scouting has been acquired young. You cannot teach a man to
> scout in a suburb or from a text-book …[3]

Contemporary accounts, regardless of whether they are Canadian, Australian or
New Zealand, convey this vision of naturally gifted volunteer soldiery. Any faults are
shrugged off or portrayed as strengths of individuality and initiative. Each colony
believed without question that they alone provided the best-looking soldiers and best
fighters in South Africa, who were far superior to their regular British counterparts.
In this chapter we re-examine the achievements of the Australian, Canadian and New
Zealand contingents in the war in South Africa. I will argue that outstanding colonial
achievement is as much a part of the mythology of the war as the belief that the same
colonial governments showed unhesitating support to Empire.[4]

The war in South Africa was the first one where Britain employed colonial forces on a
large scale. They had been used before in the Empire's wars, but in minuscule numbers.
South Africa was different. In addition to some 60,000 colonial forces enlisted from
within South Africa, 30,000 volunteers came from other parts of the Empire. These were
the so-called 'Irregular Forces' consisting of units of men raised specially for the South
African war and 'disbanded at or before its close'. It was an impressive show of support
for the Empire. By the war's end Canada had dispatched three contingents totalling at
least 7368 personnel, including 1238 personnel specially enlisted for the South African
Constabulary.[5] The Australian colonies despatched 16,378, including 6274 from New
South Wales, 3641 from Victoria, 2852 from Queensland, 1524 from South Australia,
1229 from Western Australia, and 858 from Tasmania. The sixth and final contingent,
consisting of eight battalions of the Australian Commonwealth Horse, were the first
post-Federation Australian units and the first Australian units to wear the rising sun
badge. The Australian Commonwealth Horse arrived in South Africa from March 1902,
with only the first two battalions seeing active service before the peace treaty was signed.
New Zealand dispatched ten contingents totalling 6416 personnel.[6]

In 1899 this was a far from universally popular war within the Empire. Canadian
opinion was split over support for Britain's ambitions in the Transvaal and Orange
Free State. French Canada was 'unanimously hostile to Canadian participation', and
English Canada was far from unanimous in its support.[7] The Liberal Government of Sir
Wilfred Laurier initially thought it could avoid military involvement, but was mistaken.
Joseph Chamberlain, Secretary of State for Colonies, wanted Canadian support to
give the war an imperial dimension, rather than for any practical value a Canadian
contingent may have had. Chamberlain's request, which Laurier initially refused, was

matched by pressure from Major-General Edward Hutton, a seconded British officer who commanded the Canadian Militia, to send a force. The ambitious Hutton wished to lead a Canadian contingent in South Africa, and planned and schemed accordingly. This, combined with pressure from a strongly organised pro-war lobby, saw Laurier reluctantly agree to send 'a certain number', the total 'not to exceed 1000 men'.[8]

There was the same reluctance in the Australian colonies, which reacted equally cautiously and at first rejected Chamberlain's suggestion that they should offer contingents for South Africa. This was in spite of the recommendations of the commandants of each of the colony's volunteer forces, who in response to overtures from London suggested to their respective governments that a combined force of some 2000 volunteers be sent to represent Australia. This was turned down by Britain, which wanted small groups of only 125 men in strength, which could be attached to existing British units. Finally it was British pressure on the New South Wales government that broke down colonial diffidence. It reluctantly agreed to send the contingent of New South Wales Lancers that was in England, at its members' own expense, competing at military tattoos. After this there were flurries of offers from Australian colonies as they were swept along on an initial tide of fervently jingoistic public opinion.

Even the Empire's man in New Zealand, Premier 'King Dick' Seddon, made sure he had public support behind him before offering a New Zealand contribution. Only then did he try to be first in a race with the Australian colonies to dispatch a contingent.[9]

Indeed, London itself was not sure what it actually wanted from the colonies in the way of contingents. It certainly wanted a show of imperial support, but was not sure how irregular soldiers could best be used in South Africa. This question perplexed the designated Commander-in-Chief, General Sir Redvers Buller. He did not want colonial cavalry, considering it 'would be quite useless',[10] and while he preferred infantry units of company strength he was prepared to accept mounted infantry.

On 3 October 1899 the Colonial Office cabled the colonies outlining the conditions under which the War Office would accept contingents for service. Raising, equipping and getting them to South Africa was to be at the colony's expense. Once disembarked the colonial contingents would be paid for by the British Government. The colonies responded with fervour and both Australia and New Zealand offered mounted riflemen. Australian 'Bushmen' or New Zealand 'Rough Riders', as they became known, were sent off 'for a year, or such longer period as their services might be required' with the cheers of the population ringing in their ears.[11]

In New Zealand thousands volunteered for the first two contingents, and with only 214 men required for the First Contingent and 240 for the Second, selection standards

A sergeant of the Fifth New Zealand Contingent ready to go on trek in South Africa. *(F-49721-1/2, Alexander Turnbull Library, Wellington, NZ)*

were rigorously enforced. At first the qualifications were so strict that it was 'impossible to get the necessary number'.[12] Each man had to pass a riding and shooting test, and if an applicant was not a member of a volunteer corps he was accepted on probation. There was only time for selection and parades before the contingents sailed. It was the same in Australia, with the first two contingents from Western Australia and Queensland raised from part-time militia and volunteers.

Only Canada ignored the British request for small contingents to be attached to existing British units and sent the 2nd (Special Service) Battalion Royal Canadian Regiment, the 1st being Canada's only regiment of permanent militia. The newly raised regiment was 1000 strong, organised into two infantry battalions each of 500 men, together with two Maxim machine guns mounted on artillery carriages. Each of the eight infantry companies was drawn from one of the Canadian provinces, and permanent militia formed a high proportion of its officers and NCOs. Commanded by a permanent officer, Lieutenant-Colonel William Otter, it was structured as a self-contained Canadian force with a regimental headquarters staff that included a quartermaster, paymaster, transport officer, chaplains, medical officers, nurses, instructional officers, an historical recorder, and later a postal corps.

It was sent as a self-contained national force and although Britain would undertake to pay its members on arrival in South Africa, Canada supplemented the difference between the lower imperial pay rates and those of the Canadian active militia as well as providing a separation allowance to families. In dress, equipment and administrative organisation it was distinctly Canadian. Its commander, Lieutenant-Colonel Otter, had to provide written reports weekly to both Canadian and British authorities, and questions of appointments, promotions and transfers of officers required the approval of the Canadian General Officer Commanding (GOC) in Ottawa. Any misunderstanding over administration of the force between Otter and his British superiors had to be referred to Ottawa, where if necessary the matter would be taken up with London on a government-to-government basis.

This first Canadian contingent was the forerunner, albeit in miniature, of the dominion expeditionary forces sent by Australia, Canada and New Zealand to the First World War. As Carmen Miller concludes, it was a defining moment in Canadian military history, and was the 'crucible of the Canadian Army'.[13] It suffered only from being raised and dispatched in 16 days without sufficient time for preparation or training. Despite careful selection nothing could disguise the fact that it, like the other colonial contingents, was made up of largely untrained amateurs with a minimum of military experience. What training they did before embarking and en route to South Africa was all the training they got. On arrival the series of British reverses of 'Black Week' saw colonial contingents sent straight into the field on operations under Lord Roberts, who replaced the unsuccessful Buller. As the Commissioners examining the war were later told, this method of 'sending untrained men straight into the field would be dangerous against most enemies', and so it proved in South Africa.[14]

The first colonial contingents took part in the series of engagements that were fought during the advance on and taking of Pretoria in June 1900. Each colonial force had its moments of recorded glory: the West Australian Mounted Infantry at Slingersfontein and a combined force of Victorians and South Australians at Pink Hill in February 1900, and the First New Zealand Contingent as part of Major-General French's Cavalry Division at Jasfontein Farm on 18 December 1899. It was here that Farrier G.R. Bradford became the first New Zealander to be killed.

They were in action again at Slingersfontein Farm on 15 January 1900, where the defence of 'New Zealand Hill' by Captain W.R.N. Madocks won French's praise in an action that saw Lieutenant Hughes awarded New Zealand's first DSO.[15] The New South Wales Mounted Rifles, and more particularly the infantry of the Royal Canadian Regiment, were in action at Paardeberg in February 1900. Despite being the best organised of the contingents, the Canadians demonstrated all the weaknesses of untrained infantry. Only the scale of the British victory at Paardeberg disguised the difficulties the Canadians had experienced in this their first major battle. Nevertheless, colonial achievement at Paardeberg and other actions grew in the telling, and was willingly accepted by the public at home.

After Paardeberg the war entered a new phase of guerrilla warfare where there were never enough mounted infantry to protect the long columns of British infantry and supply wagons against swift-striking Boer commandos of mounted horsemen. In response Britain asked the Empire for skilled horsemen who were also good shots. The Canadian third contingent was raised and largely paid for by Lord Strathcona, Canada's wealthy High Commissioner in London. Lord Strathcona's Horse, as it was known, was organised on British cavalry lines into a regiment of three squadrons. It was drawn from western Canadian horsemen, and commanded by Colonel Samuel Benefield Steele, formerly a superintendent with the North West Mounted Police. Steele was a sound leader and capable administrator who had the measure of the hard-riding, hard-living horsemen under his command. Lord Strathcona's Horse arrived in March 1900 and the men initially served as scouts to Buller's Natal Field Force.

The Australian colonies raised 'Bushmen' contingents funded in part by public subscription to form the third and fourth contingents in March and April 1900. In the same way New Zealand raised the Third, Fourth and Fifth Contingents of New Zealand 'Rough Riders', recruiting men who could ride and shoot, and funded by public conscription. Canada also raised a Second Contingent, which was again structured as a self-contained national force of two battalions of Canadian Mounted Rifles, and a brigade of three batteries of Royal Canadian Field Artillery numbering eighteen 12-pounder guns; together with headquarters staff these numbered 1289 men. Despite Canada's wish that it act as a united force, this did not happen in South Africa. It and the other colonial contingents were increasingly used in mobile columns, usually drawn from a number of colonial contingents and operating with British infantry.

After Lord Kitchener became Commander-in-Chief in November 1900 the colonials became involved in the guerrilla phase of the war, attempting to subdue small bands or commandos of Boers who could draw supplies from the farms. In this way comparatively small numbers frustrated and evaded the much larger British forces which, when Kitchener took over command, numbered some 210,000 and 'was overwhelming

Civic welcome in Dunedin to the First Contingent on its return from South Africa, 23 January 1901. *(18796-1/2-1/2, Alexander Turnbull Library, Wellington, NZ)*

only on paper'.[16] The bulk of the British forces were tied down protecting the railroad and towns in scattered and isolated garrisons supplied by large, vulnerable columns of bullock wagons that also had to be protected. Comparatively few members of this British force were actually involved in pursuing the Boer commandos. Only columns of mounted horsemen could do this effectively and as these were few in number, despite the colonial contingents, they were used to the point of exhaustion.

The members of the early contingents usually had some military background either as volunteers or as militia, but this experience became rarer as the recruiting of contingents continued. Although of excellent potential, the contingents usually suffered from a lack of skilled leadership among their officers and NCOs. The colonies had to take what talent was available. Major Alfred Robin, who commanded the First New Zealand Contingent, was selected because he was undoubtedly the 'smartest Commanding Officer in the Colony'.[17] Robin would demonstrate that this was but one of his talents as he performed more than competently in South Africa, becoming a national celebrity whose portrait appeared on commemorative medals, post office stationery and Christmas cards. However, a general lack of experienced leadership at every level within contingents was a critical factor. If available, professional imperial officers were seconded for service and placed in senior command appointments, but all the colonial contingents were limited by the nature of colonial volunteer forces. In New Zealand Volunteer officers and NCOs were elected to their positions by the votes of their men. In the later contingents Seddon, who was both Premier and Defence Minister, decided officer appointments and was seen to be influenced by friends and politicians lobbying on behalf of sons and acquaintances.

The cost of such selection methods had to be paid for in South Africa, where inexperienced officers and NCOs could not cope with the need to provide for the care and welfare of their men. Too often they had accepted the privileges of rank without the responsibilities that went with it. Contingents were generally enlisted for one year, which the British Forces in South Africa interpreted as meaning one year's service in South Africa. This generally meant that by the time contingents had learned their trade as soldiers the hard way on trek, it was time to send them home to be replaced by newly arrived and inexperienced men.

The colonials lacked the normal support one could expect in a Regular battalion. Most had no paymasters, and inexperienced quartermasters. With the exception of the Canadians, there were no administrative staffs to ensure that when men returned from weeks on trek tent lines were established, hot meals were prepared, and stocks of clothing and equipment were available to replace that worn out or lost on trek. More important was the issue of pay so that men could go into the nearest town and wash down the dust of weeks of hard soldiering. Failure to be paid was always the subject of great discontent. Men who were detached from their regiment, left behind sick, or on detached duty, as most of them were at one time or another, 'found great difficulty in drawing their pay' as they were usually given no proof of when and how much they were last paid.[18]

Men also wanted mail and newspapers from home, and word from hospital on the condition of the sick and wounded. None of this happened. Only the best of Volunteer officers understood that the care and welfare of his men was his first duty. In contrast, when a British column returned to base the Regular battalions would have tent lines established, cooks preparing food, a pay parade and the issue of mail, a sick parade in front of a medical officer for those needing it, and fodder and horse lines established. The colonials who rode in with them would be given a bare patch of ground and told to get on with it.

This was not the fault of the British; it simply reflected the way the contingents had been raised, with no understanding of how they were to be administered. It was no wonder that colonial discipline, while regarded as satisfactory on operations, was indifferent in camp. British authorities accepted that colonial contingents 'hastily raised' would always have difficulties with discipline, and they recognised the poor administration of colonial contingents, but the link between the two was rarely made.

At times the men took matters into their own hands, such as at Knights Farm in June 1901 when the men of the Sixth New Zealand Contingent found that once again no provision had been made for them except for a patch of bare ground, no food, and no pay. Disgruntled troopers called a meeting and a 'general strike throughout the regiment was decided upon'.[19] This was very much citizen soldiers taking steps to right a wrong as they would have done in the shearing sheds, mines or factories back in New Zealand, but such actions in the British Army were mutinous. As a result WO2 H. Davis of D Squadron, 6th NZMR, 'while on the line of march was tried and convicted for insubordination and was sentenced to be reduced to the ranks, discharged, lose all medals and gratuities and five years penal servitude'.[20] Davis's sentence was later remitted, but discontent and mutterings were common in most contingents where inexperienced leadership could not cope with the lack of administrative and organisational structure needed to care for the health and welfare of the men.

Even the Canadian contingents, which were provided with a full administrative staff, found that the inexperience of the staff led to similar problems. In the same way, Volunteer contingent commanders often had no experience of the Army Act in disciplining their men. Punishments were often arbitrary and unauthorised. Sometimes it was easier to get rid of the troublemakers by discharging them as unsuitable simply by saying so, but without informing the higher British authorities or the colonial authorities. Couple this with the nature of the warfare, which saw columns carry out a scorched earth policy, burning farms, killing stock and herding Boer families into centres so that the menfolk could not draw upon them for supplies and shelter, it was a wonder the reputation the contingents maintained in the field was as good as it was. In every contingent looting was part of the business, but both the Australian and the New Zealand contingents apparently had to acknowledge the skills of the Canadians who they regarded as perhaps the 'most accomplished "looter" in all the world'.[21] Irregular units like Lieutenant Harry Morant's Bushveldt Caribineers, which had been raised from colonials who had taken their discharge in South Africa, went beyond the rule of law and openly murdered Boer civilians. Morant and his deputy, Lieutenant Handcock, would pay for such deeds with their lives in front of a British firing squad on 27 February 1902.

It was during this guerrilla phase of the war that the colonial mounted contingents showed their worth in countering the Boer commandos. The colonials were employed on large sweeps to deny support to the Boer commandos or to track down the elusive

General de Wet, who kept the war going months after the remaining Boer resistance had ceased. This involved weeks of hard riding across the veldt:

> … day after day, almost without the bare necessaries of life, of our being in the saddle fifteen or eighteen hours at a stretch, and night after night on outposts without blankets, or else with wet ones … One's vitals aching for want of food and no visible way of getting it; the lips cracking from thirst, and one's whole frame so strained for want of sleep, that men nodded in their saddles, whilst others at every few minutes' halt would throw themselves on the ground and fall asleep almost before they got stretched out.[22]

Major engagements were few. The Canadian Second Contingent had heavy fighting as part of Major-General Smith-Dorrien's column at Van Wyk's Vlei and at Liliefontein in November 1900. In the latter fight, two Canadians were killed and 11 wounded in a running battle in which the isolated Canadian rear-guard prevented the ambush of the infantry and supply wagons of the main column. As a consequence of this action the Canadians were awarded three Victoria Crosses.

The Australians were involved in actions at Elands River in August 1900, Rhenosterkop in November 1900, and Haartebeestefontein in March 1901. The 5th Victorian Mounted Rifles were humiliated at Wilmansrust in June 1901 when the camp was surprised and 18 Australians were killed, 42 wounded and 50 fled to avoid capture while the Boers seized 100 of the Australian horses and killed a further 100.

The New Zealanders were involved in fighting at Mokari Drift in September 1901, at Zwartwater in January 1902 where 28 New Zealanders were captured, and at Langverwacht Farm in February 1902 where, of the 80 or so members of the Seventh New Zealand Contingent, 24 were killed and 41 wounded in heavy fighting against General de Wet's column. These were very high casualties for this phase of the war.

Disturbing reports of poor administration, 'strikes' and discontent within contingents led New Zealand and the newly formed Commonwealth of Australia to follow Canada's example with later contingents. These were formed as national units and organised with a headquarters and administrative staff capable of ensuring that the care and welfare of the men could be met within national resources.

In New Zealand the Eighth Contingent was raised to replace the Sixth and Seventh Contingents. It was 1000 strong, and divided into two mounted rifle regiments, one from the North Island and one from the South. Both regiments were under a brigade headquarters commanded by Colonel R.H. Davies CB, who emerged as one of the outstanding New Zealand field commanders of the war. His headquarters included pay staff, quartermasters and chaplains, as well as sheep and cattle dogs to assist in gathering Boer stock during the sweeps. Each regiment was officered by experienced men who had shown ability in the field.

The contingent was designated the 1st New Zealand Mounted Rifles Brigade. It was intended that both the 1000-strong Ninth and Tenth Contingents, which were organised on similar lines, would concentrate under Davies' command and work as a New Zealand formation. The Eighth Contingent was the only one to see active service. No men were lost in action although 16 were killed in a railway accident en route to the front and a further 20 died of disease. The Ninth and Tenth Contingents arrived during the peace negotiations, although one officer of the Ninth was killed and another wounded in a clash with a party of Boers after peace had been signed.

The Commonwealth of Australia formed the Australian Commonwealth Horse as the first units of the newly formed federal government. Eight battalions were raised from every state and territory under guidelines laid down by the GOC Australian Military Forces Major-General Edward Hutton, who had been instrumental in raising

Kitchener employed a scorched-earth policy in fighting the Boer commandos: farms and crops were burnt, stock rounded up or killed, and women and children concentrated into camps where because of overcrowding and lack of sanitation hundreds died from sickness and disease. (*National Army Museum, Waiouru Collection*)

the Canadian contingents before commanding a brigade in South Africa. Hutton no doubt applied that experience to the raising of the Australian Commonwealth Horse, and it too was designed to operate as a national column. However, only two battalions saw active service before peace was signed.

Of the 16,175 Australians who are known to have gone to South Africa, 251 were killed in action or died from wounds, a further 267 died from disease, and 43 were reported missing. Five Australians were awarded the Victoria Cross and one the Queen's Scarf for Bravery. Of the 8372 Canadians known to have served in South Africa, at least 244, some say 270, were killed in action, died of wounds or died from disease. Four Canadians were awarded the Victoria Cross and one the Queen's Scarf for Bravery. New Zealand sent 6495 soldiers to South Africa; 70 were killed in action or died of wounds, 25 were accidentally killed and 133 died of disease. Trooper Henry Coutts was awarded the Queen's Scarf for Bravery[23] after rescuing a wounded NCO under fire at Sannah's Post in March 1900. He was one of four colonials to be awarded the Queen's Scarf, specially knitted by Queen Victoria for distribution to the four most distinguished private soldiers in the colonial forces of Canada, Australia, New Zealand and South Africa.

For the Australians, Canadians and New Zealanders the Boer War marked the birth of their military reputation, the courage and initiative of the mounted riflemen marking them out from their British counterparts. The reported exploits of the contingents in South Africa saw a resurgence of volunteering enthusiasm in each country, and a belief by the public that the part-time militias and volunteers had proved they could respond effectively when the Empire needed them.

The public praise that Britain was quick to give, especially when more horsemen were needed, shielded the colonies from the reality of indifferent leadership, untrained soldiery, and poor administration. Few recognised that the colonial contingents that could go into action reasonably effectively in a guerrilla campaign against the Boers certainly could not play a similar role against an army of a European power. In that sense the Boer War was an aberration. The South African experience showed the promise that was there in the volunteers from Australia, Canada and New Zealand, but the discerning eye discounted colonial dash and initiative, and instead assessed how good they could be if properly trained, officered and administered.

The official reports recognised the need for some uniformity of organisation in the colonial forces if they were to be properly utilised again 'on the occasion of a big war in which contingents on a large scale are furnished by a number of colonies'. Those who had dealt with the colonial forces believed that administration needed to be improved and standardised, and certain 'broad lines upon which Colonial Forces, should be raised should be laid down beforehand, and details of establishment and pay, forms of attestation and discharge, etc, should be fixed and adhered to'.[24] If colonial resources were to be used effectively there was a need for imperial uniformity that should be supervised by an 'Inspector-General' who could periodically inspect 'recruiting centres and base and regimental depots' and see that a common standard was being achieved.

New Zealand proposed establishing an Imperial Reserve at the 1902 Colonial Conference, but this was opposed by both Australia and Canada in the belief that rather than fostering an elite for imperial service it was better to make citizen volunteers more efficient.[25] In 1902 that required more than the citizen volunteers and publics of Australia, Canada and New Zealand were yet prepared to give.

THREE

AT THE EMPIRE'S CALL: NEW ZEALAND EXPEDITIONARY FORCE PLANNING 1901–1918

In June 1913 Colonel James Allen, the New Zealand Minister of Defence in William Massey's Reform Government, wrote to his Prime Minister outlining the state of New Zealand's defence preparations, and the role New Zealand expected to play within the Empire should the need arise.[1] The Adelaide-born Allen wrote that in the 'future our most valuable aid can be given if we have everything ready to the minutest detail, to dispatch a force, the strength of which is known, at the shortest notice, fully equipped and organised on the same basis as the British Army'.[2]

Since 1909 New Zealand had developed its military forces into a provincially based Territorial Force founded on compulsory military training. This 30,000-strong force was designed to meet both the needs of home defence and also the provision of an expeditionary force of approximately 9000 men to be drawn from volunteers from the ranks of the Territorial Force. Equipment and supplies were being purchased and stockpiled, mobilisation plans drafted and the likely employment of the force assessed. In August 1914 the New Zealand Defence Forces were still some two years short of being fully effective, but pre-war planning enabled the swift and efficient deployment of the New Zealand Expeditionary Force (NZEF), with an advance party seizing German Samoa in August, and the Main Body sailing in October 1914.

Contrary to popular belief, New Zealand has never been better prepared for war in its history than it was in August 1914. Unlike Australia, which improvised and adapted to meet the needs of mobilisation in 1914, and very different from the chaos that surrounded Canadian mobilisation, New Zealand followed the guidelines that its military staff had established, and relied upon its existing Territorial units to provide both the recruiting structure and the principal source of volunteers for the NZEF.[3] That is not to suggest that New Zealand was ready for war in every respect, but the outline was in place and able to meet the enthusiastic surge of volunteers who flocked to the Territorial drill halls to enlist.

New Zealand's mobilisation provides an interesting comparative study when placed beside the more ad hoc solutions used by Australia and Canada in raising their forces for Empire service in 1914. There was not the unchecked expansion of the NZEF in the First World War that occurred with the Canadian and Australian forces. In 1914, with a population of one million people and some 250,000 males of military age, New Zealand had already assessed the likely size of force it could maintain overseas. This planning was to govern wartime expansion and provide the necessary arguments to put a brake on prime ministerial enthusiasm in the face of constant War Office pressure for more men.

New Zealand's defence preparations and manpower planning during the First World War have been the subject of two important studies: Ian McGibbon's *The Path to Gallipoli: Defending New Zealand 1840–1915* (1991) and Paul Baker's *King and Country Call: New Zealanders, Conscription and the Great War* (1988). This chapter does not attempt to cover the same ground. There is no examination of naval policy, which McGibbon covers in detail. Instead the focus is on the evolution of expeditionary force planning within New Zealand before 1914; how effective this planning proved to be on the outbreak of war in August 1914, and how the provision of new units and reinforcements evolved during the war to meet the insatiable demands of the Gallipoli Campaign in 1915 and of the Western Front from 1916 to 1918.

John Mordike's *An Army for a Nation* (1992) argues that Australia's defence history before 1914 was a contest between two ideologies, where the imperial interests of those who wanted to shape the Australian forces into an expeditionary force for overseas service won out over those who wanted to develop the force primarily for the defence of Australia. This is also a theme in Jeffrey Grey's *The Australian Army* (2001).[4] There was no such debate in New Zealand. As the New Zealand parliamentary records show, it was accepted almost without question that if the Empire asked then New Zealand would respond with an expeditionary force.[5]

Let us look at the evolution of New Zealand expeditionary force planning. To be ready to respond to the Empire's call was a matter of pride for the dominion of New Zealand. The country's Boer War experience had demonstrated the difficulties involved in raising contingents for overseas service. The quality and performance of the later contingents in South Africa was inferior to the first contingents, which included those few with military background and experience. Poor leadership and training threatened the reputation won by the first New Zealand contingents. While there was a generally held public belief in the natural ability of the New Zealand volunteers, the *Report into the War in South Africa* was rightly critical of the quality of many of the officers. The organisation, administration and logistics of the contingents were faulty at best. As discussed in the previous chapter, to overcome these deficiencies the last three New Zealand contingents (Eighth, Ninth and Tenth, each 1000 strong) were planned to operate as a self-contained and self-administered brigade under specially selected officers who had already proved themselves in South Africa.

The end of the war meant that only the Eighth Contingent saw active service, but the need for sound organisation of New Zealand's military forces was self-evident to the more discerning New Zealand officers who served in South Africa. Many of these, such as Robin, Davies[6] and Bauchop,[7] were appointed to positions in the Permanent Militia on their return to New Zealand. In 1902 the New Zealand premier, 'King Dick' Seddon, was keen to capitalise on New Zealand's role in South Africa and championed the formation of an Imperial Reserve drawn from the colonies. New Zealand for its part was willing to raise a 600-man 'New Zealand Regiment' for service in India as the basis for a 5000-strong Imperial Reserve. This was partly an expression of an emerging New Zealand nationalism that found its voice in a willingness to be seen to serve the Empire and, like many of Seddon's proposals, lapsed after he had milked it for all the publicity he could get from it, both in New Zealand and in Britain.

At the beginning of the twentieth century the New Zealand military forces consisted of a minuscule permanent militia, and myriad volunteer corps of all shapes and sizes, all of dubious military worth.[8] Its military efficiency was made even more questionable by the practice of electing officers and NCOs to appointments within the various corps. In defence issues New Zealand sheltered comfortably under the shield of the Royal Navy, and while the invitation to join the Australian Commonwealth had been made, New Zealand had no interest in substituting Australia for Great Britain. Japan's victory in the Russo-Japanese War and the beginning of the naval race with Germany made the dominion of New Zealand increasingly aware of the deteriorating strategic position of the Empire in the Pacific, and of the inadequacies of New Zealand's military forces.

The Liberal governments of Richard Seddon (1893–1906) and Sir Joseph Ward (1906–1911) were reluctant to change the system from one based on volunteers to one based on compulsory military service, as was being increasingly advocated in some circles in New Zealand. Some improvements were made to the volunteer system after 1901. Pay for attendance was introduced, and the various volunteer companies were gradually formed into provincially based battalions, but as the annual reports to Parliament show there was still little training of any military worth, and no suggestion that the lessons learned by hard experience in the Boer War had taken permanent root.

The formation of the Imperial General Staff in Britain in 1907 was followed by attempts to standardise staff and organisational procedures throughout the Empire. The role of the dominions in imperial defence was raised at the 1909 Imperial Conference, which was attended by Prime Minister Sir Joseph Ward and the Inspector-General of the New Zealand Defence Forces, Colonel R.H. Davies. The naval threat from Germany had seen New Zealand offer Britain a 'Dreadnaught' for the Royal Navy and a second if necessary. Similar improvements were now seen to be equally necessary to its land forces.[9] Ward asked the Chief of Imperial General Staff, General Sir William Nicholson, to recommend a plan for New Zealand's military forces that would include the number of properly trained troops considered necessary for the 'local defence of New Zealand, the method and organisation of such troops and the organisation of the Expeditionary Force'.[10]

In response to this Nicholson produced a 'Scheme for the Reorganization of the Military Forces of New Zealand'. This document established the guidelines for a radical reorganisation of New Zealand military structure and became the guiding document for the formation of the New Zealand Territorial Force. It examined New Zealand's strategic situation and drew conclusions and made recommendations on the size and organisation of an army necessary for home defence, expeditionary action and, most important of all, how the peace establishment would cope with the provision of reinforcements in war. Nicholson's scheme was to determine New Zealand's level of contribution during the First World War, and shaped the structure of the New Zealand Defence Forces for the next 50 years.

In his proposals, Nicholson accepted 'as a fundamental axiom that Sea Power is essential to the existence of the British Empire'. As long as Britain was able to maintain its superiority at sea, 'the safety of the component parts of the Empire cannot be seriously threatened or their integrity permanently endangered by organised attack from overseas'.[11] However, the relative isolation of New Zealand meant that it had to provide 'a military force adequate, not only to deal promptly with small raids, but also to ensure local safety and public confidence until our superiority at sea has been decisively and comprehensively asserted'.[12] Nicholson's planning was based on the premise that local forces should be big enough to make an invasion impossible for a small force and dangerous for a large one. An invading force would have to be of such a size that its passage could be identified and intercepted by the Royal Navy and that the very risk of this taking place would 'render the operation extremely hazardous if not impracticable'.[13]

Using *The New Zealand Official Yearbook 1908* as a guide, and assisted by the New Zealand Inspector-General, Colonel R.H. Davies, the General Staff estimated that New Zealand could sustain an army of 30,000. This calculation was based on the existing male population of 500,000, with 160,000 of these between 21 and 40 years of age (86,000 in the North Island and 74,000 in the South Island).[14] It was estimated that this would force an enemy to embark at least 10,000 men for any serious operation. The preparations necessary to ship such a force, together with naval escorts, would alert British authorities and enable the Royal Navy to deploy and intercept the threat. What was of equal importance, from an Imperial point of view, was that an army of 30,000 'would enable the Government of New Zealand … to employ some portion of that force for Imperial purposes outside the dominion without seriously dislocating the organization for home defence'.[15]

In detail it was planned that New Zealand's principal ports of Auckland, Wellington and Lyttelton needed to be defended and mobile forces raised to deal with any raids made against them. There was a laid-down formula for the number of garrison artillery and engineers needed for the defence of the major ports, and a mobile force of some 7500 all arms was suggested as sufficient to deal with raiding parties landed by warship. A strength of 30,000 could meet these local defence requirements and also release a 'force of about 10,000 all ranks for the general purposes of Empire without any dislocation of the normal arrangements for home defence'.[16] The proposed structure would also supply the organisation and numbers to provide the 'machinery for creating a reserve that would augment the peace establishment of the force and supply the wastage of war at home or overseas'.[17]

The scheme recommended that New Zealand be formed into four military districts, two in the North Island and two in the South. Each district would form the following units, totalling 30,848 personnel:

1 Headquarters Mounted Brigade
3 regiments Mounted Rifles
1 Field Artillery brigade
1 Infantry Brigade including Headquarters
1 Infantry Brigade Signal Company
1 mixed Brigade Supply Column
1 Field Ambulance

1 Mounted Brigade Signal Column
1 Mounted Brigade Supply Column
1 Mounted Brigade Field Ambulance
Artillery and Engineers for fixed armaments, lights and guns
(variation of strength depending on coastal defences).[18]

These units, organised on British establishments, were to be regionally or provincially based, and affiliated to local cadet corps and rifle clubs. Each unit would provide a quarter of its strength towards a regional unit of the expeditionary force. That is, each provincial brigade would provide a regional battalion that would take the identity of the military district. The willingness with which volunteers came forward during the Boer War convinced the planners that there would be no difficulty in voluntarily recruiting one in four of the anticipated strength of the force. It was planned that the four districts would together provide a brigade of infantry and a mounted rifles brigade that would make up an expeditionary force totalling approximately 9000 all ranks. Nicholson and his staff assumed this structure would be formed from the volunteer force as existed in New Zealand at the time, but noted that a change to a compulsory training system would perhaps allow a greater percentage of the organisation to be committed to overseas service.

A territorial force of 30,000 could ideally provide one quarter of its strength as volunteers for the Main Body, and then use the remaining three-quarters to provide reinforcements while drawing in additional numbers to make it up to 30,000. Any expansion of an expeditionary force over and above the recommended 9000 required a proportional increase in trained manpower to reinforce it.

What is interesting about Nicholson's scheme is the secret Appendix F, which assessed the likely scale of reinforcements needed to replace the 'wastage of war' once an expeditionary force was dispatched overseas. This appendix would become a critical influence on New Zealand expeditionary force planning. It noted that the casualty rates to both sides in the Russo-Japanese War reached almost 95 percent annually of the forces engaged, and chillingly noted that it 'is impossible to assume that we should not prepare to suffer to the same extent'.[19] Using the Russo-Japanese War as a worst-case scenario, the General Staff arrived at a replacement-planning figure of between 65 and 75 percent per annum. Given that a first reinforcement of 10 to 20 percent of trained men were needed to travel with an expeditionary force when it sailed, the anticipated casualty rates meant that New Zealand with an army of 30,000 required 44 percent or 13,200 trained reinforcements in the first six months to sustain it on operations.

Similarly, an expeditionary force of 10,000 would require 6600 in the first six months, or 9500 replacements in the first year.[20]

As we shall see, New Zealand's Gallipoli experience would bear these figures out. Even before New Zealand embarked on operations, however, the wartime Minister of Defence James Allen determined that the General Staff assessment of 1909 would provide the guidelines for both the likely size of an expeditionary force, and the reinforcements necessary to sustain it.

Nicholson estimated that in the first year of a war under European conditions the likely wastage would be: 80% of the infantry strength, 70% of the mounted rifles, 60% of the artillery, 40% of the engineers, 30% of the staff and departmental services, and 20% of the lines of communication troops. To meet this wastage, reinforcements would also be drawn from an Army Reserve made up of those who had completed their training commitment with units.

In 1909, when Nicholson presented his scheme to Ward, there was no way the existing hotchpotch of volunteer units in New Zealand could meet any of these requirements. If New Zealand was serious in playing a role within imperial defence, a complete reorganisation of the New Zealand military forces was necessary. Ward accepted Nicholson's recommendations, but as a former volunteer officer he was wedded to the voluntary system. It was with great reluctance, and only after gaining assurances that the country would agree to the move, that he accepted that volunteering alone would not be sufficient to sustain a Territorial Force of 30,000.

While the 1909 Defence Act was introduced by Ward's Liberal administration, it found equal favour with William Massey's Reform administration of 1912. The Act established a Territorial Army based on a system of compulsory military training. However, its implementation was delayed until after the visit of Field Marshal Lord Kitchener in February 1910. Kitchener confirmed Nicholson's recommendations, with some amendments, and these were incorporated into a Defence Amendment Act in 1910, which was again further refined in 1912.

Service was compulsory for all males from 18 to 25 years of age, with a further five years' service in the Reserve. A system of Junior and Senior Cadets was also established. The Junior Cadet system was abolished in 1912 but the Senior Cadet scheme for youths aged between 14 and 18 years was retained, with training emphasising elementary drill and musketry. Compulsory Territorial training requirements were minimal. Each soldier was obliged to do 30 drill parades a year consisting of six-day parades, a seven-day camp, and an annual musketry qualification course. This could only provide the thinnest coating of military experience, but what were important were the organisation

Lord Kitchener inspects New Zealand Cadets and Volunteers in 1910 before recommending a way forward for New Zealand defence, while the New Zealand Premier, Sir Joseph Ward, in top hat, looks on. *(Wilson and Horton Collection)*

and procedures that were set in place for the recruiting, administration, training and mobilisation of a military force.

A British officer, Major-General Alexander Godley, was appointed General Officer Commanding the New Zealand Military Forces. Highly ambitious and without private means, Godley came to the Antipodes to make his name. The New Zealand Territorial Force became his achievement, with an expeditionary force the ultimate goal. The period between 1910 and 1914 saw unprecedented military expansion in New Zealand. General Headquarters was reorganised, expanded, and largely staffed by British officers on loan. A New Zealand Section of the Imperial General Staff was established, and New Zealand officers sent on secondment and for staff training to Great Britain. Godley proved adept as a trainer and administrator of the Territorial Force, and was equally skilled as a politician, touring New Zealand to explain to the public the need for compulsory military training.

Agreement was reached with Australia to train future officers by sending ten cadets a year to the newly established Royal Military College at Duntroon and, in addition to the existing Corps of Royal New Zealand Artillery, the New Zealand Permanent Staff and New Zealand Staff Corps was formed to provide a cadre of professional NCOs and officers to administer the system and train the force.

Mobilisation planning began in August 1912, and as there was no provision for compulsory overseas service under the 1909 Defence Act, 'each unit of the Territorial Force should furnish to the expeditionary force a quota of volunteers equal to a quarter of its establishment; the vacancies left by these volunteers to be filled up from the reserve'.[21] Godley kept in close contact with the Imperial General Staff in Whitehall, and briefed his minister James Allen on how the General Staff considered a New Zealand expeditionary force could best be used. This makes interesting reading. A short war was forecast, because anything more would be disastrous for the economies of Europe.

> It is obvious so far as the war policy of nations is concerned that, in all cases where universal service has been adopted, every effort will be made to bring the war to a conclusion as quickly as possible. A war between France and Germany would cost over 1,500,000 [pounds] per diem, while the whole manhood of both nations would be taken from productive employment which would bring to a standstill a very large proportion of the productive industries with the consequent losses to both capital and labour … The issues at stake then are enormous, taking into consideration the loss of life, of capital, the hindrance to production etc. Every nation therefore endeavours to be ready for war at a moment's notice, and to put the utmost possible force into the field of action.[22]

The fruits of New Zealand's forward mobilisation planning. Soldiers of the New Zealand Samoan Expeditionary Force go through basic rifle training on the deck of their troop transport in August 1914 in anticipation of having to fight to seize German Samoa. *(F-66833-1/2, Malcolm Ross, later NZ Official War Correspondent, Alexander Turnbull Library, Wellington, NZ)*

Godley confirmed the need for a Territorial Force that had sufficient numbers trained and equipped to provide a quarter of its strength as volunteers. As far as he was concerned there would be no time to engineer a system of mobilisation once war was declared. It was important to have everything planned for and the procedures in place, ready to be put into effect. Allen was also a man for meticulous detail and agreed with Godley that these matters were too important to be left to chance.

> It is therefore necessary to have the complete plans (organization, transport, equipment etc.), of any overseas Expeditionary Force thoroughly worked out in peacetime, for the value of any assistance, however willingly and enthusiastically given, will be greatly lessened, if not altogether nullified, by waiting till the actual outbreak of hostilities.[23]

Godley also briefed Allen on the likely enemy that New Zealand might face and the role it might be called on to fulfil. Existing alliances ruled out France and Russia as potential enemies, and therefore of the 'large Continental powers there remains Germany who is our probable opponent in the next great war'.[24] With Germany as the obvious foe, New Zealand might be called on to carry out all or one of a series of options: attack a German overseas territory, reinforce a British expeditionary force, and/or carry out operations in Egypt to protect the Suez Canal. Examining each of these in turn, Godley estimated that the seizing of German Samoa as a subsidiary operation was the only likely activity New Zealand would be asked to undertake against a German possession. There was also the prospect of an expeditionary force being used 'to advantage' in Egypt to meet a Turkish advance, but '[it] would seem best that the Dominion Troops should be given the opportunity of fighting with the British Expeditionary Force in the main theatre of operations'.[25]

On this basis Godley recommended that as soon as it was safe to sail a New Zealand force should be dispatched to Egypt for further training and then on to the front in Europe, which would inevitably be the major campaign theatre. New Zealand could play its part in carrying out these tasks but, as Godley concluded, it 'is of the utmost importance that there should be some definite understanding on this matter between the Home Government and the Government of New Zealand, so that these proposals can be worked out in detail'.[26]

It also made sense to discuss mobilisation planning with Australia. The means by which equipment, training procedures and other issues relating to how Imperial Defence preparations could be standardised was discussed in London between dominion representatives and the Chief of Imperial General Staff in June 1911.[27] In late 1912 Massey agreed to discussions being held between Godley and his Australian counterpart, Brigadier-General Joseph M. Gordon.[28] These were held in Melbourne, and it was concluded that there was little need to assist each other with home defence other than in the area of manufacturing of military equipment and intelligence sharing; the most productive area of cooperation was in the area of expeditionary forces.[29] This led to the joint recommendation that 'the Commonwealth and the Dominion should make a joint contribution in the form of an Australasian division, or, as an alternative, an Australasian mounted force'. The Australasian division was to consist of 17,476 men of all ranks, the Commonwealth contributing 11,423 and New Zealand 6053.[30]

The discussions also concluded that of the neighbouring German territories, the Commonwealth of Australia should plan on seizing outlying possessions of any probable enemy in the Bismarck Archipelago 'and the Dominion [of New Zealand] might deal with Samoa'.[31]

Raising the Union Jack in front of the Post Office, Apia, German Samoa, on 29 August 1914 with the men of the Advance Party of the NZEF on parade. (*Wilson and Horton Collection*)

Allen was not totally happy with these recommendations, as he believed New Zealand was being asked to do too little. During his visit to London in 1913 he discussed possible options with General Sir John French, the Chief of Imperial General Staff, Brigadier-General Henry Wilson, Director of Military Operations, and Brigadier-General Launcelot Kiggell, Director of Staff Duties. As a result of these discussions a revised figure of some 8000 soldiers was suggested as appropriate for New Zealand's contribution to a combined force. This was effectively the size of force originally suggested by Nicholson in 1909. Cabinet approved the recommendations on 21 June 1913, and formal planning was initiated to put them into effect. Godley also visited London for further discussions on these issues in 1913. Allen mooted the prospect of specifically earmarking 8000 volunteers for special training on the proviso that they agree in advance to volunteer to become part of any expeditionary force. Godley disagreed with this, as he believed it would form an elite, while he considered it more important to raise the overall standard of training in the Territorial Force. It was an issue that was pre-empted by the outbreak of war.

As a result of discussions at the 1911 Imperial Conference, where it was decided that the services of an Inspector-General of the Overseas Forces would be made available to assess the efficiency of dominion forces, General Sir Ian Hamilton made a tour of inspection to Australia and New Zealand in February to May 1914. Hamilton reported back to London and also to the respective Ministers for Defence in Australia and New Zealand. His report on each country's forces was searching and perceptive.[32] After reviewing a series of practical field exercises held at divisional annual camps throughout New Zealand, where he inspected some 36,675 Territorial soldiers and cadets, 70 percent

Members of the Eleventh Taranaki Company of the Wellington Infantry Battalion packed and ready to sail for war in August 1915. *(Wilson and Horton Collection)*

of the existing Defence Forces, he concluded that 'the military machine in New Zealand had been subjected to a severer trial than that of any portion of the Empire' inspected by him. Hamilton assessed the New Zealand Territorial Force as 'well equipped and well armed; the human material is second to none in the world; and it suffers as a fighting machine only from want of field work and want of an ingrained habit of discipline'.[33] These shortcomings could never be made good unless it was mobilised for war and trained as a body for a period of time.

The 1909 Defence Act determined that the 'New Zealand Territorial Force (including the Territorial Reserve) is the first line of defence of the Dominion after the Imperial Navy … [and] must be able to take the field at once on the outbreak of war'.[34] In August 1914 the outbreak of war allowed these plans to be put into effect. On 7 August 1914, on receipt of a request from London, a force of 1413 all ranks was mobilised to seize German Samoa. Drawn from Auckland and Wellington units of the Territorial Force, it paraded fully equipped on the Wellington wharves ready to embark on 11 August 1914. It was a further three days before transports and escorts were ready, but on August 29 this force rowed ashore at Apia and seized German Samoa, one of the first German territories to surrender to the Allies in the First World War.

Mobilisation of the Main Body of the NZEF was equally swift, and the force was complete by 28 August. Its dispatch was delayed because of New Zealand's reluctance for it to sail without sufficient escorts given the threat of the German East Asia Squadron. It finally sailed on 16 October 1914, numbering 8574 men, with 3818 horses. It consisted of an infantry brigade of four battalions, a mounted rifles brigade of three regiments plus an independent mounted rifles regiment, a field artillery brigade of three four-gun batteries together with signal, medical and supply units, ten million rounds of small arms ammunition, and 6000 rounds of artillery ammunition.[35]

New Zealand was the only member of the Empire, with the exception of the British Expeditionary Force to France, to mobilise its forces on the basis of pre-war planning. Australia utilised part of the existing procedures but considerably expanded its anticipated contribution. Canada's eccentric and dictatorial Defence Minister Sam Hughes deliberately ignored existing planning and professional advice and proceeded to raise the Canadian Expeditionary Force (CEF) under his personal direction. This had chaotic results that led to unchecked expansion, duplication and triplication of effort, and myriad systems of administration all dependent on Hughes' whim.[36] Given this chaotic birth, it is paradoxical that the Canadian Corps became the most professional and skilled formation in the British armies on the Western Front in the First World War, superior even to the Australian Corps of 1918 (for more on this see chapter eight).

As planned, the NZEF joined with the AIF convoy in Western Australia and sailed for Egypt to become the Australian and New Zealand Army Corps (ANZAC). For eight months between April and December 1915 it bore the brunt of New Zealand's efforts during the Gallipoli Campaign in Turkey. In all, 8556 New Zealanders landed on Gallipoli during the eight-month campaign. Casualties numbered 2721 dead and 4752 wounded, a total of 7473, most of which occurred in the first four months on the peninsula. It was a graphic confirmation of the wastage that New Zealand could expect in modern war. Coupled with the numbers of sick, New Zealand casualty rates on Gallipoli reached nearly 150 percent of those involved.[37] This paralleled the experience of the British Expeditionary Force in France, which, after four months of intense operations in the opening battles of 1914 and in the struggle to hold Ypres, lost 96,000 of its original strength of 100,000.[38]

It proved impossible to keep the NZEF on Gallipoli up to strength, and for most of the campaign there were more soldiers in hospital and convalescing in Egypt, Malta and England than in the trenches.[39] Every New Zealand community felt the impact, with few households being unaffected. New Zealand's military administration was sorely tested, with delays in casualty reporting severely affecting the political credibility of Massey's government.[40] The difficulties experienced in sustaining the strength of the NZEF on Gallipoli confirmed to Allen the validity of the wastage rates anticipated by Nicholson in 1909. It also convinced him that there could be no unchecked expansion of NZEF numbers, unless it was determined beforehand that there were sufficient reserves of manpower available in New Zealand to sustain the increase in strength.

Gallipoli also confirmed that, contrary to initial expectations and planning, this would not be a short war. If New Zealand were to play its part within the Empire it would have to maintain its contribution at full strength for an indeterminate number of years. Already Otago and Canterbury, the less populated of the four military districts, were having difficulties meeting their reinforcement quotas.[41] The dangers of unchecked volunteering were also becoming increasingly obvious, with underage students from Otago Medical School being ordered back to New Zealand to finish their training.

The Gallipoli Campaign acted as a spur to recruiting, with volunteers flocking to the recruiting halls in both Australia and New Zealand. Australia embarked on an unchecked and unplanned expansion of formation and units to meet the number of volunteers coming through the doors, with little or no thought as to how these new units would be sustained with reinforcements.[42] Canada followed a similar approach, with its Defence Minister Sam Hughes reverting to the system used by the Union in the American Civil War, with locally raised battalions for overseas service officered by

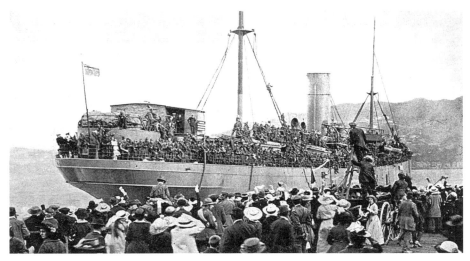

From the uttermost ends of the earth: cameras snap and the cinematographer on his stand winds his camera as a crowded troopship steams away from Wellington for war. *(Wilson and Horton Collection)*

those who raised them, with their own peculiar dress and equipment. Canada found itself mobilising 150 battalions more than it needed to meet its expeditionary force establishment, then had to go through the 'slow, awkward, inefficient, and sometimes ugly process' of disbanding them.[43]

Allen in New Zealand took the opposite approach. He agreed to the formation of the Trentham Regiment of four infantry battalions under the patronage of the Governor, the Earl of Liverpool.[44] This would provide the third infantry brigade needed to bring the organisation of the New Zealand and Australian Division in line with other divisions. This expansion of the NZEF was done with Nicholson's wastage rates always in mind. Allen knew that if New Zealand's contribution to Empire was to count, whatever the country raised had to be sustained and seen to be still effective when victory was gained.

Formation of the New Zealand Division

In February 1916 New Zealand reluctantly agreed to increase its contribution to that of an infantry division for service on the Western Front, as well as maintaining a Mounted Rifles brigade in Egypt for service in Sinai and Palestine. The planned expansion of the AIF from two to five divisions meant that the 4th Australian Infantry Brigade was no longer available to be part of the mixed New Zealand and Australian Division, so New Zealand had little choice but to fill the gap.[45] The initial feeling in New Zealand was that this was beyond the country's resources. Allen was unwilling to expand New Zealand's contribution until he was sure that he could maintain it at full strength and at the Gallipoli attrition rates.

Allen believed that the additional monthly reinforcement bill could only be met under a compulsory system, particularly as at that time New Zealand was committed to providing 20 percent of its total infantry numbers a month as reinforcements. This had been increased from 15 percent because of the heavy casualties suffered on Gallipoli.[46] Any increase would also impact on training, equipment and shipping.[47] Allen replied to the Army Council's request on 3 February 1916, saying that while the 'New Zealand Government is most anxious to do what it can to assist the Empire', it wanted to know where the suggestion had come from and if the Army Council agreed that the additional troops were necessary. Allen asked if three brigades could be maintained, with reinforcements for two brigades' worth, until August 1916 and stated that the 20 percent per month that New Zealand was currently providing for two brigades was not sustainable for the larger force of three brigades. Allen was also conscious of the time lag that would occur before reinforcements for the third brigade could reach the front as they could only be called in and commence training at the beginning of July 1916.[48]

The expansion of the NZEF was only agreed once Allen was convinced he could provide sufficient forces for the duration. As one can see from his reply to the Army Council, Allen suspected the initiative to form a division came from Godley. The latter's unpopularity with the New Zealand soldiers had filtered back to New Zealand, and his personal ambitions were seen as not necessarily coinciding with New Zealand's interests. Allen saw the reinforcement of the NZEF as a problem that needed to be addressed in national terms on a long-term basis. The Territorial system of recruiting based on district quotas was adjusted to a national monthly recruiting target. Godley objected to this because he saw it breaking the existing links with the provincially named infantry battalions and mounted rifles regiments. However, the adjusted 15 percent monthly reinforcement figures required to meet the wastage rates gave Allen no other option. Both provincial and personal agendas had to give way to national need.

Allen made it clear to Godley that while he as Minister for Defence was:

> ... very glad indeed that New Zealand has been able to provide a Division and the reinforcements thereon ... it is a very large task for us and I do hope that you will not without the very gravest consideration suggest that more be done by New Zealand. We have supplied considerably more than our share

of soldiers as compared with the Commonwealth or with Canada, and the willing horse cannot be worked till it drops.[49]

As a result New Zealand did not share in the unplanned and unchecked expansion of divisions that was a feature of the CEF and AIF in 1915–16. Despite ongoing pressure from the War Office, Allen was always mindful of the Nicholson statistics of 1909 and conscious of the political implications if New Zealand, having committed a force, could not sustain it until victory was won.

New Zealand would have to provide reinforcements annually that equated to 100 percent of its force strength overseas for the duration of the war. This required a system of reinforcement training and administration that would effectively eke out New Zealand's manpower for an unknown number of years. Volunteers could not rush to the Colours and get away on the next boat. Instead, on enlistment they were enrolled then sent home to await call-up in batches of 2000 at monthly intervals to go into camp for 14 weeks' training. Those who failed the fitness and musketry requirements were held back for the next intake or until they reached the required standard.[50] Pre-war planning had established the organisational machinery to do this based on compulsory military

A New Zealand Reinforcement Draft forms up at Liverpool before entraining for Sling Camp in late 1917. *(Wilson and Horton Collection)*

training of its Territorial Army. Extending this compulsion to overseas service for the Empire became the logical extension of this policy under the 1916 Military Service Act, which became law on 1 August 1916. The first ballot to conscript for overseas service was conducted on 16 November 1916.[51]

Even during the worst years on the Western Front in 1917 there was little or no questioning on New Zealand's part on how its Expeditionary Force was used. Strategic employment was an imperial matter and tactical employment a matter for the theatre commander. New Zealand's concern was that its forces were maintained at full strength, effectively trained, and that the performance of its soldiers reflected credit on the dominion that had sent them. Maintaining this contribution was a matter of national pride. Britain had declared war on New Zealand's behalf and in 1914 there was no resentment at being asked to contribute to the Empire's need. New Zealand's concern was to be able to fulfil its task as effectively and efficiently as possible. Where resentment arose was when it was found in 1917 that New Zealand was being asked to send a larger percentage of reinforcements than Australia. As a result there was government anger and growing public questioning of the fact that New Zealand was being penalised because of the efficiency of its reinforcement administration.[52]

There were requests from the War Office for New Zealand to increase its contribution. In late 1916 New Zealand was asked to raise a second division. This was strongly resisted by Allen, but Prime Minister Massey, on a visit to France, had boasted to Haig of New Zealand's reserves. As a compromise a fourth infantry brigade raised and trained from reinforcements in Britain was added to the existing division. This was not popular with Allen, or with Major-General Sir Andrew Russell, the New Zealand Divisional Commander, and was agreed to only on the understanding that 'additional Reinforcements were not asked for or the supply of Reinforcements to the original New Zealand Division was not interfered with'.[53] Allen in particular was conscious of the mood of the public and the growing war weariness, which led to increasing disenchantment with the constant requests for more men.[54] He was determined to eke out the resources that were available, with the priority being the maintenance at full strength of the New Zealand Division and of the New Zealand Mounted Rifles Brigade.

The addition of a fourth brigade made the New Zealand Division the largest division in the British armies on the Western Front, but it also made it the odd one out, being the only division with this structure. The additional brigade was generally used as a corps or army labour resource out of the line, which Russell believed was a misuse of an asset that should remain under his control, training for the next operation.[55] It was disbanded after the heavy New Zealand casualties incurred at Passchendaele in October 1917.

During 1918 the men of the disbanded 4th Brigade became an invaluable reinforcement pool of trained officers, NCOs and soldiers, enabling the New Zealand Division to remain at full strength with three infantry brigades, each of four battalions. This was at a time when British divisions were reduced to three brigades of three battalions. The Canadian Corps achieved similar results when it disbanded the Canadian Fifth Division, which was based in England. It too retained four battalions in its infantry brigades because the Canadian Corps commander, Lieutenant-General Sir Arthur Currie, knew from experience that it was essential to sustain the strength of his infantry formations if they were to be effective.[56] The New Zealand Division was one of the few divisions among the British armies in France that had the strength and guaranteed supply of reinforcements to sustain the hard fighting needed to defeat the Imperial German armies in 1918.

This was not the case with the AIF. It disbanded the 6th Division, which was being formed in England, and intended to turn one of its five divisions in France into a 'depot division', although this was never implemented. Totally dependent on volunteers, who were no longer coming forward to fill the ranks, the Australian Corps was committed to hard fighting with under-strength units, with no prospect of reinforcements to sustain them. This meant that when an Australian soldier was wounded he faced being returned to the line after convalescence, when his wound and service record should have seen him returned to Australia. The success of the Australian Corps in 1918 was won at the cost of increasing exhaustion within its ranks and disillusion at the burden they were expected to perform. The operations after 8 August 1918 effectively destroyed the Australian Corps as a fighting formation.[57]

The dominion of New Zealand was a junior partner of Empire. The size of force its population of one million could raise for war would never be of sufficient magnitude to have a decisive influence on world events. It could not influence the strategy or the tactics employed, but it could ensure that once committed its expeditionary force would be maintained at full strength, and reinforced with trained and equipped soldiers for the duration of the war.

By November 1918 New Zealand had sent 100,660 men to war and 550 nurses, at a cost of 59,483 casualties. Nicholson's assessment in 1909 had proved chillingly accurate. It had required 20,000 men a year to maintain a 20,000-strong expeditionary force on active service. Both the New Zealand Division in France and the New Zealand Mounted Rifles Brigade in Palestine were maintained at full strength. At the Armistice on 11 November 1918 the 17,434-strong division had 10,000 trained reinforcements available to it in France and the United Kingdom, and a further 10,000 training in New Zealand.

The NZEF was the only Empire force that could guarantee to maintain its contribution at full strength into 1920. This was no small achievement. It was almost entirely due to the vision of two men, Godley as Commander of the New Zealand Defence Forces until 1914 and then of the NZEF from 1914 to 1919, and Allen as Minister of Defence. Godley established the organisation and procedures necessary to raise and train the Territorial Force between 1910 and 1914, so that by the outbreak of war an effective system was in place and mobilisation plans drawn up to meet the anticipated contingencies. Allen as Minister of Defence had the strength of purpose not to be bullied into doing what was beyond New Zealand's means.

In consequence New Zealand public opinion was not split asunder with the political turmoil and dissent that was the legacy of the ill-planned and insufficiently thought-through reinforcement procedures of Australia and Canada. The principle of equality of sacrifice was put into practice. In the context of the times it was a rare example of effective planning and execution in a small country's national interest in the face of constant pressure from London for more men.

FOUR

THE INEVITABLE GALLIPOLI CAMPAIGN

But if the actual conduct of operations is held up to obliquy [sic] and most of all if the people of Australia and New Zealand feel their sacrifices went for nothing, then never expect them again to have any sort of truck with our superior direction in preparation for future wars.[1]

General Sir Ian Hamilton

The Gallipoli Campaign continues to haunt those who study it with 'what ifs'. Could it have succeeded? Would a continuation of the naval assault after 18 March have broken through into the Sea of Marmara? Would the Turkish Government have surrendered had the Allied fleet appeared off Constantinople? Of course all of this is uselessly tantalising, because the Allied Gallipoli Campaign failed and with it the dreams of a quick end to the First World War.[2]

The Gallipoli Campaign was part of the inevitable process of a Liberal administration in Britain, which found itself reluctantly at war, searching for other options to the Western Front in a strategy that was more in keeping with Britain's maritime strength. The seizing of the Dardanelles Straits had been the subject of ongoing staff studies over the years, and once Turkey entered the war as a German ally it was again examined as one of a range of options involving the projection of British naval power.[3] Despite a continuing commitment to the Allied force in Salonika, the failure of the 1915 campaign on Gallipoli confirmed that this war had to be decided on the Western Front against the primary enemy, the armies of Imperial Germany. It was in the West that the war was fought to a conclusion over five long years, during which the growing professionalism of the wartime mass citizen armies of both Britain and France eventually led to the defeat of the German armies in the field in 1918.

Could Gallipoli have succeeded? Churchill's scheme of 'knocking Turkey out of the war' envisaged passing a fleet through the Narrows of the Dardanelles into the

Sea of Marmara. This involved the passage of the 65-km-long straits, dominated on their western shore by the heights of the Gallipoli Peninsula. By anchoring off Constantinople (now Istanbul) the fleet would force the surrender of the Turkish Government, thus opening the sea route to the Black Sea and an all-weather supply route to Russia. An Allied advance would follow this route across the plains of Hungary against Austria-Hungary in concert with the Russian armies and those of the Balkan states won over to the Allied cause by the Gallipoli success.

All bold schemes that were believed possible by some of those taking part. Major-General Sir Alexander Godley, commanding the New Zealand and Australian Division, wrote to his wife immediately before the landing that he had packed his kit, leaving the large items to go through the Dardanelles and be available for him in Constantinople, 'if I am fortunate to get there'.[4] He also spoke of leaving the Australian Light Horse and New Zealand Mounted Rifles behind in Egypt, as they and their horses would not be needed until the advance across the Hungarian plains. It was the optimism of soldiers, many with considerable colonial war experience like Godley, who had yet to see and appreciate the ponderous bloody reality of mass citizen armies against a similar mass. In the case of the Gallipoli landings, it would in fact be a mixed force of Regulars and citizen volunteers against the Turkish Regular Army, many of whom had fought through the Balkan Wars of 1912–13.

When originally conceived, this was a naval operation entrusted to an Allied fleet of largely pre-Dreadnought class battleships. They proceeded to bombard the outer forts on the Aegean coast in February 1915, and followed this up with shore landings by parties of Royal Marines to confirm the damage. All this served to warn the Turks of the vulnerability of their coastal defences and inspire frantic preparations.[5]

An attempt to break through on 18 March 1915 failed because of a row of 20 mines that had been missed by the minesweepers. These sank three battleships, and a combination of artillery fire and mines badly damaged three others. General Sir Ian Hamilton, who had been appointed by Kitchener to command the Mediterranean Expeditionary Force (MEF), decided in concert with Vice-Admiral J. de Robeck, the naval commander, that it must become a combined Army/Navy operation. De Robeck had said he was prepared to make another attempt, and was confident that it would succeed after some days of bombardment. All he needed before he could begin a second attempt was the support of aeroplanes to direct fire across the peninsula at the howitzer gun positions in the Narrows and a new, more effective minesweeping organisation to clear the minefields.[6] However, by 22 March de Robeck was not so confident, and in discussions with Hamilton it was decided that a combined army and naval operation provided the better option. The general plan of operations after 18 March was to 'secure command of the Dardanelles' with the Navy tasked to 'landing the Army and supporting it till its position is secure, after which the Navy will attack the fortifications at the Narrows, assisted by the Army'.[7]

What would have happened if the Allied fleet had got through the Dardanelles? There was not the submarine threat that would become a factor from May onwards, and despite the presence of the *Goeben* and the *Breslau*, the Allies had the measure of the Turkish fleet. What would have happened had a line of Allied battleships threatened the Turkish capital with their guns? This was a question that was posed to the Turkish admiral who was the keynote speaker at a history conference in Ankara to mark the 75th anniversary of the campaign. It was during the opening session, with the Turkish Cabinet seated in the front row, backed up by the admiral's peers from all three services in the row behind. On receiving the question the admiral looked as if he had been asked to have his teeth pulled without anaesthetic. However, after a long pause, during which he was clearly asking the views of his peers in front of him — without using words, but rather by his facial expression — he nodded and said that he believed the Turkish Government would have surrendered. From the expressions and nods of his peers it was clearly a view they shared.

This is generally borne out by contemporary reports from Constantinople, which suggested that the arrival of an Allied fleet off Constantinople would spark a 'revolution' against the Young Turk administration. This was also the view of Enver Bey, Chief of Staff to the German Admiral Souchon who commanded the fleet at Constantinople. Lieutenant Commander Baltzer, a German naval officer on Souchon's staff, shared this view and believed: 'Turkey would have made peace.'[8] Not all agreed, but the reports of the 'state of excitement' of the government and public in Constantinople at the time indicate that the Turkish admiral's assessment in 1990 might have had some validity.

By his contemporaries and the British public, General Sir Ian Hamilton was regarded as a thinking general with experience in the Mediterranean, and judging from his writings, he was one who had an understanding of modern warfare. He seemed an ideal choice for the Gallipoli venture, although even his supporters at the time expressed some doubts about the suitability of his temperament for such a command. The Prime Minister, Herbert Asquith, who pushed for Hamilton's appointment to the MEF, described him 'as a sanguine enthusiastic person, with a good deal of superficial charm … and much experience of warfare … but there is too much feather in his brain'.[9] This was to be borne out during the campaign.

Hamilton would achieve a brilliant stroke of tactical surprise with his landing plan, but he lacked the steel to overrule his subordinates and to argue with Kitchener in insisting on the supplies and support his campaign needed to achieve success. He seems to have been too conscious of Kitchener's difficulties to impress upon his superior the real nature of his own problems and the needs of his force. Obsessed by the need for secrecy, he did not understand the need to communicate his designs to the citizen soldiers who would have to carry them out. Hamilton continued to act as if he was waging a colonial war against an inferior enemy with a professional force of soldiers who needed no more urging than to be directed what to do.

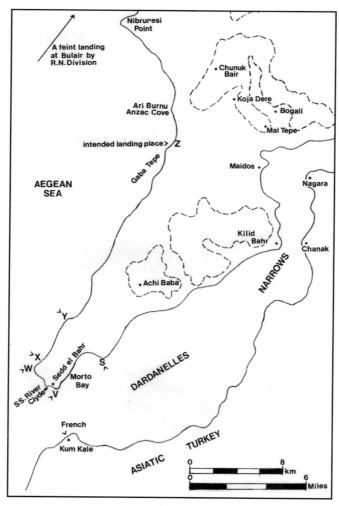

General Sir Ian Hamilton's plan for the amphibious landings on the Gallipoli Peninsula of Turkey on 25 April 1915.

Hamilton's MEF totalled some 70,000 men. It consisted of the 29th Division, commanded by Major-General A.G. Hunter-Weston, the sole Regular division not committed to the Western Front; the Royal Naval Division under Major-General Paris; the 29th Indian Brigade under Brigadier-General Cox; Lieutenant-General Sir William Birdwood's Australian and New Zealand Army Corps (ANZAC), which was made up of the 1st Australian Division under Major-General W.T. Bridges and Godley's New Zealand and Australian Division (NZ&A Division); an under-strength division consisting of two infantry brigades, one New Zealand and one Australian; and a French Expeditionary Force of two divisions.

In terms of support on land, it was the assessment of Hamilton and his staff that his army could assist 'the Fleet to force the Dardanelles by capturing the Kilid Bahr plateau, and dominating the forts at the Narrows'. Today the Kilid Bahr plateau is rarely mentioned, but to those who have visited the peninsula its imposing bulk is very evident both from Anzac to its northwest and from the south at Cape Helles. The Turks recognised its importance, and it was developed into a key component of their defensive plan. In contrast, Achi Baba to the south of Kilid Bahr is a low hill dominating the southern approaches to the small village of Krithia, a mere stepping stone on the way to what seems a much more difficult objective.

In 1915 Kilid Bahr was never seriously threatened. Hamilton's main thrust from the south had to first secure Achi Baba, which overlooked the southern coastal plateau. Further north Birdwood's ANZAC Corps had to secure the Sari Bair range that began inland and immediately north of the Gaba Tepe promontory and climbed steadily towards the heights of Chunuk Bair and Point 971. Both proved to be beyond Hamilton's grasp during the campaign, and the question of whether his force could then have seized Kilid Bahr has never been addressed. Assessing the ground it seems unlikely that Hamilton could have seized Kilid Bahr with the force at his disposal unless there had been a Turkish collapse. Even the initial objectives set for the landing could only have been gained and held had there been minimal Turkish resistance and a laggard response by Turkish reserves.[10]

Hamilton's first concern was to land his army, but he was well aware that the bombardments and the Royal Marine landings had alerted the Turks to the likelihood of an invasion. In the limited time available for his staff to plan the operations he made good use of aerial and naval reconnaissance and correctly assessed Turkish dispositions. He decided to mount two major feints to tie down Turkish forces and keep them away from his landing beaches. Hamilton used the transports of the Royal Naval Division to mount a feint landing off the major defensive lines at Bulair, where the peninsula was at its narrowest point. He also planned for the French Expeditionary Force to land at Kum Kale on the Asiatic shore at the entrance to the Narrows. Once the main landing was secured the French would re-embark and land at Cape Helles 'preparatory to the general advance of the Allied Forces against the enemy's army in the Gallipoli Peninsula'.[11]

It was a clever plan, with the two feint attacks intended to confirm the preconceptions of General Liman von Sanders, the German commander of the Turkish V Army. Meanwhile Hamilton's forces would land on every available beach, thus gaining time and space before the Turkish forces known to be to the north and east of the peninsula could be redeployed. In von Sanders' assessment the most likely objectives were the narrow isthmus of Bulair, where the peninsula reached its narrowest point before linking with the European mainland, and the plains of Thrace and Kum Kale on the Asiatic shores at the mouth of the straits protecting the plains of Homer's Troy. He positioned his forces accordingly. The Turkish XV Corps, with two divisions numbering 20,000 men and 50 guns, protected the Asiatic shore. The bulk of von Sanders' army, some 50,000 strong and consisting of the veteran III Corps, protected Bulair, with elements deployed on every anticipated landing beach, while the 19th Division held in reserve north of Maidos, the present-day Eceabat.[12]

Despite the alertness of the Turkish defenders Hamilton's plan achieved the tactical surprise intended, and on 25 April 1915 there were comparatively few Turkish forces close to the landing beaches used by the force. The main landings were in the south at Cape Helles by the 29th Division, at 'S', 'V', 'W', 'X' and 'Y' beaches. The aim was to seize Achi Baba, the securing of which would provide an effective beachhead from which to continue the advance.

The ANZAC Corps would land at 'Z' beach immediately north of Gaba Tepe, advance across the peninsula and cut off the roads running north-south.

> Gaining such a position, the Army Corps will threaten, and, perhaps, cut the line of retreat of the enemy's forces on the Kilid Bahr plateau, and must, even by their preliminary operations, prevent the said plateau being reinforced during the attack of the 29th Division ... the results of which should be more vital and valuable than the capture of the Kilid Bahr plateau itself.[13]

It is important to remind ourselves of the success of the landing plan. The tactical feints by the transports of the Royal Naval Division off Bulair and the landing of the

The SS *River Clyde* with sally ports cut into its side and ramps positioned for the infantry to run down onto a bridge of barges for the attack on 'V' Beach at Cape Helles on 25 April 1915. *(Royal Military Academy Sandhurst Collection)*

French Expeditionary Force at Kum Kale achieved their aim and convinced von Sanders that his defensive dispositions were sound. This gave Hamilton's landing parties the time and the opportunity to establish themselves had they been bold enough and trained sufficiently. Hamilton and his staff had grappled with the difficulties in terms of the timings of the landings, the comparatively few landing beaches, and how to get his forces ashore. Innovation was evident with the use of the *River Clyde*, as the forerunner of a large Landing Ship Infantry (LSI), at 'V' beach. It was a brilliantly conceived plan that might have achieved success had it been conducted by Regular divisions of the standard found with the British Expeditionary Force in France in 1914, but Hamilton's force did not have the capability to carry it through.

It is here that the gulf emerges between Churchill's strategic intention of knocking Turkey out of the war and the tactical ability of Hamilton's forces to achieve the operational objectives of the campaign. Hamilton recognised that the occupation of the Kilid Bahr plateau would allow him to dominate the Narrows. His forces would land south and north of this objective, but any appreciation of the ground raises serious questions about the size and ability of the forces he had available to gain and then to hold on to what they had won.

This highlights the difficulties he and his staff faced in the time they had to prepare, between the last week of March and early April when the plan first appeared in draft. It also highlights their particular blindness to the logistic and administrative needs of the landings. As Birdwood noted ruefully:

> The Adjutants-General, the Director of Medical Services and the Quarter Master General probably knew less about the destination and purposes of the expedition than anyone in Egypt, and no attempt was made to enlighten them.[14]

To quote a former colleague, 'Tactics is the art of the logistically possible,' and this is one critical area where the needs of the operation had not been assessed with any degree of practicality.[15] Birdwood and the divisional commanders voiced their doubts, but Hamilton's enthusiasm pushed these to one side. Greater involvement by his logistics staff might have brought a cold dose of reality to the planning, by bringing up issues such as the availability and speed of arrival of reinforcements and replenishment of artillery ammunition. Hamilton's plan, like the naval plan that preceded it, was always a best-case scenario. This discounting of difficulties was predicated on an overly ambitious assessment of what his soldiers could achieve, and was matched by a corresponding underestimation of Turkish fighting capabilities.

The difficulty as Hamilton saw it was getting his troops ashore; too little consideration was given to the fighting qualities of the Turkish soldier. This also applied to the assessment of likely Turkish reaction to the landings, and how quickly they could reinforce in comparison with Hamilton's ability to build up his forces. What was seen as a poor performance in the Turkish attempt on the Suez Canal in February 1915, and the ease with which the Royal Marines had landed on Gallipoli Peninsula in February, gave the impression that once pushed the Turks would collapse. No questions seemed to be asked about what the MEF would do if they did not.

The most glaring deficiency was in the comparative strengths and capabilities of the two sides. Their numbers were similar, but von Sanders was given the best available of Turkish Regular formations, the core of which, III Corps, had served in the Balkan Wars of 1912–13. Hamilton's army was an amalgam of everything available in theatre or in Great Britain that had not yet been committed to the Western Front. Its centrepiece, the Regular 29th Division, was a division in name only and formed from British battalions drawn from garrison duties in India, who had not operated or trained as a division. It was no different with the Royal Naval Division, which consisted of two brigades of spare seamen and stokers together with a brigade of Royal Marines, cobbled together into units officered by keen amateurs and lacking all the essentials of a divisional force, including artillery.

The two divisions of Birdwood's ANZAC Corps were no better. They had been in existence barely three months, with the last of Godley's two infantry brigades, Monash's 4th Australian Infantry Brigade, arriving in February 1915. The Australian battalions and formations had been raised from scratch since August 1914, and while the New Zealand units had been based on existing Territorial units, these were two citizen armies with the barest veneer of military experience. While the material was potentially first class, it lacked training and discipline at every level, particularly among the Australian infantry battalions raised from the working-class suburbs of Sydney and Melbourne.

The bedrock of potential was there, but the officers and NCOs lacked both knowledge and training. 'Quite good enough,' as Kitchener answered Asquith, 'if a cruise on the Sea of Marmara was all that was contemplated.'[16] Kitchener's assessment was chillingly accurate. Despite the accolades showered on the Anzacs by the British official journalist Ashmead-Bartlett and others, the reality of the Anzac landing was of a force over-matched by the objectives they were set, and thrown off balance by unexpectedly difficult terrain and the tenacity of an outnumbered Turkish defence. An amateur force found itself fighting a professional army. What is more, they were fighting an enemy who had everything to fight for, correctly believing that the Allies would give Turkey in Europe, including their capital, Constantinople, to the Russians as part of the spoils.

At Anzac an error in landing on the wrong beach compounded the problems for both sides. Fearing a Turkish thrust from the direction of the Kilid Bahr plateau, the leading brigade commander ashore directed the second Australian brigade to land to seize 400 Plateau to the south, thus diverting it away from its objective on the vital high ground of the Sari Bair range to the north. This meant that the ANZAC corps' strength on this northern flank, which faced the vital ground, was dangerously weak during the first critical day of the landing.

As it turned out, the landings at Ari Burnu, or Anzac Cove, caught the Turkish defenders off balance as this was the least likely point on which to expect a landing. It was defended by less than a company of soldiers. Major Zeki Bey commanding 1/57th Regiment, 19th Division, 5th Army Reserve, told C.E.W. Bean in 1919 that they 'had not anticipated a landing at Ari Burnu, as it was thought the ground was too broken, and the ships could not support an attack there. The landing, therefore, came as a surprise, and no dispositions had been thought out for it.'[17]

However, as part of their preparations for the expected invasion the Turkish defenders had been trained to attack disembarking troops at the 'moment of landing', and if

Anzac Cove from the sea: Rhododendron Ridge leading to Chunuk Bair is on the extreme left skyline. Below it is Walker's Ridge climbing to the sharp point of the Sphinx, which was the Anzac northern perimeter. The flat top of Plugge's Plateau protects the 800-metre-long cove, which sheltered an Army Corps Headquarters, two divisional headquarters and all the supply and medical units needed for the 30,000 Anzacs crammed into 400 acres on a hostile coast. (*Royal Military Academy Sandhurst Collection*)

forced back, they were to move to prepared positions and hold out until reinforced.[18] During training Turkish formations had practised counterattacking against anticipated landings, and it was the speed of the Turkish reaction that disrupted and overcame the advantages the Anzacs had gained by their unexpected choice of landing beach.[19]

At Anzac it was Lieutenant-Colonel Mustafa Kemal who assessed the seriousness of the landing, and who committed von Sanders' reserve division on the peninsula. He knew the ground intimately, having been stationed here during the Balkan Wars. His counterattack by two battalions of the 57th Regiment, launched down the line of the coastal ridge, hit the ANZAC Corps where it was at its weakest. Some 1200 men were launched against an expanding perimeter of 12,000 men of the 1st Australian Division, but the Turkish axis of attack saw them initially engage not many more than 200 Australians who were holding that part of the line on Baby 700. This counterattack locked the ANZAC Corps into a perimeter that would remain largely unchanged until August.

In the south, two Turkish companies at 'V' and 'W' beaches also conducted a determined defence. At 'V' beach the bombardment by the HMS *Albion* alerted the defenders, who met the landings from ships' boats and the SS *River Clyde* with heavy fire. At 'W' beach the Lancashire Fusiliers met with greater success but took heavy casualties in establishing a beachhead. At 'X' and 'Y' beaches the forces landed successfully but did not display the urgency and initiative necessary if Hamilton was to seize critical ground before Turkish reinforcements arrived.

At every level at both Helles and Anzac the Turks showed a skill and professionalism that the invaders lacked. They knew the ground, knew their role, were skilful snipers and trained in grenades, and were intent on delay at all costs until reinforced.

In contrast, few officers of the invading force displayed Kemal's skill and initiative. At Helles, while there was the opportunity to occupy Krithia and advance on Achi Baba, little initiative was shown and time was given for Turkish reinforcements to meet, delay and eventually hold the southern thrust short of Achi Baba.[20] Neither could soldier keenness compensate for lack of training and basic skills. At Anzac and Helles the willingness to attack was not matched by the ability to hold ground. Only hard experience would show that modern war demanded that the pick and shovel be recognised by soldiers as equal in importance to the rifle and bayonet.

Thanks to the pre-war planning of the Australian and New Zealand governments, the AIF and the NZEF were relatively well-equipped, but as Gallipoli would demonstrate, you cannot create staffs and armies overnight and expect them to function effectively.[21] It was the same at Helles; there was no questioning the bravery of the soldiers, but these were Regular battalions drawn from garrisons in India, and initiative was not their hallmark.

Hamilton's staff achieved miracles of planning in getting the army ashore, but once ashore they found both the terrain and the Turkish defence more difficult than they had imagined, and the implications of the task much greater than anyone had anticipated. Once Turkish resistance failed to collapse, the complexity of what was demanded was beyond the imagination and resources of raw, inexperienced formations and their staffs.

Success depended on what was achieved in that first day ashore. The Turkish defences were at breaking point, both at Helles and at Anzac on 26 April, when von Sanders' concern about further landings meant that he was not prepared to release the forces he had committed in the defence of Bulair and Kum Kale. However, Hamilton had already committed his available forces and they were not enough for the objectives that had already been set.[22]

Hamilton's immediate reinforcements in theatre were limited to the 29th (Indian) Brigade, and questions over their willingness to fight against Moslems led to them being held in reserve until success was assured. In addition he had three battalions of the Royal Naval Division, and the potential to use the Australian Light Horse and the New Zealand Mounted Rifles in Egypt as infantry, which together amounted to the strength of an infantry brigade. Anything more than this would have to be released from forces in training in England. The readily available reinforcements needed to capitalise on success were not available; had the breakthrough occurred Hamilton would have lacked the resources to exploit it.

By 2/3 May 1915 British losses numbered 13,979 and Hamilton's formations were 40 percent under-strength in infantry, with 29th Division reduced in strength to that of a single brigade. In contrast the Turks were able to reinforce and did so. After the first 24 hours, 'Turkish reinforcements commenced to arrive in considerable numbers.'[23]

The same lack of foresight also limited the availability of artillery ammunition. Too much was expected of naval gunfire support. Howitzers were the ideal artillery piece for the terrain but like everything else were in short supply. Birdwood had one four-gun howitzer battery at Anzac and its ammunition holdings were limited to what had been brought out from New Zealand, with the nearest reserves in England. Because of this the howitzers were limited to two rounds per day. The most common field piece was the 18-pounder field gun. Here too there were limitations. There was no high-explosive shell for this weapon, only shrapnel, and the force's 56 guns, later built up to 72, never had more than 23,000 rounds stockpiled. This meant that after retaining 10,000 rounds for emergencies the force was limited to 12,000 rounds or approximately 160 rounds a gun. This in turn had to be eked out at 10–20 rounds a day until further stocks could be brought from England. It was the same with medical resources, and trench and engineering stores. The Turkish defenders faced the same shortages of artillery ammunition, but their defence with manpower and rifles proved effective enough and they demonstrated a skill in developing trenches that was far superior to their opponents.[24]

In every sense the greatest empire on earth embarked on a poor man's war where everything needed was in critically short supply. All of this should have been anticipated and greater contingencies made, but this is easy to say in hindsight. The reality is that regardless of deficiencies the operations would have gone ahead. Everything was predicated on a Turkish collapse, but even then there were insufficient resources and manpower available to take advantage of it. A handful of professionals both citizen and Regular, but mostly the latter, prevented disaster, and so by trial and error the soldiers ashore learnt the business of soldiering. A parallel learning experience was being undergone by the Allied formations on the Western Front.

It is customary to decry the stupidity of the Turkish attacks at Anzac on 19 May 1915, which determined to drive the invaders into the sea. These failed at tremendous loss, and as we now know the cost of holding the British attacks at Helles in early May came close to breaking the Turkish resistance. This was not appreciated at the time, however,

Hamilton being more conscious of the cost to the MEF.[25] The Allies were equally blind in their launching of suicidal frontal assaults, such as those mounted by Hamilton's force at Helles in May and June and at Anzac, particularly with the feints during the August offensive. The Allies knew what machine guns could do to Turkish attacks, yet they never credited the Turks with the same defensive power, even though they demonstrated their skill in the defence during the April landings.

One can excuse Hamilton for the lack of time he had in April, but one cannot blame a lack of time for the planning failures of the August offensive. Hamilton's aim was 'to break out with a rush from Anzac and cut off the bulk of the Turkish Army from land communication with Constantinople'.[26] This was the task of Birdwood's ANZAC Corps and not of Stopford's IX Corps, which was to land at Suvla and 'incidentally to secure a winter base for Anzac'.[27]

Hamilton's obsessive secrecy crippled the effective evolution and coordination of the August plan. Birdwood's planning for the August breakout showed that he and his staffs had also learnt little in the three months they had been ashore. Their assault plan showed little understanding of the ground, and they misused the troops that were

Australian soldiers guarding a working party of Turkish prisoners of war at Anzac Cove. The Turkish soldier was a hardened and determined veteran trained and determined to defend his homeland from the invader. *(Royal Military Academy Sandhurst Collection)*

available. Although weakened by dysentery and disease, the veteran formations had learnt the bloody business of fighting in their months ashore. They knew the ground and how to use it. The Territorial and New Army divisions that reinforced Birdwood's columns for the breakout did not have these skills. While they were fit and enthusiastic, they were similar to the untried Anzacs who had landed on 25 April and, like the Anzacs then, they did not have the skills to carry out the tasks they were given. Furthermore, Hamilton's obsession with secrecy meant that from commanding officer to private in each battalion they had no idea what they were meant to do once they got ashore.

There were enough veterans available but these were thrown away on wasteful feints. This was recognised by both Walker, who temporarily commanded the 1st Australian Division after Bridges' death in May, and his successor Major-General J.G. Legge, who assumed command of the division on 24 June. Walker again assumed command on 26 July when Legge was posted to Egypt to command the 2nd Australian Division.[28] Both protested against the scale of the Lone Pine attack on 6/7 August. Both considered the Australian formations would be better used to some purpose more clearly connected with the major thrust. The nature of the Lone Pine assault could not achieve anything more than a feint. While initially successful it became the Hougomont of Gallipoli. Like Jerome's thrust at the Battle of Waterloo it was a feint that developed a life of its own, drawing in and destroying veteran Australian battalions that would have been better used supporting the columns advancing on Chunuk Bair.

It was the same with the assault itself. Birdwood's series of attacks frittered away the forces needed to exploit success. When reinforcements were needed all that were available were the newly arrived soldiers of 13th Division, who found the demands of Gallipoli beyond them. Indeed, all the mistakes seen in the planning in April were repeated. The gulf between the strategic intention of cutting off the Turkish Army by advancing across the peninsula, and how it was to be done once Chunuk Bair was captured, was never bridged. No one could have asked more of the soldiers; it was simply inadequate planning by staffs that had yet to learn their business. It would be early 1917 before there was clear evidence that they had started to understand their trade, but that was little consolation for the 12,000 casualties at Anzac in August 1915.

Lieutenant-General Stopford's failure with IX Corps at Suvla was a relative failure in that it reflected poorly defined objectives, insufficient training, and an almost total lack of information given to keen but inexperienced troops about the tasks they were set. History has unfairly blamed the events at Suvla for the failure of the August offensive. The greater failure was at Anzac; by now ANZAC Corps staff had both experience and knowledge of the ground, but little of this was evident in the planning and execution of the attacks. In a demonstration of the power of the media and of film in particular to create a mythology, the blame for failure at Anzac has shifted to IX Corps, whose objective was always 'incidental' to that of the ANZAC Corps.[29]

In war successful commanders make their luck by the quality of their preparation and planning, and the leadership and training of their men. On Gallipoli in April 1915, Hamilton's landing plan succeeded, but his strategic intention foundered on a lack of resources and a lack of understanding on his part that the continuation of the campaign, even if his initial landings had succeeded, would have demanded more resources than he had available. Predicating all on a Turkish collapse was poor generalship on his part. In the August offensive the reverse was true: the resources were there but Hamilton's subordinate staffs, principally that of Birdwood and his ANZAC Corps, did not have the skills to use them effectively, and so it failed.

By August de Robeck's belief in a successful naval passage of the Dardanelles had gone, and the willingness of the Turkish Government to capitulate after their successes was questionable. Any success in August at Gallipoli would have been but a step in a much longer campaign on a long and difficult road to Constantinople, with no guarantee that the Royal and French navies would have provided support to a land advance from the Sea of Marmara.

Luck was with the Turks but, as noted above, luck in war is earned. They were forewarned and used the time given to prepare and practise to defend their homeland. They were professionals, and demonstrated their skills at every level of command. Unlike Hamilton's forces, the willingness and enthusiasm of the Turkish soldiers was matched by officers of the calibre of Mustafa Kemal who used their initiative in the interests of their country. Theirs was a deserved success against the overconfident invader, and Gallipoli was the outstanding Turkish victory of the First World War.

FIVE

THE NEW ZEALANDERS AT ANZAC

The eight-month-long Gallipoli Campaign began with the landings on 25 April 1915 and ended for New Zealanders with the final evacuation on 20 December 1915.[1] It was the 'baptism of fire' for the NZEF in the First World War, and it saw the highest percentage of casualties suffered by New Zealanders during any campaign in New Zealand's history. Major-General Sir Alexander Godley's New Zealand and Australian (NZ&A) Division, as part of Lieutenant-General Sir William Birdwood's ANZAC Corps, left Egypt on 10 April 1915 for Mudros Harbour on Lemnos Island, which became the base for the Gallipoli landings. Godley's division consisted of the New Zealand Infantry Brigade commanded by Colonel F.E. Johnston and the 4th Australian Brigade commanded by Colonel John Monash, together with its divisional artillery and supporting units. Left behind in Egypt was the New Zealand Mounted Rifles Brigade, together with the Otago Mounted Rifles Regiment and the 1st Australian Light Horse Brigade.

The role of Birdwood's ANZAC Corps was to carry out the northernmost of a series of landings by General Sir Ian Hamilton's 70,000-strong Mediterranean Expeditionary Force. Birdwood's ANZAC Corps was to land at 'Z' beach, immediately north of the Gaba Tepe promontory on the western coast, and advance across the Maidos Plain to the Dardanelles Straits that separated the Gallipoli Peninsula from the Asiatic shore. This would cut off Turkish reserves from responding to the main landings in the south at Cape Helles. The initial landing was to be carried out by Major-General W.T. Bridges' 1st Australian Division. Its leading brigade, the 3rd (All Australian) Brigade, was to be towed ashore in ships' boats and barges at 4.00 a.m. on the morning of 25 April 1915. (The landing was originally planned for 23 April but bad weather forced its postponement.) It was to act as a covering force and seize a bridgehead, which would be expanded by the next two brigades ashore which were to consolidate on an arc encompassing the three main ridges that ran south from the highest point of Koja Chemen Tepe (or Point 971 as it was known, from its spot height on the map) to the Maidos Plain and from there to the promontory of Gaba Tepe.

Godley's NZ&A Division had the supporting role. It was to land after Bridges' Australians and be held in reserve before advancing across the peninsula to seize the small feature of Mal Tepe, which dominated the junction of the Maidos Plain with the Dardanelles Straits. Godley anticipated that there would be little for his two infantry brigades to do in the initial landings. So confident was he of this that he was content to wait until the New Zealand Infantry Brigade had landed before seeking a replacement for its commander, Colonel F.E. Johnston, who had gone sick the day before. It was an ambitious plan for two divisions covering a large area of ground, which relied for its success on the surprise of a pre-dawn landing and a delayed Turkish response.

As we know, nothing went according to plan. Although the reasons are still debated today, it seems a mistake by the Royal Navy set the first wave of the 3rd Australian Brigade over 1500 metres north of the intended landing beach. Instead of a low rise covering the beach then the expanse of the Maidos Plain, the Australians landed around the headland of Ari Burnu at the northern tip of the yet unnamed beach that is today known as Anzac Cove. Inland the Australians faced a tangle of ridges and gullies. Turkish opposition was slight, but an initial thrust by the Ottoman 27th Regiment on the 400 Plateau led to a change to the plan by the leading Australian brigade commander. This saw the first two brigades ashore both tasked with securing the southern flank, leaving the northern series of crests climbing to the 971 feature only weakly occupied.

It was on this axis that Lieutenant-Colonel Mustafa Kemal (later known as Kemal Ataturk, and first president of the Turkish Republic) launched his initial counterattacks. These took place mid-morning on 25 April, just as the first elements of the New Zealand Infantry Brigade were wading ashore at Anzac Cove. Kemal commanded the Turkish 19th Division, which was the Turkish Army Commander, German General Liman von Sanders', reserve on the peninsula. Kemal intended to exercise one of his regiments near Point 971, and on hearing news of the landing he moved at the head of the regiment to the critical height of Chunuk Bair. At 10.30 a.m. he counterattacked down the ridge. Although outnumbered by the total number of Anzacs now ashore, Kemal's counterattack threatened to overrun the weak Australian line on the Baby 700 feature at the junction of First and Second ridges.[2]

Temporarily commanded by Brigadier-General Harold 'Hooky' Walker, Birdwood's Brigadier-General General Staff, the New Zealand Infantry Brigade was placed under the command of the Australian Division and fought for the next 24 hours under Bridges' command. The New Zealanders were committed from midday on to reinforce the Australians on the threatened left flank, with the 16th Waikato Company of the Auckland

Battalion the first New Zealanders to see action. This became the battle for Baby 700, involving in turn elements of the Auckland and Canterbury battalions supporting the Australians in a seesaw battle for the heights. So critical did the situation seem that by late afternoon when the Otago Battalion landed it was used to secure the plateau above Anzac Cove (later known as Plugge's Plateau) as a defensive bastion should evacuation be necessary. Casualties were heavy, particularly among officers and NCOs; Lieutenant-Colonel D. MacBean Stewart, the commanding officer of the Canterbury Battalion, was killed, and in the 16th Waikato Company all the officers and all but one of the Senior NCOs were either killed or wounded. It is estimated that of the 3100 New Zealanders who landed on Anzac Day some 600–700 became casualties.[3]

When the Wellington Battalion, the last New Zealand battalion to come ashore, landed in the late afternoon of 25 April the battle for Baby 700 had been lost. Fragmented groups of Australians and New Zealanders held pockets of ground along Second Ridge where niches in the ridge offered protection from Turkish fire. The nearest of these to Baby 700 would later be known as Quinn's Post, but on that first night it was held by Major T.H. Dawson of the Auckland Battalion with a mixed garrison of Australians and New Zealanders. A handful of machine gunners from the Auckland Battalion held the saddle later known as The Nek. Any coordinated Turkish attack would have been disastrous for the ANZAC Corps. However, Kemal's soldiers were as exhausted and disorganised as the Anzacs and the opportunity was missed.[4]

At Anzac Cove the growing number of stragglers, the chaotic evacuation of the wounded and the increased Turkish artillery fire, which forced the transports to stand further out to sea, led Bridges in consultation with Godley to halt the landing of the artillery and recommend the withdrawal of the force. Walker, who accused Bridges of cowardice, hotly opposed this, but his divisional commanders' concerns led Birdwood to recommend evacuation to Hamilton. As Godley explained in a letter to his wife:

> We have had a devil of a time, and on Sunday night it was touch and go whether we could stand it for the next day … Bridges and I had to tell Birdwood it was touch and go, and he decided that we must let Sir Ian know … He [Hamilton] replied that there was no question of doing anything except sticking it out and the Admiral said that in any case it would be impossible to re-embark us.[5]

From the evening of Anzac Day there was little prospect of breaking out from the Anzac perimeter. In the days that followed the ANZAC Corps consolidated on the two ridges, dominated at their junction by the Turkish-held Baby 700. Godley's NZ&A Division became responsible for the northern part of the perimeter (Nos 3 and 4 Sections), which stretched from Courtney's Post and Quinn's Post across the head of Monash Gully to Pope's Hill, a spur leading off Baby 700, then across to what was later known as Russell's Top, which faced Baby 700 at The Nek. Godley's line continued along Russell's Top, down Walker's Ridge to the sea, then north again along Ocean Beach to a number of isolated positions, known as Nos 1 to 3 Outposts, movement to which was impossible by day.

Bridges' 1st Australian Division became responsible for the Anzac line in Nos 1 and 2 Sections to the south of Courtney's Post. The irony of this disposition on the ground is that it condemned the larger Australian force ashore to a secondary role for the remainder of the campaign. It soon became evident that any breakout would have to involve securing the high ground to the north of the Anzac perimeter, which was opposite Godley's NZ&A sector of the front. Because of this Godley's division would be tasked with the primary role in the planned breakout, which developed over time into the August offensive.

The 800-metre-long stretch of beach at Anzac Cove, bounded by the headlands of Ari Burnu to the north and Hell Spit to the south, became the supply lifeline and stores depot for the ANZAC Corps. Above the beach the gullies of Plugge's Plateau became the site for Birdwood's ANZAC Corps Headquarters as well as those of his two divisions. Around them were crammed field ambulances and supply and ordnance depots, interspersed with artillery battery positions firing in defence of the Anzac front line. There was not enough room for the artillery, and the 3rd Battery NZFA was one of five Anzac batteries employed at Cape Helles.[6]

The raw amateurism of both divisions was evident at Anzac in April and May 1915, and in sniping and entrenching the Turks outmatched them.[7] An attempted breakout by Godley's NZ&A Division to seize Baby 700 on the night of 2/3 May 1915 was defeated, with heavy casualties to both the New Zealand Infantry and the 4th Australian brigades. Overly ambitious, it lacked both planning and coordination, the soldiers' bravery being unable to compensate for poor staff work at both Johnston's and Godley's headquarters. Heavy losses among officers and NCOs saw a decline in morale and a breakdown in cohesion among those battalions that suffered most. This was particularly so in the Otago Battalion which, until reinforced, was effectively destroyed as a combat force.[8]

Already certain personalities had emerged whose determination and leadership became critical to the holding of the Anzac perimeter. Principal among these was Lieutenant-Colonel W.G. Malone commanding the Wellington Battalion. It was he who consolidated the defensive arrangements on Walker's Ridge and Russell's Top in late April when it threatened to collapse.[9] Equally prominent was the expert marksman Captain J. Wallingford NZSC, whose presence alone was enough to reassure frightened men.[10] It was Wallingford who, with Captain J.M. Rose NZSC, machine gun officer of the 4th Australian Brigade, developed the system of mutually supporting machine guns whose interlocking arcs swept no-man's land between the posts at the head of Monash Gully. It was this that ensured the failure of the Turkish counterattack on 19 May 1915.

The ANZAC Corps' failure to expand and break out of their tiny bridgehead confirmed to Hamilton that an advance in the south from Cape Helles supported by naval gunfire held the only prospect for success. A series of costly and ultimately fruitless daylight attacks to secure the village of Krithia was launched by Major-General Hunter-Weston's 29th British Division and the French Expeditionary Force but failed to capture the heights of Achi Baba. To support this Hamilton ordered their reinforcement by a brigade each from Godley's and Bridges' divisions, and on the night of 5/6 May the 2443-strong New Zealand Infantry Brigade and the 2568-strong 2nd Australian Brigade, the two strongest brigades within the corps, embarked at Anzac Cove and were transferred to Cape Helles.

On 8 May both were committed in poorly thought out and hastily mounted attacks at Hunter-Weston's direction. At 11.00 a.m. Johnston's four New Zealand battalions began their advance from the British support lines, alone and unsupported by either artillery fire or by other British formations. It was a doomed assault by a single infantry brigade on the obvious axis of attack against a prepared and dug-in enemy. The brigade received heavy casualties even before its leading elements reached the forward British trenches, and its advance beyond this was stopped by Turkish fire after 200–300 metres. Its resumption was ordered and also failed.[11] The 2nd Australian Brigade suffered a similar fate in an equally forlorn lone attack that afternoon. The combat effectiveness of both brigades was destroyed. The New Zealanders suffered 770 casualties and were now some 1700 strong, having lost 2800 casualties since the landing on 25 April 1915. The Wellington Battalion at half-strength was the strongest of the four battalions.

Helles demonstrated the inability of British and Anzac commanders at divisional and brigade level to adapt their thinking on how to overcome the growing strength and complexity of the trenches the Turks were constructing. Bravery alone was seen as sufficient, and there was little evidence of planning. Malone of the Wellingtons was scathing in his criticism, telling Johnston that a night advance would have been far more effective, with far fewer casualties.[12]

At Anzac two half-brigades of the Royal Naval Division replaced the New Zealanders within Godley's NZ&A Division, until they too were relieved on 12 May by the arrival of the New Zealand Mounted Rifles Brigade commanded by Colonel A.H. Russell and the 1st Australian Light Horse Brigade commanded by Colonel H. Chauvel. Fighting as dismounted infantry, and with each brigade barely as strong as two infantry battalions, Russell's brigade took over No. 4 Section and immediately sapped forward the defensive line on Russell's Top. However, this was still incomplete when the Turks launched a major counter-offensive on 19 May. Its destruction by Wallingford and Rose's machine guns and the rifle fire of the Anzac defenders left no-man's land carpeted with Turkish dead. They joined the Anzac dead from April and 2/3 May in making the front trenches unbearable as bodies decomposed in the sun.

It was decisive proof of the power of the machine gun and rifle in defence, but despite this, it took Russell's protestations to stop Godley ordering a counterattack at The Nek over the same ground on which the Turkish attack had just failed. On 26 May an armistice was held in a futile attempt to bury the thousands of dead, with both sides taking advantage of the opportunity to spy out each other's trenches.

The Anzac perimeter was now under a state of siege. Turkish defences crisscrossed the forward slopes of Baby 700 and effectively barred any advance, while Turkish snipers made supply of water, rations and ammunition up the main artery of Monash Gully particularly hazardous. The Turks commenced mining operations under Quinn's Post. They were generously supplied with a German-designed hand-grenade, while the Anzacs had to manufacture their own from empty jam tins. This reflected a general shortage in all areas; artillery shells were limited to two rounds per day, and there were no supplies of timber or corrugated iron with which to build trenches.

None of this had been anticipated or planned for as it had been imagined that by now Hamilton's force would have secured the peninsula and occupied the British-built Crimean War defences at Bulair. Battalions acting on their own initiative sent away to England to purchase field telephones out of regimental private funds, as there was none available on the peninsula. In developing the defences at Anzac everything had to be improvised or, with the connivance of their officers, stolen from stores stacked at the depots on the beach if release was otherwise refused by zealous quartermasters. To reduce the effectiveness of the Turkish snipers, trench periscopes were built from boxwood and ship's mirrors, and an English-born Australian, Lance-Corporal W.C.B. Beech, devised a periscope rifle that could effectively hit a man at 300 metres without exposing the firer. This became an essential weapon in holding the Anzac line.[13]

The heat, general conditions and lack of replacement clothing saw soldiers reduced to cut-down trousers, vests and headgear of every description. By necessity it became a ragtag army, creating the legendary image of the 'Anzac' soldier. Food was limited to the essentials of bully beef, biscuits, tinned cheese and jam. There was no provision for fresh vegetables, and water had to be barged in from Greek islands off the coast. The sheer mass of men within the tiny perimeter, the lack of sanitation, the dead bodies buried everywhere among the living, together with those lying out in no-man's land, saw dysentery endemic and sickness widespread. Only vaccinations prevented the decimation of the ANZAC Corps from cholera and typhoid. As the summer months progressed, the strain of trench warfare, lack of rest, inadequate food and insufficient water saw the health of the Anzacs decline to the point where a fit man was one who could stand in a trench and hold a rifle. Men died from dysentery after being refused evacuation by doctors who had been directed to keep all but the worst cases in the trenches.[14]

The ANZAC Corps looked for a way out. Russell's New Zealand Mounted Rifles, holding No. 4 Section, began patrolling and reconnoitring the coastal ridges north of Anzac to see if this offered a possible route to the high ground of the Sari Bair range. These were men who readily adapted the skills of scouring the Canterbury high country slopes to the business of war. Scouting parties personally led by the Boer War veteran Major P.J. Overton of the Canterbury Mounted Rifles established that the foothills were lightly guarded and that a night advance onto the heights was possible. There was the potential to advance up the coastal foothills onto the high ground at Chunuk Bair, outflank the Turkish defences and then attack down the ridge taking Baby 700 from the rear.

This became the basis of planning for an offensive that would involve a series of attacks both at Anzac and at Cape Helles, together with a landing by a fresh British corps at Suvla Bay to establish a base for winter operations and if possible support the Anzac attack. It was planned for August, which was the earliest Kitchener's New Army divisions could arrive from England.

In May the New Zealand Infantry Brigade returned from Helles and was placed in reserve on Wellington Terraces, below the Sphinx, and in Reserve Gully between Russell's Top and Plugge's Plateau. In early June the near success of the Turkish attacks on Quinn's Post and Courtney's Post saw it replace the now exhausted 4th Australian Brigade. Conditions in the front line on Second Ridge beggared description, the Turk having gained the moral superiority and his mining under the Anzac line threatening to blow the linked posts of Quinn's and Courtney's, each barely of tennis court size, into Monash Gully. A series of raids on the Turkish trenches to destroy tunnel entrances simply added to the casualty list and further lowered morale.

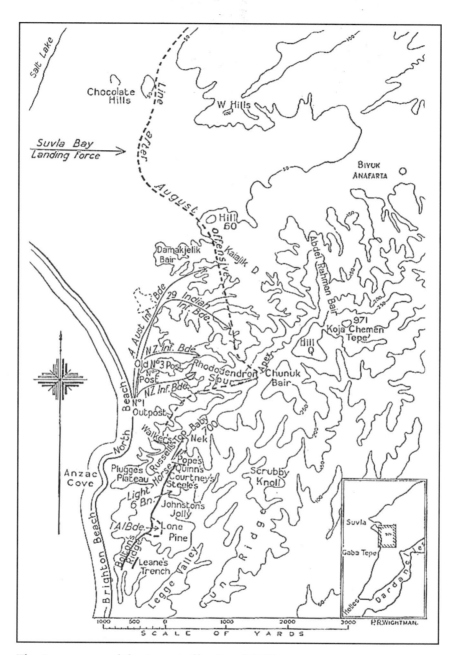

The Anzac area and the August offensive of 1915.

It was a crisis point in the siege of Anzac, which was resolved by the determination of one man: Malone of the Wellington Battalion. Malone believed that 'The art of warfare is the cultivation of domestic virtues', and he demonstrated this with his achievements first at Courtney's Post and then at Quinn's Post in June 1915. Each post was put into a proper state of defence; the front trenches were covered over as a defence against Turkish grenades, and communication trenches connected the front trenches with terraces below the crest where bombproof shelters were erected to protect the garrison. Latrines were dug, sanitary arrangements strictly enforced, and an aggressive defensive policy adopted. Malone was determined to dominate the Turks. Three jam-tin bombs were returned for every Turkish grenade, and Turkish fire was met by intense rifle and machine-gun fire.[15] Malone transformed an untenable piece of ground into an impregnable fortress. One only has to stand on Quinn's and see how small it is, and how dominant are the Turkish positions on three sides of it, to appreciate his achievement.

In no-man's land the work of New Zealand and Australian snipers, drawn from the crack shots within the ranks, was now coordinated to overcome Turkish ascendancy at the head of Monash Gully. Led by Lieutenant T.P. 'Maori' Grace of the Wellington Battalion, himself a skilled shot, they stalked and killed their Turkish opponents so that by late June mule supply trains could move unmolested up Monash Gully to replenish the front line.

At the same time a network of mine shafts was dug under Second Ridge to intercept the Turkish tunnels and prevent them being dug below the Anzac trenches. This was the work of professional miners drawn from the battalions, who now used their civilian skills to counter Turkish attempts to tunnel under the Anzac front line. Now it was the Turk who feared occupying the trenches opposite Quinn's. This transformation, which was due almost entirely to one man's bloody-mindedness and determination, finally secured the Anzac position at the head of Monash Gully. Malone was made Post Commander at Quinn's and the New Zealand battalions were rotated through under his command.

By late July preparations had been made for the August offensive, in which Godley's NZ&A Division had the major role. The seizure and loss of what would become the old No. 3 Outpost by the Canterbury Mounted Rifles in late May had seen the Turkish defences in the foothills strengthened. Overton's patrols had established likely routes, but Birdwood's plan was unnecessarily complex and took little account of the difficult country to be traversed. With reinforcements in the form of the 477-strong New Zealand Maori Contingent in early July, and at the end of the month by the 13th New Army Division and 29th Indian Brigade, the plan involved the seizure of the foothills by two brigades including Russell's New Zealand Mounted Rifles Brigade. This was to be followed by an advance onto the Sari Bair range by two assaulting columns. The left, consisting of Major-General H.V. Cox's 29th Indian Brigade and Monash's 4th Australian Brigade, was to seize the 971 feature, with the right, Johnston's New Zealand Infantry Brigade, seizing Chunuk Bair.

Feints by Walker's 1st Australian Division would concentrate Turkish attention on Australian attacks along Second Ridge, the main one being launched on the Lone Pine feature on the night of 6/7 August. This would be followed by further attacks at The Nek and from Quinn's the next morning, to coincide with the final advance by Godley's columns on the high ground. This bold undertaking promised to break the deadlock at Anzac; the question yet to be answered was whether the now exhausted veterans could carry out the task before them.

There is a scene in Peter Weir's film *Gallipoli* in which the AIF runner, a young Mel Gibson, is in the presence of an Australian general, in a headquarters on Anzac Cove, with a request that after the bloody failure of the first attempt any further attacks at The Nek be cancelled. Plainly harassed, the general turns to his signallers and asks for a report on the progress of the British landings at Suvla, only to be told that the British soldiers are ashore but have stopped and are drinking tea. Blame for the failure of August and the sacrifice of the men of the 3rd Australian Light Horse Brigade at The Nek is clearly established. It is another British blunder that the dominion forces have paid for with the blood of their bravest and best. However, it is important to remind ourselves that, despite the passionate beliefs of generations of Australians and New Zealanders who have seen this film, Weir got it wrong. The first-light attack at The Nek was not to support the Suvla landings, which was a subsidiary operation, but rather was a feint to support the main purpose of the August offensive, which was the assault by Major-General Sir Alexander Godley's NZ&A Division onto the critically important heights of the Sari Bair range.[16]

Weir would have been more correct if he had had his signaller say that the New Zealand Infantry Brigade was some 500 metres short of the crest of Chunuk Bair, but had stopped for breakfast on Rhododendron Ridge while their Brigade commander, the New Zealand-born Brigadier-General F.E. Johnston, vacillated as to whether he should attack or not. New Zealand soldiers sheltering between the thorny ilex and rhododendron bushes that covered the spur were witnesses to the destruction of the Australian Light Horse attacking Baby 700. After the failure of the August offensive, Lieutenant-Colonel Hart of the Wellington Infantry Battalion recorded that the Australians had now christened The Nek 'Godley's Abattoir'.[17] As the old saying goes, you cannot fool children or soldiers. After the August failure Godley was a far more justified target for criticism than the 61-year-old General Stopford and his untried Kitchener New Army and Territorial divisions of IX Corps that landed at Suvla.

During the August offensive of 1915 the major attack was entrusted to Godley. This reflected the reality of Godley's mixed NZ&A Division's position in holding Sections 3 and 4 on what was the left, or northern flank, of the Anzac perimeter. Attempts to open a direct route up the ridge line to the critical heights of the Sari Bair range by the capture of Baby 700 had failed in early May. By August the crisscross of Turkish trenches on its forward slopes had earned it the nickname the 'Chessboard' and made it the most strongly held position in the Turkish line surrounding Anzac.

To the discerning military eye on the Anzac perimeter, the coastal foothills north of Anzac offered a possible route to the high ground of Chunuk Bair and the 971 feature beyond. This was first suggested by Lieutenant-Colonel W.G. Malone of the Wellington Infantry Battalion in early May, in discussion with the staff of the Royal Naval Division at Helles after the failure of the attacks on 8 May.[18] Independently of this, it was also given impetus by the arrival at Anzac of the New Zealand Mounted Rifles Brigade and the Australian Light Horse in early May. Serving as infantry, they garrisoned the left flank of the Anzac perimeter including the outposts along the beach. Patrols coordinated by the Boer War veteran Major Percy Overton, Second-in-Command of the Canterbury Mounted Rifles, established that the coastal foothills to the north were weakly held and that the ridges and deres, or valleys, in between offered potential routes for infantry onto the heights. Overton's reconnaissance also showed that the Sari Bair ridge north of Battleship Hill, including the heights of Chunuk Bair, Hill Q and 971, were neither entrenched nor defended.

The ANZAC Corps Commander, Lieutenant-General Sir William Birdwood, Skeen, his principal planning officer, and Godley formulated a plan that was presented to General Sir Ian Hamilton, commanding the Mediterranean Expeditionary Force (MEF), in late May. It envisaged a feint from Anzac towards Gaba Tepe in the south, simultaneously with a flanking night advance to the north through the foothills to seize Chunuk Bair. The seizure of the highest point on the ridge, '971' or Koja Chemen Tepe, was excluded initially on the basis of reports from Overton's patrols, which considered a seaward approach impossible because of the sheer nature of the ravine that divided '971' from Hill Q to its south. Overton's assessment was ignored in Birdwood's final plan. This may have been because Birdwood was flush with troops and driven by the belief that if enough parties of men were sent towards the heights then one of them would get through. Because of this Monash's brigade was dissipated on an impossible task when his experienced battalions may have made the critical difference had they been available to reinforce the New Zealand assault on Chunuk Bair.

Birdwood wanted the attack mounted as soon as possible, before the Turks reinforced their defences on this flank. He planned for June/July, and asked for another 3000–4000 reinforcements to bring his corps up to strength. He requested Brigadier-General H.V. Cox's 29th Indian Brigade since 'it is ideal country for Gurkhas', and planned to use the New Zealand Mounted Rifles Brigade as the spearhead because they knew the ground and were the freshest troops available to him. Birdwood accepted the difficulties:

> A night attack will involve a certain number of troops losing their way. This, however, is not a matter of consequence, as they know they all have to press upwards … My plan would be to attack the ridge with three brigades of a total of about 8000 men and occupy the position Hill Q-Chunuk Bair-Battleship Hill … When secured, I should hope to move down the ridge with at least one brigade, to take the enemy's trenches facing my present position in rear.[19]

This was in the first 24 hours and would be followed by the securing of Third or Gun Ridge, which included the Turkish Headquarters on Scrubby Knoll.

Birdwood's plan offered Hamilton the chance to gain mastery of the Straits and also cut the north-south land communications to Liman von Sanders' Turkish Fifth Army. Hamilton accepted the concept but wanted to guarantee success by having sufficient troops on hand to exploit Birdwood's gains. He asked for reinforcements and tasked Birdwood to consider how more troops could be employed. At the same time he allowed the British VIII Corps at Helles to persist in battering away at Achi Baba, squandering men that he would later need to mount feints to support the breakout.

It was the same at Anzac. Activities by Russell's Mounted Rifles on the coastal plain in late May saw increasing Turkish interest in the foothills below the Sari Bair range. Mustafa Kemal, commanding the 19th Division, had become increasingly alarmed at the activity north of Anzac and pressed Essad Pasha, commanding the Turkish forces, to increase the defences on Sari Bair to guard against any attack through the coastal foothills. Essad discounted this threat but at Kemal's insistence increased the garrison watching the Sazli Dere, which led to the base of Chunuk Bair. Kemal noted that Chunuk Bair remained 'the most important point in our defences and the most inadequately manned'.[20]

There was growing concern among the Anzacs that the opportunities for a flanking movement were rapidly vanishing. Nevertheless, both Hamilton and Birdwood remained optimistic. Hamilton had asked for four divisions and Kitchener promised a total of seven divisions, the first three of which would be available in July.[21] It was more than Hamilton expected, but he willingly accepted what was offered and then had to assess how best to use them. Birdwood's plan for a speedily mounted flanking movement had grown into a major undertaking that could not now be mounted until early August when the phase of the moon offered the least light.

At Hamilton's direction, and with the promise of reinforcements, Birdwood enlarged his original plan to include seizing 971 as well as Hill Q and Chunuk Bair. To achieve this, feints were planned at Anzac with a major thrust towards the south by Walker's 1st Australian Division at Kanli Sirt or Lone Pine. This was planned to draw Turkish reserves onto the Anzac perimeter and leave open the ridge to the north, but was strongly opposed by both Legge and then by Walker, who replaced Legge after he returned to Egypt to command the newly raised 2nd Australian Division. Both considered the 1st Australian Division would be better used in the advance on Chunuk Bair, however Birdwood was adamant on the need for a series of feints from the Anzac perimeter and overrode their objections. The limited space in Anzac and the difficulties of providing water meant that Birdwood could employ only one of the New Army Divisions as part of the Anzac breakout, and he suggested using some of these resources in a subsidiary landing at Suvla to seize the 'W' Hills from which a Turkish battery shelled the Anzac perimeter.[22]

In the revised plan Suvla became a major operation in which a division would land, advance and seize the ring of hills guarding the plain. This division would be part of a corps of three New Army Divisions that would provide a firm base at Suvla, large enough to seize the ring of surrounding hills and also support Birdwood's assault on Sari Bair. However, through a series of discussions between Hamilton and General Stopford, who as Commander IX Corps would undertake the operation, the support to the Anzac assault was lost sight of. The main purpose evolved into seizing Suvla Bay as a sheltered harbour for a winter base on what would become an increasingly inhospitable coast. The forces at Helles would also mount a major attack to retain Turkish forces in the south.

By now the plan had grown until in the minds of many of the commanders the aim of the offensive had become obscured. Hamilton always intended that: 'Anzac was to deliver the knockout blow. Helles and Suvla were complementary operations.'[23] Now, however, as Hamilton's staff wrestled with the difficulties of planning this new offensive, this priority of effort was lost sight of in the minds of those who had to carry it out. Planning was limited to Hamilton's small operational staff, and his administrative and logistic staffs were left out. It was the same for the corps staffs who were to mount the operation, who were told nothing. Hamilton and his staff were determined there would be no repeat of the situation that existed before the April landings when every seaport in the Mediterranean knew of the projected invasion.

This obsession with secrecy backfired because his staff made no allowance for consultation and coordination with the three corps staffs involved, and permitted only the most cursory of reconnaissance by corps and divisional staffs. Discussion between commanders and staffs were forbidden, and false maps were issued of Asiatic Turkey that were never withdrawn. Corps and divisional staffs of Stopford's IX Corps who were to conduct the Suvla landings were not briefed until late July and no thought was given to allowing commanding officers time to brief their battalions. This was left until the day the troops embarked for the landings, and many battalions scrambled ashore at Suvla Bay without their commanding officers having seen a map of the area. The planners took no account of the difficulties of the terrain or the inexperience of the troops, particularly those of the New Army with green officers and NCOs trained for static warfare in France.[24]

The assault force on Sari Bair consisted of Godley's NZ&A Division supported by Brigadier-General Cox's 29th Indian Brigade, and Shaw's 13th New Army Division, which was smuggled ashore in the 48 hours before the advance and hidden within the already crowded Anzac perimeter. Godley's task was to seize the Sari Bair ridge. His advance was in two stages. The New Zealand Mounted Rifles with the Maori Contingent and one of Shaw's brigades would act as a covering force that would open the door and seize the foothills in a silent night attack on the night of 6/7 August. That same night two assault columns would pass through the covering force and advance up the deres and spurs onto the Sari Bair ridge. In the north, the left assaulting column consisted of two brigades commanded by Major-General H.V. Cox; these were Cox's 29th Indian Brigade and Monash's 4th Australians, who were to seize '971', or Koja Chemen Tepe, and Hill Q. On the right, Johnston's New Zealand Infantry Brigade was to seize Chunuk Bair. It was estimated that it would take six hours of darkness to reach the heights, and the plan demanded that dawn 7 August 1915 would see Godley's force secure on the crest.

At Anzac on the evening of 6 August the covering force moved out. With rifle and bayonet Brigadier-General Andrew Russell's New Zealand Mounted Brigade and Brigadier-General Travers' 40th Brigade seized the coastal foothills in a carefully planned and brilliantly executed operation. It showed the same careful appreciation and planning by Russell that he would later demonstrate as a divisional commander on the Western Front. The covering force battle started at 9.30, when the searchlight beam from the destroyer HMS *Colne* outlining the Turkish position at Old No. 3 Post was switched off. This had been the pattern for the past few weeks. 'Every night exactly at 9 p.m., the *Colne* had thrown the beam of her searchlight on the redoubt, and opened fire for exactly 10 minutes. Then, after a 10 minute interval, she had repeated the performance ending precisely at 9.30 p.m.'[25] It was the signal for Zero Hour for Russell's covering force. The Auckland Mounted Rifles had closed right up below the sandbags marking the Turkish trench during the *Colne*'s bombardment. Now there was a 'tremendous cheer, then clambered over trench ... Were through to rear trenches by 9.15. No live Turks [except a few prisoners taken] on position after 9.30.'[26] Findlay's Canterbury Mounted Rifles and Bauchop's Otago Mounted Rifles seized Bauchop's Hill, during which Bauchop was mortally wounded. Meldrum's Wellington Mounted Rifles took Destroyer Hill and then Tabletop, the sheer sides of which were scaled in the dark. By 11.05 p.m. the Tabletop was reported clear. The flashes of Turkish rifle fire, the cheers of Russell's 'En Zeds' and the war cries of the Maori platoons attached to each regiment established the rate of the Mounteds' advance. At 1 a.m. on 7 August 1915 Russell reported his objectives secure. Bean later wrote: 'By this magnificent feat of arms, the brilliance of which was never surpassed, if indeed equalled, during the campaign, almost the entire Turkish defence north of Anzac was for the moment swept aside and the way cleared for the infantry to advance up the valleys to Chunuk Bair.'[27]

The two assaulting columns closely followed this up. In the left assaulting column Monash's 4th Australian Brigade was to make a sweeping left hook and seize '971', while two battalions of Cox's Indian Brigade were to seize Hill Q. Birdwood's tasking for the left assaulting column ignored Overton's reports that the terrain was impassable as a route to 971. Despite being guided by Overton, Monash's column fell behind schedule and the next day confusion as to direction and location, and stubborn opposition by scattered Turkish troops, saw it held up in the foothills. Cox's preoccupation with Monash's lack of progress over the next two days diverted him from the progress his own battalions were making towards Hill Q, and so a potentially successful advance on Hill Q did not get the command attention it deserved.

Planning in Brigadier-General F.E. Johnston's right assaulting column did not match that of Russell's brigade. In part this was due to Hamilton's obsessive secrecy and prohibitions on reconnaissance. Nevertheless, Johnston's plan showed little understanding of the approaches or of the capacity of the ground to deploy his columns, all readily perceivable from observation posts within the perimeter. When one looks

The Narrows of the Dardanelles from the site of the New Zealand Memorial on Chunuk Bair taken in 1920. This was the left of the New Zealand line held by Malone's Wellington Batttalion on 8 August 1915. *(IA 1, 32/3/136, Photo No. 7, Archives New Zealand)*

at Rhododendron Ridge from the Anzac perimeter today and traces out Johnston's instructions it is obvious that his planning was simply a map exercise totally detached from any reality presented by the ground.

The objective of the right assaulting column was the line Point 161, Chunuk Bair, to the head of Kur Dere in the saddle between Hill Q and Chunuk Bair. The intention was then to advance down Second and Third ridges to the line Scrubby Knoll, to coincide with the breakout from Nos 3 and 4 Sections at Quinn's Post and The Nek. It was an ambitious plan that relied on strict timings being achieved in a night advance over difficult ground. Johnston divided his brigade into two assault columns that were to move by night from a concentration area in Happy Valley, on the coastal edge of the Anzac perimeter, along the 'Sap' to No. 2 Outpost, and then advance up the Sazli and Chailak deres onto Rhododendron Ridge and from there onto Chunuk Bair.[28]

Malone was highly critical of the Brigade plan. This was a continuation of an ongoing running battle between Malone and the commander and staff of the New Zealand Infantry Brigade. Malone wrote:

> The Brigadier will not get down to bedrock. He seems to think that night attack and the taking of entrenched positions without artillery preparation is like 'kissing one's hand'. Yesterday he [Johnston] burst forth. 'If there's any hitch I shall go right up and take the place myself.' All as it were in a minute and on his own! He says there's to be no delay.[29]

Malone was right to be concerned. On the night of 6/7 August the Mounted Rifles did not clear the foothills until 2 a.m. Isolated pockets of Turks and congestion in the narrow deres meant it was dawn before the struggling columns of New Zealand infantry found themselves on an apex of the spur some 500 metres from Chunuk Bair. The Wellington Battalion alone was in position to attack, with Johnston's Brigade Headquarters following behind. Further behind again the Otago Battalion was scattered and straggling up the slopes, and there was no sign of the Canterburys who had moved independently up Sazli Dere.

The Apex at the junction of Cheshire Ridge and Rhododendron Ridge was secured, but with Chunuk Bair all but deserted of Turkish defenders the New Zealand column failed to attack. Johnston was not prepared to attack until he received additional support, and while the 3rd Australian Light Horse Brigade was being massacred at The Nek, the New Zealanders sacrificed a priceless opportunity to seize the crest. Birdwood had personally briefed officers of the attacking force and told them that, in the event of delays and columns being split, it was critical that isolated units still push on and seize their ground. On the morning of 7 August on the slopes below Chunuk Bair this was not done. Johnston, the New Zealand Brigade commander, was a sick man and rumoured to be drunk that morning from rum in his water bottle, which he had been sipping through the night. There was tension and distrust between Temperley, the Brigade Major, and the battalion commanders. It was the setting for a part farce but mostly tragedy. By day Rhododendron Ridge was exposed to observation and fire from the slopes of Hill Q to the north and Battleship Hill to the south, both of which overlooked it. The massed column of infantry wending its way up had little hope of cover; the only option was to push on but, suddenly conscious of being forward and unsupported, the New Zealand commanders faltered and did nothing.

Unknown to the New Zealanders, the crest was controlled by no more than 20 Turkish infantry and an artillery battery. Rather than push on as ordered Johnston waited for the remainder of his brigade to come up. Turkish reinforcements reached Chunuk Bair first. Once a field telephone line was established to Godley's headquarters at No. 3 Outpost, Johnston was ordered to attack. At 11 a.m. an assault along the ridge gained 100 metres and saw the Auckland Battalion cut to pieces, with the Brigade Commander incoherently waving them on until his staff dragged him to shelter behind the start line. Malone refused Johnston's order to renew the attack with his Wellington Battalion in daylight, and after consultation with Godley it was agreed that the brigade would attack before dawn the following day. Losses to the New Zealand Brigade on 7 August had effectively destroyed two of its four battalions, and the remainder were exposed throughout the day to Turkish machine gun and sniper fire from Hill Q to Battleship Hill.

For the British, 7 August 1915 was a day of promise crippled by difficult country, an overly complex plan, and commanders whose fitness and mental toughness did not match the spirit of the men they commanded. The same cannot be said of the Turks. Liman von Sanders, caught off balance by Hamilton's plan, immediately ordered reinforcements to the Suvla and Anzac front. Heavily outnumbered, elements of Kemal's 19th Division stopped the New Zealand attack on Chunuk Bair, while Major Willmer's Anafarta group, made up of paramilitary policemen, tied down IX Corps at Suvla. Both at Suvla and on Rhododendron Ridge it was a day of fatal inactivity. At his headquarters at No. 2 Outpost above the beach Godley accepted the delays and ordered a further assault on the heights by each of his columns before dawn on 8 August.

For the attack on 8 August Godley reinforced Johnston's column with the Auckland Mounted Rifles, the Maori Contingent from Russell's Brigade, and the 7th Gloucesters and 8th Welsh Pioneers from Shaw's 13th Division. Brigade Headquarters issued orders at 9.45 p.m. for an attack with Zero Hour at 4.15 a.m., preceded by a preliminary bombardment commencing at 3.30 a.m. The leading wave was to be two battalions, with the 7th Gloucesters on the left and the Wellingtons on the right. The 8th Welsh Pioneers were in the second line, followed by the Auckland Mounted Rifles and the Maori Contingent.

Once again there was little evidence that the attack plan had been arrived at by a study of the ground. The frontage from the Apex to the Pinnacle and across the Saddle to the twin knolls of Chunuk Bair would accommodate a tightly packed platoon at best. Malone planned accordingly. He sent his best scouts forward to reconnoitre the route and issued his orders.[30]

At 4.15 a.m. the Wellingtons advanced in a column of eight tightly packed files, two companies leading each with four platoons in single file, Wellington West Coast on the left, Hawke's Bay on the right, followed by Taranaki and Ruahine. Tightly packed in close column, they advanced on a frontage little wider than a cart track towards the heights above. After 80 metres they passed through the remnants of the Auckland Battalion who waited, expecting the Wellingtons to be swept away in a storm of artillery and machine-gun fire. Nothing happened. The Wellington column moved through them into the slight saddle before climbing up the slope towards the crest. The head of the column paused briefly below the crest for their supporting artillery fire to stop and then went in without firing a shot. 'Killed some Turks others cleared. We occupied trench — could see Dardanelles.'[31] Amazingly, the crest was all but deserted, the artillery bombardment having driven the garrison down the eastern slopes into the valley towards the Straits. Malone's New Zealanders had seized the vital ground. As dawn broke, his men, filling sandbags and deepening the half-metre deep Turkish crest line trench, could see the Narrows. 'A thin streak of blue haze about 600 feet up in the air marked the complete course of the Dardanelles … We could see Turkey in Asia above and below the blue haze.'[32]

Malone dug in with two companies occupying the Turkish trench that ran along from crest to crest on Chunuk Bair facing towards the Narrows. The battalion frontage covered some 200 metres between the twin knolls, which are today marked by the New Zealand Memorial on the left, now joined by a brooding statue of Kemal Ataturk, and the Turkish Memorial on the right. This was the centre of what can be described as a horseshoe-shaped feature formed by Hill Q as its northern arm, with the twin crests of Chunuk Bair in the centre, and a prominent spur running southeast to become Gun Ridge forming its southern arm.

The Wellington position on the crest covered the only seaward approach where it linked with Rhododendron Ridge. This was the lifeline to the sea up which reinforcements, ammunition and water would have to be carried if the advance was to be sustained. Section-strength standing patrols were sent forward from the two forward companies to occupy a line of empty howitzer pits some 30–40 metres down the slope in the centre of the horseshoe, immediately below where the New Zealand cemetery now stands on the eastern slopes. The crest itself, except for the area around each knoll, was some 20–25 metres across before the ground fell steeply away. Indeed, a soldier lying down in the shallow crest line trench would not see a man advancing towards him until he was ten or so metres away. It was only on each flank where the crests broadened out onto the ridge that the field of fire extended out to 30–50 metres. Malone was conscious that a supporting battalion would be positioned on each of his flanks, and so to give depth to his position his remaining two companies dug in a support line on the seaward slope immediately below the crest.

The Ottoman trench was little more than half a metre in depth in stony ground, and the entrenching tools carried by each soldier made little impact. The 30 picks and shovels allocated to each company were used to dig in as best they could, and each man filled and stacked his two sandbags on the parapet in front of him. There was little time for development. Within half an hour the Wellington line came under fire from Hill Q and from Battleship Hill. This growing Turkish fire played havoc with the two British battalions following up the Wellington advance.[33] The companies of the 7th Gloucesters attempted to extend the Wellington line towards Hill Q and advanced over the crest to occupy it but were driven back. It was the same with the 8th Welsh Pioneers, who suffered heavily in making their way onto Chunuk Bair. They were to extend the defence onto the southern arm of the horseshoe but on moving into position immediately broke and withdrew in panic behind the Wellington support line, cowering in the dead ground formed by the junction of Rhododendron Ridge with the main ridge. Some were eventually led into the right of the Wellington line, but at about 10 a.m. watchers at the Brigade Headquarters on the Apex of Rhododendron Ridge saw them break and fall back into the gully, 'and men in the trenches were turning round and shooting them down'.[34]

The two British battalions made little further contribution to the defence of the hill. They shared in the glory of the stand, and indeed gained more recognition in decorations and awards than Malone's men, but did little if anything to earn it. The two battalions of 13th Division lacked the training and leadership to cope with what they faced on the slopes. They had been trained for trench warfare in France and nothing had prepared them for the exhaustion of a night advance and a daylight attack under the conditions presented by Chunuk Bair. From the outset Malone and his Wellington

Battalion alone dictated success or failure on Chunuk Bair. It was Malone who would fight the brigade battle, and in turn Godley, isolated at No. 2 Outpost, surrendered the initiative to fight the divisional battle to Johnston at the Apex. There was no initial contact with the brigade and Corporal Cyril Bassett would win New Zealand's single Gallipoli VC for being one of the brave band of signallers who got a field telephone line forward to the Wellington position at midday.

The forward Wellington trench was counterattacked at about 6 a.m. and the defenders 'practically annihilated after inflicting enormous casualties on the enemy who came up in close order'.[35] After the destruction of the forward Wellington companies, the crest line, except on the right where the more open ground around the southern knoll of Chunuk Bair allowed the support line to run along its edge, became no-man's land, cleared in turn by Wellington and Turkish counterattack. Each drove the other back in hand-to-hand combat with rifle and bayonet, with the Wellingtons being inspired by the example of their commanding officer, who led them in charge after charge. Fire from Battleship Hill and Hill Q onto Rhododendron Ridge allowed only a trickle of reinforcements to get forward to the Wellington line on the heights.

The Wellington Battalion fought on alone, supported by the gunfire of a New Zealand Howitzer Battery firing from within the Anzac perimeter, until reinforced by the Auckland Mounted Rifles at about midday. At nightfall what was left of the battalion still held its position although Malone was dead, killed by what was probably a New Zealand artillery shell at about 5 p.m.[36]

After dusk the surviving New Zealanders on Chunuk Bair were reinforced by the Otago Infantry Battalion and Wellington Mounted Rifles. There was little left to reinforce. Of the Auckland Mounted Rifles only 27 answered roll call out of the 288 who had started the advance. 'Of the Wellington Battn all but 3 officers were casualties and only 50 odd men were left in the trenches.'[37] The Fifth Reinforcements for the Wellington Battalion, some 280 strong, took up stores and were kept forward in the firing line. Lieutenant Colonel Hart, who assumed command of the battalion in September, estimated that the Wellingtons suffered 737 casualties on 7/8 August: 113 killed, 284 missing and 340 wounded, with almost all the missing later reported killed.[38] He wrote to Malone's widow stating that after the battle, 'Not a single officer remained of the original force and only a very few of the men. The total strength was only 186 notwithstanding the fact that the 5th Reinforcements 270 strong had arrived on the 7th August.'[39]

The Brigade Major, Temperley, no fan of Malone, made a point of noting in the Brigade War Diary that: 'This Battn and the Welsh assumed that they were to be relieved and withdrew without orders.'[40] Temperley also took out his spite on the dead. For his

Looking at the heights of Chunuk Bair where the New Zealand Memorial now stands from a Turkish attacker's perspective. The crosses mark the graves of the unknown, above the visible ledge where the Turkish gun pits provided an outpost line for the Wellington Battalion on 8 August 1915. Malone's front line was a Turkish trench on the skyline sited to cover the seaward approach. *(IA 1, 32/3/136, Photo No. 6, Archives New Zealand)*

actions this day, Malone would be praised for his bravery, yet bore the responsibility in Hamilton's dispatches for wrongly positioning his trenches on the reverse slope of Chunuk Bair, thus leading to the loss of the crest. In the view of the professional Regulars it was all one could expect of a conveniently dead New Zealand Territorial officer. Temperley's influence is evident in the wording of Hamilton's dispatches.

> Also many officers are of the opinion that they had not been well sited in the first instance. On the South African system the main line was withdrawn some twenty-five yards from the crest instead of being actually on the crestline itself, and there were not even look-outs posted along the summit. Boer skirmishers would thus have had to show themselves against the skyline before they could annoy. But here we were faced by regulars taught to attack in mass with bayonet and bomb. And the power of collecting overwhelming numbers at very close quarters rested with whichever side held the true skyline in force.[41]

As we have seen, this is wrong in almost every detail. The existing crest line trench had been occupied as the main defensive line and was then only surrendered after the machine-gun fire from each flank and the counterattacks out of the valley to the east had killed its garrison. Lookouts had been posted and gave early warning but the limited depth of the crest line meant there was no option but to put the supporting companies on the seaward slopes below the crest. There was nowhere else for them to go, and as we have seen they fought on all day and turned the crest into no-man's land where no one, Turk or New Zealander, could pause and live. Temperley wrongly damned Malone's actions and Hamilton recorded his views for posterity.

For this epic, which was equal in every respect to that of Lone Pine and of far more tactical significance, the Wellington Battalion's share of honours and awards amounted to a single Military Cross and a number of mentioned-in-dispatches. In contrast, Hamilton's dispatches gave 'great kudos' to the gallant 7th Gloucesters whose achievements on the crest were anything but. As a jaundiced Wellington officer who survived Chunuk Bair wrote: 'Their Colonel got the C.M.G. and I think they got a D.S.O or two and some military crosses.'[42]

However, on 8 August 1915 the New Zealand toehold on Chunuk Bair was the only success, and strong leadership was demanded to capitalise on what Malone had won. It was not forthcoming. Johnston's brigade headquarters was overloaded with 11 units to command through the course of the battle, while Godley remained isolated and preoccupied with the progress of the left assaulting column at his divisional headquarters at No. 2 Outpost.

On 8 August it was clear that Chunuk Bair was the vital ground, and that all of Godley's efforts should have focused on how to enlarge the perimeter that Malone had seized. Godley intended to reinforce the Wellington position on the night of 8/9 August and commit Baldwin's 38th Brigade from 13th Division to enlarging the perimeter by attacking through the Wellington position on the crest towards Hill Q. Baldwin's brigade would be the main thrust. At the same time the 1/6th Gurkha Rifles of Cox's Indian Brigade and part of the 6th South Lancashire Battalion from 38th Brigade would assault Hill Q from the seaward slopes. A conference was called to plan the attack at Johnston's headquarters at the Apex on Rhododendron Ridge. Tragically, neither Godley nor any of his staff attended. Despite advice to the contrary from his staff, Johnston insisted on changing the route of 38th Brigade's approach from Rhododendron Ridge to a route up Chailak Dere to a ledge of ground known as the Farm — a route that had not been reconnoitred and was even then crammed with wounded and reinforcements. It was not possible to push a brigade through the packed gully; only by advancing in column at night up Rhododendron Ridge and attacking from the New Zealand trenches in the direction of Hill Q was there any prospect of success. Even then it was essential to have dug in on the ground won before morning or Turkish machine-gun and artillery fire, limited as the latter was, would drive troops in the open off the crests. There was simply no possibility of that being achieved by attempting to advance up the gullies. The New Zealand brigadier's forceful advice to Baldwin sealed the fate of the offensive.

On the immediate seaward slope of Chunuk Bair the Wellington Mounted Rifles held the centre of the 300-metre-long trench line with Otago infantry on each flank. At 11 p.m. on the evening of 8 August Lieutenant-Colonel Moore of the Otagos was wounded and Lieutenant-Colonel W. Meldrum, of the Wellington Mounted Rifles, assumed command. The Otagos numbered some 400 men and the Wellington Mounted Rifles 183. 'We had only one trench about 5'6" deep ... We were digging all night till daylight. In [the] centre we were about 25 yards from the [unmanned] Turkish trench [on the crest].'[43]

Meldrum's force on Chunuk Bair had a relatively undisturbed night and by morning had developed a strong position, with machine guns providing enfilade fire from each flank. This shows what could have been accomplished had Baldwin's brigade used Rhododendron Ridge as the route forward and attacked out of the New Zealand bridgehead. Instead Baldwin's soldiers got bushed in Chailak Dere and at dawn were

Lieutenant-Colonel W. 'Fix Bayonets' Bill Meldrum, CO
Wellington Mounted Rifles, later GOC New Zealand Mounted
Rifles Brigade in Palestine. *(G-14410-1/1, Earle Andrew
Collection, Alexander Turnbull Library, Wellington, NZ)*

still struggling towards the Farm, well short of their objective on the heights above. This
meant the failure of Godley's planned breakout attempt of 9 August.

At dawn Major Allanson's 1/6th Gurkhas and the South Lancashires of Cox's left
assaulting column attacked and briefly gained the saddle between Hill Q and Chunuk
Bair. This is vividly told in Michael Hickey's *Gallipoli*, in which he declares that it is
'doubtful if any other unit under Birdwood's command on that terrible evening behaved
with the classic professionalism of the 1/6th Gurkha Rifles'.[44] But this is a battle where
Australian, British and New Zealand historians become gripped with the emotion of
the moments they describe, and I for one would argue that Meldrum's defence of the
Chunuk Bair slopes was the critical success of that day and one that overshadows all
others. However, more important to events was the fact that Baldwin's brigade was
still struggling to clear Chailak Dere and never reached the crest. Godley's main attack
was never launched. Supporting British and New Zealand artillery fire fell on both the

Gurkha and New Zealand positions and drove the Gurkhas back off the crest. Only the New Zealand foothold remained.

On 9 August Hamilton met with Birdwood and Godley and offered them a further division to renew the offensive. It was refused. The scale of operations had overtaxed a logistic system attempting to sustain the attack up what was a narrow ridge line no wider than a road, and the two clogged gullies on either side. The evacuation of wounded had broken down and the supply of water was insufficient to meet the minimum needs of the troops presently engaged.

On Chunuk Bair the fighting continued throughout the day. 'Here we were men falling all about, wounded men groaning, water and food run out …'[45] Meldrum sent runners requesting ammunition and reinforcements. At midday '40 odd of the 6th North Lancs got into the trench just in front of Meldrum … Only one of them fired a shot during the day— they lay in the bottom of the trench — The NZ officers kicked some of them to try and stir them up … there is a morale effect in the reinforcements coming in but the actual men were worth nothing.'[46] Meldrum was confident his men could hold, and the Turkish attacks waned with the day. 'Our men on left could see Turks attacking on our right. Our right could shoot across to left … and we kept this going all day.'[47]

Three Turkish divisions, each of brigade size, had been consumed in the fighting, and the supporting artillery fire, despite taking its toll on the defenders, denied the crest line to the Turks as effectively as Turkish machine guns denied it to any New Zealand advance. Turkish artillery support was limited to two guns, one at Anafarta and one at Gaba Tepe, and it was these that caused the heavy casualties on the crowded slopes of Rhododendron Ridge.

At 11 a.m. General Shaw of 13th Division assumed command of the sector and requested recommendations on the strength of garrison necessary to relieve Meldrum's force. Johnston recommended a garrison of two battalions and asked that the New Zealanders be relieved that night as his men were spent. That evening at 8 p.m. 500 men of the 6th (Loyal) North Lancashire Regiment relieved the New Zealand garrison. The Wellington Mounteds lost 110 of their 183 men on top of the hill. The Otago's losses were equally severe, Lieutenant W.G.A. Bishop being the senior surviving officer with the battalion. Of the 583 New Zealanders, 280 survived to walk off the hill. They withdrew carrying as many of their wounded as they could, and the body of Major J.M. Elmslie of the Wellington Mounted Rifles, whom Meldrum recommended for 'special distinction'.[48]

The 5th Wiltshires were also directed to garrison the hill but were delayed in the crowded gullies with the leading elements not getting forward until 1 a.m. on 10 August. The 6th Leinsters already in position on the Apex were proposed as a replacement, but this Shaw refused. It was not until 3.30 a.m. in the pitch black of night that the exhausted Wiltshires staggered up the slopes. There was little or no Turkish fire. The men piled arms and slept the sleep of exhaustion in what seemed sheltered ground, where Rhododendron Ridge linked with Chunuk Bair behind and below what had been Meldrum's trench line.

Meldrum had briefed the incoming commanding officer of the North Lancashires on his defensive line and told him he had enough men to hold the position, but that the 'trouble will be to get enough trenches to cover your men. I'd keep them digging all night — you're safe until then.'[49] A garrison of 900 replaced half that number of New Zealanders in what was now a strong, albeit exposed, defensive position. Meldrum left half a dozen of his best scouts forward with the incoming garrison, together with his machine guns dug in and positioned on each flank. Although the replacement garrison was exhausted by the approach march, their survival depended on their digging in and enlarging what the New Zealanders had held. But while Temperley expressed his confidence in what a Regular commanding officer would achieve compared to the New Zealand amateurs, the North Lancs' and Wiltshires' commanding officers and their subordinates lacked the drive, initiative and experience to see that their survival depended on ensuring the battalions were dug in and ready for the inevitable counterattack at first light. Nothing was done to prepare the Wiltshires for battle, and the men were allowed to sleep where they lay.

As we know, Mustafa Kemal, placed in command of all Turkish forces north of Battleship Hill, counterattacked and consolidated the position at Suvla on 9 August. Now, on the evening of 9 August, he was determined to secure the heights. At dawn on 10 August Kemal's counterattack of three regiments included the last Turkish reserves on the peninsula. His attack followed the pattern of the previous day, as forecasted by Meldrum before he retired down the hill, and should have been expected. Despite this no effort seems to have been made by the garrison to anticipate and withstand the attack. The Wiltshires were still sleeping in the gully by their piled arms. Only the North Lancashires were manning the trenches with outposts along the crest, but they were unnerved by the line of Turkish rifles and bayonets that surged over the crestline towards them, only metres away. To each man it must have seemed that he and he alone was facing the charging mass. The North Lancashires offered no resistance but broke and ran. The sleeping Wiltshires were engulfed in the tide and died where they slept.

One of the New Zealand scouts whom Meldrum had left forward on the crest later reported to his commanding officer that the Turkish attack was not of the same intensity as the day before. This time they had attacked without the shower of grenades that had preceded previous attacks, and had not thrown more than 60 bombs before they came with rifle and bayonet. The scout told Meldrum that 'he was revelling in it shooting for all he was worth [until he] … looked along and saw men bolting from the left'.[50] It was time to go and he too joined the exodus. The Pinnacle fell and the Apex was threatened. Panic spread and threatened to collapse the British line all along the front. Temperley described the scene that unfolded in front of the New Zealand Infantry Brigade headquarters on the Apex:

> I saw 300 or 400 of them running forward to the Turks with their hands up. To save a disaster of the first magnitude and to prevent the whole front collapsing I gave orders to the machine guns of our brigade to open fire upon them and at some cost in life the movement was checked and they ran back to their lines.[51]

Wallingford, the New Zealand Machine Gun Officer, threatened to shoot any man who ran, while the exhausted New Zealanders were called back and consolidated the line on Rhododendron Ridge. 'On the evening of the 10th all the heights, with the exception of the insignificant elevation of Chocolate Hill, were firmly in the hands of the Turks.'[52] Given the scout's report, one has to ask whether the overwhelming Turkish counterattack painted in the British official histories grew with the telling, which both recognised the military achievement of the president of the Turkish Republic and disguised the debacle and lack of resistance of the British battalions. Had Meldrum been relieved by Walker's or Monash's Australians would the position have fallen? We will never know, but Kemal's successful counter-offensive confirmed the British failure.[53]

The failure of the August offensive was a failure in command. Birdwood's original concept was sound, and as events showed correctly identified a route to the vital ground, but he and his staff made no true assessment of the size of the force that was needed and how the seizing of the heights would be exploited.

The seeds of failure were contained in Hamilton's plan and staff procedures, and Birdwood's and Godley's failure to temper the expanded concept with an assessment of what was possible on the ground. A simple flanking movement had grown into three independent battles on three separate fronts, each distracting commanders from the central purpose of seizing the vital ground of Chunuk Bair. What was attempted was far too ambitious, and there was never a possibility of achieving the laid-down objectives.

Chunuk Bair alone would have been enough. If one looks at how it dominates the Turkish perimeter at Anzac one can see that, as the New Zealanders proved, taking Chunuk Bair was achievable, and if properly exploited may have provided a turning point in the Gallipoli Campaign.

Stand at the New Zealand Memorial on Chunuk Bair and see for yourself. The Sari Bair ridge extends like a horseshoe on either side, ahead are the Narrows protected only by the round hill of Mal Tepe in the distance. This narrow ridge was the last major obstacle before the Straits. However, it needed the best soldiers available and it was here that Birdwood and Godley's planning was fatally flawed. It was beyond the capacity of the newly arrived British battalions, who needed to be seasoned into the realities of campaigning on the peninsula. In August they were no better or worse than the Anzacs had been on 25 April; sadly they lacked an Ashmead-Bartlett or a Peter Weir to create their legend, and have suffered for it. They have become history's scapegoats for a command and staff failure within the ANZAC Corps.

Walker was right to criticise the scale and purpose of the Lone Pine attack; it became the Hougomont of the August offensive, employing seasoned soldiers who would have

The unveiling of the New Zealand Monument on Chunuk Bair. Standing among the Turkish officials are Sir James Allen, New Zealand Minister of Defence during the war, a New Zealand veteran sounding the Last Post, General Sir Alexander Godley towering above the crowd, and Major-General Sir Andrew Russell on Godley's left.(*IA 1, 32/3/136, Archives New Zealand*)

been better employed supporting the Chunuk Bair assault. The same is true for Cox's left assaulting column, Monash's 4th Brigade and the 29th Indian Brigade, both of which would have been better employed in expanding the Wellington foothold on Chunuk Bair. Had veteran Australian formations, no matter how exhausted, backed up the original New Zealand assault, had Walker instead of Godley commanded on this flank, who knows what may have eventuated. Godley himself wrote in his reminiscences:

> Had General Russell, who knew the ground better than anybody else, been given, in addition to his own New Zealand Mounted Rifles, the Australian Light Horse, whose attack at the Nek met with such disaster, I have no doubt that he would have gained the ridge on the first night without difficulty. The New Zealand, 4th Australian, and Indian, Brigades could then have relieved him, and established themselves on Chunuk Bair and Hill Q.[54]

As Godley goes on to say this is being wise after the event, but the possibilities tantalise. August was a soldiers' battle and no commander, Allied or Turk, could have asked their men for more, but bravery alone was not enough. What distinguished victory from defeat was the conduct of commanders in the battle for Chunuk Bair. Godley must take the brunt of the criticism. The course of events showed that he, like Birdwood, had no tactical grasp of the operation and allowed himself to remain isolated in his headquarters at the base of the ridge while overloading his brigade commander with the resources of a division. Indeed, in this battle first Malone, then Meldrum the following day, fought the brigade on Chunuk Bair, while Johnston made decisions that were more properly Godley's. The critical conference on 8 August, which neither Godley nor his staff attended, resulted in decisions that foiled the attack by Baldwin's brigade on 9 August. Hamilton's August offensive was lost on Chunuk Bair. Godley should have moved to the sound of the guns and positioned himself with his brigade commanders on the Apex of Rhododendron Ridge. His moment of greatness was to have been Chunuk Bair — but he missed it. As he later wrote:

> I have never ceased to regret that I did not stick to my original intention of going to see the ground for myself. I feel sure that I should have insisted on the advance [of Baldwin's brigade] being made by the high ground, and it is possible that it might have succeeded.[55]

A veteran returns: Fred Rogers, former CSM, 8th Southland Company, Otago Infantry Battalion, addresses the gathering in front of the Chunuk Bair Memorial on 25 April 1990 on the 75th anniversary of the Gallipoli landings. *(NZ Defence Force)*

It has been said that the Sari Bair range was only one of a series of ridges that had to be taken before Birdwood's corps could reach the Narrows. Standing on Chunuk Bair one can see how wrong this assessment is. It is the last major range before the Dardanelles and its taking would have seen the possibility of major advance. Whether that could have been translated into anything more than a local success that enlarged the Anzac bridgehead is questionable. The fighting capabilities of the Ottoman Army in defence of their homeland had been ably demonstrated, and German submarine activity made it unlikely that a further naval attempt could be mounted to capitalise on such gains. The likelihood that the Turkish military government would surrender, extremely probable in March, had gone by August 1915, and a campaign up the peninsula and around the shores of the Sea of Marmara was beyond Hamilton's resources.

What was left of Godley's division was withdrawn to Lemnos on 15 September for rest and reinforcement. Rested but still at less than half strength, it returned to Anzac and took over the sector below Chunuk Bair in early November. Hamilton had been removed and his successor General Sir Charles Monro was convinced that an evacuation was the only option to end the stalemate. Both sides dug in for winter. Birdwood assumed acting command of the MEF with Godley commanding the ANZAC Corps and Russell the NZ&A Division. The approach of winter and the consciousness of failure ate into the force. Godley wrote to Allen that 'our impotence here fills one with shame, especially in view of the magnificent gallantry displayed by these troops, and the frightful casualties we have incurred.'[56]

The evacuation of the Anzac and Suvla positions began on 8 December. Major-General Sir Andrew Russell, who had made his name with the night attack in August, and proved equally successful in command of the NZ&A Division, commanded the rearguard at Anzac for the final two nights of the evacuation. Coordinated by the Australian officer Brigadier-General C.B.B. White, who was Brigadier-General General Staff (BGGS) on the Headquarters ANZAC Corps, it was a masterpiece of planning and was successfully completed by 20 December 1915.

> The men were splendid. They were very angry at having to go, but once they realised that it had to be done, they all played up thoroughly, and every man was a policeman … their silence and orderliness was quite remarkable, and from first to last there was no panic, and no undue haste to get into the boats as they filed down onto the beaches under the noises of the Turks on the heights above.[57]

The successful evacuation was little consolation for the failure of the campaign. Helles was equally successfully evacuated by 9 January 1916. Despite a commitment to the campaign in Salonika, the Gallipoli Campaign ended the search for a feasible alternative to the Western Front, and confirmed that it was in France and Flanders that Germany had to be defeated in the field.

Gallipoli cost New Zealand 7473 casualties including 2721 dead – 87 percent of the 8556 New Zealanders who served on the peninsula.[58] When those evacuated with dysentery and diseases are included the New Zealand casualty rate was approximately 150 percent. It forecast the likely cost of what was now inevitably a long war and one that determined New Zealand's decision to commit no more than an infantry division to the Western Front and retain the New Zealand Mounted Rifles Brigade in Sinai and

Palestine. This, as circumstances were to prove, was the maximum New Zealand could sustain. Australian casualties numbered 26,111 including 8141 killed. British and French casualties numbered some 147,000, while it is speculated that the Turks lost 218,000; some authorities put this figure much higher.[59]

In New Zealand terms the Gallipoli Campaign forged a unique kinship with Australia, but it also demonstrated how different we were to each other as peoples. It also showed that a citizen force had to be totally professional in its approach if it was to survive the stresses of war. Enthusiasm was no substitute for careful planning and preparation under capable leadership, matched by thorough training and detailed administration including, most importantly of all, the regular supply of trained reinforcements. These were the lessons the NZEF took to the Western Front.

SIX

THE NEW ZEALAND MOUNTED RIFLES BRIGADE IN SINAI AND PALESTINE 1916–18

Who could have dreamed when the Regiment left Auckland that men of it, before they returned, would stand ... on Christendom's holy place? Who could have imagined that the paved street of Bethlehem would resound with the march of [Australian and] New Zealand horsemen as they moved forward to the conquest of Jericho?[1]

C.G. Nicol, *The Story of Two Campaigns*

After the evacuation from Gallipoli the New Zealanders returned to Egypt. When the New Zealand Division went to France in April 1916 the New Zealand Mounted Rifles Brigade together with brigades of the Australian Light Horse formed what became known as the Australian and New Zealand, or ANZAC, Mounted Division. Two-thirds Australian and one-third New Zealanders, this body of horsemen became a key part of the mobile fighting force of the British army protecting the Suez Canal against the Turks in the Sinai Desert. It was as 'rough riders' that New Zealanders had first won a reputation as fighting soldiers during the Boer War. As we have seen, it was a reputation that was not initially matched by a national organisation of training and reinforcement, but it led to the growth of Mounted Rifles Territorial units in New Zealand. These would prove their worth again in the Sinai deserts and the high country of Palestine. Unlike British cavalry, who still carried the sword and lance as weapons, the Mounted Rifles fought with rifle and bayonet, and machine gun — the horse being the means of taking this firepower forward at speed to the battlefield where the mounted trooper would dismount and fight on foot.

In an earlier examination of New Zealanders and military discipline in the First

World War, I drew a parallel between the New Zealand experiences in the Gallipoli Campaign and in the campaign in Sinai and Palestine.[2] In both cases the comparative lack of civilian population, and the demands of climate and terrain, made these campaigns very different from that waged in the trenches on the Western Front. On the Gallipoli Peninsula and in the arid wastes of the Sinai self-discipline was everything, as conditions 'ruthlessly exposed and exploited any weakness in a man, and only the strong-willed survived'.[3]

This chapter examines the evolving effectiveness of the New Zealand units that served in the Sinai and Palestine Campaign, and compares it to the New Zealand experience on the Western Front. In both cases the personality of the commander is essential to an understanding of the discipline of the force. The New Zealand Mounted Rifles Brigade and the various other New Zealand units that formed the NZEF (Egypt) conformed to the standards set by their commander, Brigadier-General E.W.C. Chaytor, who commanded the New Zealand Mounted Rifles Brigade in 1916 before succeeding Chauvel in command of the ANZAC Mounted Division.[4]

In 1916 the 47-year-old Chaytor was a professional soldier of the New Zealand Staff Corps. Known as 'Fiery Ted', he had receding red hair and lean features, a prominent Roman nose, sharp blue eyes, jutting jaw, resolute mouth and moustached upper lip. Chaytor had earned a reputation as a skilled commander of mounted rifles on operations during the Boer War, where he commanded the Third New Zealand Contingent before being severely wounded and invalided back to New Zealand. He returned to South Africa in February 1902 as a Brevet Lieutenant-Colonel commanding the 2nd Regiment, or South Island Regiment, of the Eighth New Zealand Contingent. When the war ended in May 1902 Chaytor returned to New Zealand with a reputation as a soldier who was respected by his men for always being close to the action. The first New Zealander to graduate from the British Army Staff College Camberley, in 1907, Chaytor was highly regarded by Godley for his staff work and administrative skills, and was appointed Assistant Adjutant General (AAG) on the headquarters of the NZEF on mobilisation for war. Chaytor was again badly wounded on Gallipoli, and his conduct in hospital in England showed his willingness to break rules and regulations to meet the needs of men recovering from wounds and the rigours of Gallipoli service.[5] Chaytor had the balance of staff and command skills that Godley saw as necessary for the independent role of commander of the New Zealand Mounted Rifles Brigade and the other New Zealand elements that formed part of the ANZAC Mounted Division in Egypt in 1916. Both ANZAC Corps had sailed for France, and the NZEF administrative base shifted from Egypt to the United Kingdom.[6]

Colonel (later Major-General, Sir) Edward Walter Clervaux
'Fiery Ted' Chaytor, GOC New Zealand Mounted Rifles in Sinai,
and GOC ANZAC Mounted Division from 22 April 1917 for
the remainder of the Palestine Campaign. *(F-44189-1/2, L.F.*
Wilson Collection, Alexander Turnbull Library, Wellington, NZ)

Chaytor was supported by the calibre of his commanding officers who were all men of character; both in their understanding of men and in the determination of each to produce the finest regiment of mounted rifles. John Findlay commanded the Canterbury Mounted Rifles (CMR). 'Old John' was a farmer from South Canterbury who had seen service in South Africa and had been brought back from the Reserve to command the regiment on the outbreak of war. He had proved his ability on Gallipoli and would command CMR for the duration of the war.

Charles Mackesy from Whangarei commanded the Auckland Mounted Rifles (AMR). A noted horseman and rifle shot, 'German Joe' was already a legendary figure in the NZEF. The number of his family that were in the regiment led to the 11th North Auckland Mounted Rifles (NAMR) being known as 'Nearly All Mackesy's

Lieutenant-Colonel Charles E.R. 'German Joe' Mackesy, CO
Auckland Mounted Rifles. An accountant and land agent in
Whangarei, where the 11th North Auckland Mounted Rifles
(NAMR) was known as 'Nearly All Mackesy's Relations'.
(C22394, Alexander Turnbull Library, Wellington, NZ)

Relations'.[7] Mackesy lost a son on Gallipoli and had a name for being fiercely protective
of the welfare of his men. His reputation continued to grow in the ANZAC Mounted
Division. Word soon spread during the advance into Palestine: 'when the Auckland
regiment reached the boundary line, the old colonel halted his men, rode on alone past
a boundary pillar, took off his hat, and thanked God that he had at last been permitted
to enter the Holy Land'.[8]

William Meldrum, a 51-year-old lawyer farmer from Hunterville, commanded the
Wellington Mounted Rifles (WMR). Meldrum had commanded the 6th Manawatu
Mounted Rifles in New Zealand before the war. He proved to be an excellent regimental
commander during operations on Gallipoli, particularly in his regiment's seizing of the
'Tabletop' feature during the night advance on Chunuk Bair on 6/7 August and with his

leadership on Chunuk Bair on 9 August. Meldrum commanded the NZMR Brigade in the closing phase of the Gallipoli Campaign, and he was the obvious person to take over command of the Brigade in 1917 when Chaytor succeeded Chauvel to command the ANZAC Mounted Division.[9]

On the return of the ANZAC Corps to Egypt in early 1916 and on the formation of the New Zealand Division, the New Zealand Mounted Rifles Brigade became one of the brigades of the Australian and New Zealand (ANZAC) Mounted Division. It remained with this division for the remainder of the war, seeing service in Egypt, Sinai and Palestine. The division was formed from three brigades of the Australian Light Horse — 1st, 2nd and 3rd Light Horse Brigades — and the New Zealand Mounted Rifles Brigade. There were no ANZAC artillery elements available, and indeed the lack of artillery in the ANZAC infantry formations before they sailed for France saw veterans transferred from both the Light Horse and the Mounted Rifles to make up the required numbers in recently formed artillery batteries. Four British Territorial Army batteries of the Royal Horse Artillery (RHA) were allotted to the division and these English and Scottish gunners became completely identified with the mounted brigades; the New Zealanders were supported by the Somerset Territorial Battery RHA for almost the entire campaign.[10]

Chaytor's New Zealand Mounted Rifles Brigade consisted of a brigade headquarters and three regiments of Mounted Rifles: Canterbury, Auckland and Wellington, with the 1st NZ Machine Gun Squadron, an NZ Mounted Field Ambulance, an NZ Mounted Signal Troop and No. 2 NZ Mobile Veterinary Section. The strength of the brigade was approximately 2373 men and horses, although the arduous nature of the campaigning meant the brigade was always under-strength in manpower.

It was a comparatively small, tight-knit family of horsemen, and the provincial roots of each of the mounted regiments emphasised these close bonds. Each regiment numbered 24 officers, 499 other ranks and 616 horses, and was drawn from the military district whose name it bore. Each of the three squadrons within the regiment was recruited from and identified with one of the Territorial regiments of Mounted Rifles from the district.

So the Auckland Regiment consisted of the 3rd, 4th, and 11th Squadrons coming from their parent regiments, 3rd [Auckland] Mounted Rifles, 4th [Waikato] Mounted Rifles, 11th [North Auckland] Mounted Rifles. The Wellington Regiment was composed of the 2nd, 6th, and 9th Squadrons coming from Queen Alexandra's 2nd [Wellington West Coast] Mounted

Rifles, 6th [Manawatu] Mounted Rifles, and the 9th [Wellington East Coast] Mounted Rifles. And the Canterbury Regiment consisted of the 1st, 8th and 10th Squadrons, from their parent regiments the 1st Mounted Rifles [Canterbury Yeomanry Cavalry], the 8th [South Canterbury] Mounted Rifles, and the 10th [Nelson] Mounted Rifles.[11]

During the course of the campaign the following New Zealand units were raised and attached to British and Australian formations. The 15th and 16th Companies of the Imperial Camel Corps were raised and formed part of the 4th Battalion of the Imperial Camel Corps Brigade. The Camel Corps was later disbanded in Palestine and the New Zealand members were then formed into the 2nd NZ Machine Gun Squadron, which was attached to the 5th Australian Light Horse Brigade. The NZ Engineer Field Troop was part of the 1st (ANZAC) Field Squadron of the ANZAC Mounted Division, and No. 4 Company NZ Army Service Corps was part of the ANZAC Mounted Divisional Train. A New Zealand Rarotongan Company was raised as a Labour Corps and served with XXI British Army Corps. 'These Islanders were employed on the lines of communication, and did yeoman service in unloading stores in surf boats, and in handling heavy shells in ammunition dumps. They gained the reputation of being the smartest and strongest body of men on this work on the whole front.'[12]

An Australian Regular officer, Major-General Harry Chauvel, commanded the ANZAC Mounted Division. A brigade commander on Gallipoli in Godley's New Zealand and Australian Division, Chauvel had much in common with Chaytor, his New Zealand subordinate commander. Both were Regular officers with grazier backgrounds, and both had seen active service in South Africa commanding volunteer mounted regiments in circumstances 'where more than rank was needed to obtain quick and willing obedience'.[13] In temperament the two men were much alike. Chauvel's biographer wrote of him: 'A degree of shyness and reserve masked a nature that was warm and friendly; but these characteristics combined as they were with his simplicity and self-possession were sometimes mistaken in Chauvel for aloofness.'[14] This could also have been written of Chaytor. The two had known each other in South Africa, and a close working relationship developed throughout the Sinai Campaign of 1916. Chaytor was the only one of Chauvel's brigadier-generals to whom Chauvel would willingly entrust his division, and he recommended Chaytor to succeed him as divisional commander in 1917 after being appointed to command of the Desert Mounted Corps in the rank of Lieutenant-General.[15] This was in spite of there being three brigades of Australian Light Horse to the single brigade of New Zealand Mounted Rifles in the division, but in this case it was too important for the best man available not to get the job. Chaytor thus followed Russell, who commanded the NZ&A Division on Gallipoli, in being the second New Zealander to exercise command of an ANZAC force at divisional level. Chaytor's command was significant in that although a New Zealander he commanded three times as many Australian troops as he did New Zealanders.[16]

His men did not love Chaytor, but he was respected as a disciplinarian and a tactician. The wound he had received on Gallipoli often troubled him and made riding difficult. This did nothing for his temper and he was sometimes seen as aloof and demanding, with outbursts of anger directed at officers and units that did not meet his expectations. While the New Zealanders had nicknamed him 'Fiery Ted' for his once flaming red hair, he also earned it by fighting as furiously for the welfare of his soldiers against the restrictions and seeming blindness of higher headquarters as he did in his demands on his subordinates.

The NZMR Training Regiment and Base Depot was at Moascar, and nearby was the NZ Convalescent Home 'Aotea', which had been established by Lady Godley at the beginning of the Gallipoli Campaign. The latter served New Zealand troops in Egypt for the remainder of the war.

The New Zealand Mounted Rifles returned from Gallipoli at half strength and then faced losing many veterans to the New Zealand Division; 50 officers and 2000 men were provided to infantry and artillery units from the brigade and mounted reinforcements. 'This forceful and rigorous policy depleted the Brigade of some of its best officers and "Main Body" NCOs and men.'[17] Many of these were in the details camps, just out of hospital and recovering from wounds and sickness incurred on the peninsula, and were summarily transferred to batteries, transport or infantry battalions. 'NCOs of long experience as mounted riflemen were reduced to the ranks where privates or gunners only were required, and were not given a chance to volunteer; nor was the Brigade Commander given a chance to call for volunteers, for the men were seized while in the training camps.'[18]

Officers such as Major George Augustus King NZSC, who was transferred to command the NZ Pioneer Battalion, were hard to replace, and many veterans were still recovering from 'Gallipoli strain' — the exhaustion of their seven months of combat in the most trying conditions. This combat stress was recognised by the officers and soldiers, if not always by higher command. Training, sports and a spell in the Aotea Home would work for many, but a number would never recover and were evacuated to New Zealand or posted to training appointments at Moascar. It was in these first months of 1916 that Chaytor's regimental commanders gripped their units, absorbed reinforcements, and with hard work and strict attention to detail in constant training, practised and honed their troopers' skills to prepare them for their mounted role.

During the Gallipoli Campaign an ANZAC training depot, which controlled the schools of instruction and the training of reinforcements, administered the Australian and New Zealand troops in Egypt. It was commanded by a British officer, Major-General J. Spens. This was his first experience of citizen soldiers, and he recorded:

> ... the situation was a novel one for all, and the general handling of both Australians and New Zealanders whose ideas of discipline were certainly more elastic than which Regular Officers are accustomed to, has been tactful and carried out with little friction; the credit is not all on one side, for both Australians and New Zealanders, officers and men, exclusive of the conduct of a considerable number of 'rowdies' who would disgrace any nation, have generally shown themselves ready and willing to adapt themselves to the severe restraint of military discipline, so suddenly placed upon them.[19]

Spens noted the uneven nature of the training of Australian reinforcements, which varied between periods of two to three weeks for some individuals and six or seven months for others. In the case of rifle shooting, all Australian units and reinforcements were regarded 'as recruits, irrespective of any rounds previously fired in Australia, and it was necessary to put them through a complete course of 75 rounds'. In contrast, New Zealand reinforcements had received a 'much more level standard of 4 months training'. Knowledge of the New Zealand training syllabus allowed Spens' staff to carry on the New Zealanders' training from the point at which it ceased on leaving home. Almost all New Zealand reinforcements had completed a course of range practices, and 'the standard attained has been found so high as to warrant the elimination of further range instruction, from their course of training in Egypt'.[20]

The standard of these reinforcements is further evidence of Allen's and Brigadier-General, later Major-General, A.H. Robin's achievement in New Zealand. The establishment of a structured call-up and training system ensured all reinforcements achieved a set standard before they were passed fit to proceed overseas. This mirrored the differences that existed in the basic training methods and supply of reinforcements in Australia and New Zealand.

There was competition to join the Light Horse and the Mounted Rifles, which were seen as the elite, but as on the Western Front Australia found it increasingly difficult to maintain the flow of trained reinforcements to the AIF in Egypt. The variation in standards that Spens noted for the AIF in 1915 remained for the duration of the war.[21] It was accentuated in 1918 when Australian formations were desperate for recruits, and the reinforcement situation became so parlous that in 1918 some Australian reinforcements could not ride a horse.[22] At the end of the Gallipoli Campaign Spens gave up his role when each force established its own training depot in Egypt.

In New Zealand, reinforcements for the Mounted Rifles trained at Featherston, and had to pass tests of horsemanship before being released for the front. After the departure of the New Zealand Division for France all reinforcements for the New Zealand Mounted Rifles Brigade and its subsidiary units were sent to Sydney or Melbourne and were transhipped from there in transports conveying troops from Australia to Egypt.[23] In Egypt they were sent to their respective reinforcement depots. In all, 17,723 personnel left New Zealand to maintain the brigade's strength of 102 officers and 2271 other ranks over the three years of the campaign.

Despite their training in New Zealand the reinforcements still had much to learn, and it was at the New Zealand depot at Moascar that a rigorous culling took place in the Training Details Squadrons: 'Horsemanship being an essential accomplishment for success in mounted work, daily riding tests were made, and much care, judgement and patience were exercised in the selection of suitable men from the reinforcements to complete establishment.'[24]

Reinforcements were drilled in the basics of musketry, gas drill and mounted fieldwork. Sufficient horses were available to mount one squadron at a time, and the new men had to be deemed proficient as horsemen before they were passed fit to join the regiments in the field. The instructors were veterans on rotation for three months from the brigade, and this served to ensure the depot was current with operations in the field as well as providing a rest for combat-weary officers and NCOs. As a result the troopers were prepared for the standards expected of them when they reached their regiments in the field.

Chaytor and his commanding officers spent the first months of 1916 training and exercising the brigade at regimental and brigade level so that units knew what they could do and could work with each other. The basic skills were there, and these were refined and honed by veterans who married the Gallipoli experience to what they remembered from the veldt in South Africa, then adapted it to the even more demanding terrain of the Sinai Desert. Chaytor rebuilt his brigade by concentrating on the basics: 'rifle shooting, machine gun shooting, tactical exercises, boxing matches, swimming in the canal, filled up the days — and happy days they were'.[25] All contributed to bringing the brigade back to strength and tactical fitness.

This all produced a tight-knit body of horsemen, as is reflected in the remarkably small number of courts martial for New Zealanders in this campaign — a known total of 97 for some 20,000 New Zealanders during three and a half years of soldiering under difficult conditions. Only three are listed for 1916;[26] it is likely there were more in this year, but the records are incomplete. Yet even if the figures reached into the thirties, which are the averages for 1917 and 1918, they are still very low for a period when the Mounted Rifles were being reformed, trained and first committed to operations in the Sinai.[27]

The comparatively few courts martial also indicated a continuation of the less rigorous enforcement policy of King's Regulations and Routine Orders that had been evident in the ANZAC Corps after its return from Gallipoli. A great deal of latitude was accepted from the veterans in some aspects of discipline, and this was reflected in the punishments awarded. While this was tightened up in preparation for the infantry divisions' move to France, it never reached the rigorous standards demanded by the British armies in France.[28] This disciplinary policy continued in Egypt throughout the war. Nevertheless, as the statistics show, it was in Egypt while troops were in training that most of the courts martial occurred. This was often due to the weeding out process that was taking place during reinforcement training at the Moascar depot. Outbreaks of insubordination, drunkenness and absence without leave often became the escape for soldiers who found themselves under pressure because they could not achieve the required standard.

This pattern of offences paralleled what happened during training in New Zealand.[29] It is assumed that it was mirrored in the AIF, and that this will be confirmed once research is completed on Australian disciplinary statistics for Egypt and the Sinai and Palestine Campaigns. Wahlert's study into the ANZAC Provost Corps shows that the military police of the Egyptian Section of the AIF had the highest percentage of criminal offences of any unit of the AIF in Egypt, Sinai and Palestine. This reflected the ability of the commanding officer, who was removed, the selection process, and perhaps the ongoing first-hand contact with temptation.[30]

There were few serious cases. The single proven case of desertion was of a trooper of the Wellington Mounted Rifles under training at the New Zealand depot in December 1917. He received seven years' penal servitude, which was the most severe punishment awarded to a New Zealander in that theatre. A sentence of two years' imprisonment with hard labour for theft was the next most severe punishment, also meted out to a trooper of the Wellington Mounted Rifles under training.[31] Soldiers convalescing after sickness or wounds also featured in the statistics by breaking out and 'going on the town'. Two

New Zealand lance corporals, irked with hospital regulations, supposedly joined in a mutiny and 'combined with others to absent [themselves] from the 1600 Roll Call of the patients of "V" Block'.[32] Sanity prevailed and both were found not guilty. Perhaps the most unusual case was that of a trooper of No. 1 NZ Machine Gun Squadron who went AWOL from the depot at Moascar and gave himself up in Cherbourg in France a month later. This mirrored attempts to desert to Gallipoli in 1915, and received an equally light punishment of 31 days' forfeiture of pay for the time the trooper was absent.[33]

Egypt was also the destination of soldiers on leave from the front, and many of the courts martial relate to altering entries in pay books to wangle more money for leave. This crime was particularly prevalent among New Zealanders in the Camel Corps, and got the offenders up to twelve months' imprisonment with hard labour. Theft, absence without leave, drunkenness, being out of bounds in the women's quarter, and 'Conduct to the prejudice of good order and military discipline in that he at Ismailia … created a disturbance in a brothel'[34] all feature in the register. These parallel the pattern in France, but not with anywhere near the same intensity.

Unless one was lucky enough to get into the rum while on operations, the 'En Zeds' did not have the constant temptation that was available to the soldiers of New Zealand Division, with the attraction of the estaminets and billets in the villages of Belgium and France. Leave in Cairo was a rare luxury for a Mounted Rifleman, and on leave he played hard and caused the same problems as his counterpart on leave in France and Great Britain. Periods of leave in Egypt were mirrored by a steep rise in the rate of venereal disease, and this was no different in France. More often than not, however, rest and recreation for the Mounted Rifle Brigade was a spell in a tented camp on a beach behind the lines, where good food, a beer canteen and lots of sport were the only forms of relaxation. Gambling was endemic and something that officers and NCOs turned a blind eye to, as in the evening men would gradually move out of the camp to a secluded spot in the dunes, where the schools were in full swing.

> The tastes of Australians and New Zealanders ran more to 'Two up' and 'Crown and Anchor' but these games were not allowed to be carried out within the lines, so in dusk the 'school' assembled out in the sandy wastes where the faint light of their few candles could not be seen from the camp. Especially after a pay day, the 'schools' would boom at night, when various schemes were adopted by rival 'ringmasters' to attract custom. Some would have free biscuits and lemonade distributed amongst their patrons at intervals during the evening; others would have a free issue of cigarettes

and chewing gum, while their exhortations to the motley crew who were in various states of dress and undress, and composed of men from the four corners of the earth urged their patrons to stake their piastres on their fancy in a manner that would have turned an American sideshowman green with envy — 'Shower it in thick and heavy,' they urged, 'You pick 'em and I'll pay 'em,' 'I'll hide 'em and you find 'em,' 'Throw it in my lucky lads, they come here in wheelbarrows and go away in motorcars.' 'Speculate and accumulate,' 'Pour it in, lads. We are the Good Samaritans you read about.' 'Here's where you get the oscar for your next trip to Cairo.'[35]

The ANZAC Mounted Division's approach to discipline followed on from that set by Birdwood in the ANZAC Corps prior to its departure for France. In February 1916 a memorandum on disciplinary policy stated that the Commander-in Chief 'does not consider that detention is a suitable punishment [even when it can be carried out] on active service under present conditions'. Field punishment was to be awarded in its place; at the same time, however, it was stated that field punishment as laid down in Field Regulations would not be carried out but that it 'was preferable in every way that some useful work should be found for men undergoing Field Punishment'.[36] This was very different from France, where it was the most common punishment for summary offences and for courts martial, and sentences were carried out both in the unit and in the divisional field punishment centres in both the NZEF and the AIF.

Field Punishment No. 2, which involved pack drill, loss of leave privileges, and being placed on roster for all menial tasks, remained a summary punishment for commanding officers to award. However, there were few awards of Field Punishment No. 1, which included being chained or roped to a post or support for two hours a day, as well as the other restrictions imposed by Field Punishment No. 2.[37] Field Punishment No. 1 was commonly awarded by the New Zealand and Australian divisions in France, but rarely awarded and hardly ever carried out in Anzac units in Sinai and Palestine. In December 1916, in response to the investigation into abuses in the conduct of Field Punishment No. 1 that had been reported in France, HQ Southern Section in a signal to the ANZAC Mounted Division directed that while Field Punishment No. 1 would be retained as a punishment it was to be reserved for the 'more persistent and troublesome offenders, Field Punishment Number 2 being awarded as the general rule'.[38]

The NZEF (Egypt) Courts Martial Register records four awards of Field Punishment No. 1 and 15 of Field Punishment No. 2, in contrast to 36 awards of Imprisonment with Hard Labour (IHL) or Penal Servitude (PS).[39] Three of the four awards of Field

Punishment No. 1 were to privates of the Rarotongan Labour Company supporting XXI British Corps. They were court-martialled in April 1918 on charges of neglecting to obey camp orders and drunkenness; found guilty, they received sentences ranging from 28 to 56 days' Field Punishment No. 1. The sentences were carried out. The only other award of Field Punishment No. 1 was to a trooper of the Canterbury Mounted Rifles who on return to his regiment from leave was found to have falsified the entries in his pay book. Soldiers under training in Egypt had received sentences of up to 12 months' imprisonment with hard labour for similar offences. This trooper's award of 60 days' Field Punishment No. 1 was commuted to 60 days' Field Punishment No. 2, then quashed. The different fate of the Rarotongan soldiers who appeared before a British Field General Court Martial (FGCM) may have reflected XXI Corps policy, but it may also indicate the generally harsher punishments meted out to native troops in the common belief that this was necessary because of their lower position in the human scale. The British soldier's general attitude to native troops, including Rarotongans, had led to incidents and fights that had been the subject of NZEF complaints in Egypt, but on operations detached units such as the New Zealand Rarotongan Company were at the dictates of corps policy.[40]

The disciplinary system underpinned performance in battle. On operations it was the bond between man and horse that determined the discipline of the New Zealand Mounted Rifles Brigade. The structure of the regiments, and the conditions in which the horsemen operated, meant that an ill-disciplined man did not last. A trooper in the Mounted Rifles was at constant war with the elements of the Sinai Desert or the Jordan Valley. His horse was essential to his survival, as was the cooperation of the other three men in his section. The lazy, careless or dishonest man who may have been able to survive and find his niche in a battalion in France did not make it past the Details Squadron at the depot in Egypt, and if he did the demands of operations soon exposed him and led to his inevitable rejection. It was a hard and demanding war where only the best survived, and even they became worn down and exhausted. Teamwork and 'mateship' were essential to survival in Sinai and Palestine.

> The section of four men being the smallest working unit of a mounted regiment, one man generally attending to the commissariat, and did the cooking and tea-making in mess-tins and billies, while the other three looked after the four or more horses … Newcomers in reinforcement drafts reaching the Brigade for the first time quickly had selfishness knocked out of them, and under the rough chaff and good-humoured patience of their

experienced comrades, quickly learnt the necessity of co-operation in all things, and the valuable lesson of always helping others beside themselves.[41]

The horse always came first.

> On the order to dismount being given, built-up ropes would quickly be taken off the horses' necks and up into one long line. Then while the horseholders in each section looked after the horses, the remainder would set to work with pick, shovel, and bayonet to stretch and anchor down the horse lines. This done, the horses would be tied on the line, off-saddled, perhaps given an opportunity to roll, if the ground was soft, groomed, and then fed. The patient animals always knew the order 'feed up' which was greeted with a chorus of hungry whinnyings and much pawing of the ground.[42]

It was only then that the men would set to and attend to their own comfort.

> Bivvies would spring up all over the area like magic, often supported, if sticks were scarce, on two bayoneted rifles, the bayonet being driven into the ground, while the butt of the rifle carried the canvas or blanket. As dusk fell, hundreds of tiny fires would flicker brightly in the gathering gloom, as shadowy figures moved about in preparation of the indispensable billy of tea to wash down 'hard tack' and 'bully'.[43]

It was on such foundations that the reputation of the Mounted Rifles was made. It was the combination of sound leadership and thoroughly trained soldiers of good calibre; Chaytor and his subordinate commanders worked hard to forge a totally professional 'amateur' mounted force that was capable of enduring sustained operations under trying conditions. This was tested to its limits in the Sinai in the summer of 1916 during the Turkish advance on the Suez Canal.

> By mid-May, the heat raged across the sand; the sharp outlines of the dunes seen in the early morning light would melt into shifting, simmering mirages as the sun climbed higher or be blotted out in the dust of the khamsin, which frequently blew for three days and sometimes longer. Man and horse were tested to the limit when temperatures rose above 120° Fahrenheit in tents under the palms ... Sometimes men were so parched when they

reached camp that they would fling themselves from their horses and drink the brackish water from the same troughs.[44]

It was a time of small patrols and reconnaissance work, 'and there were many casualties from heat stroke among the unseasoned troops, as yet learning their first lessons in nomad life and gaining experience in the problem of desert transport.'[45]

The Battle of Romani in early August 1916 proved the calibre of the ANZAC Mounted Division. It was at Romani on 4 August that the Turks sought to outflank the ANZAC Mounted Division's positions. Chaytor's aerial reconnaissance of the Turkish advance was an innovative and decisive act by a brigadier-general who was to prove that he and his brigade were the finest available in a division of fine brigades. Meldrum of the Wellington Mounted Rifles confirmed the tactical skills and leadership in battle that he had displayed on Gallipoli, as his regiment held the tactically important Wellington Ridge against repeated Turkish attacks. Told to defend the Anzac camps that were covered by the ridge Meldrum, who would become known to his men as 'Fix Bayonets Bill', replied with typical panache: 'If they get through my line here they can have the damned camps.'[46]

The Turkish attempt to seize the Suez Canal was defeated by hard fighting, but it confirmed the Anzac soldiers' admiration for the fighting qualities of the Turkish soldier. The war in the desert was also a war where principles were maintained. 'On the 25th [July 1916] there came a polite note dropped from a German aeroplane warning our ambulances that their red cross flags were not sufficiently visible from the air, a matter to which the ambulances gave serious attention.'[47]

The defeat of this Turkish thrust in the battles of August 1916 led to heavy losses in the brigade, particularly the Canterbury Mounted Rifles. The exertions had a cost that would be repeated with every period of sustained operations.

> The months of September, October, and November [1916] were a period of outpost duty, rest, training and organization. Sanitary effort was not neglected, although the sickness wastage of the Mounted Division would have been considered very high on the Western Front, as it averaged from 12 to 14 per 1000 per week.[48]

The Romani operations had confirmed the abilities of the ANZAC Mounted Division and their superiority over the British yeomanry regiments, who had not worked hard enough to adapt to conditions faced in the Sinai and who tended to be too cumbersome and slow. The key to the Mounted Rifles' and Light Horse's approach was speed in movement onto tactical ground, and then effective infantry tactics once dismounted. The lessons of Romani were absorbed and refined in training in the latter months of 1916 and Chaytor drilled his units to overcome what he saw was a lack of speed in getting into battle. He drove his men hard so at times they looked forward to operations to escape his demanding training for battle. The brigade was fortunate that it retained a solid core of experienced command at all levels and did not suffer the turnover through losses that hampered the evolving professionalism of the division in France.

Russell became seriously concerned when the sickness rate in the New Zealand Division in France reached eight per 1000 a week. This was inevitably accompanied by an increase in courts martial as exhausted men and tired battalions experienced an increase in drunkenness and the accompanying sins of absence and insubordination. This was not the case in Sinai and Palestine. Men who broke down featured as statistics in the sickness rates, but rarely in the disciplinary statistics; drunkenness was not an option, absence difficult, and insubordination settled within the section or troop by men who needed each other to survive. Men got on with each other or were got rid of.

It is difficult to establish the pattern of courts martial in the New Zealand Mounted Rifles Brigade because there were so few during field operations. Between 1916 and 1919 the three Mounted Rifles regiments and the Machine Gun Squadron of the Brigade had a total of 48 courts martial, which were almost evenly shared between the major units: 15 in the Auckland Mounted Rifles, 12 in the Canterbury Mounted Rifles, 13 in the Wellington Mounted Rifles, and eight in No. 1 NZ Machine Gun Squadron. Yet almost all were for offences committed during periods of training in Egypt or while soldiers were on leave; only one each occurred on operations with the Auckland and Canterbury Mounted Rifles. There were none on operations in the Wellington Mounted Rifles, and four in the Machine Gun Squadron. Discipline was the preserve of the commanding officers and they maintained it with rare recourse to court martial. The most serious punishment awarded was six months' imprisonment with hard labour for a Farrier Corporal of the NZ Mounted Field Ambulance who was found guilty of two charges of absence without leave and breaking out of arrest. Disobeying a lawful command, theft, resisting arrest, drunkenness and losing a horse were some of the other offences, but they do not stand comparison with the number of offences and severity of punishment meted out in France.[49]

It is interesting to note that most offences occurred in the smaller units such as the two companies of New Zealanders attached to a battalion of the Imperial Camel Corps, and in the Machine Gun Squadron, including that raised to support the 5th Australian

Light Horse Brigade. Part of this was a reflection of the limited disciplinary powers of the major or captain in command, but perhaps it was also a result of the isolation from the main body of New Zealanders and the problems of welfare and administration that arose from that. It is not that New Zealanders could not integrate on operations with the Light Horse and vice versa, but Sinai confirmed what New Zealanders had learnt on Gallipoli; the two nationalities are different, as they are different again from British troops, and these statistics may be yet another indicator of that difference.

Operations in the Sinai were night marches in long columns of horsemen enveloped in clouds of dust. Tired men on equally tired horses, 'the shuffling of horse' feet … the clink of stirrups and bits … Some men fall asleep in their saddles and are carried on in uneasy oblivion by their understanding mounts — others remain awake in a world of moving shadows and distorted images.'[50] It called for energy, resource and endurance from all ranks, as regiments would cover 40 miles of heavy sand in 30 hours.

In December 1916 the division was grouped with British yeomanry units and the Imperial Camel Corps to form the Desert Column under Lieutenant-General Sir Philip Chetwode. This was all part of General Sir Archibald Murray's Egyptian Expeditionary Force (EEF). The Desert Column occupied El Arish on 21 December, and on 23 December captured Magdhaba. These operations made extreme demands on men and horses, with great distances covered over long periods without water. The growing professionalism of the division was indicated by the New Zealand Mounted Rifles and Light Horse capturing Turkish infantry positions with rifle and bayonet. Once again, it was demonstrated how Chaytor's regiments had moulded themselves into skilled fighting units that seamlessly transited from swiftly moving bodies of horse that rode for covered ground before dismounting, and then became small groups of riflemen working forward in rushes covered by the fire of the Hotchkiss machine-gun teams. With one in every four troopers committed to horse-holding tasks, the holding of a defensive line or the conduct of an attack demanded skill in infantry movement over ground and cover by fire. This was not achieved by dash alone but by constant rehearsals and training. In action, surprise was achieved by the speed with which the brigade moved and the relatively short time it took to mount an attack, all of which kept the Turk off balance.

A period of rest by the sea at El Arish in late December 1916 was necessary to rebuild the tired men and horses of the brigade. January 1917 saw the invasion of Palestine, led by the Desert Column under Chauvel. It consisted of five mounted brigades: two Australian Light Horse brigades, the NZMR, the 5th Yeomanry, and the Camel Brigade. This resulted on 9 January in the Battle of Rafa, an important tactical outpost on the Ottoman border with Egypt. The encirclement of the Turkish position by the NZMR and its attack on the Turkish rear led to 1500 prisoners being taken at a cost of 467 casualties to Chauvel's Desert Column, including 124 New Zealanders; a heavy loss given the size of forces engaged.[51] Chaytor's abilities were superbly demonstrated in this battle, which marked the end of the Sinai Campaign. After a hard day's fighting Lieutenant-General Philip Chetwode was aware that Turkish reinforcements were on their way, and he ordered his units to withdraw from their attack on the town. 'Chaytor, about to launch an attack with his brigade, chose to ignore the order; in the ensuing attack the town's defences were overrun and Rafah [or Rafa] was taken.'[52] Chetwode was full of praise for Chaytor's performance in battle, and wrote to Godley:

> The Rafa show was really won by the New Zealand Mounted Rifles Brigade under Chaytor, who is far the best man of the lot ... a better soldier than any of them, with a real eye for the ground and a fight ... We were quite stuck up in the open, about 400 yards from the trenches, about 3 p.m., and I ordered the New Zealanders to work round the rear and assault the principal work from the rear. This was brilliantly done by Chaytor and his N.Z. lot. They were to have been helped by the Yeomanry but the latter were late in getting round, and the New Zealanders took the bit in their teeth and stormed over the hill yelling like fiends and sent the Turks flying. After which the rest soon collapsed. It was a most inspiring and gallant sight. In both cases we only dismounted about 4000 rifles which when the many protecting detachments were deducted (rendered necessary by the presence of a large number of hostile Bedouins) left none too many to assault 2,000 men in trenches. In fact it was a pretty cheeky performance altogether. General Cox is a fine fighter, as is also Royston ... but both are not a patch on Chaytor.[53]

In addition to the skills the Mounted Rifles had demonstrated in the battles preceding Rafa, this success indicated that what was becoming a superb fighting machine was matched by the eye and skills of its commander. At Rafa, Chaytor showed his eye for ground, demanded speed from his regiments and exploited their infantry skills in the final attack. He knew their capabilities and exploited them to the limit. As Chetwode noted, these skills marked him out from the other brigade commanders who had the dash but did not have Chaytor's eye for ground or his ability to see the big picture. Once again Rafa showed how comparatively more quickly the Mounted Rifles and Light Horse could respond and move compared to the British Yeomanry brigade, which lacked the drills, skill and command drive to match their Anzac counterparts.

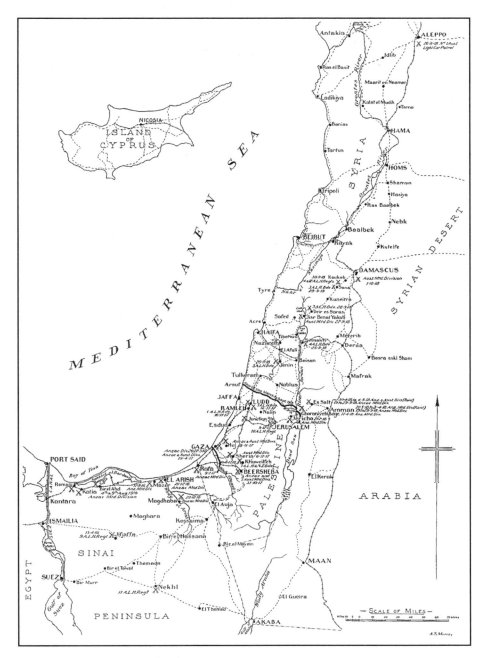

The campaign in Sinai and Palestine.

This success was followed by the frustration of the first battle for Gaza on 26 March 1917. After a day's hard fighting the Australians and New Zealanders who had fought their way into the outskirts of the town were ordered to retire, and withdrew in a 'confused night of intense darkness, the Khamsin blowing; the troops disheartened by lack of success; horses and men exhausted'.[54] For the men who had fought their way into the town, victory was surrendered with the battle almost won. Brigadier-General Granville Ryrie commanding the 2nd Light Horse Brigade wrote of his surprise at being given the order to withdraw and refused to pull back until he had it in writing.[55]

The attack on Gaza had been preceded by weeks of careful reconnaissance. Patrols went out by night to lay up by day on stony outcrops to study the ground in front of Gaza, so the Desert Column would be able to move across the formidable obstacle of the Wadi El Ghuzze, a deep, dissected dry watercourse that barred the way to Gaza. It was this sustained patrolling, or 'picnics' as the Mounted Rifles termed them, that built up a detailed picture of the ground and underpinned their success. They could move comparatively swiftly because they knew where they were going and had studied and anticipated the obstacles they would meet. This was achieved because of the work of night patrols that spent sleepless nights 'on top of a sand hill far from their Regiment … to be shot at by a hostile patrol in the morning'.[56] All of this hard work was frustrated by the failure of First Gaza. The division knew they were winning, and saw victory snatched away from them by the order to withdraw. It was the task of their COs to rebuild their morale after their 'spirits went down to zero, and a period of dark depression was ushered in'.[57]

General Sir Archibald Murray's lack of imagination and lack of grip that had been evident at Romani and in the first battle of Gaza was demonstrated again in the second battle of Gaza where his scarce infantry conducted a predictable frontal assault and were shot to pieces by the now well-entrenched Turks. This would lead to Murray's recall and his replacement by General Sir Edmund Allenby as Commander of the EEF. Allenby would revitalise the campaign, and in this his mounted forces would play a critical role.[58]

As Coates records in his impressive *An Atlas of Australia's Wars*, Allenby's impact on the EEF was similar to the impact Montgomery would make on the Eighth Army on the Alamein line 25 years later. He took command in June, and reorganised his army into three corps: XX and XXI Corps under Lieutenant-Generals Chetwode and Bulfin respectively, and his strike force, the Desert Mounted Corps, commanded by Lieutenant-General Chauvel, consisting of the ANZAC, Australian and Yeomanry mounted divisions.[59] Chaytor was promoted to Major-General in command of the

ANZAC Mounted Division, and Meldrum to Brigadier-General to command the New Zealand Mounted Rifles Brigade.

While Allenby planned and waited for reinforcements from England, operations stagnated in front of Gaza throughout the hot summer. The Turks established an entrenched line over 30 km long to Beersheba, and limited the Desert Column to a war of 'outposts, trench digging, reconnaissance and patrolling'. The constant patrols, or 'stunts' as they were known, 'although of a minor nature in the whole scheme of operations were very trying on the men who performed them'.[60] A man would be on patrol one day, starting with the usual 'stand-to' about three o'clock in the darkness before dawn, travelling over arid dusty country all day, and not returning until after dark. Outpost duty would claim him the next night, to be followed, if he were lucky, by a spell of sorts the next day. Then the cycle of duty would commence again, week after week.

> Their bodies would be but half covered in sleeveless shirts or singlets, always open at the neck, round which was slung the heavy bandolier. Rifles would be carried across the front of the saddle or slung over the left shoulder. Many would be unshaven, with red-rimmed eyes peering from faces darkened by sunburn and dust. The horse's coat would be rough and streaked with sweat, and horse and rider would be smothered in dust from the day's march.[61]

Sickness rates soared, reaching 20 per 1000 per week in the New Zealand Mounted Rifles Brigade. The jaded and war-weary veterans needed rest, and June and September 1917 saw recreation camps established on the beaches. Men rotated through on ten-day spells to build them back to strength with sea-bathing and better food. However, Meldrum ensured that in tactical terms his brigade retained its edge and most of September was spent in 'strenuous training and practice of all kinds'.[62]

The summer months of 1917 climaxed in the Battle for Beersheba. This was the key to Allenby's plan to outflank Gaza by capturing Beersheba and then advancing northwest across the plains, cutting Turkish lines of communication and splitting the Turkish Seventh and Eighth Armies, leaving Gaza surrounded and with no option but to surrender. The attack on Beersheba on 31 October 1917 concluded with the charge of the 4th Australian Light Horse Brigade late in the afternoon. This was made possible by the taking of Tel el Saba, the key to the Turkish position, by the New Zealand Mounted Rifles Brigade led by the Auckland Mounted Rifles. Under their CO, Lieutenant-Colonel J.N. McCarroll, the brigade attacked the hill by clever use of the many dry watercourses.

The squadrons dismounted at various distances from the hill, with the troops moving forward section by section by fire and movement as covering fire was provided by the Hotchkiss machine guns and the artillery of the Somerset Battery. A total of 133 prisoners were taken in this cleverly fought action, which demonstrated the tactical skills of the Mounted Rifles under an experienced commander. McCarroll had joined the unit as the commander of 11th Squadron on its formation in August 1914 and had served with it through Gallipoli and Sinai, being twice wounded.[63] Casualties in the Auckland Mounted numbered six killed, including Captain S.C. Ashton commanding 3rd Squadron, and 22 wounded. The latter included Lieutenant W.H. John, a Main Body man and Gallipoli veteran, promoted from the ranks in May 1916, who was mortally wounded.[64] The battle was against the elements as much as the Turks, as men had to endure days of patrolling and fighting on as little as half a pint of water per man per day; in some cases their horses went without water for 72 hours.[65]

The strength of the brigade was its ability to replace these men from within its ranks with men of equal experience. At the same time trained reinforcements were trickled forward to make good the losses. This was ensured by McCarroll's predecessor Colonel C.E.R. Mackesy, who now commanded the training depot in Egypt. With his strict discipline, keen eye for horsemanship and attention to detail, Mackesy ensured the high standard of reinforcements coming forward to the brigade.

The New Zealand Mounted Rifles Brigade advances through the Hills of Juda towards Bethlehem in early December 1917 during the campaign in Sinai. (F-66833-1/2, L.F. Wilson Collection, Alexander Turnbull Library, Wellington, NZ)

This was followed by the fighting north of Beersheba on the coastal plain in the advance towards Philistia. In this battle lack of water and determined Turkish rearguard actions made Allenby's considerable and impressive victory less than he had hoped. At Ayun Kara on 14 November 1917 the New Zealand Mounted Rifles had 44 killed and 81 wounded. It was a hard fight against a determined enemy made up of Turkish cavalry and infantry who mounted a series of clever counterattacks that took all the skill of the Mounted Rifles to overcome.

> When it is remembered that a mounted rifle regiment dismounts for action only a little over two hundred men and that the Regiment was far from full strength, the eighty nine casualties suffered by Auckland give some indication of the fierceness of the engagement. There were probably not more than one hundred and thirty or one hundred and forty men in the line.[66]

Losses were heavy, particularly among the officers. Lieutenant-Colonel McCarroll was wounded, and the Boer War veteran Captain F.M. Twistleton MC was mortally wounded. Turkish casualties numbered 160 dead and some 250 wounded.[67] November 1917 continued to be a month of hard fighting north of Jaffa, and the brigade was again exhausted when it was rested in early 1918 among the vineyards and orchards of the Jewish settlements of Richon le Zion. Chaytor ensured that oranges were issued to the men to supplement the standard diet of corned beef and biscuits, and the same pattern of reinforcement and retraining occurred to bring the New Zealand Mounted Rifles Brigade back to fighting fitness.

'Eight months campaigning in the Jordan Valley with two raids into the mountains of Moab, the first a partial, the last a complete success, concluded the operations of the NZMR Brigade … in the victorious year of 1918.'[68] This brief statement summarises a difficult final year of operations for Chaytor's ANZAC Mounted Division and the NZMR Brigade.

Allenby's plan to mount a decisive spring offensive was dashed by the Germans' March offensive of 1918. His Egyptian Expeditionary Force was gutted of 60,000 infantry to reinforce Haig's armies. While he rebuilt his force with Indian Army units a series of raids was mounted across the Jordan River threatening Amman, the important rail junction at Deraa, and the capture of the grain harvest around Amman and Es Salt that was so important to the Turkish logistic effort. The raids and the capture of the harvest were also planned to assist the spread of the Arab revolt in which T.E. Lawrence played so prominent a part.

Hard men of the New Zealand Mounted Rifles. *(National Army Museum, Waiouru Collection)*

In February 1918 the ANZAC Mounted Division began operations in the Jordan Valley. This climaxed in late March with the raid on Amman; it was a failure. The Turks reacted strongly to the threat and poured in reinforcements that threatened to cut off the long narrow salient thrust into the Jordan hills. The mounted formations relied on their speed of movement, but in this case the difficult going and the intensity of the Turkish reaction highlighted the intrinsic lack of numbers and lack of artillery support that was the reality of independent mounted operations. Against fierce resistance in cold wintry weather and over difficult mountainous terrain the Mounted Rifles had heavy casualties. While the rearguard held its ground the wounded were evacuated tied to horses, lashed face down head to tail; 'some had penetrating wounds of head, thorax or abdomen — and the firing line held fast for a precious three hours until all were brought away'.[69]

There was a second raid on Es Salt between 30 April and 4 May. Es Salt was captured, but the Turks sent in reinforcements and the raiders found themselves again threatened on all sides in a dangerous salient, and had to fight their way out. Allenby wanted pressure applied on this flank and Chaytor met his demands. It was infantry country but the Mounted Rifles, Light Horse and Camel Corps responded, despite lack of numbers and insufficient artillery support. They skilfully conducted operations in hills unsuited for horse operations against a determined enemy where units with less cohesion and leadership would have met with disaster.

The raids convinced the Turks that Allenby intended to advance east of the Jordan, leading them to concentrate the Turkish Fourth Army, a third of their total force, on this flank, while the Seventh and Eighth Armies defended Samaria and the Plain of Sharon.[70] For the rest of the summer and early autumn the ANZAC Mounted Division was in 'bivouac in the weird depths of the Jordan Valley, 266 fathoms below sea level, where no Europeans had ever dared to live in summer time before. But the Anzacs were not Europeans and they stuck it out somehow'.[71]

Allenby's Battle of Megiddo called on Chaytor Force — consisting of the ANZAC Mounted Division reinforced by an infantry brigade, two battalions of British West Indians, and two recently formed Jewish battalions — to remain in the Jordan Valley with the task of convincing the Turkish Fourth Army that an offensive was to be mounted across the Jordan River towards Amman. On the coastal plain Bulfin's XXI Corps was to break through the Turkish defensive line, allowing Chauvel's Desert Mounted Corps to thrust deep behind the Turkish defences and cut them off. Aircraft of the RAF completely dominated the skies. A deception plan saw empty camps erected in the Jordan Valley, while mules dragging sleighs created dust clouds along roads, convincing Turkish observers that forces were being massed on this flank.

Megiddo began at 4.30 a.m. on 19 September, 'almost to the day and in the same spot that Richard Coeur de Lion had defeated Saladin'.[72] The attack totally surprised the Turkish defenders. Bulfin's infantry broke in with hard fighting and Chauvel's Desert Mounted Corps, moving in mass, broke through and swept in a wide left hook behind the Turkish lines of communication. Critical crossing points on the Jordan River were seized, with the Turkish Commander, the German General Liman von Sanders, narrowly escaping capture in his pyjamas from his headquarters in Nazareth.

Chaytor Force in the Jordan Valley harried the Turkish Fourth Army and kept on its heels as it began to withdraw. The force held the crossings on the Jordan and, supported by aircraft strafing and bombing the Turkish columns, advanced and seized Es Salt and Amman. It also prevented the Turkish garrisons to the south escaping up the Hejaz Railway. By 30 September the Maan garrison of 4600 had surrendered. It was a brilliantly executed operation. In Hill's words:

> Chaytor's bag of prisoners for the period of less than a fortnight was 10,322,
> besides guns and machine guns and other booty; the casualties of his entire

> force were only 139 … Such figures reflect more than the collapse of Turkish
> morale; they show the skill with which Chaytor commanded his Force
> in operations where the enemy always had the advantage in ground and
> observation.[73]

Chaytor's ability was matched by the tactical skill of his subordinate commanders, who led veteran units inured to the demands of difficult, stony country and the privations forced by the difficulties of supply over such going.

The demands of this fast-moving campaign pushed Chaytor's brigades, both men and horse, to the point of collapse. The sudden change from the intense heat of the Jordan Valley to operations around Amman saw men collapse with fever. This was accentuated after the collapse of the Turkish forces; as many as 190 men went sick overnight, totally overloading the medical services that were at hand. There were no ambulances, so the men were evacuated in lorries. The victory over the Turks was followed by the swift victory of disease over the New Zealand Mounted Rifles Brigade. 'In the first 12 days of October the ambulance admitted over 700 cases of malaria, most of it malignant. The New Zealand Brigade lost at least a third of its strength.'[74]

It was a time of madness all round. Men of the ANZAC Mounted Division had to band with their Turkish prisoners to hold off Feisal's Arabs, who were intent on revenge and murder against the defeated Turk.[75] Large gambling schools flourished unchecked, funded by enormous stocks of paper money looted from a train captured in the Barada Gorge on the route north from Damascus. When the horsemen found the money was no longer accepted by Damascus tradesmen:

> … soldiers broke into an orgy of card-playing for high stakes. The sky was
> the limit on a single throw at two-up or a hand at poker. One player would
> casually bet a hundred pounds on three aces, and the next player would
> calmly say, 'Your hundred, and up another hundred,' and the stakes would
> ultimately stagger the Jubilee Plunger [a notorious gambler] had he been
> present. Thousands of pounds would change hands at a sitting.[76]

The exhausted brigade regrouped near Richon and longed for home. It was an unsettled period, during which the Canterbury Mounted Rifles were sent as part of the British garrison to Gallipoli. The Armistice saw disturbances and outbreaks in Egypt as men in the training depots liquored up and then looted the bars. Chaytor saw this as a failure in command on the part of the CO of the training depot and sacked him.[77] As far as he was concerned it was the officers who had to rise to the circumstances brought on by the end of the hostilities and maintain a grip on their units.

On the night of 10 December 1918 the New Zealanders were involved in one of the worst incidents of the war involving British troops, when they raided the Arab village of Surafend and a nearby Arab encampment and killed some 38 Arab men.[78] The attack was sparked by the murder the night before of Trooper L.T. Lowry of the 1st New Zealand Machine Gun Squadron, who was killed after disturbing an intruder in his tent. Footprints seemed to lead in the direction of the nearby village of Surafend, and when it seemed the military police could find nothing that incriminated the village, the Mounteds decided to deal with it. Armed with pickaxe handles and bayonets, men of the New Zealand Mounted Rifles and Australian Light Horse cordoned off the village, pushed out the women and children, then beat to death all the men they found before tumbling their bodies down wells and setting the village on fire. A nearby Arab settlement was treated in the same manner. Despite the highly coordinated way in which the attack was conducted, no officers intervened. The camp picquet arrived only after the attackers had dispersed, finding the village on fire and some badly beaten Arabs with broken limbs, who had been lucky to escape death.[79]

Chaytor was incensed and blamed his subordinate commanders. A court of inquiry failed to identify any of the perpetrators, but Chaytor knew that an episode on this scale would not have gone unnoticed, and saw it as a failure in command. Allenby was equally irate. He paraded the ANZAC Mounted Division and berated them as cold-blooded murderers. 'Once I was proud of you,' he said; 'I am proud of you no longer.'[80] Chaytor disciplined his officers by stopping their leave; Allenby went further and refused to include the names of the officers and men of the ANZAC Mounted Division camped at Surafend for honours and awards in his Peace Dispatches. This struck at the heart of what the NZMR had achieved in the closing campaign, and became the subject of a series of submissions to have the names forwarded for recognition, only some of which were recognised belatedly.

Surafend was a vicious act which, as I wrote many years ago, 'was a blot on the reputation of the New Zealand Mounteds. They acted out of tribal loyalty, in revenge for what had happened to one of their own, and their own officers tacitly accepted their actions. Surafend cannot be condoned, but it can be understood.'[81]

During the war the New Zealand Mounted Rifles Brigade and attached units suffered a death toll of 1166; 476 of these occurred in the eight months of the Gallipoli Campaign. The breakdown for fatalities in units of the New Zealand Mounted Rifles Brigade is detailed below.

- Brigade Headquarters: 2
- AMR: 333
- CMR: 333
- WMR: 324
- NZ Company ICC: 44
- NZ Engineers: 11
- NZ Machine Gun Corps: 56
- NZASC: 2
- Rarotongan Company: 11

Casualties during the Sinai and Palestine Campaign numbered 44 officers and 596 other ranks who died from all causes, with 88 officers and 1058 other ranks wounded; a total of 1786.

It was not a swift return home for the New Zealand Mounteds. The nationalist uprising in Egypt led to delays in sailings and growing frustration among the men who remained. An outburst of looting took place on the night of the peace celebrations in July 1919 and a number of New Zealanders were court-martialled and received imprisonment with hard labour. Eighteen courts martial occurred in 1919, and this included three troopers of the Canterbury Mounted Rifles who were found not guilty of rape.[82]

While the men eventually returned home to New Zealand, quarantine regulations made that impossible for their horses. Those not destined for British or Egyptian army units were led out into the sands and shot by their riders rather than risk them suffering maltreatment by Egyptian purchasers. It was all a sad anti-climax to what had been a superb, disciplined performance in a difficult campaign.

The basis of the success of the New Zealand Mounted Rifles Brigade paralleled that of the New Zealand Division. Selection and training in New Zealand and an equally rigorous training and selection process in the New Zealand 'Details Squadrons' in Egypt guaranteed a high calibre of mounted horseman. The self-discipline imposed by the routine of man and horse, the teamwork of the mounted sections and troops, and the experienced leadership at brigade and regimental level determined the high standards of the New Zealand Mounted Rifles Brigade. This was demonstrated time and again in battle under the superb leadership of Chaytor, his successor Meldrum and their subordinate commanders. Success in battle was met with the inevitable attrition of experienced officers and men, and could not have been sustained without the supply of trained reinforcements and constant retraining that occurred during every period of

Lonely graves on the Roman road to Jericho. *(F-106342-1/2, Alexander Turnbull Library, Wellington, NZ)*

rest. The horsemen alone were not enough; their quality had to be matched by the strict discipline and tactical skills of veteran commanders who could read ground and knew how far mounted horsemen en masse could be pushed. The finale was always dependent on their tactical ability as infantry working in small units supported by their own machine guns and always with limited artillery support. As we will find in our study of the Western Front, small-group fire and movement underpinned the horsemen's tactical success in the same way as it was central to an understanding of how the trench deadlock was broken in France and Flanders.

The New Zealand Mounted Rifles Brigade has become the forgotten story in New Zealand's military history, yet by whatever measure one chooses, this was one of the finest fighting bodies that New Zealand has ever raised.

SEVEN

'Flotsam on the fringe of hell':
Discipline and Morale in the NZEF

Pity for the tired men,
Up the line and down again
Tramping where their comrade fell.
Flotsam on the fringe of hell.[1]

M.E. Hankins, 3rd Battalion Wellington Regiment, NZEF

In 1991 I published *On the Fringe of Hell: New Zealanders and Military Discipline in the First World War*. One of the first studies of its kind, it is now but one of a growing body of literature in the field. Yet it is still the only study that examines the range of punishments available and their use within a division as a microcosm of the British experience on the Western Front, throughout the course of the campaign from 1916 until the armistice and beyond into demobilisation in 1919. Crime and sickness rates have been the traditional measures of the discipline and morale of a unit, and are still used for that purpose today. In tracing the evolution of a New Zealand disciplinary system in this chapter I have concentrated on courts martial statistics, which are but one measure of the changes occurring within the NZEF during the First World War. Statistics alone do not tell the whole story, but when judged against the peaks and troughs reflecting the periods of combat intensity and relatively quiet periods in the trenches or in training out of the line, they form an interesting and consistent pattern. This pattern traces the evolution of the New Zealanders of the NZEF into a professional fighting force, which is one of the principal themes of this book.

Where figures are available I have compared the New Zealand performance with those of the AIF and the Canadian Expeditionary Force (CEF). One sees a parallel pattern in all three forces as they journey from ill-trained citizen armies to professional bodies hardened in warfare. The disciplinary statistics of the three dominions diverge during the intense fighting of 1918, and it is here that one sees the impact of combat exhaustion on under-strength units. This is particularly evident in the AIF, and is seen to a lesser extent in the CEF.

When the New Zealand Division arrived in France in 1916 its inexperience was reflected particularly strongly both in the front line and in its administration. Inexperienced commanders overreacted to disciplinary breakdowns, and this was reflected in the courts martial statistics. As Cathryn Corns and John Hughes-Wilson's perceptive study *Blindfold and Alone* confirms, the harsh sentencing policy of the New Zealand Division was balanced by the Commander-in-Chief, General (later Field Marshal) Sir Douglas Haig's 'desire to punish only in the interests of group discipline and wherever possible, by Haig's desire to give a man another chance'.[2] Dominion disciplinary zeal was tempered by the checks and balances built into the administration of military justice in the British armies in France, and as recent studies show, Haig was far from the ruthless hanging judge of legend.[3] In condemning Haig in this way, as is still the fashion, we overlook the fact that 2694 of the 3040 British soldiers sentenced to death were not executed. If the policy of Haig and his army commanders in their review of New Zealand courts martial is consistent with other divisions in the British Armies in France, it raises questions about the findings of those writers who seem to look no further than the fact that the soldiers were executed, rather than place this in the context of the times.[4] It is only with the recent study by Corns and Hughes-Wilson that we have

The New Zealanders arrive in France: the First Auckland Infantry Battalion, led by their Commanding Officer, Lieutenant-Colonel Arthur Plugge, the last of the original COs of the Main Body NZEF, march through the streets of Marseilles. (*Wilson and Horton Collection*)

a study of capital punishment in the British armies in the First World War that sees beyond the polemic.

The General Officer Commanding the New Zealand Division, Major-General Sir Andrew Russell, was a man of his time. He and his officers, who in the main were wartime volunteers reflecting the society from which they came, accepted the need for capital punishment as the final sanction. However, this was increasingly balanced by an understanding of the men they commanded, a striving to improve the administration of the division, and a realisation that all men had their limits. Most of all, one sees their appreciation that under-strength units could not perform effectively and that this inevitably impacted on discipline and morale. It was this that compensated for an ageing and less flexible group of reinforcements and the growing war-weariness of 1918 so that despite the demands made on the division, its fighting performance was matched by superb discipline, as is reflected in the statistics.

The New Zealand Expeditionary Force sailed to war in October 1914 with its officers and men as blind to the realities of the war they would fight as they were ignorant of the King's Regulations that would dictate the discipline and procedures that governed their lives for the next four years. New Zealand's 1909 Defence Act made the members of the New Zealand Expeditionary Force subject in every respect to the British Army Act. The implications of this were never considered in 1914. It was a citizen army with little training and a smattering of experience. Nowhere was this lack more obvious than among the Territorial officers who filled most of the command appointments. During mobilisation in New Zealand in the first months of the war these deficiencies were overlooked because of the 'discipline of enthusiasm' that bound the volunteers together. Experience was limited to the Regular Officers of the New Zealand Staff Corps and Imperial Officers on secondment. It was these officers, under the direction of the force commander Major-General Sir Alexander Godley, who dictated the standards of the force. The settling in process started on the voyage overseas, which gave the citizen soldiers a taste of the monotony of military life. This continued during training in Egypt, where the New Zealand Expeditionary Force was linked with the 1st Australian Light Horse Brigade and Monash's 4th Australian Infantry Brigade to form the NZ&A Division. This, with the 1st Australian Division, became part of Sir William Birdwood's ANZAC Corps. Egypt was hard training, where the citizen soldiers would learn the basics of their new trade.

Godley demanded perfection and his soldiers cursed him for it. 'Heaven help us when and if I ever become popular,' he responded.[5] Godley never did become popular, but the standards of administration and discipline that he set in the NZEF became guidelines that continued for the rest of its existence. Indeed, an appreciation of Godley's influence in Egypt and later on Gallipoli, his successor Russell's influence in France, and Brigadier-General (later Major-General) E.W.C. Chaytor's influence on the New Zealand Mounted Rifles in the Sinai and Palestine Campaign is essential to an understanding of the discipline of New Zealanders in the First World War. Their influence proves again the truth of Napoleon's maxim that there are no good or bad battalions, only good or bad commanding officers. Standards are set at the top and it is the calibre of leadership at this level that dictates the performance of the force.

It was in Egypt that the first courts martial were held. These were military tribunals made up of three to five officers who sat in judgement on offences under the British Army Act that were too serious to be dealt with summarily by commanding officers. The initial policy was for 'incorrigibles' to be returned to New Zealand in disgrace. This action had a positive effect that lessened once soldiers experienced combat and, having seen war's reality, some men sought any excuse to get 'Home'.

The benefits of training in Egypt were demonstrated on the Gallipoli Peninsula. The weak link for New Zealand units proved to be officer inexperience, but the men showed an adaptability and intelligence that came to be seen as a characteristic of the 'Anzac' soldier. The Gallipoli experience was unique in that self-discipline was everything. If a man lacked it, he died of a sniper's bullet or collapsed from enteric fever and dysentery. The campaign is remarkable for the very few courts martial among New Zealanders and Australians. Seven New Zealand courts martial were held on the peninsula out of 41 New Zealand courts martial held in theatre during the eight months of the campaign.

It was different in France. The New Zealand Division had been in existence for two months when its three infantry brigades landed at Marseilles in late April 1916. Like its Australian counterparts it was a raw, untrained division with inexperienced officers manning divisional headquarters, brigades and units. The Gallipoli experience was concentrated in the original 1 NZ Infantry Brigade, with a cadre of officers and NCOs providing a basis of experience for the reinforcements that made up the strength of 2 NZ Infantry Brigade. The last two battalions of 3 NZ Rifle Brigade arrived in Egypt just before the division sailed for France, and this brigade had no time to carry out brigade training with its four battalions. As events would show, it was neither ready nor fit for combat.

The New Zealand-born divisional commander Major-General Sir Andrew Russell was conscious of his division's inexperience and hoped to train his formations in France before going into the trenches. This did not happen. By late May 1916 the divisions of the ANZAC Corps were occupying the Armentières sector, a nursery where new divisions were blooded on the Western Front. It was too soon. Battalion officers and NCOs were sent on courses to learn the ways of trench warfare and battalions occupied the front line with an average of 11 officers available for trench duty in each battalion of 1000 men. There was a lack of direction and communication in units, which was exacerbated by the demands of the Somme offensive. The demand for large-scale trench raids and the inevitable artillery bombardments these raids drew in response added to the pressure on the troops.

In June and July 1916 some New Zealand battalions spent up to 32 days continuously in the front line. The strain of this experience showed in the sickness statistics and the high rate of offences, particularly the number of courts martial, and combat-weary Gallipoli veterans featured prominently. The billeting of troops in the villages behind the lines also emphasised the differences from Gallipoli. Estaminets were everywhere and drink cheap and plentiful. Men who could not face the thought of returning to the trenches found their escape in alcohol. Drunkenness, absence without leave, and insubordination became prevalent offences and remained so for the duration of the war.

In response a commanding officer could summarily award a maximum punishment of 28 days' field punishment. More serious offences were subject to Field General Courts Martial convened by the brigade commander and consisting of three officers, the senior, usually a major, being president. The niceties of military law were just another skill

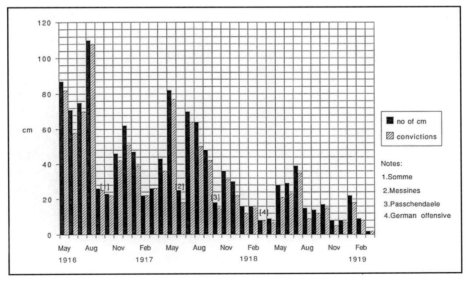

Courts martial in the New Zealand Division, 1916–19. *(NA WA 22/6/10)*

for Territorial officers to learn; the courts were swamped with offences, and standards suffered accordingly. The chart opposite below shows the number and pattern of courts martial in the New Zealand Division during the war.

As one can see, in 1916, except for the two months of the Somme offensive, there were more courts martial in the division each month than the total number of New Zealand courts martial for the entire eight months of the Gallipoli Campaign. The men of the now much larger force, consisting of raw troops with inexperienced leadership, regardless of their potential, were not able to handle the stresses placed on them by the conditions they experienced on the Western Front. This first experience of trench warfare almost broke the New Zealand Division. August 1916 saw 110 courts martial and seven death sentences awarded by New Zealand courts as inexperienced commanders responded to breakdowns in communication and administration with a tightening of discipline.

In many cases the offence was a symptom of a failure in command on the part of an officer or NCO. In Russell's view this did not pardon the offence or mitigate the severity of the punishment. He took steps to improve the calibre and training of his officers and NCOs, but continued to demand strict discipline. In every respect he was determined to have the best division in France, as he made clear in September 1916 in a letter to James Allen, his Minister of Defence:

> The discipline of the Divn is fair. I can't say more. There are 70% first rate fellows, 20% weak and 10% who are born to give trouble. We should be a better fighting unit without the 10% … Bad characters do not make good soldiers. With our men we might well earn the title of being the best division in France. That we shall not do so will be partly my fault, partly the fault of the 10%.[6]

Russell was determined that the ten percent would not tarnish his division's good name, and it was he who set the standards for his New Zealanders. Throughout the war he monitored levels of punishment in his brigades and battalions, and demanded that serious offences receive the maximum sentence. Guidelines were issued to his brigadier-generals and commanding officers to ensure this was carried out.

As the chart shows one's chance of being acquitted by courts martial in the New Zealand Division were slim indeed, and Russell's influence is evident in the pattern of courts martial in the New Zealand Division from 1916 to 1919 seen in the previous chart. The troughs reflect periods of intense activity, while the peaks indicate periods of training out of the line where the offence rate soared as men went on a 'drunk' and committed the related crimes of absence and insubordination. This was also the time when offences committed during the periods of intense activity were caught up with and formal disciplinary procedures carried out.

As the declining numbers of courts martial indicate, New Zealand discipline improved as the war progressed. This was in spite of changes from a volunteer to a conscript reinforcement, the increasing age of reinforcements and the mobilisation of married men. Improved discipline was a reflection of the sound initial training of the New Zealand soldier, the insistence on trained and experienced junior officers and on the careful selection and regular replacement of commanding officers. Russell closely monitored his subordinate commanders' performances and removed or rested them by spelling them in training appointments when they showed signs of exhaustion. Equal care was given to the selection and training of junior officers and NCOs, and by 1918 50 percent of all officers who served in the New Zealand Division had risen from the ranks. Maintaining a balance between reinforcement with Territorial officers from New Zealand and commissioning from the ranks was a subject of fierce debate and concern among veteran rankers in the division, but Russell recognised that both sources were necessary. He did not want to commission and therefore take away from the ranks of his battalions all of the better NCOs, a balance of whom were needed as future CSMs and RSMs.

Most important of all was the ongoing attention to the care and welfare of the men. In his first conference after the Somme in 1916 Russell noted in his diary: 'Divisional Conference — Outlined policy — Men's comfort and safety first, the rest nowhere.'[7] As he informed his Minister for Defence, '[I] have told Brigadiers and Commanding Officers to forget about the Germans of a few days and devote their minds and energies towards establishing a good system of interior economy, and improving the discipline of their Units.'[8]

The New Zealand success on the Somme in 1916 was due to the performance of the New Zealand 'Digger'. The emphasis Russell placed on training his division in the latest tactical drills paid dividends. This compensated for the lack of command and staff experience at the New Zealand brigade and divisional headquarters. Russell recognised this inexperience and appreciated that it was the cause of many of the difficulties his division had suffered at Armentières. He realised he could not demand standards without giving in return, and from this time on the care and welfare of his men became his principal concern.

Canadian experience had an important influence on the ANZAC Corps' operational and disciplinary policy. On their arrival in France in 1916 both I and II ANZAC Corps sought advice from the Canadians on all aspects of trench warfare, and this was passed down to divisional staffs. The rigorous policy practised by the Canadians in their field punishment centres was adopted by both Birdwood's and Godley's corps. Indeed, all three dominions showed a common approach to disciplinary policy that was characterised by the same zeal recorded in the New Zealand statistics.

New Zealand courts were manned by New Zealand officers drawn largely from the Territorial Force or, as the war progressed, from the ranks of the division. In dispensing justice the members of the court mirrored the society from which they came. There were no shades of grey in the New Zealand approach, and this had its origins in the New Zealand criminal code. Capital punishment was not an issue. In New Zealand murderers faced the hangman's noose. Sex offenders and molesters faced imprisonment and flogging or whipping. 'Boys under 16 could be whipped for all the offences in the Crimes Act 1908 for which adults could be flogged.'[9] This view was transferred to the military code and punishment was meted out as a deterrent to others.

Twenty-eight New Zealanders were sentenced to death, 27 by courts martial in France, and 25 of these by New Zealand courts. Twenty-six charges were for desertion (including one of leaving his guard), one for mutiny, and one for sleeping at his post. Five men in the New Zealand Division were executed: Privates Frank Hughes, John

Major-General Sir Andrew Russell inspecting a billet in France. Out of the line it was the 'Men's comfort and safety first, the rest nowhere', which underpinned the discipline of the New Zealand Division. (*National Army Museum, Waiouru Collection*)

Sweeney and John Braithwaite in 1916; John King in 1917; and Victor Spencer in 1918. Braithwaite was the only one of the five who was sentenced to death by a British court martial. Two of the five, Sweeney and King, were Australians serving with the New Zealand Division. In the division the pressure to execute came from within and was not imposed on a reluctant dominion force by outside pressure from above.

Hughes, Sweeney, King and Spencer were guilty of the offences for which they were charged, but in hindsight Sweeney, King and Spencer were combat exhaustion cases who should never have faced the firing squad. They died because they were the outsiders in their units and because the division had nothing positive to say about them to the British headquarters that reviewed sentence. This was the determining factor between life and death.

New Zealand courts made five recommendations for mercy, all of which were accepted by the British High Command. Indeed, what stands out in a study of the New Zealanders sentenced to death is the willingness of the army and Haig's General Headquarters to commute death sentences despite strong recommendations from the division to have a man shot. It is true to say that New Zealand disciplinary zeal was ameliorated by the judicial checks and balances set in place by the British High Command. This is also reflected in Corns and Hughes-Wilson's findings in their study of British cases.[10] Godefroy's study of the 25 Canadian soldiers sentenced to death during the First World War comes to a different conclusion in that he finds that recommendations for mercy by Canadian courts martial were overruled by higher command. On closer study, however, in these cases there was usually disagreement between unit, brigade and division within the CEF over whether the sentence should be recommended or not, and in the context of 1916 and the Somme, this usually swung the pendulum towards execution.[11] The cases of capital punishment in the CEF show similarities with the New Zealand experience, in that desertion in battle, repeat offenders or prolonged absence usually saw sentences confirmed. This was the situation in 1917, and in 1918 all of the seven Canadians executed were repeat offenders.[12]

Like New Zealand, Australia and Canada believed in the necessity for capital punishment. Both Canada and New Zealand sentenced and executed their soldiers in France. The AIF readily sentenced its soldiers to death, and did so in the belief that the British Army Act extended to the AIF 'without qualification', but had it pointed out by the British High Command that a provision in the 1903 Australian Defence Act required the concurrence of the Australian Governor-General before the sentence could be confirmed.[13] The initiative to remove this obstacle came from Australian commanders, who saw the failure of the Australian Government to agree to this change as having a serious impact on disciplinary standards.[14] In this they were supported by the Army commanders under whom they served; Rawlinson, commanding the 4th Army, and Gough, commanding the 5th Army, both supported Birdwood and his divisional commander's requests.[15] Throughout 1916 there was a concerted campaign by Australian commanders to have the death sentence imposed on their soldiers and have the AIF come under the British Army Act in every respect. They, like their Canadian and New Zealand contemporaries, were men of their time and saw the death sentence as essential for effective discipline.

Regt No	Rank	Name	Unit	Civ Occupation	Age	Born	Offence	Date CM / Auth		Sentence CM
10/549	Pte	John Robert DUNN	WIB	journalist	26	NZ	sleeping at post	18.7.15	NZ&A Div	death /mercy
24/2041	Pte	Thomas C.MORRISON	2CIB	labourer	38	NZ	leaving guard	4.8.16	2NZ Bde	death
13/3246	Pte	William BARNETT	1AIB	labourer	28	NZ	desertion	11.8.16	1NZ Bde	death
24/2008	Pte	Frank HUGHES	2CIB	labourer	28	NZ	desertion	12.8.16	2NZ Bde	death
12/2132	Pte	Charles THOMAS	1AIB	labourer	28	NZ	desertion	24.8.16	1NZ Bde	death
12/3197	Pte	James T.WILLIAMS	1AIB	carrier	31	NZ	desertion	24.8.16	1NZ Bde	death
12/2881	Pte	William WELSH	1AIB	labourer	41	England	desertion	24.8.16	1NZ Bde	death
8/3281	Pte	Alexander HAMPDEN	2OIB	chemist	25	UK	desertion	30.8.16	2NZ Bde	death
8/1384	Pte	John J.SWEENEY	1OIB	labourer	37	Australia	desertion	13.9.16	1NZ Bde	death
24/1521	Pte	John BRAITHWAITE	2OIB	journalist	35	NZ	mutiny	11.10.16	Brit GCM	death
21940	Pte	John BURT	2 BN NZRB	rabbiter	26	NZ	desertion	1.12.16	3NZ R Bde	death
23/1227	Pte	Harold H.WALKER	1 BN NZRB	bootmaker	32	NZ	desertion	1.12.16	3NZ R Bde	death
12 2018	Pte	Thomas LOWRY	2AIB	coach painter	28	Ireland	desertion	26.12.16	2NZ Bde	death
17751	Pte	John W.BLACK	1OIB	labourer	33	NZ	desertion	12.4.17	2NZ Bde	death
6/1209	Pte	Constantine RUMMEL	2WIB	labourer	20	NZ	desertion	16.6.17	1NZ Bde	death/mercy
4/1563	Pte	Edward R.CRAWFORD	NZ Tunnelling Coy	labourer	29	Australia	desertion	3.7.17	VI Br Corps	death
12/1142	Pte	Frederick J.BAKER	1AIB	carter	26	NZ	desertion	4.7.17	1NZ Bde	death
14864	Pte	John RAYNOR	2AIB	bridge builder	33	Australia	desertion	3.8.17	1NZ Bde	death
6/1598	Pte	John KING	1CIB	miner	33-39?	Australia	desertion	5.8.17	2NZ Bde	death
11401	Pte	William BLACK	2OIB	compositor	40	Scotland	desertion	30.8.17	2NZ Bde	death
12547	Pte	William A.KERR	2AIB	labourer	38	Australia	desertion	4.9.17	1NZ Bde	death/mercy
6/4610	Pte	Thomas GEORGE	2OIB	shepherd	22	NZ	desertion	8.10.17	2NZ Bde	death/mercy
23011	Pte	Alfred H.MORGANS	2OIB	farmer	22	NZ	desertion	8.10.17	2NZ Bde	death/mercy
24143	Pte	Henry O.DAIKEE	1CIB	labourer	22	NZ	desertion	19.10.17	2NZ Bde	death
7/1594	Dvr	William E.BASHAM	NZFA	carpenter	22	NZ	desertion	3.1.18	CRA NZ	death
8/2733	Pte	Victor M.SPENCER	1OIB	engineer	20	NZ	desertion	17.1.18	2NZ Bde	death
12/3728	Pte	Louis H.MEYRICK	2AIB	ironmonger	24	NZ	desertion	6.4.18	1NZ Bde	death
7/1563	Pte	Charles H.CLOSE	1CIB	labourer	25	NZ	desertion	10.5.18	2NZ Bde	death

Regt No	Rank	Name	Unit	Sentence Awarded	Promulgated	Remarks
10/549	Pte	John Robert DUNN	WIB	remitted	5.8.16	KIA 8.8.15
24/2041	Pte	Thomas C.MORRISON	2CIB	commuted 5yrs IHL suspended	15.8.16	KIA 24.8.18
13/3246	Pte	William BARNETT	1AIB	commuted 5yrs PS suspended	18.8.16	WIA16.9.16 sentence put into effect 17.7.18
24/2008	Pte	Frank HUGHES	2CIB	confirmed	24.8.16	shot 25.8.16
12/2132	Pte	Charles THOMAS	1AIB	re-assemble AWOL 2yrs IHL	13.9.16	sent to prison
12/3197	Pte	James T.WILLIAMS	1AIB	re-assemble AWOL 2yrs IHL	13.9.16	sent to prison
12/2881	Pte	William WELSH	1AIB	re-assemble AWOL 2yrs IHL	13.9.16	sent to prison KIA 5.10.17
8/3281	Pte	Alexander HAMPDEN	2OIB	quashed	22.9.16	
8/1384	Pte	John J.SWEENEY	1OIB	confirmed	1.10.16	shot 2.10.16
24/1521	Pte	John BRAITHWAITE	2OIB	confirmed	28.10.16	shot 29.10.16
21940	Pte	John BURT	2 BN NZRB	commuted 10yrs PS	12.12.16	sent to prison
23/1227	Pte	Harold H.WALKER	1 BN NZRB	commuted 10yrs PS	12.12.16	sent to prison
12 2018	Pte	Thomas LOWRY	2AIB	commuted 15yrs PS	5.1.17	sent to prison
17751	Pte	John W.BLACK	1OIB	commuted 10yrs PS suspended	24.4.17	KIA 6.5.17
6/1209	Pte	Constantine RUMMEL	2WIB	commuted 10yrs PS	22.6.17	sent to prison
4/1563	Pte	Edward R.CRAWFORD	NZ Tunnelling Coy	commuted 5yrs PS suspended	14,7,17	SIW 22.1.18
12/1142	Pte	Frederick J.BAKER	1AIB	commuted 15yrs PS suspended	23.7.17	WIA 17.8.17sentence put into effect7.11.17
14864	Pte	John RAYNOR	2AIB	commuted 10yrs PS suspended	9.8.17	WIA 23.11.17,WIA 1.9.18,DOW 7.11.18
6/1598	Pte	John KING	1CIB	confirmed	18.8.17	shot 19.8.17
11401	Pte	William BLACK	2OIB	commuted 10yrs PS	17.9.17	sent to prison
12547	Pte	William A.KERR	2AIB	commuted 10yrs PS	13.9.17	sent to prison
6/4610	Pte	Thomas GEORGE	2OIB	commuted 2yrs IHL suspended		KIA 12.10.17
23011	Pte	Alfred H.MORGANS	2OIB	commuted 2yrs IHL suspended		WIA 12.10.17
24143	Pte	Henry O.DAIKEE	1CIB	quashed	3,11,17	
7/1594	Dvr	William E.BASHAM	NZFA	commuted 10yrs PS	10.1.18	sent to prison
8/2733	Pte	Victor M.SPENCER	1OIB	confirmed	23.2.18	shot 24.2.18
12/3728	Pte	Louis H.MEYRICK	2AIB	commuted 5yrs PS suspended	16.4.18	
7/1563	Pte	Charles H.CLOSE	1CIB	commuted 15yrs PS	12.6.18	sent to prison

Death sentences in the NZEF, 1914–18. (*NA WA 22/6/10 and JAG Files*)

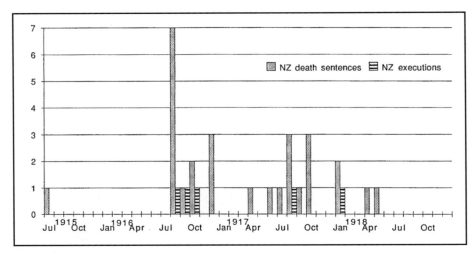

New Zealand death sentences and executions in the First World War. *(NA WA 22/6/10)*

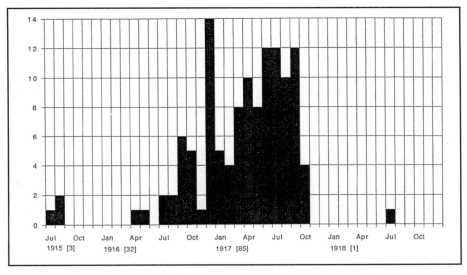

Australian death sentences in the First World War. *(Ashley Ekins,* Taming the Diggers: The Other Face of the Anzac Legend*)*

Today many Australians take a somewhat 'holier than thou' attitude because no Australians were executed on the Western Front. This is based on the comfort of ignorance. At the time Australian commanders did not initially appreciate the fact that there was an impediment to executing Australian soldiers, and they showed an equal willingness to sentence Australians to death in the belief that these sentences would be carried out. It

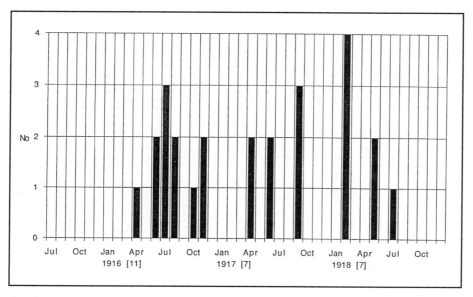

Canadian executions of the Western Front, 1914–18. *(PRO WO 93/44)*

was British legal advice from the Judge Advocate General on Haig's Headquarters that made it clear to Australian commanders that a clause in the 1903 Australian Defence Act meant that while the death penalty was permitted for mutiny and for desertion to the enemy, it could only be confirmed and carried out with the ratification of the Australian Governor-General. This was politically impossible, and led to a concerted campaign by Australian citizen commanders to have the Australian Defence Act changed so that the AIF, like the Canadians and New Zealanders, would come under the British Army Act without qualification. The Australians feared that failure to do this would lessen their ability to enforce the necessary disciplinary standards, and have the performance of their soldiers suffer by comparison to the other two dominions.

Penal servitude and imprisonment with hard labour were reserved for the more serious offences, and particularly where a soldier appeared a second time before a court martial. New Zealand courts readily passed sentences of imprisonment, but the voracious demands for manpower in the trenches meant that it was very difficult to get a man sent to prison. Cases were reviewed at corps, Army and at Haig's GHQ, and as the graph on the following page shows only a third of those sentenced to terms of imprisonment actually went to prison; the remainder had their sentences commuted to field punishment, or suspended under the Suspension of Sentences Act 1915.

Suspension of sentence kept a man with his unit under the threat that if his performance deteriorated his suspended sentence would be put into effect. Russell disliked this suspension policy as it led his men to believe they had got off 'Scot free'. The lift in the New Zealand graph showing men committed to prison in August 1917 illustrates a deliberate measure to remind his 'Diggers' that prison remained an option that could be enforced. The Canadians and Australians followed a similar policy. However, the AIF increased the length of sentences to life imprisonment when it was known that death sentences would not be carried out. Australians convicted of desertion, which may have incurred the death penalty, tended not to have their sentences considered for suspension, and this accounts for the steeply rising numbers of Australians in military prisons from 1917 onwards.[16]

All three dominion forces readily awarded field punishment, including Field Punishment No. 1 which involved tying a man to a fixed object such as a wagon wheel or a tree trunk for no more than two hours on any single day. Twenty-eight days' Field Punishment No. 1, could be summarily awarded by commanding officers, and a Field General Court Martial could award a maximum sentence of three calendar months. Field punishment was the preferred punishment on the Western Front because it kept a man with his unit, and even when offenders were committed to divisional field punishment centres they could be quickly returned to their units to take part in a forthcoming offensive. The 537 sentences of field punishment awarded by New Zealand courts totalled 59 percent of courts martial convictions in the division.

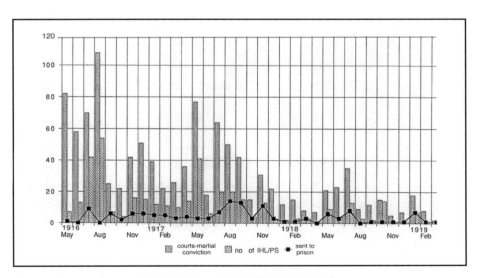

Prison sentences and commitals, NZ Division, 1914–18. (*NA WA 22/6/10*)

New Zealand officers tended not to be court-martialled. They were more likely to be invited to resign their commission and sent back to New Zealand. Russell was constantly weeding out his 'empties', and he was conscious that these were often good men who had seen too much war and who were now a danger to the

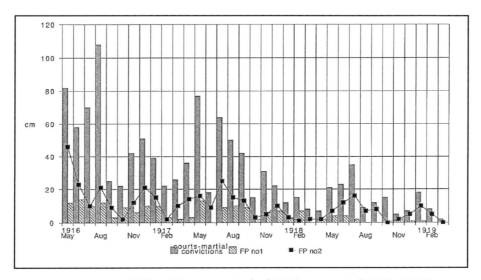

Court-martial sentences of field punishment, New Zealand Division, 1916–19. (NA WA 22/6/10)

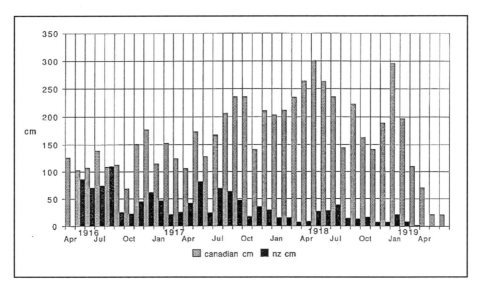

Canadian and New Zealand courts martial on the Western Front, 1916–19. (Canadian: FGCM, PRO WO93/45: New Zealand Division: NA WA 22/6/10)

men they led. Fifty-three officers were court-martialled in France, and seven were found not guilty. Officers appeared before a General Court Martial consisting of five officers and a judge advocate, which provided a certainty of procedural standards not available to soldiers at a Field General Court Martial. Drunkenness was the most common offence and 17 officers were charged with this, seven being dismissed with ignominy from His Majesty's forces. Other offences ranged from 'scandalous conduct' to 'being in possession of a camera and took photos'.[17] Russell used two measuring sticks to determine the health of his division. These were the sickness rate and the offence statistics. Abnormally high rates in either of these would see units rested, a build-up of reinforcements in a unit or a brigade to dilute the number of veterans or, if necessary, a change of commanding officer or brigade commander. Russell recognised that his most valuable asset was the private soldier who would do anything that he was asked to do if he knew the reason why and considered the task properly planned. Russell knew his men, paid particular attention to their welfare and administration, and matched this with his tactical planning. He rarely repeated mistakes, and on operations the New Zealand Division sustained a reputation as one of the finest fighting divisions in France for the two and half years of operations from the Somme in 1916 to the Armistice.

A measure of Russell's success can be gauged by comparing the number of New Zealand courts martial with that of the Canadian divisions. In 1916 the New Zealand rate nearly equalled the rate for the three Canadian divisions. Statistics show that the rate in Australian divisions in the same period also equalled that of the New Zealanders.[18] By 1917 the rate in the four infantry brigades of the New Zealand Division was in proportion to that of the four Canadian divisions. In late 1917 and throughout 1918 this changes; the Canadian rate escalates while the New Zealand rate declines, and the Australian trend exceeds both dominions. As Ekins' study of the Australians at Passchendaele and in 1918 shows, combat exhaustion impacted on sickness and discipline rates in the grossly under-strength units of the Australian Corps.[19] As Brigadier-General H.E. 'Pompey' Elliot, one of the outstanding brigade commanders in the AIF, recorded: 'They have not the same spirit at all as the old men we had. The difficulty once was to restrain their impatience for action … now we find men clearing out to avoid going into the front line at all.'[20]

In 1918 the forces of the three dominions were regarded as among the best fighting formations in France. The strains of 1918 had a major impact on all three forces, however, and after August 1918 this was most evident in Australian and Canadian formations. Professionalism alone could not compensate for declining numbers in both forces.

Conscription maintained the New Zealand Division at full strength and provided reinforcements who had completed 10 months' training by the time they reached the front line. The New Zealand Division was able to top up its battalions after each major action.

In contrast, the Canadian conscription system was not fully effective until after August 1918. Lieutenant-General Sir Arthur Currie compensated for this by disbanding the full-strength 5th Division, which was still in England, to ensure that his battalions were up to strength.

The Australian volunteer system could not meet the manpower needs of the AIF and men of low calibre were being sent, many of whom had received little or no training. In the case of both Australia and Canada, but particularly the former, under-strength battalions were over-committed during the battles of 1918, despite their professionalism. Success after success was won at the cost of diminished combat effectiveness and exhausted survivors, as units dwindled to 150 bayonets or less. By October 1918 the Australian Corps had ceased to be an effective fighting formation, and its court-martial rate was but one expression of this combat exhaustion.[21]

On the Western Front there was a consistency of approach in the Canadian, Australian and New Zealand forces. Each was determined to be the best, and this led to a disciplinary zeal that was tempered by the judgement of the British High Command. Although current mythology suggests dominion divisions cared little for the niceties of dress and saluting, this is not evident in the Routine Orders of any dominion division that you care to examine. With the exception of the AIF as discussed above, with regard to capital punishment all three forces served under the British Army Act, and the disciplinary approach was dictated by the calibre of the commanders. New Zealand was particularly well served by Sir Andrew Russell. He sustained the fighting effectiveness of his division by his operational skill and his insistence on sound administration. He recognised that if the men were properly led and administered then disciplinary problems would be minimal. This is reflected not only in the disciplinary statistics, but more importantly in the performance of the New Zealand Division in 1918.

In September 2000 the New Zealand Parliament passed the Pardon for Soldiers of the Great War Act, which pardoned the five soldiers who were executed while serving as members of the NZEF. Its purpose was 'to remove, so far as practicable, the dishonour that the execution of those 5 soldiers brought to those soldiers and their families'. The Act sought to recognise that the soldiers did not deserve to die, and that their punishment resulted from 'the harsh discipline that was believed at the time to be required', and 'application of the death penalty for military offences being seen at that time as an essential part of maintaining military discipline'.[22]

One can understand the emotional commitment of the families in seeking such a pardon. There is no question that Russell believed the death penalty was an essential part of maintaining military discipline, but I question whether it resulted from 'harsh discipline that was believed at the time to be required'. Indeed, Sir Edward Somers' review of the death sentences was 'unable to conclude that there is sufficient evidence of a miscarriage of justice in any of the five cases'.[23]

I have outlined the evolution of the disciplinary system in the New Zealand Division as the war progressed. In the beginning it was harsh because it was punishment inflicted without recourse to circumstance by an amateur force that had yet to learn its job. This changed as Russell and his subordinate commanders grew in professionalism. What stood out about the New Zealand Division in 1918 was that despite the demands of a hard campaign, after two exhausting years of fighting on the Western Front the disciplinary record continued to improve. The strict discipline imposed was matched by sound administration and an understanding on the part of the officers that the care and welfare of the men was the first priority.

To call the discipline of the New Zealand Division 'harsh', with its suggestion of being 'cruel, unkind, unsympathetic, insensitive, callous, ruthless, inconsiderate and unforgiving', is to ignore the context of the times and to negate Russell's achievement. As we have seen, some of those words might fit in some circumstances and at some time and some place. However, righting perceived wrongs with grand gestures, however well intentioned, risks placing labels on an age. History is too complex for that. Sometimes it is better to leave the past as an ugly scab for all to see and scratch at, to remind ourselves that we as New Zealanders did these things. We must ask what it tells us about ourselves as a society and as a people, and in what circumstances could we do the same again. 'The past, which as always did not know the future, acted in ways that ask to be imagined before they are condemned, or even simplified.'[24]

EIGHT

LEARNING FROM THE CANADIAN CORPS ON THE WESTERN FRONT

You can have an entirely civilian army and, if it's entirely civilian its members will be dead before they are good.[1]

Brigadier-General (later General) A.G.L. McNaughton

There is a curious paradox about the Canadian Corps that is summed up in this quotation from *Canadian Brass*, Stephen J. Harris's study of the evolution of a professional army in Canada. How did this military organisation become so effective in war, considering the background it had and the structure that supported it for most of its existence? This model of tactical excellence was born amid the chaos of Canadian Minister of Defence Sam Hughes' egomaniacal control at Valcartier Camp. It was beset by jealousies, political backhanders, corruption and influence peddling, and saddled with favourites as incompetent officers who at best were 'very weak' and had 'no power or habit of command'.[2] Hughes determined to ensure that no Regular soldier received a command appointment, and instead put in his favourites. These were drawn from the citizen militia, whose ability was summed up by the young iconoclast and future military theorist J.F.C. Fuller, who remarked that the Canadians had potential only 'if the officers could all be shot'.[3] Yet the Canadian Expeditionary Force (CEF) rose above this administrative nightmare, even if its impact continued to haunt the force for most of its existence.

By 1918 the Canadian Corps was the most effective fighting formation among the British armies on the Western Front, superior in performance to its vaunted Australian contemporary in terms of organisation, tactical efficiency and staying power. This was in large measure due to the guiding hand of perhaps the most brilliant corps commander of the war, the unlikely, diffident, corpulent figure of Lieutenant-General Sir Arthur Currie.

Recent historical studies in Australia, Canada and New Zealand demonstrate that we are at last moving away from what Jeffrey Keshen calls 'the cult of the superior soldier',[4] one where 'Johnny Canuck' or 'Tommy Cornstalk', the 'Aussie', 'Digger', 'Fernleaf' or 'Pig Islander' of Australia and New Zealand dominates the popular imagination of national achievement and identity in each country's mythology of the First World War. Read C.E.W. Bean's Australian official histories,[5] or Pierre Berton's *Vimy*, and parallel images are displayed, of a fierce, individualistic, rough-around-the-edges soldier who is also somehow self-disciplined and fearless in battle; a soldier who is seen as uniquely Australian or uniquely Canadian. As an aside, the New Zealanders knew they were unique, but never had the prophets to proclaim it quite so vehemently, although Robin Hyde's image of James Douglas Stark in *Passport to Hell* comes close.[6] As I have argued in earlier chapters, something more than distinctive national traits accounts for success in battle. Examinations of experience on the Western Front show that Australia, Canada and New Zealand followed parallel paths in the evolution of professional citizen expeditionary forces during the First World War.

A formidable pair: Lieutenant-General the Honourable Sir Julian Byng, talking to his successor as GOC Canadian Corps, the unlikely corpulent figure of Arthur Currie. Both were tactical and organisational innovators who forged the Canadian Corps into the outstanding premier corps on the Western Front. (*Royal Military Academy Sandhurst Collection*)

This chapter examines some of the points of contact between the three dominions' forces in the Great War, and highlights the influence of the Canadian experience. One should not assume that the title is influenced by my receiving a Canadian Studies Grant for 1998; rather it reflects the simple reality that the Canadians got to the Western Front first, while the Gallipoli Campaign sidelined the Anzacs in 1915. When the Anzacs arrived in France in March 1916 the Canadians were already veterans in theatre. They had demonstrated their prowess in holding the line under gas attacks at the second Ypres, when the 1st Canadian Division formed part of British V Corps in April 1915.[7] While the 'sideshow' of the Anzac landings on Gallipoli were occurring in the same week, they were not considered to have the same significance as they were far removed from what was regarded as the primary theatre of conflict.[8] Ironically, the formation of the ANZAC Corps was used as the precedent for the drive to form the Canadian Corps after the arrival in France of the 2nd Canadian Division in September 1915.[9]

On 5 June 1916, two months after Lieutenant-General Sir William Birdwood's I ANZAC Corps arrived in France, the first formal Australian trench raid on the German lines was mounted by combined parties of 26th and 28th Battalion of 7th Brigade in the Armentières sector of northern France. The raid was carefully planned and, as C.E.W. Bean recounts:

> The whole party was withdrawn for a fortnight to a rear area, and there went into training after the fashion of a football team before an important game. This included a sharp course of physical training, and close practice in carrying out its raid. A replica of the enemy's trench, which had been photographed from aeroplanes, was dug on the training ground and the operation was rehearsed again and again until it went almost automatically.[10]

This was the first of a series of raids mounted against the German lines, as preparations for the Battle of the Somme further south grew in intensity. The British Commander-in-Chief, General Sir Douglas Haig, was demanding every effort all along the trench lines held by the British armies to prevent the Germans thinning out numbers and sending reinforcements south to the Somme front. In taking over the line forward of Armentières, the Australians and New Zealanders were very conscious of their amateur status. The independence that marked the Gallipoli Campaign was gone, since in France this was regarded as a sideshow and no test of worth. Instead, they now numbered five of the 50 British and dominion divisions of the British armies facing the real enemy in the form of the German Imperial armies in the trenches of the Western Front.

In mounting this first raid the Australians sought outside expertise, requesting assistance from the Canadian Corps; as 'the Canadians were the pioneers in enterprises of this kind, two of their officers were borrowed from the 1st Canadian Division to assist in training the team'.[11] The New Zealand Division sought similar assistance from the Canadians in mounting their first raid; the training notes and lesson plans used by the New Zealand Division in training young officers in patrolling in no-man's land, and in the techniques of trench raids, were drawn from Canadian Corps experience.[12]

The Anzacs had already benefited from their experience after receiving grim reports of the Canadian difficulties with inadequate camp facilities and the resulting breakdown in health during their training on the wintry Salisbury Plains over Christmas 1914. This had been a significant factor in the decision to assemble and train the ANZAC Corps in Egypt instead of proceeding on to the United Kingdom. Both the Australian and the New Zealand Divisions of the ANZAC Corps also requested and received reports on operations, administration and discipline. This included visiting Canadian field punishment centres, as reported in this visit to the 1st Canadian Divisional Field Punishment Station at Westhof Farm on 31 March 1916.

> Prisoners had their heads clipped as soon as possible after being admitted … They were not allowed to have tobacco, rum, beer, lights, or matches, nor were they allowed any other food than that issued to them, and in order to avoid prisoners smuggling such things into their sleeping quarters, it was necessary to search each prisoner returning from working parties or parades … Any man found guilty of insubordination or breaking any rules during the days, or who in any way gave trouble — such as reporting sick without sufficient cause or being found with forbidden articles in his possession when searched — was tied up after returning from work at night. On one occasion during stormy weather some of the prisoners refused to work, but the extra punishment of being tied up out of doors in a storm and afterwards solitary confinement in a dark cell on a diet of bread or biscuit and water, prevented recurrences of this nature.[13]

The draconian methods practised by the Canadians impressed the Anzac visitors, and were adopted by both the Australians and the New Zealanders in the running of their field punishment centres. Both Birdwood's I ANZAC Corps and Godley's II ANZAC

Corps were conscious that the Canadians were the veterans among the dominion forces on the Western Front.

There had been little pre-war contact; unlike Australia and New Zealand, Canada had followed the British system of a voluntary militia and had not brought in compulsory military training for its citizen army. From the outset it had been employed in the primary theatre of war on the Western Front, and with the arrival of the 2nd Canadian Division it became the Canadian Corps in September 1915. The continued *ad hoc* expansion of the Canadian Corps beyond the resources of the Canadian population to effectively sustain it occurred in parallel with the expansion of the original ANZAC Corps into two corps. In July 1915 the Canadian Government planned for an expeditionary force of 150,000. In October 1915 this was increased to 250,000 and on New Year's Day 1916 the Canadian Prime Minister, Sir Robert Borden, announced that Canada would raise an army of 500,000.[14]

The dangers of this unchecked growth were seen by Major-General Willoughby Gwatkin, the Canadian Chief of General Staff, who warned the government that Canada might not be able to find the men to sustain the force once it was raised. This warning was ignored by Hughes, who bulldozed his demands through, assuring the prime minister that the 'third division in an army corps was almost always in reserve and immune from casualties'.[15] Equally important and equally difficult was finding the staffs needed to oversee these fighting formations. Experience was lacking at every level but was particularly evident within each of the 12 infantry battalions from commanding officer to private.

This was also the Anzac experience. In spite of the Gallipoli Campaign the rapid growth of the AIF and the NZEF into two corps dangerously stretched the limited command and administrative abilities within both the Australian and the New Zealand forces, particularly when the first elements were dispatched to France barely six weeks after being raised. Early May 1916 saw them in the trenches in the 'nursery' sector at Armentières conscious of their lack of experience, determined to do well, and keen to seek advice. That they turned to the Canadians for this was inevitable. It too was a dominion citizens army raised in similar circumstances to their own.

The Kitchener New Army divisions, which had been raised in similar circumstances, had been found wanting in Anzac eyes on the Gallipoli Peninsula. Being British divisions they did not face the unique demands of establishing administrative bases for reinforcement and training in the United Kingdom, or of dealing with national concerns of pay, mail, administration, welfare and the provision of reinforcements. Both Anzac forces were keen to learn from Canadian mistakes. While administratively the Canadian system in Britain was initially a chaotic bottleneck, exemplifying Hughes' interference and meddling, the Canadians' fighting reputation became the benchmark to aspire to. Both the AIF and the NZEF were determined to match the Canadian achievement and have the best divisions on the Western Front.

The 'nursery' experience of May to August 1916 was anything but easy for the two ANZAC corps. They were ill-prepared for the demands placed upon them by the Somme offensive. The constant raids, the extended divisional frontages, and prolonged tours of duty in the trenches came close to breaking the inexperienced divisions. They were learning the hard way what the Canadians had learnt in the previous 12 months; that poor administration and a lack of leadership led to disciplinary problems characterised by skyrocketing courts martial, principally for absenteeism and drunkenness. As we have seen, inexperienced Anzac officers attacked the symptoms rather than the causes, and by tightening discipline rather than improving welfare and administration saw disciplinary statistics continue to rise. When the ANZAC corps arrived in 1916, courts martial in the Canadian divisions averaged 40 a month compared to over a hundred in each of the Australian and New Zealand divisions. However, this disciplinary pattern exactly paralleled the Canadian experience of 1915; they too had problems in the first 12 months, until the Canadian Headquarters improved its skills in managing its growing force of what were now three divisions, a fourth joining by late 1916.

Twelve months later, in 1917, with more experience and better administration, the Canadian, Australian and New Zealand divisional disciplinary statistics were similar. Each national force was fiercely competitive and determined to improve. Each was aware that standards were judged not only by performance in battle, but also by standards of drill, discipline and saluting. Despite what one would like to believe today, each national force demanded conformity within its ranks to the standards of the British armies in which they served.

On the Western Front in 1916 and 1917 the dominion forces were made up of hard men facing hard times, and as the description of the Canadian field punishment centre shows, if soldiers did not conform they were broken as an example to the rest. This also applied to capital punishment, which saw soldiers who were found guilty of capital offences such as mutiny and desertion risk facing the firing squad. All three national forces were equally hard on those who deserted and threatened their good name. All three displayed a willingness to impose the death sentence by courts martial made up of citizen officers of each force standing in judgement of their own.

Tactically the Canadians showed a superiority gained through their longer experience

Tangled banks of barbed wire covered by rifle, artillery and machine-gun fire from the shelter of trenches presented a tactical problem that had to be solved if infantry were to attack successfully on the Western Front. *(National Army Museum, Waiouru Collection)*

on the Western Front. In 1916 both the Australians and the New Zealanders showed their lack of command and tactical skills. The attack at Fromelles on 19–20 July at a cost of 5533 casualties was a disaster for 5th Australian Division, one that would take the rest of the year and a change in command to recover from. Equally, on the Somme the calibre of the men could not compensate for poor command and staff skills in the Anzac formations. All three dominion forces employed the stereotyped infantry wave tactics, which although successful when employed with the developments in artillery tactics such as the creeping or rolling barrage, came with a fearful cost — an average on the Somme of 7400 in each division.

Popular belief portrays the Western Front as a place where unimaginative generals, totally out of touch and secure in their chateaux kilometres behind the front line, sent soldiers to their deaths in frontal assault after frontal assault. 'Lions led by donkeys' and 'Butcher Haig' are clichés cemented in public consciousness. In recent years there has been a sea-change in thinking among military historians. In discussing the influence of the Canadian Corps on Anzac thinking, and indeed on the British armies as a whole, let me first explain the revolution in tactical doctrine that occurred on the Western Front, one that irrevocably changed the nature of warfare. It was a revolution in tactics that was overseen by the 'donkeys' of generals who we still identify as 'butchers', and perhaps suggests that they achieved more than we credit them with. This is certainly my belief, so let me expand on this.

The problem the British armies faced on the Western Front was one that had been evident to discerning military minds since the American Civil War. The advent of massed rifle fire increased the effective infantry killing range from 80 metres for a musket to 250–300 metres for a breech-loading, magazine-fed, bolt-action rifle. This has not changed, and at the beginning of the twenty-first century this is still the laid-down killing range for infantry personal weapons.

The British Army appreciated this after the hard lessons of the Boer War, and section rushes (essentially 'fire and movement', which is the essence of military tactics today) within half companies, there being no platoon organisation, became the tactical means of closing with an enemy. The firefight had then to be won by massed rifle fire and British infantry were trained to fire 15 rounds rapid in the first deadly minute, with their bolt-action Lee-Enfield rifles, before the final attack on the enemy with rifle and bayonet. This was matched by a change in organisation in the infantry battalion from the eight-company structure — so effective for the linear formations that had been the underpinning strength of British drill and tactical manoeuvre from Wellington's successes in the Napoleonic Wars and in the colonial wars that followed — to four double-strength companies, each of four platoons. This was the organisation with which the British armies and the dominion expeditionary forces went to war.

This was a radically new organisation that put a junior officer or subaltern in charge of 40–50 men, who were further subdivided into four sections, each of 10–12 soldiers under the command of an NCO. Platoons had not existed in the British battalion organisation before this, and how it was to work was still being evolved when the British Army went to war in 1914.[16]

The small British Expeditionary Force (BEF) demonstrated the benefits of both the organisation and their tactical skills in the opening defensive battles of Mons and Le Cateau, and again in the struggle to hold on to Ypres in October and November 1914, which led to the destruction of this professional elite. The dominion expeditionary forces mobilised to reinforce the BEF initially trained in these skills in 1914. As photographs in the Alexander Turnbull Library show, the Wellington Infantry Battalion, for example, practised section and platoon rushes over the sand dunes near Miramar where

Wellington International Airport now stands. Those who now decry what they see as outdated Boer War tactics, blaming them for the formalised slaughter on the Somme in 1916, fail to realise that the evolution of these same tactics of section and platoon rushes to avoid presenting the defending riflemen with a massed target was the secret of the British armies' success in 1918. It was the British failure to retain these tactical skills in the raising and training of the mass citizen armies that led to the slaughter on the Somme on 1 July 1916. The small-group tactical doctrine used in the British Army of 1914 was perfectly suitable for closing with the enemy on the Western Front, but it was a skill that was lost with the destruction of the professional army at Ypres and had to be relearned and reapplied through hard experience.

Regular British soldiers at Mons and Le Cateau in 1914 were surprised that the attacking German formations made little attempt to advance across the fire zone by fire and movement in section and platoon rushes, as the British had been taught. Instead they attacked in massed ranks and suffered for it. The German attack method showed the reality of the state of tactical skill of a European conscript army, but one where a lack of tactical skill within regiments was compensated for by the higher-level operational and administrative skills of its General Staff. Those British Regulars who survived the first months of fighting would see the level of training and skills that they took for granted within their battalion become diluted and deteriorate to the same levels they

The machine gun formed the backbone of the defensive fire plan as it was capable of placing a wall of fire effective out to 1800 metres, through which infantry had to pass if they were to gain the German trenches. (*Royal Military Academy Sandhurst Collection*)

witnessed in the German ranks in 1914. It takes time to train a small group to work in pairs, with one soldier firing as the other rushes forward, and with a section of 10–12 men working in pairs rushing forward while covered by the rifle fire of other sections. Replicate this with the platoons moving forward in the same manner, covered by other platoons, and the same at company level, and you begin to recognise the degree of professional skill required to do it in battle army wide. The British Army of 1914 had this skill; its successors from the Territorial and New Armies did not, and had to find it, but before they could do so they had to appreciate its importance; all of this evolved by trial and error.

Kitchener's New Armies were made up of the finest material ever seen in a British army. It was of a calibre that would never been seen again, certainly not in the Second World War where the competing demands of the Royal Navy and the RAF, and the growth of specialist arms in the army, meant the infantry arm received what was left over after the cream had been skimmed off. The vast potential of Kitchener's citizen armies was fitfully used. The army administration that existed in Britain was barely able to house and feed the influx of recruits let alone provide the degree of training needed at every level from soldier to commanding officer.

A citizen army whose training had to be entrusted to long-retired veterans unfamiliar with the tactical evolution that had occurred since the Boer War was trained in mass and used in mass in the linear formations of the nineteenth century. The trainers had not the knowledge or the experience of the tactics that had evolved since the end of the war in 1902, and they trained the New Armies in those drills that had been effective in the small colonial wars that had been their experience. They had never experienced the four-infantry-company-strong battalion organisation, nor were they familiar with the new platoon organisation. They were used to operating in companies and half-companies and were too old to change. The so-called 'Boer War' tactics of section and platoon rushes standard in the Regular Army and aspired to by the dominion forces were allowed to lapse, and were replaced by the formalised lines of advancing infantry that were shot down in their rows by German machine guns on the Somme on 1 July 1916.

The infantry assault was a task made much more difficult by the defensive firepower of the machine guns that now formed the backbone of the defensive fire plan in the trench lines along the Western Front. Belt-fed, effective out to 1800 metres and firing on fixed lines by day or night, they provided a continuous stream of bullets through which flesh and blood had to pass before men could attempt to cross the belts and tangled mass of barbed wire that protected the German trenches. A man could stand up and walk forward, laden with 30 kg of webbing, equipment, accoutrements, ammunition, grenades, rifle and bayonet, but did not have the training or the tactical skill to suppress, isolate and destroy the machine guns that barred his way. Enthusiasm was not enough, and even this vanished after the first slaughter to be replaced by an overwhelming desire on the part of every individual to survive and return home. Weight of materiel in the shape of massed artillery fire was the answer to opening the way for infantry to advance, but on the Somme this was still a blunt instrument. There was little coordination — only a blind belief that the sheer weight of shellfire must destroy the German defences. Artillery techniques improved markedly as the Battle of the Somme progressed. These started to provide the essentials needed to keep the attacking infantryman alive as he advanced by first destroying the wire that blocked his advance, then by suppressing enemy artillery fire while he advanced and secured his objective, and also by giving him covering fire to mask his movement while he moved forward.

Yet artillery support was only one of the key elements in achieving tactical success on the Western Front. Artillery fire cannot be brought down closer than some 130 metres from your advancing troops. Think about what that means if you are attacking across a boggy, recently ploughed paddock towards a distant fenceline representing the German front line. Now picture yourself with a rifle and bayonet, webbing, water bottle, 200 rounds of ammunition, entrenching tool, grenades, iron rations, and so on, all weighing

Success on the Western Front was brought by a marriage of improved artillery and infantry tactics and organisational changes that took advantage of technical developments. Here a New Zealand 18-pounder gun team loads its limbers for the next mission. (*Wilson and Horton Collection*)

175

about 30 kilograms. How long would it take you to walk or jog this distance? Three or four minutes? More? Artillery fire has covered your approach up to this point, but if it continues to fire as you go forward you run the real risk of being killed by the explosion of your own shells. At 130 metres it has to lift and move away from you. How long will it take you to cover this distance and what is the enemy at the fenceline likely to be doing? In essence, that is the problem that faced attacking infantry on the Western Front; at some point when close to the enemy they had to advance over the last critical metres of ground without artillery support.

The importance of fire and movement at platoon level was the tactical revolution that led to the breaking of the trench deadlock. The skills of 1914 and the lessons of the Boer War had to be relearned by amateur armies commanded by Regulars who had never had to think on this scale, so it was a learning process for all.[17] The story of the First World War on the Western Front is one of the evolving professionalism of citizen armies over four years from 1915 onwards, and the dominion forces shared that process with the Canadian Corps leading the way.

The best of the divisional and corps commanders evaluated the Somme experience

A 'female' Mark III Heavy Tank (armed with machine guns as opposed to a 'male', which was armed with six-pounder cannon) struggling over a trench during the Arras offensive in April 1917. Tanks were too slow and mechanically unreliable to be an effective breakthrough weapon, but provided valuable support to infantry in crushing barbed wire and destroying machine-gun posts. (*Royal Military Academy Sandhurst Collection*)

and profited from it. This was certainly true of Lieutenant-General the Honourable Sir Julian Byng's Canadian Corps. Bill Rawling's detailed study in *Surviving Trench Warfare* shows the growth in tactical development between the Somme and the Canadian attack on Vimy Ridge in April 1917. Rawling's careful evaluation, which minutely examines both relative success and failure, is a record of outstanding Canadian achievement that places it at the forefront of the tactical revolution that was occurring in the British armies on the Western Front.[18]

The Canadians were fortunate in the calibre of their British corps commander, 'Bungo' Byng, who took command of the corps in May 1916 after his predecessor proved more expendable than failed Canadian divisional and brigade commanders.[19] With a reputation of being a 'cheerfully unintellectual cavalryman', Byng proved to be anything but, demonstrating a tactical grasp that places him at the forefront of British generals on the Western Front.[20] It is clear from his directives that he was a practical, thinking general who in his eight months in command of the Canadian Corps was determined to work out how to attack successfully at minimum cost. Equally importantly, he understood the particular nature of the men he commanded. He recognised that a citizen army had to be treated and trained differently from Regulars, noting that it was important for senior officers to become involved at levels that would not be contemplated in a Regular formation but, 'when so many Senior Officers in Battalions are still inexperienced, the interference even of Corps and Divisional Commanders in the training of the Platoon was beneficial'.[21]

Directives from above were not enough when inexperience at every level of command down to private soldier meant that the few professionals who knew what to do had to get involved and by hands-on involvement and advice teach staffs and units the business of both how to manage fighting and the business of fighting itself. This was the reality in every dominion force. Byng also recognised and preached that it was at platoon level that the key to tactical success in breaking the trench deadlock was to be found. He was not alone. Throughout Haig's armies commanders and staffs were assessing the lessons of the Somme, and fighting and thinking commanders at army, corps and divisional level were suggesting changes. Led by Haig, his army commanders Plumer, Rawlinson and even the much-maligned Gough in Fifth Army knew there had to be a better way and groped towards solutions.

The Canadian Corps staff, pondering on the lessons of the Somme, sent Major-General Arthur Currie to visit the French at Verdun and assess their organisation and training. As a result organisational changes were made to the platoon structure within the infantry battalions that would anticipate army-wide changes in the months ahead.[22]

Currie's report from Verdun, as Hyatt explains in his incisive biography of this little-appreciated general, was not just a record of what he saw of the French organisation and tactics. It was more an evaluation of what the Canadians had learnt from what they had done wrong in the fighting around Pozières after replacing the Australians in late September 1916. It was a thoughtful assessment of how the organisation, communication and training had to improve within the corps, both in terms of the infantry who carried out the attack and in what the artillery needed to do to ensure they could get forward.[23] Currie's notes are rich in detail that one recognises became integral to British tactical doctrine; indeed, much of it was already being practised and experimented with. He summarised the primary factors behind successful French offensive operations as 'careful staff work', thorough 'artillery preparation and support', the 'element of surprise', and the 'high state of training in the infantry detailed for the assault'.[24]

Currie was impressed by the fact that the French were producing what he termed '"storm" troops on a large scale'. If one looks at its subsequent adoption in the British armies, one can see that by late 1917 every British soldier was trained in the tactical skills of fire and manoeuvre. It is this scale of training that marks the critical difference between the Allied approach and that of the Germans, where the *Stosstruppen*, or specialist storm-trooper, remained an elite and the German Imperial Armies suffered for it.[25] Crucial to this was the need to improve tactical skills within the infantry battalions. Currie noted in his report:

> Too often, when our infantry are checked, they pause and ask for additional [artillery] preparation before carrying on. This artillery preparation cannot be quickly and easily arranged for and is often not necessary. Our troops must be taught the power of manoeuvre and that before giving up [and asking for more artillery support] they must employ to the utmost extent all the weapons with which they are armed and have available.[26]

Both Byng and his Canadian subordinates appreciated that the Somme fighting had demonstrated 'that the present organization and training of our Infantry have not succeeded in developing the maximum offensive firepower bestowed by the weapons with which it is now armed'.[27] Where it was going wrong was with a lack of effective fire and movement at platoon level. The critical problem was that you could not keep artillery firing until the infantry reached the enemy trenches because if you did, you would kill your own men. As discussed above, the closest the infantry could come was 130 metres before the supporting artillery had to lift and move away from the attacking troops. This was the problem facing any attack on the Western Front, as these minutes gave the enemy time to react and man his trenches and machine guns. It was in these critical minutes that the infantryman had to fight his way forward with the weapons he had at hand; artillery could no longer directly assist him. It was Byng's assessment that once the supporting artillery fire lifted then success or failure depended on how effectively the platoons dealt with the machine guns and obstacles in front of them. As he wrote:

> The largest unit that, under modern conditions, can be directly controlled and manoeuvred under fire by one man is the Platoon. The Platoon Commander is therefore in most cases, the only man who can personally influence the local situation. In fact, it is not too much to say that this is the Platoon Commander's war. Realizing this, it becomes the duty of the Company Commander to see that each Platoon is trained by its leader to act either with independence or as a component of the Company. In each case the fullest development of all the various Infantry weapons should be the object to be achieved.[28]

The problem was that the existing four-platoon structure in a rifle company based on 50-strong platoons was too inflexible. It became a means of administration rather than an effective command, giving the platoon commander 'no command worthy of the name and little or no opportunity of training either his men or himself to realize their capabilities'. Changes were needed to the platoon organisation, making it smaller and more adaptable yet still giving it both the numbers and the specialist skills needed to make best use of the weapons technology available.[29] Inexperienced commanders both at company and platoon level did not know what was required of them, and fell into the trap of centralising command at company level and not using the platoons as tactical and organisational sub-units within the company.

Byng directed that in the Canadian Corps infantry platoons were to consist of a platoon headquarters and four sections with a maximum strength of 44, and at least 28 strong, which he regarded as the working minimum. Each of the four sections had to have 'its own leader, and an understudy'. One section was to be Lewis gunners, to give the immediate fire support with the Lewis light machine gun to the other three sections; one was to be a bombing section armed with hand grenades; while the other two sections were to be riflemen, and would also include a number of rifle grenadiers firing rifle grenades. In effect there was one fire support section based on the Lewis gun to give covering fire, with three manoeuvre sections to fight their way forward covered by that fire. The gas-operated magazine-fed Lewis machine gun gave the British a genuine man-portable weapon with the firepower to assist infantry in the attack. Its adoption revolutionised the fire support available within a platoon. Its firepower more than matched the rifle fire of the entire platoon; the principal problem was carrying enough of the 47-round-capacity circular magazines to keep it firing.

Byng saw it as essential that 'the Platoon should constitute a unit for fighting and training, and should consist of a homogeneous combination of all the weapons with which the Infantry is now armed'. The key to success was maintaining the strength of the rifle platoons. Battalions out of the line had to give priority to platoon training, and ensure that platoons were kept up to strength, avoiding the tendency to drain off platoon manpower for appointments in battalion. Corps schools were set up to train instructors, and to train officers and NCOs in the skills that were required. In particular Byng wanted to achieve the following levels of expertise:

(i) Train the Platoon Commander in handling his Platoon, not only in a set piece previously rehearsed, but in dealing with unforeseen situations such as must occur both in attack and defence.

(ii) Train every man in the platoon to act in case of necessity as specialist, i.e., as a bomber, rifle grenadier, or Lewis gunner.[30]

This platoon-level revolution was adopted army-wide in February 1917 with directives from Haig's General Headquarters. It was these directives that led to the new platoon structure being introduced into the New Zealand Division and its Australian counterparts in I and II ANZAC Corps, but as we have seen the Canadians had already anticipated its need and introduced its recommendations.[31] Once again it is easy to direct from above, but it was the willingness to adopt these changes and make them effective within the division that marked out the better divisions. How difficult this was for a British division in the line is captured by Lieutenant Colonel Cecil Allanson, who commanded the 6th Gurkhas in the August offensive of 1915, where he was wounded and recommended for the Victoria Cross. In early 1917 he was GSO1 of the 57th Division that was just arriving in France when he was informed of the changes to the platoon organisation. He was very critical that this instruction had not reached him in England 'so that our final training could have been carried out under these conditions. With a division spread out along miles of trenches, reorganisation is difficult, and will receive but scanty attention — from force of circumstance — by experienced officers.'[32]

Canadian soldiers skylined as they move forward in their platoon tactical formations to seize the strongly defended Vimy Ridge on 9 April 1917. *(Royal Military Academy Sandhurst Collection)*

It was here that the Canadians took the lead, and with Byng's drive ensured that the changes became standard in all four Canadian divisions. This was possible because the Canadian Corps was unique in having a fixed homogeneous grouping. The only other corps similar to this were the two ANZAC corps, but even in these, additional divisions were attached for operations and Australian divisions were interchanged between I and II ANZAC. But it was not only having the willingness to change that was essential; divisions such as the 57th Division also needed the time, and inevitably this was often left to training periods out of the line.

The Canadian Corps' attack on Vimy on 9 April 1917, Easter Monday, as part of the Arras offensive, showed what an infantry-based army could achieve with detailed preparation and planning and the coordination of all available resources. It was a demonstration of how much Byng and his Canadians had learnt from the mud and chaos of the Somme fighting. The Vimy Ridge north of Arras was critical ground on which the German defensive line hinged. It had successfully denied a series of French attacks at bloody cost. The four Canadian divisions advanced side by side in battle for the first time under a creeping artillery barrage, assisted by specially dug communication tunnels that allowed the attacker to move close to the German front lines. Counter-battery fire silenced the German artillery, and most of the critical ground except that on which the Vimy Memorial now stands was gained in the first few hours of battle. The toll exacted was high: 3598 killed and 7004 wounded.[33] But the Canadian victory at Vimy showed that it was possible to break in and seize heavily defended ground with

181

platoon-based tactics assisted by engineering skills, and the skilled use of artillery in destroying the wire, providing an effective creeping barrage and counter-battery fire.

Limited gains at heavy cost, which historians today believe to be part of Haig's battle of attrition mindset, were the reality of manoeuvring an infantry-based army dependent on fighting their way forward on foot in a geographically restricted area defended by mass armies. Both attacker and defender were able to stockpile and use materiel and technology, but by its nature the ground gave greater advantages to the defender. The tank, which was introduced for the first time on the Somme on 15 September 1916, was a major technological advance but lacked the robustness and manoeuvrability to make it a battle winner. It could not keep up with infantry over broken ground, and its lack of suspension and poor exhaust extraction meant that its crew was unfit for combat after one hour's cross-country travel. Until this problem was overcome the role of the tank was limited to infantry support.

Breaking through the trench lines of the Western Front was by necessity a battle of tactical-level small-scale manoeuvre, but because it was not one of sweeping breakthroughs this manoeuvre has not been recognised for what it was. Improved offensive tactics, particularly in the use of artillery, saw the evolution of German defensive doctrine from the fixed trench lines of the Somme to defence in depth by zones based on a chequerboard pattern of concrete bunkers or pillboxes, protected by wire obstacles often hundreds of metres in depth. These channelled the attacker into the mutually supporting crossfires of this matrix of mini-forts, behind which specially designated infantry units were held ready to counterattack.

Fighting forward in short dashes covered by the fire of the Lewis gun team was an exhausting business even without the need and the strain of taking out each German machine-gun position and bunker. Each required a platoon attack within the framework of a company attack which was in turn part of a battalion attack within the brigade plan that was part of the divisional attack, and so on through corps to army! It was the means by which infantry could take on the dug-in enemy successfully and keep going forward. It was physically demanding work that burnt up the energies of the individuals taking part, so after each bunker or trench had been taken platoons had to leapfrog through each other to keep the advance progressing. This meant that what each battalion could achieve in terms of metres of ground gained (with its four rifle companies each of four platoons) was by necessity very limited.

An infantry division of three brigades usually attacked with two brigades side by side, each having its battalions echeloned in depth so that each took a bite out of the objective the brigade had been given, fighting its way forward behind the artillery barrage to a predetermined line. At this point it paused and consolidated while the next battalion passed through and continued to fight forward. From above this would appear to be a dispersed series of antlike columns edging forward, but this was the reality of an organised mass of men across a frontage of a kilometre or two, biting its way into a highly sophisticated defensive system that was designed to impede and kill. Thousands of men were needed to achieve hundreds of metres, not through ignorance on the part of their commanders but through the reality that at the fighting edge of this advance, small groups of 30 or so infantrymen were fighting their way forward platoon by platoon, section by section, in small difficult bites across this front.

Artillery fire was critical in allowing the infantry to move forward. Four things were essential to any attack, and these were things that artillery had to provide. The wire obstacles protecting the German defences had to be cut to allow the infantry to get through. The infantry had to have covering fire so that the German defenders were forced to keep their heads down to the last possible moment, but equally importantly the German artillery had to be suppressed by counter-battery fire while the attack was in progress. Infantry were at their most vulnerable while they were above ground, so the planning staff had to ensure that for the critical period of the attack, during the infantry advance, every effort was made to stop the German artillery from firing. Finally, defensive fire had to be available to destroy German counterattacks while the attackers consolidated and put into a state of defence the ground they had won in the attack.

Covering fire was achieved by the evolution of the creeping barrage that became standard procedure in the British and French armies from the Somme on. This became a sophisticated mix of a moving line of exploding artillery shells, sometimes mixed with smoke shells that lifted in 25-, 50- or 100-yard leaps and moved forward as a curtain of fire and explosions ahead of the infantry who had been trained in and had practised moving forward behind this covering fire.

A limiting factor in how far an attack could go was the range of the artillery. The standard supporting field gun in British divisions was the 18-pounder. For most of the war its effective range was 6500 yards. Even if positioned as far forward as possible, this could be 1000–2000 yards behind a front line. The planning staff also had to factor in being able to effectively use artillery to defeat German counterattacks while the attacking infantry consolidated the ground they had won. Artillery had to be able to reach out and fire on the German attackers in front of the newly won positions. There was no guarantee that artillery would be able to be moved forward into new positions to provide this support, so objectives had to be within range of existing artillery positions. If one allows 1000 yards as the minimum distance that was needed in front of the furthest advance then one can see that by subtracting from the field gun's 6500-yard planning range the 2000–3000 yards that is the combined length of the distance of the guns to the front line and the distance that the guns had still to cover after the infantrymen had reached their farthest objective, what is left is a maximum 3500-yard template within which to plan the infantry attack. Often this was in fact much less, commonly 1000–2000 yards. If one wanted to achieve more than this then the attack had to be carried out in stages so that provision could be made to get artillery forward so that it could support a further advance. Balanced against this was the sophistication of the German defences, whose series of defensive zones could cover a depth of six to ten kilometres. Taking all this into account, the scale of the problem facing the attacker on the Western Front becomes obvious. The Germans looked at the distance from which British artillery could support an attack and did everything in their defensive planning to frustrate it. The Germans provided an 'onion skin' defence in layers that the attacker had to piece and work his way through, each layer being separated by belts of barbed wire covered by machine-gun fire. While he was doing this he would be subject to German artillery fire and infantry counterattacks.

Getting artillery forward through these layers was a major undertaking that required roads to be built through what was often a churned up, trackless waste blocked by the obstacles of enemy wire, trenches in depth, and the fact that the German artillery was now bombarding the ground that they had lost. Horses had to drag the guns forward, together with the hundreds of rounds needed for each gun, as well as the timber needed to build stable platforms in the ground to prevent guns sinking into the earth each time they fired. Moving the mass of materiel needed was a major engineering and logistic undertaking that demanded staff planning and direction of the highest order. It was where corps staff proved their mettle. The Canadian Staff was a mix of British professionals and Canadian officers, some professional, some not, but the Canadians also had the benefit of experience. It was with this combination that the Canadian Corps in 1917 proved greatly superior to its two ANZAC Corps counterparts.

All of this was the reality of achieving infantry manoeuvre at foot pace. Its cost in manpower and materiel, or more evocatively 'attrition', was far higher than if one could have devised a way of getting round the German defences and attacking them from the flank or rear, but the Western Front did not allow this. The Belgian coast and the Swiss frontier fixed the parameters. Manoeuvre had to be achieved within the context of a frontal attack that had the aim of breaking in and punching its way through the German lines. German defensive planning ensured that the depth of defences forced the attacker to exhaust his infantry in fighting forward and also deploy his artillery forward in stages while he was fighting through the objective, so there was no alternative but to work through the German defences in small tactical bites dictated by the range of artillery support.

The evolution of counter-battery fire techniques, with the ability to locate German artillery batteries by aerial and ground spotters, and with the introduction of flash spotting and sound-ranging techniques, was a critical part of evolving Allied offensive tactics. Byng was a driving force in having these techniques introduced into the Canadian Corps in the preparation before Vimy.[34] This allowed the infantry to get forward and survive above ground during the critical hours of the actual attack by suppressing German defensive artillery fire.

Some historians, led by Robin Prior and Trevor Wilson in their important studies of the Western Front, see this as central to explaining Allied success on the Western Front to the exclusion of all other factors.[35] The Australian historian Ashley Ekins, who is of this school, has written that:

> ... success would come to whichever side possessed the capacity to direct massive artillery damage onto their enemy's front and provide artillery cover to enable their own infantry to advance. The crucial factor was no longer the infantry, or their strength, condition, training, morale or state of discipline. Victory now depended upon the number of guns and shells and the intensity of shelling which could be applied to the chosen area of attack.[36]

I disagree. It is an argument similar to that advanced by contemporary air power advocates who believe that wars can be won by air power alone. In the twenty-first century 'smart' shells guided by lasers from guns positioned by GPS have been developed; these can guarantee that artillery can hit a pinpoint target. That was not the case in the First World War. For all the technological advances that artillery achieved, it remained an area weapon that could accurately bracket a 250 × 250 yard area with the shells of a battery, depending on calibre, weight of shell and number of guns employed, but it could not guarantee destruction. Sustained fire over a prolonged period might eventually achieve this, but what artillery could promise was neutralisation; keeping the defenders' heads down for a specified period. It is this limitation that Prior and Wilson appear to ignore. Unquestionably, the war on the Western Front was a war of materiel in which artillery was of central importance. Infantry could not succeed without artillery.

'Artillery destroys while infantry occupies' is the catch cry that emerges from the Western Front, but for infantry to occupy still demanded the skill of fighting through the objective from the point once artillery support had to lift. For, despite the increased accuracy of the guns, the introduction of the 106 fuse that allowed the 18-pounders to be more effective in cutting wire, and the greater percentage of heavy artillery that destroyed trenches and rendered German defenders in pillboxes concussed and senseless from the pounding, total destruction was impossible.

The act of occupation is not simply standing up and walking forward, as too many historians suggest. The revolution on the Western Front was one of the growing sophistication of the all arms team built around the growing skills of infantry in attack. Allied skills in massing and using artillery were a critical feature in their offensive success, but if this had not been matched by the evolution of infantry small-group tactics at section and platoon level then, once the artillery fire lifted, the infantry would have been stopped by machine guns and would have died in their extended lines as they did on the Somme on 1 July 1916.

Victory in battle depended on maintaining the balance between the artillery and its ability to 'direct massive artillery damage' onto the enemy's position, suppressing enemy artillery fire, while providing artillery cover to enable infantry to advance, and the ability of trained infantry who because of their 'strength, condition, training, morale or state of discipline' had the skills to fight their way forward from bunker to bunker. Prior and Wilson give examples of this infantry skill in their studies without crediting its importance, as in this textbook-perfect example of infantry fire and movement on 26 September 1917 in the Battle of Polygon Wood by the 5th Australian Division.

> Resistance from 'Pill Boxes' and Strong Points was encountered almost immediately, but in no case was the advance checked. In one case a strong point was encountered and machine gun fire opened on the attackers. Immediately a CSM [company sergeant major] and about half a dozen men worked round the flanks while a Lewis Gun team opened direct fire on the position drawing the enemy fire off the enveloping parties who were then easily able to work round, rush the position with bombs and the bayonet, and accounted for the occupants and captured the gun.[37]

Certainly the attacking infantry saw artillery as the key to success. It opened the way forward onto their objectives, often with minimum infantry casualties. They also knew its destructive effects when they attempted to consolidate and hold the ground they had won. The battle began in earnest once the captured position had to be defended against counterattacks. It was now that the mass of infantry that had been needed to capture the position became a liability, when the ground they occupied became the target for German artillery fire. This was something flesh could not withstand unless it was dug in with overhead protection, and this could be achieved only with time and effort.

After the Somme, thinking commanders saw the need to replace vulnerable flesh with defensive firepower in order to hold ground won and repel counterattacks. Byng factored this into his planning for Vimy; his successor Currie did the same for Hill 70 and the fighting for Lens. They were not alone, as we shall see in the next chapter when we examine the performance of Russell and Monash at Messines. Russell, the New Zealand divisional commander, wanted to halve the strength of his infantry forward once he had captured Messines because he recognised that too many men forward simply provided better targets for German artillery fire. Godley's II ANZAC Corps, wedded to the need to hold the front line in strength, which it identified in manpower terms alone, would not allow this, but Russell still attempted to minimise casualties by evacuating the centre of the town of Messines and holding it with an outer ring of machine-gun and artillery posts that would bring effective fire on any attack.

As this example shows there was limited flexibility available to a divisional commander in his planning. Much depended on the ability of the corps commander to assess the best use of the divisions that he had available, listen to his divisional commanders' views as to how they could best achieve their respective objectives, and factor this into his planning. The corps commander then had to propose, convince and if necessary argue with Army Headquarters to see that this was put into effect. Byng did this for the Canadians at Vimy. One can read of the care taken for this attack in the impressive studies of Canadian achievement by Brown, Hyatt and Rawling.[38] The careful, previously 'unheard of training' at every level from platoon through to division included a full-scale replica of the battle area over which every battalion rehearsed and rehearsed until every man knew his job in the coming attack, and detailed, specially produced maps that were issued down to section-level within platoons so that men knew where they were to go and pass back information once they got there.

Critical to Canadian success was the artillery plan; the detailed destructive shoot to destroy the wire and suppress defences in the two weeks prior to the attack, the concentration of heavy artillery giving weight to the counter-battery fire on German gun positions, and finally, despite the evidence, a fire plan immediately before the attack to provide tactical surprise for the infantry when they actually went over the top. Careful engineer and logistic preparations matched this, particularly the development of underground communication tunnels to allow a relatively safe passage of assembling troops in the attack zone.

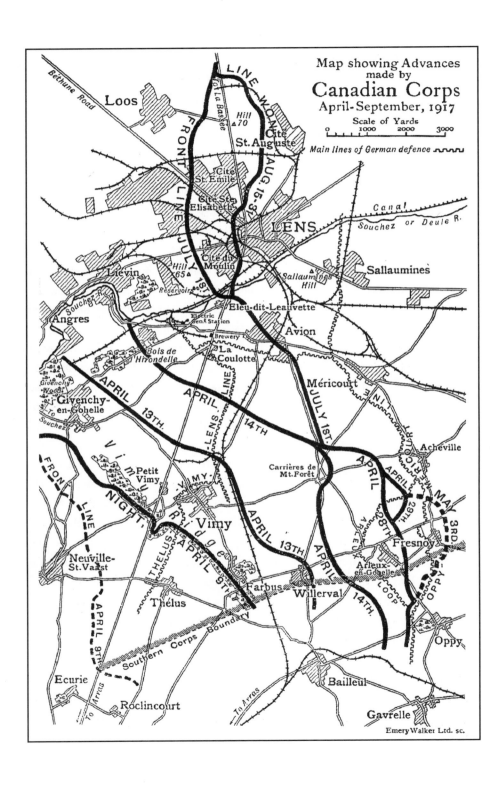

Map showing Advances
made by
Canadian Corps
April–September, 1917

Scale of Yards

0   1000   2000   3000

Main lines of German defence ∿∿∿

Bethune Road

Loos

LINE WON AUG.15-31.

FRONT LINE JULY 1st.

Hill 70

Cité St. Auguste

Cité St. Emile

Cité Ste. Elisabeth

Canal

Souchez or Deule R.

LENS

Cité du Moulin

Liévin

Hill 65

Sallaumines Hill

Sallaumines

Souchez R.

Reservoir

Eleu-dit-Leauvette

Angres

Electric Gen. Station

Avion

Brewery

Bois de l'Hirondelle

La Coulotte

Givenchy Woods

Givenchy-en-Gohelle

To Souchez

APRIL 13TH.

APRIL 14TH.

LENS LINE

Méricourt

MÉRICOURT LINE

Acheville

JULY 1st.

Carrières de Mt. Forêt

APRIL 28TH.

APRIL 29TH.

MAY 3RD.

Petit Vimy

VIMY

V i m y

R i d g e

Vimy

NIGHT, APRIL 9TH.

THÉLUS LINE

APRIL 13TH.

ARLEUX

ARLEUX LOOP

Fresnoy

Arleux-en-Gohelle

OPPY

FRONT LINE

Neuville-St. Vaast

Thélus

Farbus

Willerval

APRIL 14TH.

Oppy

APRIL 9TH.

To Arras

Southern Corps Boundary

Ecurie

Roclincourt

Bailleul

Gavrelle

Emery Walker Ltd. sc.

As Brown has argued, it was a 'not glamorous but effective' set-piece attack, which became the model for future Canadian operations on the Western Front. This in turn became a model for British armies through the dissemination of the lessons learnt by Haig's staff.

It is important to acknowledge the lead given by Haig's armies in spreading the word and seeing these techniques implemented. Plumer's Second Army was the pacesetter, and the directives and conference notes signed by Plumer's MGGS, Major-General Charles 'Tim' Harington, are a model of their kind. The Second Army preparations before Messines in May–June 1917 and then in the build-up to Passchendaele in August–September 1917 show how important an army headquarters was in setting effective artillery plans to meet infantry requirements. These included '[breaking] down obstacles which are impassable for Infantry, but in doing so to create as few new obstacles in the way of shell craters as possible', providing a protective barrage to cover the infantry advance, while neutralising 'all known hostile battery positions', before providing the consolidating on the objective with defensive fire 'which can be put down when the enemy counter attacks'.[39]

Hidden within the constraints of the set-piece attack was the vital flexibility allowed by the ability of infantry to effectively manoeuvre at platoon level. In their after-action reports on Vimy the Canadian divisional commanders were unanimous on the importance of the new platoon organisation and tactics. Major-General D. Watson, commanding the 4th Canadian Division, wrote of its 'undoubted success':

> The present platoon forms an ideal unit with which to establish strong points, to form an outpost picquet with its sentry group, to attack a troublesome hostile strong point met with during the advance, or to hold a section of hostile trench … To sum up, there seems little doubt that the intelligent handling of these self-contained platoons contributed largely to the success of the whole operation. The machinery of the Battalion in the attack worked smoothly, and minor opposition which might well have delayed the advance was usually promptly dealt with by the Platoon Commander or Company Commander on the spot with the various weapons at his disposal.[40]

In the 1st Canadian Division, Currie, who was a principal in supporting the organisational changes, wrote:

> All ranks in this Division now have every confidence in their ability to overcome hostile Machine Guns by the combined use of Lewis Guns

and Rifle Grenades, which either put the gun out of action or permit the Bombers or riflemen to get close enough to kill or capture the crew.[41]

The two ANZAC Corps had suffered the same learning experience on the Somme, but the lessons learnt by the Canadians were not as evident in Birdwood's I ANZAC Corps in the operations it conducted in early 1917. The Australians failed before Bullecourt in the two attacks on 11 April and 3 May 1917. Part of this was undoubtedly due to the determination of the Fifth Army Commander General Sir Hubert Gough to push on attacks against what he thought was a retreating enemy, despite growing intelligence to the contrary. Few subordinates in Fifth Army would oppose Gough's raging zeal to press on at all costs, and Lieutenant-General Sir William Birdwood was certainly not one of them, and so his Australians were committed pell-mell to hastily arranged attacks against strong defensive positions with inevitable results.

The operations on the Somme demonstrated Australian staff inexperience, and this was still apparent in early 1917. Brigadier-General C. Brudenell White, Birdwood's Chief of Staff at Headquarters 1 ANZAC, demonstrated his superb administrative skills in the planning of the Gallipoli evacuation, but the Somme and Bullecourt showed that this skill was not initially matched by a similar tactical grasp on the Western Front. To be fair to Birdwood's Australians they did not have the opportunities and time in early 1917 for the training and assessment that the Canadians had in the build-up for Vimy, but Birdwood was not of Byng's calibre in searching for tactical and organisational solutions to the problems raised by the Somme.

Despite the loss of some 23,000 men on the Somme, the Australians produced more of the same before Bullecourt. Brave, bold, but stereotyped with heavy losses; 4th Brigade in the 4th Australian Division was effectively destroyed, losing 2339 out of the 3000 men who took part in the attack on 11 April 1917. Despite the bravery of 6th Brigade on 3 May, the skills they showed were not evident in 5th Brigade, and coordination and cooperation among the Australian formations was lessened by tension and friction between commanders who lacked trust in each other. In 14 days of fighting I ANZAC suffered 292 officers and 7190 other ranks out of some 14,000 British casualties.[42]

The Australians blamed Gough, British flanking formations and the supporting tanks, and while the first is deserving of blame the others are more of an excuse to hide Australian deficiencies. Poor staff work and planning was evident within I ANZAC. This led to the failure of corps artillery to support the attack at critical stages on 11 April. Haste was certainly a factor, but inadequate artillery planning and support was again a key element on 3 May.[43] This was matched by command deficiencies at divisional and brigade level. As one recent study concludes, both the British and Australian formations taking part were 'riven by factional strife while their field commanders wrestled with new technology that they were unable to handle'.[44] I ANZAC did not have the opportunity to change battalion and platoon organisations to effect fire and movement within the platoon, and this tactical ineptness showed in both operations.

Tactically, in early 1917 Birdwood's I ANZAC was inferior to Byng's Canadian Corps and even possibly to Godley's II ANZAC Corps. There was no disputing the outstanding bravery of the Australian soldier, but what the Australian experience at Bullecourt showed was that the initiative and calibre of the individual soldier counted for little unless it was matched by effective command and staff skills, which I ANZAC still lacked.

In contrast, Godley's II ANZAC Corps had the opportunity and the time to assess both the lessons of the Somme and the success of the Canadians at Vimy in the preparation for the attack on 7 June 1917 at Messines. This was part of Plumer's Second Army's attack on the critical ridge holding the shoulder of the area planned for Haig's Flanders offensive. Both the now-experienced New Zealand Division commanded by the New Zealand citizen soldier Major-General Sir Andrew Russell, and the newly arrived 3rd Australian Division under Major-General John Monash, had adopted the new platoon organisations and benefited from having time to practise and rehearse these changes, an opportunity that Birdwood's I ANZAC Corps did not have before Bullecourt. We shall examine this in some detail in the next chapter.

While Messines was an outstanding success there was evidence, both during the preparation and planning and certainly in the commitment of the 4th Australian Division to exploiting the initial success and capturing the Oostaverne Line that lay beyond the ridge, that the staff work of Godley's II ANZAC was suspect. Corps coordination broke down completely, and although the ground was gained both the 3rd and 4th Australian divisions came under effective fire from their own artillery in the mistaken belief that they were part of a German counterattack.

Currie succeeded Byng as Canadian Corps Commander on 6 June 1917, at the age of 41 becoming the first non-Regular officer to command a corps in the BEF.[45] He first demonstrated his skills at this level in the planning and conduct of the Canadian Corps' attack on Lens. The purpose of the attack was to draw German attention from the next phase of the British offensive in Flanders. It was also to draw the German forces into a meat-grinder battle, destroying the combat effectiveness of as many of their divisions as possible to prevent them being sent north as reinforcements to Flanders. Currie's strength of character and determination to do what was best for his corps was evident when, unhappy with the directive and the detailed instructions given to him by General Sir H.S. Horne's First Army, he convinced his army commander that both the objective and the method had to be changed.[46] Currie was a man who had to go forward and see for himself, and from a careful study of the ground he demonstrated that the key feature dominating Lens was Hill 70, which had been placed outside the Canadian boundary in the First Army directive. Seizing this would leave the Germans no option but to counterattack it in force. Unlike Birdwood before Bullecourt, Currie refused to be rushed and repeatedly postponed the attack until weather conditions were perfect. The critical ground was seized and, as Currie had anticipated, the Germans counterattacked furiously over three days, mounting 21 separate attacks, each of which was destroyed by massed artillery fire backed up by machine guns and rifles.

Canadian losses were heavy — 9198 for the period 15–25 August against estimated German losses of 25,000–30,000.[47] All the skills that had marked Canadian success at Vimy were repeated at Lens. A successful attack was mounted under a carefully planned creeping barrage while German artillery was suppressed with counter-battery fire, allowing infantry to fight their way onto the objective with fire and movement.

Both ANZAC corps had time to prepare and rehearse before being committed to Haig's Passchendaele offensive. Working as part of Plumer's Second Army, the Australian divisions achieved a series of successes in the battles of Menin Road by 1st and 2nd Divisions on 20 September; 4th and 5th Divisions at Polygon Wood on 26 September; both I and II ANZAC corps involving 1st, 2nd and 3rd Divisions as well as the New Zealanders on 4 October, the only time both corps were used together side by side on the Western Front. Despite the image we have of Passchendaele, it saw the I and II ANZAC corps employ in battle a level of command and tactical skills equal to the Canadian Corps. With the men exhausted after Bullecourt, the period between May and September was used to good effect in building up the tactical efficiency of the AIF. It was not the quality of the soldiers alone that made the difference; rather it was how they were moulded into an efficient fighting team with hard training, matched by sound administration and leadership.

This was followed by the failure of Godley's II ANZAC in front of Passchendaele on 12 October 1917, with heavy losses to Monash's 3rd Division and the New Zealanders. Despite the skill of both divisions, lack of corps coordination on the part of Godley's staff saw both Russell's and Monash's divisions attack and fail against uncut belts of German wire. Despite Godley's success at Messines, his Headquarters II did not show the same growth in staff procedures and planning that was evident in Birdwood's

I ANZAC after Bullecourt, with the coordination problems evident in Godley's Headquarters during Messines repeated before Passchendaele.

Inadequate artillery preparation and planning at Headquarters II ANZAC led to infantry attacking uncut wire. The creeping barrages were equally ineffective because of insufficient coordination and drive by Corps Headquarters to see that the guns, material for platforms, and ammunition got forward. Despite the skills of both the New Zealand and Australian infantry, they could not reach the bunkers and were shot down in the wire. Russell's assessment was that had the wire been cut, even with limited supporting fire the attack would have been successful. As it was, the failure of 12 October confirmed that it was the all arms cooperation of artillery and infantry working together with engineer support that allowed attacks to succeed. Infantry or artillery alone was not enough.

It was now that a reluctant Currie was ordered to attack with his Canadian Corps where Godley's II ANZAC had failed. Currie had discussed with Byng the involvement of his Canadians in a surprise attack with massed tanks that would later be carried out at Cambrai. This was far more attractive than the mud of Passchendaele.

Knighted by the king: 41-year-old Arthur Currie was recognised for his ability as a divisional commander with a knighthood, promotion to Lieutenant-General, and command of the Canadian Corps, making him the first non-Regular citizen soldier to command a corps in Haig's armies. (*Royal Military Academy Sandhurst Collection*)

> Every Canadian hated to go to Passchendaele ... I carried my protest to the extreme limit ... which I believe would have resulted in my being sent home had I been other than the Canadian Corps Commander. I pointed out what the casualties were bound to be, and was ordered to go and make the attack.[48]

Having been given the job, Currie got on with it. Before Passchendaele, he did everything that Godley had not: he insisted on time for planning and preparation, coordinated the engineer effort, got his guns forward, and committed his infantry to a series of attacks that saw them seize Passchendaele, all at heavy loss.

At Passchendaele Currie found that of the 360 field guns only 220 were working but not all were in position. Key to the success was his demand that damaged guns be replaced and that the guns allocated, many of which were stuck in the mud, had to be got forward so they could contribute to the fire plan for the attack.[49] Currie and his staff went forward into the quagmire to see the conditions for themselves.[50] His planning took into account the conditions that both artillery and infantry would face fighting in such swampy desolation against a determined enemy organised in depth. It was important that the artillery creeping barrage did not run away from the infantry squelching slowly forward through the mire. In four bites on 26 October, 30 October, 6 November and 10 November, the Canadians fought their way forward against stiff resistance until they finally captured the pulverised ridge on which the village of Passchendaele once stood. The gain was a small, dangerous salient poking like a finger into the German defensive line, subject to fire from all sides. It was accomplished by Currie's corps in two weeks at a cost of 15,643 Canadian casualties. Its seizure marked the end of the Passchendaele offensive.

As the map opposite shows, Currie mounted a series of carefully coordinated attacks in impossible conditions and succeeded where II ANZAC and other corps had failed.[51] Given the conditions Currie faced, it is hard to see how this wasteland of mud could have been more cheaply gained. As we know, Currie made it clear to Haig that he did not want the task, and insisted on time and effort that Haig was initially reluctant to give. Similar demands by a British corps commander may have been overruled, but by now Currie had a professional formation, valued his men, and knew what was necessary to succeed. Haig had been instrumental in appointing Currie corps commander and would listen to reasoned argument, but, while it is clear that Currie admired Haig as a commander, the relationship between the two men was always a prickly one.

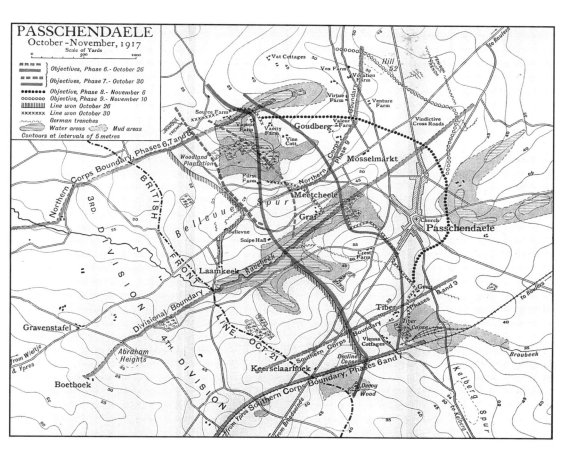

This tension underlay relations between the Canadian Corps and GHQ throughout 1917. After Currie had complained about the supply of replacement artillery before Lens in July 1917, Haig noted that 'the Canadians always open their mouths very wide!'[52] Currie, the citizen soldier, showed a willingness to speak out in the interests of his corps that was never contemplated by either Birdwood or Godley, as British Regular soldiers commanding the two ANZAC corps. While the tension between Haig and Currie was more than balanced by the tactical skill the Canadians displayed under Currie's command, the strain between the two men would surface again during the German offensive in March 1918.[53]

The tactics employed by the Canadian Corps mirrored those used throughout the British armies. The principal difference was the advantage of homogeneity, where the four divisions of the corps benefited from corps doctrine. Central to this was the figure of Currie himself. He constantly assessed the need for change, drawing on both the recommendations issued by Haig's General Headquarters and internally from his own subordinate formations. He was a commander who had to see for himself, who understood the conditions his soldiers endured, abhorred casualties, knew that exhausted men cannot fight and that battalions had to be kept up to strength with trained reinforcements if they were to meet the demands placed upon them by offensive action on the Western Front.

Unlike other corps commanders, except those of the two ANZAC corps, he was in a position to direct and oversee organisational and tactical changes in his four divisions over an extended period. British corps commanders did not have this ability to influence the organisation and training of divisions within their corps because there was no permanent allocation of divisions. Doctrinal changes and tactical evolution depended on the ability and drive of each divisional commander.

Currie's Canadians returned to the Vimy sector after Passchendaele. Despite the demands imposed by the anticipated German offensive, which it was predicted would follow the collapse of Russian resistance, Currie ensured that each of his divisions in rotation had one month out of the line in reserve training and resting, with the resolve that 'every effort should be made to bring the Corps to the highest possible fighting efficiency'.[54]

The sodden misery of victory; the Canadian front line at Passchendaele, November 1917. (*Royal Military Academy Sandhurst Collection*)

Manpower shortages led Haig to institute what he believed would be the temporary reduction of the size of infantry divisions from 12 to nine battalions throughout the British armies. By January 1918 the Canadian Corps faced a critical reinforcement situation. There were simply not enough men in the system to keep existing units up to strength. Reinforcements came from wounded and convalescent soldiers returning to their units; in many cases men who should have been returned to Canada.

> In the absence of Infantry Drafts from Canada, training has been reduced to a science, with Physical and Remedial training a very important factor. The main sources of supply for reinforcements are the convalescent Hospitals, and it has only been possible to maintain supplies for the Training Reserve Battalions by having a good system of remedial treatment at the Hospitals and physical training at the Command Depots in order that returned Expeditionary Force men might become category 'A-1' as soon as possible, and therefore available as reinforcements.[55]

Currie insisted on retaining the 12-battalion organisation within his corps. He also opposed the suggested restructuring and expansion of his corps into two Canadian corps, despite the opportunities this offered for his own advancement to command a Canadian army.[56] The bitter fighting of 1917 had reinforced his belief that infantry battalions had to be kept at full strength if they were to be effective, and that 'sending an under-strength unit into battle almost always resulted in greater losses than if that unit fought under the same conditions but at full strength'.[57]

Currie conducted a skilful political battle to achieve the retention of the existing divisional structure. He also achieved the break-up of the 5th Canadian Division, which had been retained in England, and used it to increase each battalion establishment with an additional 100 infantrymen as well as providing a much-needed pool of trained reinforcements.

The manpower situation improved in February 1918 with the arrival of the first drafts of conscripts under the Canadian Military Service Act. These reinforcements had had little training in Canada but were of good material. This and the break-up of the 5th Canadian Division meant demands from the front 'can be met by fully trained men'.[58] At the beginning of March 1918 each of the Canadian battalions was between 900 and 1000 strong and there was a small surplus of trained reinforcements in the Canadian Corps Reinforcement Camp, in contrast to the deficiency that had existed in the first two months of the year.[59]

Currie was also conscious that higher headquarters, including his own, too often saw infantry as a readily available labour force that was too easily tasked to do the myriad labouring tasks required in a combat zone instead of being given the opportunity to rest and retrain. He restructured the engineer and machine-gun organisation in his corps to lessen the demands on his infantry in battle. The three field companies of engineers that had previously supported each division were expanded to an Engineer Brigade of three battalions and a Bridging Section, greatly increasing the engineering capacity, which until now had been dependent on tasking infantry as a labour force.[60] In line with changes throughout the British armies he reorganised machine-gun companies into machine-gun battalions, and later increased the number of machine guns to 96 guns per battalion.[61]

In addition the Canadian Corps had the benefit of the 1st and 2nd Canadian Motor Machine Gun Brigades; each brigade was essentially a motorised machine-gun battalion consisting of five batteries of eight Vickers machine guns mounted in Canadian-manufactured Otter armoured cars. The concept was the brainchild of the French-born Brigadier-General Raymond Brutinel, who was Currie's Commander Canadian Machine Gun Corps. As the commander of 'Brutinel's Brigade' he would command a mobile force consisting of the two Motor Machine Gun Brigades, the Canadian Light Horse and the Canadian Corps Cyclist Battalion, together with trench mortars and artillery. This mobile force, unique to the Canadian Corps, was used with skill and boldness during the 1918 campaign. The 1st Canadian Motor Machine Gun Brigade played a critical role in covering the withdrawal of the Fifth Army during the German offensive of March 1918, and 'Brutinel's Brigade' had an equally important role in the Canadian offensive operations from 8 August 1918.[62]

In January 1918 training in Currie's Canadian divisions was built around a sequence of three weeks' training that drew its lessons from the Cambrai offensive. Every man in the platoon was expected to be an expert in all infantry weapons, and the platoon organisation was adjusted to allow for the addition of a second Lewis gun to each platoon, giving each two Lewis gun sections and two rifle sections.

Training progressed from platoon through company to battalion level. 'It is most important that these schemes should take the form of open or semi-open warfare wherein the unit advances by the aid of its own firepower and without the help of an artillery barrage. Counter-attack schemes will also be practiced.'[63] Emphasis was placed on instructing platoon commanders in the use of ground, employment of all arms under their command and efficient reporting. Tactical Exercises Without Troops (TEWT) or 'Allez-Allez' schemes were conducted to sharpen the young officers' response to the types of situations they might encounter in a fast-moving mobile battle. Making best use of technological improvements was also practised, such as the use of Stokes mortars to provide smoke in company and platoon attacks. 'Strong points may be barraged with smoke bombs to give cover for a Lewis Gun team to work around to a flank and many other similar ideas can be worked out.'[64]

Battalions and brigades practised infantry-tank cooperation and working with contact aeroplanes. The training in the Canadian Corps was innovative and impressive, but it also mirrored training that was being conducted to the same or a lesser degree throughout the British armies depending on the drive and initiative of individual divisional commanders. However, the Canadian Corps evolved its own individual approach: 'a definite Corps tactical doctrine [which] was necessary by reason of the different organisation, the greater strength, and the particular methods which characterised the Canadian Corps'.[65]

This bore fruit with the start of the expected German offensive on 21 March 1918. The Russian collapse in October 1917 had allowed the transfer of German resources to the Western Front, and General Ludendorff planned a major offensive to end the war before the United States could mobilise its manpower resources. Apart from the Battle of Verdun the Germans had been on the defensive on the Western Front since 1915, and the French and British had been the attackers, the latter taking the lead in this from June 1917. Now the roles were reversed. Ludendorff had grouped and trained an elite force of *Stosstruppen*, or storm-troopers, in platoon and section infiltration tactics tasked with penetrating the Allied defensive lines under a surprise artillery bombardment. This was similar to British and French offensive doctrine, and Ludendorff's objectives mirrored Haig's offensive ambitions.

This spring offensive was anticipated and prepared for, and the British armies copied German defensive doctrine and adopted a three-zone defence-in-depth system. The difference was that the Germans had evolved this in practice, while the British armies, on the defensive for the first time in two and a half years, adopted the form but, as its execution showed, not the substance. On 21 March 1918 the Germans achieved both tactical surprise and a deep penetration at the junction of the Third and Fifth British Armies in the Arras-St Quentin sector, particularly on the Fifth Army front.

The pressure on the Fifth and Third Army fronts saw the Canadian Corps extend its front, and the detachment on 23 March of the 1st Canadian Motor Machine Gun Brigade to support the withdrawal of the Fifth Army. With its 40 motorised machine guns it fought a brilliant rearguard action over 200 square miles of territory for some 19 days, with the loss of some 75 percent of its trench strength.[66]

As the crisis developed all four Canadian divisions were removed from Currie's command and placed under the command of two different armies, and three different corps. 'This disposition of the Canadian troops was not satisfactory, and, on receipt of the orders … I made strong representation to First Army, and offered suggestions which to my mind would reconcile my claims (from the standpoint of Canadian policy) with the tactical and administrative requirements of the moment.'[67]

Currie's determination to restore the integrity of his corps was misinterpreted by Horne, the First Army Commander, and by Haig. Both were highly critical of Currie's action, but Currie was unrepentant. He distrusted the reduced British divisional organisation of nine battalions, believing it was too weak in infantry, and knew that his Canadian divisions fought better when grouped under his command. Currie ensured that political pressure was applied through Sir Edward Kemp, the Minister of Overseas Military Forces of Canada, in London to force the return. It was this that led Haig to regroup the Canadian divisions under Currie's command, and remark angrily and inaccurately in his diary that Currie's actions kept the Canadians out of battle.[68]

By mid-April 1918 Currie had three Canadian divisions back under his command in the Vimy sector. On 7 May the Canadian Corps was withdrawn into reserve. Currie immediately finalised changes to his artillery, engineers, machine guns and signal organisations and commenced training in open warfare offensive operations.

> Many tactical schemes were carried out during May, June and July, each emphasizing some definite lesson, more particularly how to overpower resistance in an area defended by machine guns in depth, using covering fire and smoke grenades, how Batteries of Machine Guns should co-operate in assisting Infantry to get forward, and how Sections of Field Artillery could best carry out an advance in close support of attacking Infantry.[69]

The Canadians were at the cutting edge of tactical doctrinal development on the Western Front. Currie was the first to admit that Canadian skills were drawn both from their own experience and from the dissemination of lessons distributed by Haig's GHQ. 'These documents were carefully studied and, to a large extent, inspired our training.'[70] They provided similar inspiration to other thinking commanders. Monash took those lessons with him when he assumed command of the Australian Corps in May 1918 and demonstrated them in fighting his corps at Hamel, and in the battles of the Hundred Days offensive from 8 August. At last the Australian divisions had a man in command who knew the value of planning and preparation. Both the Australian and Canadian corps demonstrated the value of having homogeneous corps consisting of fixed divisions, and gained strength from that cohesiveness. It was something that Australian commanders had always recognised, but while I ANZAC was structured with four Australian divisions in August 1917 it was not until the formation of the Australian Corps at the beginning of 1918 that all five Australian divisions were grouped together.[71]

The Canadian Corps remained at the cutting edge throughout the battles of the Hundred Days, starting with the Battle of Amiens on 8 August 1918. At Amiens the Canadians advanced 14 miles at the cost of 9074 men.[72] Together with the French Army on the right flank, Rawlinson's Fourth Army penetrated seven miles and took 30,000 prisoners. It was, as Michael Howard concluded, 'the first outright and irreversible defeat that the Germans had suffered in four years of fighting'.[73] It was Currie who told Haig the battle was running out of steam against increasingly stiffening German resistance and that it needed to be either shut down or moved somewhere else.

> I further suggested that, rather than expose the Canadian Corps to losses without adequate results, it should be withdrawn from this front, rested for a few days, and used to make another surprise attack in the direction of Bapaume.[74]

It was Currie's recommendations, backed by Rawlinson, the Fourth Army Commander, that prompted Haig to widen the offensive. This produced a series of hammer blows that saw the British armies fight at what we would today term the operational level for the first time.[75] The successful attacks by the Third and Fourth Armies between 8 and 11 August and 21 and 23 August convinced Haig that the Germans were on the ropes. It was time for an all-out offensive, as he put it in his exhortation to his Army commanders on 22 August. 'To turn the present situation into account the most resolute offensive is everywhere desirable. Risks which a month ago would have been criminal to incur, ought now to be incurred as a duty.'[76]

This kept the German defenders at full stretch and off balance. The Canadian Corps played a full part in these attacks from August until the Armistice. On 19/20 August the Canadian Corps was transferred north to Horne's First Army. It was in familiar territory, facing the outer works of the Hindenburg Line at its most critical spot, the Wotan-I-Stellung or Drocourt-Queant (D-Q) position that was a critical hinge. This was one of the most strongly defended positions on the front in country that was ideal for defence. Currie had been assessing how to attack it in July 1918 and now put his plan into effect. From 26 to 28 August the 2nd and 3rd Canadian divisions and the 51st Highland

Division under command of the Canadian Corps fought their way forward with heavy casualties to the D-Q position. On 2 September the 1st and 4th Canadian divisions and the 4th British Division under Currie's control attacked this and broke through at a cost of 5662 casualties. This was 'one of the most stunning accomplishments of the Corps' triumphant Hundred Days',[77] but at the price of the 'near annihilation for the ten battalions that bore the brunt of the attack'.[78] Tough battles cost lives, and Currie was both mindful of the cost and prepared to fight his divisions to win — in 1918 there was no other easy way.[79] Harris, in his study of the Hundred Days offensive, points out that Currie almost became de facto army commander in his conduct of the offensive within the First Army. This continued what seems to have been the practice at Vimy where, as Harris suggests, Horne, the Army Commander, seems to have acquired the habit of giving all substantial offensive tasks to the Canadian Corps and leaving both planning and execution very largely to the corps commander and his staff. This was the case during the Battle of the Scarpe, which is the name by which Currie's advance and taking of the D-Q line is known.[80]

With this critical hinge taken, the Germans withdrew back behind the Canal du Nord. This was stormed on 27 September as part of a coordinated offensive by the First, Third and Fourth Armies. Once again without a preliminary bombardment on a constricted front, caused by the impassable nature of the canal for the northern half of the Canadian sector, Currie's Canadians broke in and then fanned out, capturing Bourlon Wood and pushing forward with heavy fighting towards Cambrai. Currie pushed his tired troops and drew in critical German reserves to defend the 'last organised system of defences' on the Canadian front. Cambrai fell on 9 October and the corps paused to regroup on the Canal de la Sensée on 12 October.

During the battle of Arras-Cambrai the Canadians had defeated 31 German divisions reinforced by 'numerous Marksmen Machine Gun Companies' on ground that had been specially prepared for defence over 18 months. It was a stunning achievement at heavy cost; Canadian casualties totalled 1544 officers and 29,262 other ranks between 22 August and 11 October 1918.[81] The Canadians continued to push forward, and despite growing logistic difficulties fought their way across the Canal l'Escaut. They cleared Valenciennes on 2 November and captured Mons in the early morning of 11 November 1918; the day the Armistice went into effect.

The offensive operations of the Canadian Corps showed its capabilities at every level. It was involved in sustained heavy fighting to a greater degree than any other British corps. It demonstrated a flexibility of leadership and command that took advantage of any weakness by a skilled if weakened enemy fighting stubbornly to hold successive positions. It took in turn some of the strongest positions on the Western Front. Between 8 August and 11 November 1918 Canadian Corps captured 31,537 prisoners, 635 guns, 2842 machine guns and 336 trench mortars. Between 8 August and 11 October it engaged and defeated 47 German divisions, 'that is nearly a quarter of total German forces on the Western Front'.[82] The only comparable performance on the Western Front was by Monash's Australian Corps, who under his tight and detailed direction also evolved a corps doctrine and whose battles were launched with meticulous attention to detail. This will be examined in a later chapter. Currie has never received the accolades accorded Monash, yet I see this Canadian citizen soldier as the outstanding corps commander on the Western Front and, as I will argue, superior to Monash. Canada ignored his achievements, and a vengeful Sam Hughes slandered and damned him for 'needlessly sacrificing the lives of Canadian soldiers'.[83] Today, outside of Canada, he is largely unknown and remains undeservedly in Monash's shadow.

NINE

RUSSELL AND MONASH:
TWO ANZAC DIVISIONAL COMMANDERS
ON THE WESTERN FRONT

I discussed the merits of the 18 Divisions and their respective commanders who will be under his orders so that the best commanders may be given the most difficult tasks.[1]

Sir Douglas Haig

Godley's II ANZAC Corps had two outstanding divisional commanders in 1917: Major-General John Monash, GOC 3rd Australian Division, and Major-General Sir Andrew Russell, GOC New Zealand Division. Both were officers with a citizen forces background; Monash was a civil engineer and successful businessman, Russell a sheep station owner from the east coast of New Zealand. Monash has been well served by history, both with his own writings and with two substantial biographies, *John Monash* by Geoffrey Serle and *Monash as Military Commander* by Peter Pedersen, the latter being a particularly impressive study of his military prowess.[2] Russell, by contrast, is almost unknown, both in New Zealand and in Australia.[3]

Born in Melbourne in 1865 of Prussian-Jewish descent, Monash became interested in the military while studying engineering at the University of Melbourne. He joined the Garrison Artillery, rose slowly through the military ranks, and was still a battery commander in 1907. It was his transfer to the Australian Intelligence Corps that reinvigorated his military career, and in June 1913 he was promoted colonel and given command of 13th Brigade.[4] A complex, ambitious man, Monash was eager to succeed and actively courted military advancement commensurate with his business success. On

Major-General John Monash, GOC 3rd Australian Division (later
GOC Australian Corps), a complex, ambitious personality who
proved to be a superb tactician and planner, but because of his failure
to visit the front line on the Western Front grew increasingly detached
from the men he commanded. (*Royal Military Academy Sandhurst
Collection*)

the outbreak of war Monash served briefly as deputy chief censor before being given command of the 4th Brigade AIF, which sailed for Egypt as an independent brigade with the Second Contingent on 22 October 1914. There it became part of Godley's New Zealand and Australian (NZ&A) Division, which included the New Zealand Infantry Brigade as well as Russell's New Zealand Mounted Rifles Brigade and Chauvel's 1st Australian Light Horse Brigade. For Monash this began an association with Russell that was to continue until the formation of the Australian Corps at the end of 1917.

Andrew Russell was from an old-established New Zealand family. He was born in Napier in 1868, and educated in England at Harrow and Sandhurst, graduating in 1887 as a lieutenant in the Border Regiment. He saw five years' service in Burma and India before resigning his commission in 1892, returning to station life in New Zealand under his uncle on Tunanui Station in Hawke's Bay. His grandfather had counselled him against leaving the army, and described the difficulties of a settler's life in New Zealand. 'Are you going to be satisfied in the future with the position of a small farmer running a thousand sheep on 2000 acres, and leading a solitary life in the bush, when you might be commanding a Regt?'[5] Nevertheless, Russell persevered with sheep-farming and, after a period as manager, assumed ownership of Tunanui in 1909.

Russell was a keen Volunteer officer and raised the Hawke's Bay Mounted Rifle Volunteers during the Boer War. He maintained the efficiency and enthusiasm of his squadron in the years following the war, when many of the corps that had been formed during the pitch of war fervour were disbanded. In 1909 he was promoted lieutenant-colonel, and on the formation of the Territorial Force in New Zealand quickly came to the attention of Major-General Sir Alexander Godley, GOC NZ Forces, as a Territorial officer of talent. Godley was impressed enough to offer Russell a Regular commission in the rank of lieutenant-colonel with the appointment of district commander. This Russell refused.

Russell was a practical man and as a Territorial he relished fieldwork. This experience made him conscious of the nature of the men he was to command in war:

> ... scouting, tracking and trying to do something practical, and [I] think I learn more from this sort of thing than ever we were taught on the barrack yard. It is extraordinary what you can do when you try, and how apt and keen the Colonials are. You hear the men talking after the day's work just as you hear hunting men tell their runs over and over again and discussing every point of the run.[6]

Major-General Sir Andrew Russell, GOC New Zealand Division, a practical man who grew increasingly aware that his single most valuable asset was the New Zealand soldier, and who was intent on sending him into battle fully trained with the best possible plan to ensure success. (*National Army Museum, Waiouru Collection*)

The practical bent of this Hawke's Bay farmer was balanced by his reading widely on military subjects to keep abreast of military developments in Europe.

Despite his subaltern years in an infantry regiment his Territorial experience was with the Mounted Rifles, and what he saw at the divisional camp in May 1914 made him sceptical of the effectiveness of Territorial infantry. It confirmed his views on how little New Zealand's Territorial Army knew of the business of war. His picture of a citizen army mirrored the reality not just of the New Zealand Territorial Force but, as we have seen, that of the citizen armies of Australia and Canada.

> The Infantry are without discipline, and their officers appear to have no control. It is very disappointing. It is the first time I have been in with the Infantry, and tho' I had my doubts had no idea how undisciplined they

were. The class of officer they have, tho' good enough fellows, are not up to handling men.[7]

Perhaps influenced by Russell's years as a Regular, Godley saw him as the one Territorial officer capable of handling a brigade in combat. He asked him to command the New Zealand Mounted Rifles Brigade of the Expeditionary Force on the outbreak of war in August 1914.[8] At the time Godley believed firmly that only Regular officers had the professional command and staff skills necessary to command a brigade in war, and this influenced his selection of commanders throughout; Russell was the exception to the rule.

Gallipoli made Russell's reputation, while the same campaign placed question marks over Monash's effectiveness as a brigade commander. Both served as part of Godley's NZ&A Division, Monash having landed with his brigade on the first day. Russell arrived in mid-May and commanded his Mounted Rifles Brigade in an infantry role on Gallipoli. His efforts in seizing the foothills during the night advance of the right column in the August battles made his name, Bean's history of Anzac acknowledging that this was one of the finest feats of the campaign.[9]

In contrast, Monash's performance during the August offensive is clouded with controversy.[10] Monash's 4th Australian Brigade was part of Major-General Cox's left assaulting column, which was tasked with seizing the 971 feature. Monash was unable to cope with the physical strain of the march and the demands of command. He placed himself in the middle of his brigade column and surrendered the operational command of his brigade to his leading battalion commander, defending this decision by stating that it was against his wishes but at Cox's direction. The British official historian, Brigadier-General Aspinall-Oglander, based his narrative on an account Monash provided to him after the war. In it one can read between the lines of his sceptical reaction to Monash's seeking permission from Cox, the column commander, before going forward to sort out the delays at the head of his brigade.[11]

Monash's biographers have hotly disputed accounts of what seems to have been a nervous collapse, reported by Lieutenant-Colonel C.J.L. Allanson of the 6th Gurkhas, but despite their protestations his actions appear to confirm the rumours that swirl around his performance on Gallipoli. His veteran brigade fell apart in the foothills well before it reached the high ground and he was unable to prevent its disintegration.[12] As the entry in the *Oxford Companion to Australian Military History* concludes, 'Certainly this was not Monash's finest hour. Yet it must be stressed that no action, or lack of it, could have saved the offensive. The task given the 4th Brigade was beyond the capacity of any troops.'[13] On Gallipoli Monash had the reputation of being a 'dugout king'; someone who was loath to move from his headquarters and venture into the front line trenches, and rumours of this lingered on after the campaign.[14]

When Godley became ANZAC Corps commander in November 1915 Russell was the obvious choice to succeed him in command of the NZ&A Division on the peninsula, with Monash becoming one of his subordinates. There are indications that Russell's pre-eminence rankled with the Australian, and on 12 November 1915 Monash queried Russell receiving a knighthood:

> … altho' it is a little difficult to understand the basis of the discrimination in his favour, seeing that he is junior to many of us, has units only half in number of an Infantry Brigade, did not take part in the first landing, and has done nothing specifically conspicuous in comparison with several of the Australian Brigades'.[15]

On the return of the NZ&A Division to Egypt Monash wrote of Russell that he was 'a splendid fellow and a close friend of mine … urbanity itself, without weakness'.[16] One senses that Monash liked the man, but he plainly considered he had been promoted beyond his capabilities. '[Russell] has given me an insight into the awful confusion, cross purposes, constant changes of plan and policy that characterize the higher command and get worse the higher you go.'[17] This followed a familiar pattern in Monash's correspondence, with initial praise followed by later criticism. While praising Russell as a friend Monash also damned him as a divisional commander, criticising both his command skills and his 'nonchalance' towards administration.

It was a period of considerable frustration for Monash, with the shadows of his Gallipoli performance casting doubts on his suitability for divisional command. He had to watch with anger as he was bypassed as Birdwood selected British officers to command the newly raised Australian divisions.[18] In June 1916 his brigade was posted to France as part of the 4th Australian Division, and it was in the same month that Monash was posted to command the 3rd Division, which was being raised on Salisbury Plain in England.

The formation of the New Zealand Division allowed Russell to disappear as Monash's superior from Pedersen's and Serle's narratives, and Russell as a commander does not re-emerge. There is a sense in Pedersen's biography that conclusions have been made and Russell's ability assessed. His command, the New Zealand Division, continues to feature, even if the man himself is not mentioned. On its arrival in France in late 1916

Monash's 3rd Australian Division became part of Godley's II ANZAC Corps and in each battle, almost by rote, as Pedersen states, 'The New Zealand Division, as usual, attacked on the left.'[19]

This chapter examines the operations of both divisions in 1917: the New Zealand Division under its New Zealand-born general on the left of the 3rd Australian Division under its Australian commander, who was seen by some as a suspect outsider, in the principal battles involving II ANZAC Corps; the Battle of Messines in June 1917, and the battles of 4 and 12 October before Passchendaele. Here we have two interesting commanders whose military careers ran in parallel: Russell who overshadows Monash on Gallipoli and Monash who overshadows Russell on the Western Front, emerging as one of the outstanding commanders in the British armies during the First World War. How do they compare as divisional commanders during Monash's first year in France, when they were working alongside each other in the same corps?

Monash received word of his pending appointment to the 3rd Australian Division on 24 June 1916. Given his religion and parentage he saw his promotion as a triumph over adversity, 'and it is very gratifying, in spite of these solid handicaps, and without any intrigue whatever on my part, to have got the honour on status of my present rank. I am wondering what my enemies at home will be saying.'[20] He was determined to prove wrong those whom he believed had impeded his advancement. The five months' training on Salisbury Plain ensured that his 3rd Australian Division was the best-trained formation in the AIF. No other division had the same opportunities or extended time to be prepared for battle by a now veteran commander who unhesitatingly drew from the latest experiences of the ANZAC Corps in ensuring his men were ready.

Monash, like Russell and Currie, studied intently the techniques practised by other commanders and formations in the British armies as well as what the French and Germans were doing. The importance of this was emphasised by Currie when he was Corps Commander in 1918, and could equally have been written by any of the three commanders.

> General Staff, General Headquarters, were publishing from time to time translations of captured German documents bearing of the latest tactics, and supplemented these by 'Notes on Recent Fighting', dealing with the lessons of the fighting then in progress, both from the point of view of offence and defence. These documents were carefully studied and, to a large extent, inspired our training.[21]

In addition, all three men showed an ability to assess and learn from their mistakes. Tactical training was predicated on their own experience and from recommendations of Haig's GHQ. This was assimilated in detailed preparation and planning, training and rehearsals at every level within each formation. As Pedersen concludes, '[Monash's] success rested largely on imitation rather than innovation', but in this he was in good company. As we shall see, it still required a commander of perspicacity and drive to ensure these raw citizen soldiers became skilled through a solid foundation of training at platoon and company level before progressing to battalion and brigade.[22]

In November 1916 Monash's 3rd Australian Division joined Godley's II ANZAC Corps in the line on the Armentières Sector. It was a period where his division set about 'gaining credit' by a series of raids on the German trenches. From the start, certain principles of Monash's command style emerge. Planning of raids, as in all of Monash's operations, was centralised at division, and subordinate commanders acted out Monash's plan. Monash never went forward from his divisional headquarters, depending on liaison officers' reports and a close study of the map to visualise the front line and the operational area forward of it. His GSO1 (later Major-General) G.H.N. Jackson, a British Regular officer, wrote:

> ... no Divisional Commander in France knew his line better and yet he never visited it, so far as I know. He may have gone to Brigade Headquarters occasionally but I never got him nearer than the third line and he did not seem to enjoy even that. He studied aircraft photos minutely and discussed details of the front line with me and other staff officers and acquired the most astounding grasp of local conditions. This 'seeing through other men's eyes' is to my mind not sufficiently practised in our Army.[23]

It may be because of his experience on Gallipoli during the August offensive in 1915 that Monash never again ventured into the front line. He compensated for this unwillingness to go forward by detailed planning and preparation, and by the equally detailed instructions to his subordinates at all levels that become his hallmark. His engineering background and years of study of military mapping and military science both as a coastal gunner and with the Australian Intelligence Corps now bore fruit. This 'seeing through other men's eyes' was to become a strength that he harnessed during the static periods of trench warfare and in the deliberately planned and carefully staged limited attacks in 3rd Australian Division in 1917, at Hamel in July 1918 and at Amiens in August 1918.

Monash employed a top down approach that bore similarities to the development of inter-war Soviet doctrine, where the initiative and planning was thought through in detail at the highest level and directed down to subordinate commanders who carried it out with little or no scope for initiative on their part. It was the subordinate's task to see that these plans were so imbued through rehearsals and training that they were carried out to the letter. This continued when Monash was appointed corps commander. It was an approach that needed time and thought, and was well suited to the carefully prepared 'set piece' attack. Monash had to 'see' the ground from reports before he could put himself in the position of his forward units. It was less effective in a fluid mobile battle.

In 1917 Monash was still close enough to his hands-on experience as brigade commander to understand what his men could and could not do. This was not the case in 1918. He was not one who could quiz soldiers and sense their mood. Indeed, while Monash was a constant presence in reviewing training and checking details out of the line, his brigades grew not to expect to see him in the trenches and one suspects patterned their activities accordingly. Major-General John Gellibrand, who succeeded Monash in command of the 3rd Australian Division, was far from satisfied with the state of the front-line trenches in June 1918, noting that 'it was very clear that a visit to the front line [by the divisional commander] was most unusual and most necessary'.[24] The reality with command at every level is that if you do not go forward to see for yourself you inevitably lose touch, and this happened to Monash. His first-hand experience of trench warfare was on Gallipoli, and despite his determination to see through 'other men's eyes' there was more and more he did not see and was not aware of, both at divisional level and at corps. His growing detachment from the front line would see a gulf develop between his demands and the practical capabilities of an exhausted and under-strength Australian Corps in their battles in September and October 1918.

Russell's approach was very different. He was very much a front-line commander who had to see the situation and how his men were faring himself. Russell's diary is a record of unit visits and inspections that included two to three tours of the front line a week when his division was in the trenches. Every visit would lead to a string of written suggestions and conference items, 'The GOC notes'. Nothing escaped his attention. When Monash joined II ANZAC, Russell's New Zealanders were rebuilding after the Somme, where a series of successful attacks had seen them remain in the line for the longest single tour of any division in the battle. The New Zealanders emerged with a reputation as an outstanding fighting division, but at a cost of some 7400 casualties.

Russell's aim in the winter of 1916–17 was to absorb the lessons of the Somme and to improve the administration within his division. '21 [October] Divisional Conference —

Outlined policy — Men's comfort and safety first, the rest nowhere.[25] Russell recognised that his division could not repeat its fine performance on the Somme if attention was not given to improving the standards of knowledge and leadership of his officers and NCOs, and improving the care and welfare available to his soldiers. Currently the administrative procedures within his division were poor. It was a failing for which Monash had criticised him in early 1916 and this was now acknowledged.

> … and [I] have told Brigadiers and Commanding Officers to forget all about the Germans for a few days and devote their minds and energies towards establishing a good system of interior economy, and improving the discipline of their Units. It is no reflection on the men when I say we are weak in these matters. I certainly confess that personally I have thought a good deal more about fighting than about administration, and I believe most officers would say the same of themselves, but when one sees the waste and unnecessary friction which is set up by want of administrative experience and knowledge, one realises it plays just as important a part in the success of the war as the actual fighting.[26]

Russell both implemented what he saw as necessary and saw that it was carried out. Each day he looked at some unit or aspect of his division, and the soldiers were used to him going briskly through the trenches and billets followed by his aides and subordinate commanders. Nothing was overlooked, and Russell praised or damned the unit accordingly. 'Napier Johnston and I went round the 11th Battery whose horses are a disgrace to the British Army.'[27] A daily inspection of the artillery wagon lines followed until Russell was satisfied that they were up to standard. Russell was determined to reduce the sick rate of his division and directed that commanding officers, with the RMOs (Regimental Medical Officers), 'will visit all billets, wagon lines, and cook-houses, and satisfy themselves as to the conditions under which their men are living'.[28]

Every effort was to be made to improve the men's conditions. 'Although material is scarce, this will not be taken as an excuse. Drainage is to be made, receptacles for food provided, and everything done to make their sanitation satisfactory.' Hot food containers were put on trial in order to give men hot meals in the trenches. Divisional canteens stocked fresh vegetables to allow units to supplement the monotony of field rations. A catering officer was appointed, and a divisional school of cookery established. Training courses were run for unit cooks, traditionally the post of the least employable men in the units, and the useless and dirty were dismissed. The emphasis was on preparing good hot food for the men, and making the best use of the least liked and most common elements of the field rations: bully beef, biscuits and cheese. Recipes were taught and distributed, so that, 'What was once known as the most hated portion of the Field Ration … can be turned into most appetising and tasty dishes.'[29]

Physical fitness and training was also programmed. The division organised sports days and football competitions. The first step, naturally enough, was the formation of the divisional rugby team. Players were drawn from all units in the division and were grouped at the divisional school. The priority was rugby. 'Representatives will live at the School, and, in addition to being trained as a football team, will receive instruction in Bayonet Fighting, Physical Drill and Bombing. They will be returned to their units at the end of the football season, qualified instructors in these subjects.'[30]

> By April 1917 Russell's division had recovered from the exertions of the Somme:
> I can report the Division as being in first class fighting trim. I have never seen the men look so well as they do today. The sick rate is low … Even venereal, for the time being, is a negligible quantity. I am afraid we must put that down rather to the fact that no leave is being granted to England than to any sudden development of virtue on the part of the men.[31]

This attention to administrative detail was also part of Monash's approach, and a study of his division's war diaries shows that this was reflected in carefully thought out drills and procedures in every unit.[32] This was also mirrored in both commanders' approach to training. Both divisions adopted the new platoon organisation, and the weeks before Messines were spent in intensive training at platoon and company levels to ensure that each man was efficient in all the infantry platoon weapons, and that junior commanders at both section and platoon level understood their jobs and were proficient in the drills of fire and movement.

The basis of success was the insistence 'that every soldier realises that he must be trained to use his three weapons equally well, i.e. rifle, bomb, and bayonet'. On arrival in France all New Zealand soldiers were put through individual assault practices where all weapons were used, the first time with blanks, the second with 'everything live, including bombs and firing from the hip'.[33] In platoon training it was emphasised that every man was a specialist in every weapon. 'The ideal to aim at is — that every man should be able to throw a bomb, fire a Lewis gun, rifle or rifle grenade, and use a bayonet.'[34]

The New Zealand Division shared in the platoon tactical revolution described in the previous chapter. In March 1917 the brigades reported to Russell's headquarters that each battalion 'has now been reorganised under the new system and it is in working order'. Each platoon was organised into four sections, including a Lewis gun section; although only three guns had been issued per company the fourth team was being trained so as 'to be ready when the fourth gun per company is issued'.[35] It was a mixture of learning from others such as the Canadian Corps and assessing the divisional lessons learnt on the Somme.

This was not something that occurred in isolation but part of an evolving pattern prompted, as we have seen, by directives from Haig's GHQ. As Bidwell and Graham point out in their seminal work *Fire-Power*, these directives did not guarantee 'uniformity in theory and practice'; how the organisational and tactical changes were taken up depended on the drive and initiative of individual divisional commanders. Yet it is clear from Haig's visits to training and his diary comments that it was something he was particularly interested in. This was reflected in the appointment of Brigadier-General A. Solly-Flood as BGGS (Training) at GHQ on 30 January 1917,[36] although Bidwell and Graham downplay his effectiveness, pointing out that his was a coordinating function at best.[37]

As discussed earlier, this was a time of change and evolution in the organisation and tactics of the British armies in France. Experience on the Somme had shown up the deficiencies that existed at all levels from doctrine to command. Changes had been initiated, and the tactical education of the British armies in this period is the subject of Paddy Griffith's *Battle Tactics of the Western Front*, but how central was Haig in this process?[38] Griffith notes that Haig was always anxious to multiply infantry (and indeed cavalry) by technology.[39] One of my favourite novels of the First World War is C.S. Forester's *The General*. On becoming divisional commander Forester's Major-General Curzon inspects the cookhouses of his newly raised battalions, while his predecessor was more interested in ensuring each man had a second pair of laces for his boots. Needless to say, the cooking improved.[40] Haig's preoccupation was with the preparation and planning for each attack and in the training and evolution of tactical skills within his divisions to carry this out. Given Haig's reputation and the fear with which he was regarded at army and corps level, then if the reorganisation of battalions to make better use of platoons as tactical units was what Haig wanted then it made sense to make sure he got it, even if the particular corps or divisional commander was not particularly interested. It is natural that his concerns became those of his subordinates.

In this way, by GHQ directive, Haig's visits and that particular osmosis by which things get around in armies, the level of tactical skills within British battalions improved. It is very clear that the importance of the new organisations and tactical training was given impetus by Haig's army commanders, particularly Plumer's Second Army. It was not something that had to wait for the appointment of an Inspector General of Training in July 1918; as Bidwell and Graham suggest, that appointment simply confirmed the importance of current practice and gave it more weight.[41]

It is obvious that from early 1917 thinking divisional commanders saw the issue of SS 143 'Instructions for the Training of Platoons in Offensive Action' as confirmation of many of the ideas they had already discussed and in some cases experimented with. The homogeneity of the Canadian Corps allowed it to become corps doctrine early in 1917, and as we see it was adopted in Russell's and Monash's divisions in II ANZAC in March 1917. This was at their initiative rather than at the insistence of Godley, the corps commander, who did not display the same tactical understanding and drive that Byng did with his Canadians. Godley was always a conduit rather than a director and innovator. In II ANZAC the initiatives came from Army above and from divisions below, and their import seems not always to have been fully understood at corps level.

The attack on the Wytschaete-Messines Ridge by General Plumer's Second Army was the first step in securing the southern flank for Haig's Flanders offensive. It had been in preparation for some time, and included tunnelling 21 mine shafts under the German front line, containing in total over a million pounds of TNT. Plumer with his outstanding Chief of Staff, Major-General Charles 'Tim' Harington, had evolved a plan to take the ridge with three army corps, Godley's II ANZAC tasked to secure the southern flank with three divisions, 25th British Division on the left, New Zealand Division in the centre and 3rd Australian Division on the right. In late May at comparatively short notice Major-General Holmes' 4th Australian Division was transferred from I ANZAC to Godley's corps and tasked with securing the depth objectives on the plain beyond the ridge.

Plumer's headquarters was known for its careful planning and attention to detail. Much of what both Russell and Monash did, and which Pedersen's study implies was unique to Monash — the use of the conference system, the issue of operational instructions in simple colloquial English, and even the name of the operation, 'MAGNUM OPUS' — were not Monash's initiatives but standard practice throughout the Second Army. These techniques became the pattern in both divisions and, as Bean noted in the Australian official history: 'The working out of 2nd Army's Great Plan was as smooth as that of previous British offensives had been confused.'[42]

The Army plan for Messines involved a preparatory artillery bombardment of unprecedented length — 17 days, the last four of which concentrated on destroying the wire obstacles protecting the German defences. Counter-battery fire was given equal attention. Each of the divisional commanders knew how much time they had

General Sir Herbert Plumer, GOC Second Army (left) with Field Marshal Sir
Douglas Haig, Commander-in-Chief, British Armies in France (right), and Haig's
Chief of Staff in 1918, Lieutenant-General the Honourable H.A. Lawrence standing
between them. Plumer looks the very image of a Colonel Blimp but he and his
Major-General General Staff Charles 'Tim' Harington were a superb team whose
meticulous planning was matched by an insistence that the formation under their
command be fully trained, and practised for each attack. *(Royal Military Academy
Sandhurst Collection)*

available once the ridge had been taken before German guns were likely to respond, and factored this into their planning. The weight and accuracy of the artillery plan was made possible by the employment of the latest technical innovations, including the use of the instantaneous 106 fuse that had proved so effective in cutting wire obstacles at Vimy. Overhead the Royal Flying Corps had gained air superiority, allowing aerial observation for the artillery fire plan and for counter-battery fire.

Both Russell and Monash had been forewarned of the Messines offensive in November 1916. However, it was not until late March that II ANZAC's involvement was confirmed. In the preparations for the Messines battle on 7 June 1917 Russell's division had the critical task of capturing the dominating ground occupied by the village of Messines. Russell's success or failure would determine the outcome of Godley's corps plan. In addition, as Pedersen notes, the fate of Monash's attack 'depended entirely on the New Zealander's capture of Messines and its foreslopes, for the Uhlan and Ulcer trench systems located there enfiladed the length of the 3rd Division's attack'.[43]

Russell discussed his division's task with Godley on 25 March 1917, and in 'the afternoon spent some time on Hill 63 examining Messines Ridge'.[44] After a week of study and reconnaissance with his GSO1, Russell recorded in his diary on 2 April 1917: … continued to think over the problem of the attack, which is beginning to take shape in my mind — It must be done with the smallest number of men possible so leaving a reserve for future developments.[45]

Russell devoted his attention to a detailed study of the ground to determine what he needed to do to overcome formidable German defences. His appreciation shows how a divisional commander within the framework of an army plan can still be innovative:

> The Messines Ridge — on that part of it that the New Zealand Division had to attack — is a fairly steep ridge on which the German was very comfortably entrenched with excellent observation of everything that was going on in our lines below him. He was in fact on the rim of the saucer, while we were at the bottom.[46]

Within the limits of his divisional boundaries, Russell determined how best to use the ground to achieve his aim at minimal cost. He placed his first objective beyond the German front line trenches as, 'I wish to cross NO MAN'S LAND as soon as possible, and therefore I do not wish any delay at the German 1st line trench.'

While the Somme had confirmed the importance of the creeping barrage, Russell assessed his artillery needs according to the ground:

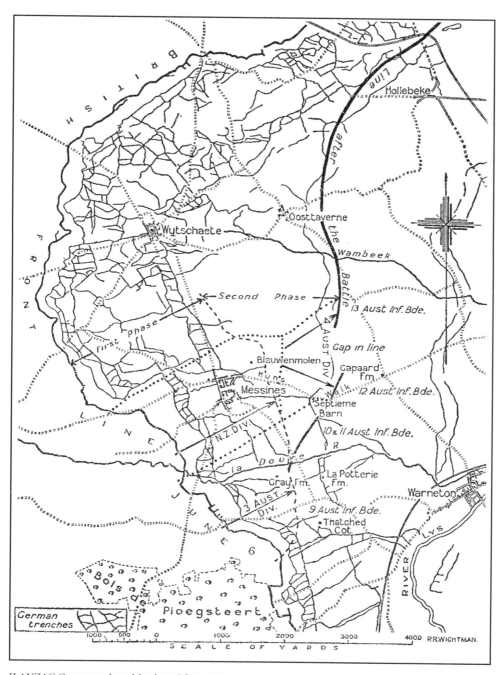

II ANZAC Corps attack on Messines, 7 June 1917.

The configuration of the ground over which I have to attack is such that the enemy can bring at one and the same time two tiers of fire to bear on my men as they advance. I therefore wish to place standing barrages both on the German front and Support Lines from the moment my advance begins … In addition to the Artillery barrage I am arranging for a Machine Gun barrage to open up on the German Support Line at zero.[47]

Following this Russell issued an outline of the divisional plan to his brigadiers. 'I propose to attack with two Brigades disposed side by side, keeping one brigade in my own hand as Divisional Reserve.' Russell talked through each brigade's task in relation to the ground, allotting objectives and analysing troops to task in terms of battalions and companies. He explained in his outline why he chose each option. His attack was a series of leapfrogs forward by battalions on a one-battalion frontage within each brigade. Fresh troops were to capture each objective and consolidate.

Russell did away with a creeping barrage to cover the advance across no-man's land, opting instead for two standing barrages. Once the German lines had been reached a creeping barrage went forward in 20 lifts to a depth of just under 2000 yards. But even here it was modified. A standing barrage fell in an arc round Messines during the time it was calculated it would take the two battalions tasked with taking the town to move through and consolidate beyond the town with two companies, while fighting through and mopping up centres of resistance within the town itself with the remaining two companies.[48]

Russell's approach was characterised by meticulous planning, both on his part and on that of his staff. His outline plan was thought out and explained two levels down to his brigadiers, who were experienced men with staffs who had fought through the Somme. Russell delegated responsibilities within the divisional plan, and his brigadiers in turn refined the plan to meet Russell's design for battle. Rehearsal after rehearsal was conducted. Each was followed by detailed discussion and, if necessary, amendments to the plan. In this way Russell's plan became one in which each brigade and battalion could also claim ownership.

April and May were days of preparation — of engineering works, trenches and accommodation. Soldiers trained for the job they had to do, and each battalion knew its tasks intimately. The procedure in 4 Battalion NZ Rifle Brigade, which had the task of capturing Messines village, reflects the detail and degree of familiarity with the plan that was the norm in most New Zealand battalions. Detailed battalion instructions were issued on 12 May 1917, allotting objectives to companies.

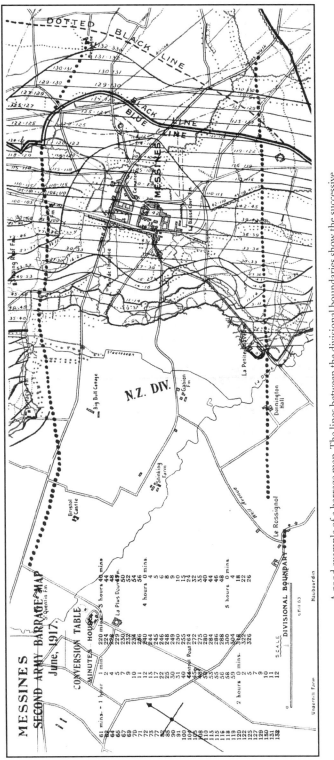

A good example of a barrage map. The lines between the divisional boundaries show the successive 'lifts' of the barrage as it moves forward in front of the advancing infantry. The 'Blue Line', 'Black Line', and so on indicate the various objectives.

> From this date onward conferences were held almost daily. The Commanding Officer thoroughly thrashed out the various problems and difficulties that might occur, with Os.C. Companies, and, in addition to tactical questions all administrative matters were gone into ... and settled well ahead.
>
> All Platoon Commanders and Sergeants were called to confer with the C.O. and each Platoon's job thoroughly talked over and all details fixed ... every individual taking part in the attack was thoroughly conversant not only with his own task, but with those of others working on either flank.[49]

Nothing was left to chance. In 4 Battalion the two companies detailed to mop up the battalion objective in Messines allotted sectors down to each platoon and each section. Landmarks were detailed and special identification worn. Two hours were allotted for clearing the village as it 'was anticipated that it would take the enemy about this length of time before he knew the Village was in our hands and start methodically shelling it'. Before the two hours were up the companies were to move forward into the trench systems beyond Messines, leaving one platoon in each case sheltering in cellars. 'During pauses in the shelling these Platoons patrolled their areas to deal with any "pockets" that might have been missed.'[50]

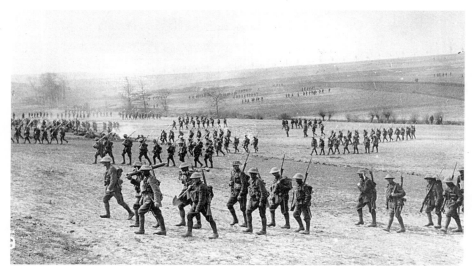

The New Zealand Division training for the attack on Messines by practising on an identical piece of ground. Russell's achievement was a superbly trained division that he ensured kept abreast of developments in tactical doctrine. That was matched by his own ability as a tactical thinker and planner. *(National Army Museum, Waiouru Collection)*

Battalions rehearsed their part in the plan and parties of officers and NCOs studied the large-scale model of the Messines area, going forward in groups to study their approach from observation posts overlooking the ground. The two-hour window of opportunity when enemy shelling was anticipated to be less effective was based on a counter-battery programme that would neutralise the German batteries or force them to move locations. This too was carefully assessed as part of the artillery plan involving 114×18-pounders and 36×4.5-inch howitzers, a total of 25 field batteries covering the divisional frontage of 1500 yards, not counting the heavy and medium guns that were also attached.

On Thursday 24 May Field Marshal Sir Douglas Haig was on the final day of three days of visits to the corps in Plumer's Second Army, where he discussed in detail corps and divisional planning for the coming battle. In each corps he followed the same pattern. Haig, with his artillery adviser Major-General J.F.N. Birch, would go through the corps plans with the corps commander and his principal staff, usually the BGGS (Brigadier-General General Staff: the principal operations officer) and the CRA (Commander Royal Artillery: the artillery adviser). After that he would visit each of the divisional headquarters within the corps, and repeat the process with the divisional commander and GSO1, the principal operations officer. After visiting Russell and his staff, Haig noted in his diary:

> He seems a most capable soldier with a considerable strength of character. His problem is a most difficult one, but he and his officers are all most confident of success … I was well pleased with their arrangements but suggested Messines Village should be taken in three 'jumps' so as to give Artillery a greater chance of producing an effect. His plan results in an awkward salient prematurely.[51]

The awkward salient is evident in Russell's artillery plan, and reflects his determination to outflank the town and commit only those troops needed to clear it while his brigades on either flank moved forward to their final objectives. Haig's concern was the New Zealand left flank with 25th Division. This had been allowed for in Russell's planning by smoking off that flank and by the impact of the mine positioned beneath Ontario Farm. Russell's left assault brigade was also to refuse that flank as the New Zealanders advanced. His intention was to get two battalions through Messines as quickly as possible and establish a firm base on the far side while the mopping up companies from each battalion cleared through the rubble that had once been the village.

A divisional commander faced with a 'suggestion' from the Commander-in-Chief would normally take the suggestion as an order to be followed. Not so Russell. He argued his case and continued with his original plan, and this registered with the Commander-in-Chief. Russell's willingness to stand by his plan may be the reason for Haig's comment about the New Zealander 'being a most capable soldier with a considerable strength of character'. Russell's own diary gives little indication of any debate, noting that 'Douglas Haig came to see Divl.Hq. He looked over plans — discussed one or two details, spoke pleasantly of N.Z.ers' work and departed.'[52]

Haig was equally impressed with his visit to the 3rd Australian Division. '[Monash] is in my opinion a clear-headed, determined commander. Every detail had been thought of. His brigadiers were equally thorough. I was most struck by their whole arrangements.'[53]

The meticulous nature of Monash's planning is well documented in Pedersen's study. Like Russell he thought through in detail how to make best use of the ground. His divisional objective was confined within an awkward triangle of ground that fell away from the principal ridge dominated by Messines. The complexity of the German defensive system saw Monash think through his attack in detail down to platoon level. His preparation and planning mirrored that of his New Zealand counterpart; nothing was left to chance and each aspect was thrashed out with his subordinates on the basis that 'we are going to talk these matters out to a finish and will not separate until we have a perfect mutual understanding among all concerned'.[54]

Monash ensured that he and his brigadiers knew the New Zealand plan in intimate detail and he, like Russell on his flank, adopted the new platoon structures and embarked on progressive training and rehearsals to ensure his division was ready for its first major attack. Where he differed from Russell was not in the detail of his planning but rather in the lesser degree of latitude he allowed his brigadiers.

Russell thought things through, stated the problem, and then with his subordinates arrived at a solution, which evolved in rehearsal and conference so that it became as much their plan as his. Monash detailed his requirements from the outset, often down to platoon level, to the point where he 'usurped the role of his brigadiers' and 'virtually stated how they must employ their battalions instead of allowing them to prepare brigade plans within the framework of a divisional scheme which did not descend beyond brigade level'.[55]

Both commanders were given the luxury of time and a degree of latitude by Godley to develop their own plans within the constraints of the corps directives for the opening phase of the battle. Haig was impressed by both men and told Plumer, '… of all the attacks which had been made under my orders, I considered the present one was the most carefully "mounted" and that all Commanders and troops were better prepared for their work than on any previous occasion'.[56]

Major-General Holmes' 4th Australian Division, which was attached to II ANZAC in May, was not as fortunate. The 4th Australian Division was tasked to seize the Oostaverne Line, which was the corps' depth objective, on the plain beyond the ridge. The division had suffered heavily at Bullecourt, losing 3289 casualties on 11–12 April. Although brought out to rest and regroup in May, it did not have the same opportunity to plan, prepare, rehearse and train for its role as the existing divisions in II ANZAC. The men resented being committed again so soon after Bullecourt and morale was low.[57] It also had a most complex task to carry out, as it was along the entire corps' front and necessitated liaison with all three divisions. It was here that it was served badly by Godley's staff. There were frequent changes of plan and inadequate corps staff liaison; Holmes' headquarters was collocated with Russell as if this would compensate, but it did not.

At 3.10 a.m. on 7 June, 19 of the 21 mines were exploded with a thunderous roar along the length of the ridge and the troops advanced as the artillery fire plan provided covering fire and suppressed the German batteries. Artillery was the key to success, as Brigadier-General W.G. Braithwaite, commanding the 2nd New Zealand Infantry Brigade, the right New Zealand assault brigade, recorded in his after-action report: 'In fact the battle may be described as an Artillery duel, with a few infantry added to clear up strong points and mop up the trenches.'[58]

> The whole of the Brigade was clear of our forward assembly trench at Zero plus 7, i.e. before the enemy's counter-barrage came down. The rapidity and ease with which the Brigade moved out of their assembly trenches and crossed NO MAN'S LAND I attribute to the fact that we had already rehearsed this advance six times over a carefully prepared position … during the period of training … where our assembly trenches and those of the enemy on the MESSINES ridge had been cut as near as possible to scale; … and so true was the representation, that when the men came to carry out the real attack, they found little difficulty in finding their way to their objectives in the German lines.[59]

There were pockets of resistance in the town that were quickly overcome by the mopping up platoons. Russell wrote that the battle 'was won by the weight of metal that was thrown onto the enemy positions, and the mettle of the men who advanced to attack them. Everything went like clockwork. The actual positions were carried at very slight expense. Our losses began to mount up after we had reached our different objectives.'[60]

Monash's division had suffered more heavily from German gas shelling on its move into the forward assembly area. Despite this his attack was successful, and as Pedersen notes, 'Messines would be the first attack by Australian troops using the revised platoon doctrine issued by GHQ.'[61] There was hard fighting for the depth objectives and some inevitable confusion on the location of forward troops.

This increased in the afternoon when after some delays the 4th Australian Division passed through. It was now that the picture became totally confused. Coordination with the 4th Australian Division failed all along the front. Russell wrote in his after-action report: 'Directly a portion of the 4th Australian Division went through us we never knew what was going on — and did not know the position in front up to the moment we came out of the line.'[62] Major-General Bainbridge of the 25th British Division, which was on the New Zealand left, was also highly critical of the performance of the 4th Australian Division and complained to Haig, when he visited after the attack, that 'detachments of the 4th Australian Division have been wandering about in his vicinity as if they had "no leaders"'. Haig noted in mitigation that the '4th Australian Division was at Bullecourt and lost many officers'.[63]

In Russell's view a far more critical failing in both Plumer's and Godley's planning was the concentration of infantry divisions that had carried out the attack on the narrow ridge that was now subject to German artillery fire. Russell wanted to withdraw one of his two assault brigades, but was overruled by corps. He wrote after the attack:

> … it appears to me that often we fail to realise the danger of leaving
> concentrated a large number of men on a position once it has been won.
> We rely, with reason, on our artillery barrages and the use of machine guns
> to break up enemy counter attacks, rather than on the number of men with
> which we man our trenches. It is seldom, if ever, that an attack is beaten off
> by actual hand to hand fighting in the trenches. Certainly the resistance we
> meet ourselves on the part of the German, once we have got to close quarters,
> is a matter of little concern. Consequently I regret very much that we were
> not allowed to thin out and reduce the number of men on the ridge after we
> had won it. Had we been allowed — as I proposed — to reduce the garrison,
> our losses would have been considerably smaller with the same result.[64]

Artillery shell fire bursting on the ruins of Messines, 7 June 1917. *(Henry Armitage Sanders, New Zealand Official Photographer, G-12776-1/2, Alexander Turnbull Library, Wellington, NZ)*

Russell was the major influence in the formulation of the divisional plan and the corps artillery supporting fire plan for his division, but there were limits to a divisional commander's power. As it was, Godley's detached method of command gave both Monash and Russell greater flexibility and tactical freedom than was granted to most divisional commanders on the Western Front. Russell, like Monash, was critical of aspects of the corps and army plan that he, as divisional commander, had no power to change:

> I do sometimes think that a non-professional mind takes a more detached view of the operations than those who have given their whole lives to the study of these problems. I suppose one ought to be content with success, but the price that one pays, though cheerfully accepted when necessary, is always a matter of careful thought, and I think we want to study economy. To have to sit down for hour after hour under heavy shelling is a severe tax on the stoutest and must mean an expenditure of nerve power. The longer men are exposed to it, the longer it takes them to recover.[65]

Within these limitations Russell did everything he could to minimise casualties. He was prepared to argue his case through at all levels, but once tasked had to get on with the job he was given. Haig noted after visiting Russell on the afternoon of the attack that he 'was holding Messines with many machine guns in great depth, all our troops being in positions around the outside of the village to avoid shellfire'.[66] Once the 4th Australian Division had consolidated their depth objective Russell also contrived to thin out his line so that only one of his brigades was occupying the actual ridge line around Messines; nevertheless, casualties from German artillery fire were needlessly heavy.

Messines was an outstanding tactical success from which both Russell and Monash emerged as divisional commanders of considerable talent. Haig recorded in his diary on 7 June: 'The operations today were probably the most successful I have yet undertaken.'[67] Pedersen notes Monash's meticulous planning and handling of his division at Messines, but faults him for dictating his brigadiers' plans at 'levels that properly belonged to his subordinates'. But, as he points out, that was Monash's way and would remain so. However, he is critical of Monash's failure to go forward to see his brigadiers when the situation was obscure in the early afternoon of 7 June, during the German counter-attack. While this was a mistake, Monash rightly took pride in his achievement in this, his first divisional battle on the Western Front.

This question of going forward is the principal difference between these two talented men; Russell's policy was to position himself where he could best appreciate the situation. He was forward in Messines on 8 June, and was lucky to escape death when a shellburst over his party killed Brigadier-General C.H.J. Brown Commanding 1 NZ Brigade and wounded Russell's ADC.[68] On 10 June Russell was reconnoitring the Warneton attack with his GSO1 when he 'nearly got bagged by a sniper'.[69] The bullet parted his hairline, and the helmet with the entry and exit holes hangs in the Russell homestead today. It was a further near-escape and there was concern among his staff that he took too many risks, but for Russell this was simply part of the job.

While Pedersen's study *Monash as Military Commander* is excellent in its detail, its one failing is that it does not place Monash in context. Messines was Monash's success, but it was Russell's even more. The New Zealander's planning, administrative preparations and tactical concept secured the corps' vital ground at little cost. At Messines Russell showed that he had learnt the lessons of the Somme, using a combination of all arms tactics, trained infantry, artillery, machine guns and tanks in support, backed by engineer effort and logistic preparations. The laying of light tramways forward onto the objective, the hot meals forward after the assault, the brigade carrying parties that supplied both the New Zealanders and the 4th Australian Division after it had passed through, the Stokes mortar teams accompanying the infantry that Monash would later 'experiment' with at Passchendaele — these were all part of the New Zealand operation at Messines. Russell also imposed his design of battle on his commanders. The administrative requirements and economy of effort in allocating troops to task gave clear parameters

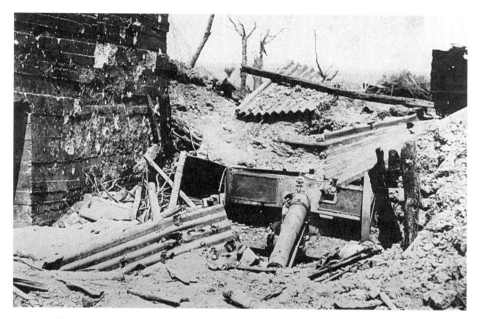

German blockhouses at Messines. The careful planning and rehearsals that coordinated the night infantry attack paid dividends by ensuring that the German machine-gun crews in these blockhouses, which now form part of the New Zealand Memorial Park, were overrun before the crews could bring out their guns and mount their weapons. *(National Army Museum, Waiouru Collection)*

to his brigadiers. Yet in the shared reconnaissance and the critiques after rehearsals the plan also became their plan. His brigadiers knew what Russell wanted, and by practice and refinement gave it to him.

The post-Messines reports of the New Zealand Division show that Russell, his commanders and his staff ruthlessly analysed the battle to eliminate mistakes and improve procedures in preparation for the next time they were committed to a major offensive. Monash followed a similar course with equal detail. The commonality of battle experience was matched by a sharing of ideas and recommendations. Both divisions conducted tactical training to counter the shellhole defence lines anchored by pillboxes now adopted by the Germans. Training techniques included the use of Tactical Exercises Without Troops (TEWT) for platoon commanders to practise in the range of situations they might have to face, live firing platoon and company attacks, developing to battalion- and brigade-level rehearsals. This mirrors the nature of the training being conducted in the Canadian Corps over the same period. It represented a rich amalgam of divisional experience, and a willingness to learn from the experience of others and profit from their successes and failures.

The Commander-in-Chief was more than a disinterested spectator in this process. A typical example is 15 July 1917, when Haig 'motored to the high ground north-east of Lumbres and saw a demonstration by a platoon in an exercise in "fire and movement," with ball cartridge. Its main object was to show all ranks the importance of good covering fire in order to help forward an advance.'[70] He noted that the young officer commanding the platoon 'had only a year's service'.[71] It is a theme that is dealt with in detail in Griffith's study *Battle Tactics of the Western Front*, but one must recognise Haig as one of the driving forces behind its implementation. His statement in July 1918 that 'This is really a platoon commanders' war' was not a bolt out of the blue, but confirmation from one who had overseen that reality.[72] It raises questions about the pessimistic assessment of the evolution of British tactical practice evident in Bidwell and Graham's *Fire-Power*, and is also a counter to the 'Germans did it first and best' school that is the principal theme of Gudmundsson, Samuels and others.[73]

After Messines Russell had to rebuild the strength and fighting effectiveness of his division. Every attention was given to the care and welfare of his men, while he assessed and weeded out unit commanding officers, his 'empties' as he termed them. These were men who had given everything to their command, but who now needed to be rested in training posts in England. Those who did not recover combat fitness were posted back to New Zealand. Russell was fortunate in having a guaranteed supply of trained reinforcements. This had led to a fourth infantry brigade being formed before Messines, making the New Zealand Division the largest on the Western Front. Russell objected to its formation because of the problems it caused in rotating his division in the line with other divisions, and the strain it placed in finding suitable staff officers and commanding officers. However, while it was also objected to by Allen, the Minister of Defence, it was a political compromise in which New Zealand agreed to raise an additional infantry brigade rather than a second New Zealand Division and, as discussed in chapter three, it was a tribute to the efficiency of the New Zealand reinforcement system.

Although both divisions were part of the essential preliminaries of the Passchendaele offensive, they were not directly involved again until the commitment of II ANZAC in early October. On 20 August 1917 Russell wrote in his diary that he had been told that his New Zealand Division was 'to go North but previously go out to rest and train'.[74] His division was withdrawn from the line and went into reserve in September for a period of intensive training for three of his four infantry brigades — 1st, 2nd and 4th New Zealand Infantry Brigades — while the 3rd New Zealand (Rifle) Brigade was detached from the division to work under the Second Army burying cable south of Ypres. The divisional training followed the pattern Russell had established in his build-up to Messines.

Full advantage was taken of the good facilities for training in the Reserve Areas, platoon, company, battalion, and Brigade training being carried out, and attacks practised from the trenches, as well as Wood and Village fighting and open warfare. Musketry training received attention and full use was made of the ranges available.[75]

This training was devised to meet the 'new Bosche [sic] tactics of shell holes and disposition in depth'.[76] Emphasis was also placed on changes within the infantry platoon organisation, and to ensure that the sections within the platoons functioned effectively; platoon training schools were set up in each brigade.[77] In the first week Russell carried out daily battalion inspections and viewed his battalions in training at company and battalion level attended by the brigade commanders. Training then progressed to formation level, with brigade inspections and brigade attack rehearsals.[78]

Haig inspected the New Zealanders on 14 September and wrote in his diary:

The 1st, 2nd, and 4th Brigades were on parade. The men were well turned out and handled their arms smartly. They are a sturdy, thick set type of man. After my inspection the troops marched past by platoons. A very fine show

Major-General Sir Andrew Russell talking to the subalterns of 2nd New Zealand Infantry Brigade with the Brigade commander, Brigadier-General R. Young, with hands behind his back, standing to his rear. (*National Army Museum, Waiouru Collection*)

indeed. Every man seemed to be trying to look his best and the whole went past in fine style. Mr Winston Churchill accompanied me and seemed much impressed.[79]

Training and planning continued throughout September, with divisional conferences on 6 and 19 September to discuss points arising from the II ANZAC conference the previous day. Russell noted that 20 September and the morning of 21 September were spent 'studying map of our projected attack'.[80] Changes in planning were then discussed with his corps commander the following day. This paralleled his daily inspections, and on 24 September Russell viewed an attack practice by Hart's 4th New Zealand Infantry Brigade, which was 'fairly well carried out, rather amateurish'. One can be sure that these shortcomings were then talked through in detail with both Hart and his commanding officers. Russell met with Plumer and Harington, his Chief of Staff, on 25 September, and also Major-General Smyth VC, GOC 2 Australian Division, 'who was on Walkers Ridge with me. He told us a lot about the attack on the 19/20 [September] and details which are useful.'[81] The next day was spent over maps, and reconnoitring the ground for the attack before motoring to corps for the latest orders.[82]

On 28 September Russell met Lieutenant-General Maxse, 'who commands the adjoining Corps to discuss matters, or rather to be talked to; he is full of his own ideas, which are good'.[83] Maxse made his name as the outstanding commander of the 18th British Division and was at the forefront of the evolution of tactical doctrine in 1916.

Review of the New Zealand Division on 14 September 1917, during the Division's training for the Ypres offensive. Field Marshal Sir Douglas Haig, saluting, is accompanied by Major-General Sir Andrew Russell, with Winston Churchill in civilian clothes in rear. *(G-129-18-1/2, Henry Armitage Sanders, New Zealand Official Photographer, Alexander Turnbull Library, Wellington, NZ)*

His re-emphasis on platoon fire and movement was a catalyst for change in the British armies. He would become the Inspector General of Training at GHQ in July 1918, but as we have seen, by then what he initiated was already standard tactical doctrine.[84] For Russell the last two days of September were taken up with corps and liaison visits to flanking divisions, discussions with his brigade commanders, and finally on 30 September a visit to Plumer 'to explain plans'.[85]

Pedersen's account of Monash's training of the 3rd Australian Division reflects in every detail the same meticulous care that was taken by the New Zealanders.[86] Monash impressed Haig, who inspected the 3rd Australian Division on 22 September:

> A very fine body of men. The parade was a great success. Some of the units had 7 miles to march to the parade ground, but everyone was delighted to do it … Every detail connected with the parade had been carefully thought out before hand, hence the parade was so successful. I think Monash has a good head and commands his division well.[87]

Pedersen outlines the confusion that accompanied the formulation of the corps plan leading up to the attack on 4 October at Passchendaele. There was a great deal of pressure on Godley and he was intent on achieving the same success that II ANZAC had won at Messines. Haig had made his intentions clear in a visit to Godley on 1 October.

> I spoke to him of the importance of making his arrangements so as to be able to exploit any success gained without delay. The guns should be placed behind Gravenstafel Hill (as soon as it is captured) for dealing with Passchendaele — and the reserve brigades of attacking divisions should be used at once to exploit a success, if the enemy counter-attacks and fails. Further reserves will be brought up by train. This is now possible, as we have three lines (broad gauge) beyond Ypres, so there must be no hesitation in using reserves on the spot.[88]

By now both Russell and Monash commanded well-drilled and experienced teams. On 2 October Russell saw his brigadiers and COs, later noting: 'I fancy we have got most of the work done and everyone seems confident — visited some of the battalion camps in the afternoon.'[89]

The attack on 4 October was successful. It was notable for the fact that it was the first time four Anzac divisions had attacked side by side. Twelve divisions in the six

Infantry of the New Zealand Division entraining for Ypres in late September 1917 after a month of intensive training. (*National Army Museum, Waiouru Collection*)

attacking corps attacked on a 13-kilometre front. The 1st and 2nd Australian Divisions of I ANZAC were in the right-centre, with the 3rd Australian and New Zealand Division of II ANZAC to their north. Russell wrote to Allen on the day of the attack:

> We've been having one of our periodical battles today: and so far have done well. Casualties not so heavy as at Messines, nor nearly so heavy as at the Somme which was the biggest battle and the heaviest fighting that we shall ever see I hope. The more I see of it [battle] the less I like it. These long casualty lists, with all they mean do not lose their effect thro' familiarity. It seems so futile, tho' one knows it isn't. Unfortunately it is raining and the sun hasn't the power to dry the ground so late in the year. We've got a very muddy time in front of us, and that means a lot. The mud is a worse enemy than the German who did not, today, put up much of a show of resistance.[90]

Monash and Russell used identical methods in this attack. Here again Russell's divisional objectives included the vital ground of Abraham's Heights and Monash's advance, as at Messines, was dependent on New Zealand success. Pedersen is incorrect in saying that 'Monash was the only one of the four ANZAC divisional commanders who prescribed intermediate objectives.'[91] Russell, like Monash, 'divided the attack into a series of progressively shorter advances, for each of which fresh infantry would be available'.[92] This battle showed both commanders and their staffs at their peak.

However, the success on 4 October 1917 was a prelude to disaster. The rain and mud prompted Gough to recommend closing down the Third Battle of Ypres.[93] In Plumer's Second Army Birdwood's I ANZAC, having successfully mounted three attacks, was exhausted. Russell's concern was the weather and its impact on the single road forward, which supplied his division. The 49th British Division relieved the New Zealanders on 6 October, and with the 66th British Division, which replaced the 3rd Australian Division, was to continue the attack under Godley's direction. Russell took his successor, Major-General Perceval, forward on foot to Spree Farm — 'wanted him to see roads'.[94] Russell's fears were realised when rain on 5–6 October made it impossible to get guns forward to the new battery positions. 'Guns out of action were in every case either completely bogged or else blocked on the road.'[95] Mud was the enemy rather than German artillery, which made little impression with few casualties.[96] At this critical time there was a lack of drive by Headquarters II ANZAC and the necessary coordination of engineer and logistic effort to see that the attack on 9 October had the necessary foundation for success was never carried out. Johnston, Russell's CRA, made this criticism of the corps: 'The advent of wet weather must have been anticipated, and even if the weather had remained dry the road was not in a state to stand the enormous amount of traffic which would follow the first advance.'[97]

New Zealand Field Artillery 18-pounders in action near Kansas Farm on 4 October 1917 in the wasteland that was the torn-up boggy ground below the Passchendaele ridge, which the rains turned into a quagmire. In the distance horse teams drag the guns forward in preparation for the next attack on 9 October. (*National Army Museum, Waiouru Collection*)

235

Most critical of all was Godley's failure to see that his artillery was able to carry out the preparatory fire to destroy the wire and had sufficient guns and ammunition forward to provide for the creeping barrage and counter-battery fire. Johnston, the CRA New Zealand Division, was highly critical of the actions of II ANZAC Corps, as his report shows:

> Men and horses worked incessantly till they were tired out when the battle of the 12th took place. Heavy and Field guns were constantly bogged, and it must be remembered that it is not only necessary to get guns forward, it is necessary to put them on stable platforms, and to make side roads by which ammunition may be brought up. Many officers seem to think that it is sufficient to get the guns forward; this is a mistake: it is equally important to have them mounted on stable platforms, ammunition clean, and the equipment in good order. The fine shooting necessitated by the modern barrage necessitates the most thorough preparation.[98]

None of this was achieved. It was worse for the British infantry of the 49th and 66th Divisions wading forward in the morass. Russell recorded in his diary that the II ANZAC attack on 9 October was a failure: '... troops held up early and arrived at Assembly point exhausted'.[99] This was not the message that Haig got. The day before he had visited General Plumer who told him that Godley 'had specially asked that there should be no postponement'.[100] On the night before the attack Haig recorded that 'a gale blew all night ... A general attack was launched at 5.30 am today ... The results were very successful ... the 66th Division advanced without barrage and took all objectives. 49th gained all except small piece on the left.'[101]

It was only the next day that these achievements by Godley's corps were qualified: 'Reports from Second Army show that progress on 2nd Anzac Corps front yesterday was not so great as first stated! The 66th Division on the right advanced a mile; the 49th Division on the left about 500 yards on an average.'[102] In fact even these limited gains were exaggerated. Both divisions were stuck on their start lines with no gain in ground. The attacking brigades were broken and demoralised, and made little or no attempt to bring in the wounded who lay dying in the shell-holes. Godley, like his two British divisional commanders, had no idea of the situation forward. He was intent only on meeting Haig's expectations, and having failed him on 9 October was even more determined to succeed on 12 October.

When Haig met with Godley on 10 October he was told:

… the 3rd Australian Division and the New Zealand Division go into the line again tonight. Godley told me that they are determined to take Passchendaele in the next attack and will put the Australian flag on it! The advance will be then over 2000 yards. But the enemy is now much weaker in morale and lacks the desire to fight.[103]

It was wishful thinking on both their parts, but it was Godley's duty as corps commander to ensure the necessities for a successful attack were in place. He failed to do this, and it is clear that his mindset brushed all obstacles aside in his determination to please his Commander-in-Chief. Godley's trump card was that his two divisional commanders, Russell and Monash, had never failed him, and he saw no reason to believe it would be any different this time despite the weather and its impact on artillery preparations.[104]

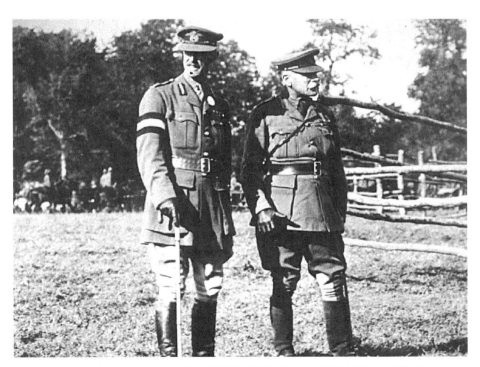

Lieutenant-General Sir Alexander Godley, GOC II ANZAC Corps, with Field-Marshal Sir Douglas Haig at the New Zealand Divisional horse show in 1918. Godley had little tactical grasp, relying on the skills of his two brilliant divisional commanders, Russell and Monash. He was intent on meeting Haig's requirements regardless of whether they were achievable or not. It was Godley's ambition and refusal to say no that led to the disastrous attacks of 9 and 12 October 1917. *(National Army Museum, Waiouru Collection)*

Russell's and Monash's divisions moved back into the line on the night of 10/11 October and both divisions assumed command of their sectors at 10 a.m. on 11 October, less than 24 hours before the attack.[105] Brigadier-General Napier Johnston, Russell's CRA, was particularly worried about the artillery situation and, after a morning reconnaissance, saw Russell in the early afternoon. 'The guns are all forward but he evidently feels uneasy about the attack — says preparation inadequate. Night dark and showers of rain.'[106]

Johnston took his concerns to Godley's corps headquarters and was assured that guns and ammunition would get forward. This was not done, and on the evening of 11 October Russell's patrols brought in the news that the wire in front of the pillboxes on Bellevue Spur was not cut. As Russell would later note to his Defence Minister, had this news been established 24 hours earlier a delay in the attack could have been requested, but in a coordinated army attack involving a number of corps it was now too late to request a delay. There was a faint possibility that the artillery fire plan would cut the wire. However, given Johnston's pessimistic assessment, Russell warned his brigadiers of the situation and told them they had to be prepared to fight their way forward with the prospect of minimal artillery support.

Russell has been criticised for not insisting on a delay. However, this ignores the wider context of the Second Army plan, Godley's determination and, given the particular wording used by Godley in telling Haig they were determined to raise an Australian

New Zealand soldiers move in towards the front line on the Ypres Salient. This road would soon give way to slippery duckboards raised on stilts over a muddy morass deep enough to drown a man. (*National Army Museum, Waiouru Collection*)

flag over Passchendaele, perhaps Monash's own belief that the attack should continue. All of this was driven by a ruthlessly tight timetable that ignored the conditions facing the attacking divisions.[107] Messines had highlighted weaknesses in II ANZAC staff procedures. Passchendaele ruthlessly exposed these deficiencies. Coordination of the corps' engineer, artillery and medical plans was lacking. On taking over the sector the day before the attack the New Zealand Division found its stretcher-bearers exhausted and its clearing stations rapidly filling because they had to collect the wounded who had been left to die by the outgoing 49th Division. Much had been promised but nothing had been done in the way of administrative preparations for the attack.

'The New Zealand Division, as usual, attacked on the left.'[108] The attack was launched 18 hours after Russell and Monash had taken over responsibility for the front line. As at Messines and at Gravenstafel on 4 October 1918 the New Zealand Division had the task of securing the vital ground that would dictate the success or failure of the corps plan. Russell attacked with two brigades up each on a battalion frontage with a series of intermediate objectives.

> Attacked this morning at daybreak — we, and indeed all other divisions, were held up from the start by M.G. Evidently the artillery preparation was insufficient, the barrage poor, and it goes to show the weakness of haste — our casualties are heavy — I am very sad — Weather conditions bad.[109]

The move up on the night of 11/12 October was hampered by drizzling rain and atrocious ground conditions. The attacking brigades were in position at 5.00 a.m. At Zero Hour, 5.25 a.m., there was a weak artillery barrage. The infantry assault was held up by enfilade fire from guns on Bellevue Spur, and the men were shot down on the continuous line of uncut wire on its forward slopes and died in the Ravebeek swamp. Monash's left flank was laid open to enfilade fire, and despite progress on his right flank the New Zealand failure prevented any further progress towards Passchendaele. A call to renew the attack at 3.00 p.m. by Godley, after he had consulted with Harington at Second Army, was cancelled on Russell's insistence.[110]

> The direct cause of failure was strong and continuous wire entanglements. When as in the operation of the 12th October, the attacking Division takes over the line only a few hours before ZERO, it is necessary that an Intelligence Staff should precede it 2 or 3 days … In the operations under review the formidable nature of the wire entanglements in BELLEVUE were

not known until the evening of the 11th by the brigade holding the line when a patrol report was received which fully disclosed it ... This information 24 hours earlier would have been invaluable.

Russell also condemned the lack of artillery support. Corps failed to provide 'the provision of means of moving forward the guns and stable platforms for them'.[111] Russell had no doubt that given sufficient artillery support his soldiers could have taken the ridge. He went forward with the relieving Canadian divisional commander on 15/16 October and noted: 'It is plain we attacked a strong position, stoutly defended with no adequate preparation, nor was the supporting barrage or rather the covering barrage such as to help us over the difficulty.'[112]

While the failure could have been blamed on II ANZAC Corps, Russell blamed himself. He emphasised this failure to his commanders and staff at the conferences following the battle: 'Divisional Conference at which I drew attention to our failure and its lessons — Notably the crime of the Division in assuming the wire to be cut which ought to have been verified.'[113]

In his diary Russell wrote that the principal fault 'applying more especially to Divl. Staff and Self, is that under no circumstances in war is one justified in assuming

A New Zealand runner making his way from a captured German bunker that as one can see from the stretcher and equipment piled outside is being used both as a headquarters and a medical aid post during the Ypres offensive. *(National Army Museum, Waiouru Collection)*

anything which can possibly be verified — and that where there are certain known conditions necessary to success it is a great risk, however justifiable, to attack before they are fulfilled.'[114]

Russell detailed this failure to his Minister of Defence:

> We as a Divisional Staff assumed that the wire had been cut. Assumption in war is radically wrong if by any means in your power you can eliminate the uncertain. This, of course, is pure theory, but we made a mistake ... We cannot always expect to succeed but I feel very sorry about it all when I think of the numbers of men who were lost. My chief fear is that the men may lose confidence in the arrangements made for them as they had been always taught that, provided the Staff arrangements are good, they are able to do anything that is asked of them ... In these days of parliamentary criticism, questions may be asked as to the operations I refer to. The somewhat bald and concise statement I have made above accurately represents the position.[115]

It is here that we see the other side to the infantry-artillery relationship. Trained infantry were needed to fight their way forward through the zones of pillboxes, but this was not possible without artillery — a balance was necessary. Russell was prepared to fight his infantry forward without the benefits of a creeping barrage if necessary, but he knew it was essential for the initial preparatory bombardment to cut the wire, for counter-battery fire to suppress German artillery, and for a defensive fire plan to be in place to break up German counterattacks. Russell and Monash recognised this fact; Godley did not. His Headquarters II ANZAC War Diaries make interesting reading. They are full of evasions, half-truths and contradictions in their efforts to explain away two failed attacks within three days. This despite the fact that it was evident before the first that major efforts were needed by corps to ensure essentials were in place for a successful attack, which could only be assured by effective artillery support predicated on a major engineering effort.

> Remark has been made on the thinness of the creeping barrage, both on October 9th and October 12th. This may be attributed first to the number of guns put out of action by hostile shelling, which could not be replaced in time, and secondly to the fact that the sodden nature of the ground made the gun platforms unstable and necessitated frequent relaying. The softness

of the ground also minimised the effect of H.E. [high explosive] a high proportion of which was necessarily used.[116]

The War Diary attempts to explain this away without attempting to explain why nothing was done to overcome these problems after 4 October when they first became evident, nor remark on why Godley kept insisting that there be no delay, despite these problems. Russell blamed himself for the failure of the New Zealand Division's attack, Godley never did; yet it was at corps that the critical coordination failed for the second time in succession.

It was the talents of his Anzac divisional commanders, Russell and Monash, that gave Godley's II ANZAC its reputation for success. His was a lazy headquarters with sloppy procedures that lacked the skill and drive to mount effective attacks in the mud of Passchendaele. The two attacks mounted by II ANZAC Corps on 9 and 12 October showed that Godley had little if any appreciation of what was required to mount a successful attack. Passchendaele showed Godley to be more intent on pleasing Haig than ensuring the basics were in place for his corps' plan to succeed.[117] He and Birdwood were of the same mould and this inevitably limited their success as corps commanders, but Birdwood benefited from a talented staff headed by his Australian Chief of Staff, Brudenell White, and learnt in the job. Godley's staff exhibited far less ability and awareness, and the nature of tactics itself remained Godley's permanent blind spot.

It can be said that both Russell and Monash demonstrated their abilities in adversity in this battle, but for Russell this was no compensation for a battle lost. Russell demonstrated a quality rare today and then: an ability to admit mistakes. While he was an ambitious man, he did not have the driving need for self-publicity so evident in Monash's writings. Passchendaele was the last battle where the New Zealand Division would advance on the left of the 3rd Australian Division.

On 1 January 1918 the Australian Corps came into existence and Monash left Godley's command. 'I have not much to be grateful to him for. I served him loyally and faithfully for nearly three years and he has done nothing for me that he could help doing. However towards the end he was very nice and amicable and gave me quite a splendid farewell banquet.'[118] Monash was one of only two Australians among the five divisional commanders in the Australian Corps and joined it with the reputation of being an outstanding divisional commander. II ANZAC Corps ceased to exist, and at midnight on 31 December 1917 Godley's Headquarters became XXII Corps, which included the 49th, 66th and the New Zealand Division holding a sector of the Ypres front.[119] Russell's New Zealanders would not fight any of the major battles of 1918 under Godley's

The October rain turned the streams into quagmires, making it impossible for mule trains carrying ammunition to get forward, with mules being trapped and drowned in the mud. *(National Army Museum, Waiouru Collection)*

command. Circumstance would see the New Zealanders attached to IV Corps in Byng's Third Army for the major fighting that year.

The New Zealand Division maintained a quantitative and qualitative superiority over any other division on the Western Front throughout 1918. Haig, impressed by Russell's performance, offered him command of a British corps in June 1918, the only dominion commander to receive that invitation. Russell's diffidence amounted to a refusal. He was suffering from a broken foot, having been thrown from his horse, and said, 'I was applying for leave to get repaired, and in any case must be allowed to choose my own B.G.G.S. so I do not know how it will be taken by D.H. [Haig].'[120] On Russell's return the offer had lapsed and Russell continued to fight his New Zealanders to the end.

Command of a British corps in 1918 would not have allowed Russell the degree of command freedom enjoyed by Currie and Monash as corps commanders of what were now national corps. Any comparison between Russell and Monash must be as divisional commanders. It can be seen that, in detailed appreciation, tactical understanding and implementation, both were highly skilled commanders. In the battles of 1917 Russell and the New Zealand Division were always given the harder tasks, a measure of the division's experience and ability. As a tactical thinker and operational commander Russell was Monash's equal, and this is also true of his administrative abilities. Where the two men differed in approach was in the willingness to go forward to see the ground and assess the situation. Monash would not go forward, and he compensated for this with detailed direction that usurped his subordinate commanders' responsibilities. This remained a feature of his approach to command both at division and later at corps level. He tried to eliminate chance through detail. This is impossible in war, and Monash's increasing detachment from the realities of the front-line experience would limit his effectiveness in the more fluid battles of 1918.

Russell, by contrast, never lost sight of the soldiers he commanded. While his planning was noted for its meticulous attention to detail, he was effective at delegating tasks to his subordinates within the framework he provided, confident that procedures and rehearsals would highlight any gaps that could then be assessed and fixed. Because of this Haig's advice to Allenby, which prefaced this chapter, held true throughout 1917 in II ANZAC. Russell's New Zealanders invariably got the hardest task because in my assessment they had the superior commander.

TEN

THE FIRST AIF: MORE THAN LARRIKINS BUT LESS THAN PERFECT?

The 'digger', as the Australian soldier had become known by the end of the war, was a citizen soldier. This fact determined many of his virtues and vices and, in turn, meant that the values formed in war would persist in peace. He did not respond easily to the discipline that was instilled in regular troops and extended to the conscript armies of the other combatants in the First World War; he showed a marked reluctance to salute and an officer had to earn his respect. Protected from the normal provisions of martial law and immune from the death penalty except for mutiny, desertion, or traitorous conduct he was more fractious that the British Tommy … He was involved in ugly scenes around the pubs. In this respect his behaviour in the company of his mates was rather like that of a football team on an end-of-season trip … On the other hand, the digger exhibited an exceptional degree of camaraderie. Among the members of the AIF there were few barriers — as a batman told a new chaplain who asked about the religion of the other chaplain attached to the brigade, 'there ain't no religion out here, sir, we're all brothers'.[1]

The year 1918 was one of achievement for the AIF. It played a prominent part in the victories in Sinai and Palestine against the Turks, and on the Western Front where the newly formed Australian Corps played a major role in holding the German offensive in front of Amiens in March 1918, and then, under the leadership of that 'painstaking engineer-turned-soldier' Lieutenant-General John Monash, played a major part in the Allied counter-offensive that climaxed with the Armistice on 11 November 1918.

The Australian Corps in 1918 constituted nearly one-tenth of the British and dominion troops on the Western Front, yet in that year they took 23 percent of the prisoners, 23 percent of the guns captured, and 21 percent of the territory regained. Stuart Macintyre, in volume 4 of *The Oxford History of Australia*, describes this Australian success as being 'as much due to their extensive experience in the management of large-scale public enterprises as it was to the celebrated qualities of courage and individual initiative'.[2] In particular it is the image of the Australian soldier or 'digger' that achieved these feats that still resonates today. The idea of the 'digger' or the 'Anzac', the two words used interchangeably for an Australian soldier, is one that Australians have grown up with since the First World War.

It is a figure we know well: 'digger' characters have included Paul Hogan as Pat Cleary in the television mini-series *The Anzacs*, Chips Rafferty in Charles Chauvel's *The Rats of Tobruk* and *Forty Thousand Horsemen* and Mel Gibson in Peter Weir's *Gallipoli*. Each depicts the 'bombastic and self-aggrandizing' larrikin soldier who was the despair of the British high command out of the trenches, yet whose fearless courage and initiative made him a superb fighter in battle — or so we are told.

As a former professional soldier who graduated into the New Zealand Army from the Royal Military College, Duntroon, in 1969 I have always had difficulty matching the obvious achievement of the Australian Corps in 1918 with the larrikin image of the soldiers who were the foundation of its success. It is certainly not how I saw the Australian Army throughout 22 years of ongoing contact. While the soldiers were still called 'diggers', I was more struck by the strict formal discipline, and the rigid code that defined relationships both between senior and junior officers, and between officers and other ranks. I was also very aware of their high degree of professionalism. Yet all of this was in an army that still prided itself on its egalitarianism, and one that believed it continued that 'digger' ethos. The traditional image was at odds with the professional reality.

Looking back on the Australian experience on the Western Front I also had difficulty relating the Anzac or 'digger' image of the individual players to the machine of which they formed a part, first within the two ANZAC corps from 1916 to the end of 1917 and then as part of the Australian Corps in 1918. Macintyre and others write of Monash's 'rare qualities of leadership in his orchestration of a vast and complex military machine', and we have Monash himself writing, 'A perfected battle plan is like nothing so much as a score for a musical composition.'[3] Yet how do you conduct a symphony with an orchestra made up of thousands of free spirits like Paul Hogan? As Eric Andrews suggests in his examination of Australian performance on the Western Front, such individualism requires a greater discipline and training to properly harness its talents.

Was this Australian success somehow built on a marriage of a unique style of national command exhibited by citizen-commanders such as Monash and the skills of these independent, egalitarian, ill-disciplined — yet somehow self-disciplined in battle — Australian soldiers? Both Pedersen, in his study of Monash, and Andrews subscribe to this belief. Or was this success due to something more akin to the traditional virtues of formal discipline, training and command that one associates with Regular soldiers, and which was demanded of the 'conscript armies of other combatants in the First World War'?[4] In this chapter we examine the nature of the AIF, and analyse its performance in battle from its first introduction to combat with the Gallipoli Campaign of 1915 to its experience on the Western Front from 1916 to 1918.

Any such analysis has to work its way past the twin barriers of C.E.W. Bean's voluminous official history of the Australians in the Great War, and the dominating figure of the Australian Corps commander in 1918, Lieutenant-General Sir John Monash. Tackling these is as formidable as any breaching of the barbed-wire entanglements protecting the Hindenburg Line. Bean's six volumes of text in his 12-volume edited history place the Australian 'digger' central to the story, describing in 'minute detail every action in which Australian troops took part, footnoting every participant of note from private to general'.[5] Yet as Eric Andrews noted in his *The Anzac Illusion*, and in his detailed examination of Bean's handling of the two battles of Bullecourt in April and May 1917, the official historian's minute detailing of the soldier's experience in battle is not matched by an equal analysis of Australian command and staff work. Indeed, the Australian divisional commanders are curiously absent from Bean's histories, particularly when things go wrong. For example, at Bullecourt British tanks and flanking units are criticised, but here and throughout the official histories the Australians are above criticism. Andrews' conclusion is that Bean is a 'chronicler rather than a competent analytical historian'.[6]

Bill Gammage's *The Broken Years*, John Robertson's study of the Gallipoli Campaign *ANZAC and Empire*, and more recently Les Carlyon's *Gallipoli* follow in the Bean tradition, all three being paeans to Australian soldiers.[7] Indeed, there has been no detailed and comprehensive study, other than Bean's, of the Australian experience on the Western Front, and we still await an examination of Australian combat effectiveness similar to Rawling's study of the Canadian Corps. Monash has been studied in detail, and in Serle's and Pedersen's work is as sacrosanct as the Australian digger. In both he is portrayed as the outstanding divisional and corps commander in the British armies on the Western Front, and when one reads his *The Australian Victories in France in 1918* it is clear that this is also Monash's own opinion.

It is only comparatively recently that Australian military historiography has wrestled with issues that provide depth and contrast to these accepted images. *The Oxford Companion to Australian Military History* has a series of excellent dispassionate assessments of the performance of the AIF and its commanders, which provide glimpses that allow us to see beyond the temple's veil. This has been supported by the *Australian Army History* series, a growing list of publications that covers the other and until now forgotten commanders of the First AIF, as well as important thematic studies such as Glenn Wahlert's *The Other Enemy? Australian Soldiers and the Military Police*. Discipline and morale in the context of AIF combat effectiveness also features in Ashley Ekins' chapter contributions to Peter H. Liddle and Hugh Cecil's anniversary volumes on Passchendaele and the Armistice of 1918. More recent still is the *Australian Centenary History of Defence* series, whose volumes include Jeffrey Grey's *The Australian Army*, which complements his earlier *A Military History of Australia*, and John Coates' impressively detailed and comprehensive *An Atlas of Australian Wars*, backed by Joan Beaumont's *Australian Defence: Sources and Statistics*.

Within this growing body of work there is also Dale Blair's *Dinkum Diggers: An Australian Battalion at War*, a seminal study that examines the experiences of the 1st Battalion of the First AIF. Blair is careful to point out that his study relates to one battalion and that this cannot be seen as typical of the AIF as a whole. He concludes that the 1st Battalion's wartime experience 'was more complex and significantly different, from the sanitised experiences painted by the "digger" stereotype of the Anzac legend'. In particular he calls into question the pervasiveness of the two central tenets of the legend, namely 'egalitarianism, and resourcefulness and initiative'.[8]

Blair presents the trials and tribulations of the 1st Battalion from its foundation, through its baptism of fire on Gallipoli and its service on the Western Front. What struck me most about his study was how it mirrored the realities of NZEF battalions that I have studied over the same period. The superb potential of the recruit was no guarantee of success or excellence at unit level, so much depending on the quality of the commanding officer and the grip he exerted in the disciplining, training and administration of his battalion. Much also depended on the fortunes of war in how the unit was used in battle, mostly factors beyond the commanding officer's control. A change in commanding officer or a commanding officer kept too long in command, too many casualties, particularly among officers and NCOs, a lack of reinforcements, or a combination of all of these could see a good battalion go bad. This cycle could be repeated over the course of the war, or not occur at all in the rare 'lucky' battalion. Australians have until now viewed the original Anzacs of the First World War as immune from these realities of battalions in wartime.

Blair's work is a long overdue reality check. He has come under intense criticism for his findings, but I read his work as confirmation that Australian historiography is finally shrugging off the stifling mantle that Bean threw over the image of the Australian soldier in the First World War. It suggests that the experience of the AIF more closely resembles that of the CEF, NZEF and BEF than the Australian public and some nationally focused historians have been prepared to accept — not unique, but founded on universal wartime realities that affect every army.

In 1914 the AIF, raised under the command of the Scottish-born Australian professional soldier Major-General W.T. Bridges, was an enthusiastic volunteer citizen force raised initially from the major centres of population on a quota basis from each state, so that in October 1914 some 20,000 soldiers were dispatched overseas. As I have already mentioned, little thought was given to how large a force Australia could sustain, and by 1916 there were five divisions, each some 15,000 strong. These were the 1st, 2nd, 4th and 5th Australian Divisions, which were in the two ANZAC corps in France, while the 3rd Australian Division was assembled and trained in Great Britain.

In 1914 there was initially just the 1st Division, which was quickly joined by an additional infantry brigade, the 4th, commanded by Colonel John Monash, and the 1st Light Horse Brigade. In Egypt these were grouped with the two brigades of the NZEF to form a composite New Zealand and Australian Division under Major-General Sir Alexander Godley, the British officer commanding the New Zealand Expeditionary Force. The two divisions combined to form the Australian and New Zealand Army Corps under Lieutenant-General W.R. Birdwood. On their arrival in Cairo the discipline of enthusiasm that sustained both forces on enlistment soon wore off, and the drunkenness and absenteeism that was rife over Christmas and New Year 1915 reflected the inevitable reality of a hastily raised force without trained officers or non-commissioned officers, dependent on the very few Regular officers and warrant officers to hold things together. Bridges, the Australian commander, was slow to get a grip and the image of the Australian larrikin soldier running amok in Cairo was there for all to see and report on, and became central to Anzac mythology.

The 1st Division was, as Grey suggests in *A Military History of Australia*, 'probably the worst trained formation ever sent from Australia's shores',[9] and there was little time to correct this in Egypt. Lack of leadership in some units, the gulf between officers and men, and inexperience are some of the underlying causes. As I have discussed in earlier chapters it was no different in the NZEF, and perhaps much worse in the shambles that was the CEF mobilisation. Improving the discipline of the force depended on how quickly the situation was gripped by those in charge.

Much of the AIF was raised in the working-class suburbs of Melbourne or Sydney, a world apart from the world of the officers placed over them in command, who were drawn from the professional and middle classes. As Blair explores in *Dinkum Diggers*, background counted for commissioned rank.[10] This was equally true for New Zealand and Canada. In the Anzac experience perhaps it was the Light Horse and Mounted Rifle regiments alone that took to war a social hierarchy that best adapted to the demands of soldiering. Inevitably there were a large number of duds, particularly among the infantry officers selected because of their professional and social backgrounds or Volunteer experience. The inadequate had to be weeded out, inexperienced officers had to learn how to handle their men, and this all had to be achieved without the benefit of any experience among their NCOs, the traditional back-up to newly appointed platoon commanders.

The same was true at every level of command and there was little time for the AIF to adapt itself for war, but by trial and error it did the best it could. Officers at all levels had to develop in the job and those who did not measure up had to be replaced, but all the while the soldiers had to bear and sometimes suffer from this learning experience. Lieutenant C.S. Algie was a platoon commander in the 6th Hauraki Company of the Auckland Infantry Battalion. A Boer War veteran, Algie was quick to praise his New Zealanders, particularly those from his hometown of Rotorua, and had a jaundiced view of Australians; nevertheless, his diaries are witness to some of the problems faced by the AIF in Egypt.

> These fellows seem to have a tremendous hooligan element among them. The other day alongside our camp we <u>witnessed</u> a most disgraceful scene from their lines. A captain remonstrated with a soldier for molesting a native whereupon the whole crowd hooked him.[11] Then another officer came to the rescue of the first and made an attempt to say something to them but the whole 'mob' again silenced him by counting him out in true ringside style. Today they were all sent back to Cairo and when their Brigadier told them they were being sent back because of their behaviour in Ismailia and on the canal they counted him out too. Truly good discipline!![12]

On 25 April 1915 Bridges' 1st Division spearheaded the landing of the ANZAC Corps on the Turkish coast at what is now Anzac Cove. The British war-reporter Ellis Ashmead-Bartlett's initial dispatch of the landing and the Australian official correspondent C.E.W. Bean's ongoing descriptions of the campaign, cemented by the release of *The ANZAC*

Book in 1916, fulfilled the Australian public's expectations of the performance of their boys. And as the casualty lists grew, ongoing stories of heroic endeavour went some way to justifying the blood sacrifice, and sustained the willing queues at the recruiting depots.

The reality ashore was very different. Here enthusiastic soldiers faced action for the first time. The veneer of training experience given to them in Egypt was not enough to cope with the wrong beach, the broken terrain and the grim determination of an outnumbered Turkish force fighting in defence of its homeland. Had experienced officers and NCOs led the 1st Australian Division this might have swung the balance, but this was not the case. Only the Turkish lack of numbers prevented a disaster.[13] As it was, enough amateur soldiers with what leadership there was did the best they could, and held on. That evening, both divisional commanders, seeing the fearful and confused stragglers crowding the beach, recommended evacuation but this was impossible, as General Sir Ian Hamilton recognised, and Birdwood's corps was told to hold on and 'dig in'. The question of stragglers, who they were and why they had come down to the beach became a contentious issue during the drafting of the British official histories. Bean objected to the initial draft, believing that it overstated the case and tarnished the Anzac image. The British Government, mindful of strains in its relations with Australia, gave ground accordingly.[14]

Birdwood's ANZAC Corps staff lacked administrative and tactical skills, and throughout the campaign never appreciated the condition and capabilities of their soldiers. As we have seen, this was demonstrated in the planning and conduct of the August offensive. While it is customary to blame the British at Suvla, Birdwood's feints from the Anzac perimeter had little chance of success. This was made worse by the tension between Australian commanders, highlighted by the rank amateurism shown by the 3rd Light Horse Brigade at The Nek.[15] The plan for the Lone Pine feint on 6 August was strongly disagreed with by Walker. Here alone, his careful planning, including the construction of communication trenches into no-man's land, provided the basis for Australian success, but the nature of the fighting led to the destruction of the 1st Brigade.

In late August 1915 Major-General J.G. Legge's 2nd Division joined the Anzacs. This was a division in name only, never having been together nor trained as a formation. Legge himself was an intellectually able but divisive personality who did not succeed in his profession where it mattered most, as an operational commander.[16] His division learnt its business as had the 1st Division before it — by trial and error. In this atmosphere outstanding leaders began to emerge and become central to AIF success.

251

Staff and planning skills also improved, as exemplified by Birdwood's Australian Chief of Staff, Brigadier-General Brudenell White, in the planning of the evacuation, which provided a gloss to a botched campaign. Despite the legend of Anzac achievement, what the Gallipoli campaign showed was that no matter the potential excellence of the individual soldier, this counted for nothing without effective leadership, training and administration. The often outstanding bravery and initiative displayed by the Australian soldier could not compensate for poor planning and inept command, either on Gallipoli or at the Western Front.

The year 1916 saw the expansion of the AIF to initially four and then five divisions. A sixth was planned but disbanded. Birdwood dreamed of an ANZAC Army, but Haig disagreed and two corps, I and II ANZAC Corps — the first commanded by Birdwood, the second by Godley — transferred to France in April and May 1916.[17] As both Pedersen and Andrews have noted in their respective studies, you cannot expand any organisation to this extent without diluting command experience at all levels. Despite the cadre of skills imported into the new divisions, all but the 1st Division were raw and untried, with little training of any worth that fitted them for trench warfare on the Western Front. This showed up in the trenches at Armentières in France.

At Fromelles on 5 July 1916 the 5th Division was cut to pieces, losing 5300 of its 15,000 men. Haking, the British corps commander, under whom the 5th Division was attached for the operation, deserves blame for an inept and ill-thought-out attack, but Major-General J.W. McCay, the Australian divisional commander, also deserves his share.[18] His was the last division to be formed in Egypt but circumstance saw it become the first to be committed to battle on the Western Front. McCay, a citizen soldier and former Defence Minister, demonstrated his skills in training his 2nd Australian Brigade before its dispatch to Gallipoli, but there was no time for the same preparation with his newly formed 5th Division before it was committed to France. At Fromelles he and Godley, his corps commander, accepted a questionable plan and carried it out without any real preparation. Half of his raw troops had never been in the front line and had little idea of where the objectives were or what they were to do.[19] The failings seen at The Nek in August 1915 were repeated, and while British command became convenient scapegoats the real failings were closer at hand. Godley demonstrated once again that he had little tactical grasp and accepted tasks without demur, while McCay's division lacked the tactical skills and the staff experience to see that the inexperienced but enthusiastic Australians were properly launched into battle.

It is unlikely, given their state of training, that the New Zealand Division or any of the other Australian divisions with the exception of Walker's 1st Australian Division would have been any more successful at Fromelles. The 5th Division reflected the loss of a third of its strength in a loss of morale, with a growing hatred and distrust of McCay, its divisional commander. He already had the reputation of being an 'unlucky' commander after the destruction of his 2nd Brigade at the Battle of Krithia on 8 May 1915. It was he who, with hundreds of Australian wounded still choking no-man's land, ordered the unofficial ceasefire, arranged by men on the ground to gather in the wounded, to end. Godley wrote of the attack and its impact:

> McCay's fellows did excellently and took their share of the enemy trenches, but unfortunately the troops on our right didn't get in so we did not attempt to stay and came away ... McCay did very well but got rather rattled at one time and I had rather a time of it quieting him! These amateur soldiers are not all joy![20]

Godley always seemed dispassionate when confronting heavy casualties, and his views on citizen command are self-evident. Within the 5th Division some of the surviving commanders broke down or were sacked after Fromelles.[21] It would take nine months and a change of divisional commander for the 5th Division to recover from this disaster.

The description in the unit history of the dissolution and collapse of the 30th Battalion during its march to the Somme in October 1916 showed how the disaster at Fromelles impacted on individual units within the 5th Division. In this instance exhausted, fully laden men at night on a wet road reacted to the commanding officer losing his way by falling out where they were. A minor incident in the context of the war, but one indelibly etched in the memories of the battalion.

> This error proved to be the last straw. Worn out by the strain of the march and with their morale broken, many men sank down on the roadside while others took cover in adjoining hedges and haystacks. The company officers, who for hours had been helping to carry the arms and equipment of their weaker men or some of the additional stores, did their best to rally them but met with little success.[22]

Fromelles was an unhappy start for the AIF, which was confirmed by its involvement on the Somme in July 1916 where Birdwood's I ANZAC fought as part of Gough's Reserve, later Fifth Army. Major-General Walker, whose 1st Division alone showed a degree of professionalism, resisted Gough's impetuosity, but not Birdwood nor his other divisional commanders. Legge's 2nd Division's attack on Pozières was rushed and failed. It drew Haig's criticism of Legge ('not much good'), his division ('ignorant') and of Birdwood's staff, who Brudenell White stoutly defended.[23] Only as the battle progressed did Walker's professional skills in the planning and conduct of the attacks first on Pozières and then on Mouquet Farm filter through to the rest of I ANZAC Corps. The calibre of the soldiers involved was excellent, but once again it was not matched by their standard of training, the tactics employed, or Australian staff and command skills at corps and division.[24] At corps level Birdwood, as he had done in the August offensive on Gallipoli the year before, showed little tactical grasp. This did not change. A year later Brudenell White, his Chief of Staff, in exasperation would describe him in a private letter to Gellibrand as 'a man of no quality'.[25] Pozières was savage, bitter attack after attack, inevitably followed by German counterattack on a narrow front under constant artillery fire that ate through the Australian divisions as the Germans determined to hold this vital ground.[26]

Pulverised by artillery far beyond what humanity could ever expect to endure, some battalions dissolved into leaderless gaggles of frightened and exhausted soldiery. Lieutenant-Colonel Iven G. Mackay, the outstanding commanding officer of the 4th Battalion, noted that the AIF battalions he relieved with his battalion at Mouquet Farm, just north of Pozières, withdrew leaving a number of wounded men as well as two Lewis guns behind in the trenches.[27] There was little scope for initiative, only endurance. At Pozières even the strongest cracked, and with them the care for one's mates that is central to the 'digger' ethos.[28]

Australian losses on the Somme numbered 23,000. If we take a battalion at 1000 men, but in reality more like 800, how do you lose the equivalent of 23 of 48 battalions and still maintain both morale and skill? This is not possible without time to absorb reinforcements and for administration and training. There was little time for this as I ANZAC wintered on the Somme battlefield. Ashley Ekins' studies show the impact of heavy fighting and casualties on Australian morale.[29] Too many losses among officers and NCOs, a change in command, and a good battalion can lose its edge. This was not compensated for by a growing egalitarianism — a brotherhood of the trenches. In fact one could argue that the reverse was true. Mackay for one knew that the only route forward for his battalion after the Somme was from amateur to professional. 'In an army formed quickly from citizens there is a great tendency to treat troops kindly and let them train without too much exertion. This is no kindness to the troops. The real kindness is to make them hard — if possible harder than the enemy.'[30]

Mackay's approach to training and administration appears to have been the norm rather than the exception in the best of the Australian battalions. 'Strict, no nonsense, but didn't throw his weight about. A good sense of humour and friendly. But above all, thorough. He was relentlessly insistent that the well-being of the men always came first.'[31] Leaf through the battalion histories and one sees the words 'strict disciplinarian' or similar, again and again, as one of the measures of effective command: A.G. Salisbury of the 50th Battalion, Maurice Wilder-Nelligan of the 10th Battalion — 'a man of great ability, bravery and originality, and, although a strict disciplinarian, who insisted on all his orders being carried out to the letter, he was loved and respected by all ranks'.[32] Lieutenant-Colonel O.G. Howell-Price of the 3rd Battalion, mortally wounded on 2 November 1916, was also loved but he too was known for his 'sternness and austerity', which matched his 'single-minded loyalty to his unit'.[33] This is mirrored in Morshead's command of the 33rd Battalion in the 3rd Division, where flair in battle was matched by a reputation for being a 'Holy Terror' with his strict discipline and demand that his officers devote their attention to the administration and training of the men.[34]

It was the same at brigade level. The legendary 'Pompey' Elliot of the 15th Brigade, as detailed in Ross McMullin's brilliant study, led from the front, was noted for his towering rages, and was a strict disciplinarian who demanded meticulous attention to detail from his officers and men.[35] Brigadier-General T.W. Glasgow of the 13th Brigade was described by Bean as the 'most forcible of the three brigadiers of 4th Division' and one who would push for the extension of the death penalty for Australian soldiers;[36] John Gellibrand of the 6th Brigade, quiet and unconventional, was a superb military manager and trainer of men who subjected his subordinate commanders to close supervision until they proved their capabilities and earned his trust, and was quick to remove those who did not measure up.[37] Examine the list of citizen brigadiers in 1918 in John Bourne's study and while many were colourful individuals, attention to detail and strict discipline can also be found among their attributes.[38]

Being 'loved' was optional. More important was the ability to command. Rather than egalitarianism, Blair speaks of the need to establish a 'rough equality' between officers and men, which meant that the men were treated fairly and consistently in the context of the times.[39] Respect was important; it did not matter if he was a 'hard bastard who would come down on you like a ton of bricks if you stepped out of line', providing he was consistent, knew his job as an officer, and did not ask the men to do anything he would not do himself. Once again these are universal measurements.

What also emerges is the need for trained reinforcements to keep the units up to strength. The unchecked expansion of the AIF was not matched by an administration that guaranteed the necessary supply of trained men. This blighted the recovery of the Australian divisions after their losses on the Somme and would eventually cripple the AIF in 1918. Mackay in the 4th Battalion was critical both of the 'merest trickle' of reinforcements that the grossly under-strength battalions were receiving after the Somme and of their poor standard of training. The latter led to his insistence during the winter of 1916 that the battalion reinforcement drafts were kept out of the front line until they were trained to handle the conditions.[40] Prime Minister Hughes' attempts to introduce conscription without splitting his Labor administration by means of a national referendum failed, and while today Australia takes pride in the fact that the members of the First AIF were all volunteers, Hughes' administration was unable to provide an alternative means of guaranteeing necessary reinforcements and the cost of this was borne by soldiers at the front.

While the statistics show 124,352 men enlisting in the AIF during 1916, enlistments for November and December that year are 5055 and 2617 respectively; 45,101 joined in 1917, and in 1918 the number reduced to 28,883.[41] What these figures do not show is the declining standards of recruits. A total of 83,084 enlistments, or just over 20 percent, did not leave Australia; 13,954 of these were soldiers in camp on cessation of hostilities in November 1918, but more telling were the 33,906 recruits medically discharged from camps during training, the 9522 discharged because they were underage or offered pressing family reasons for leaving the army, and the 18,792 who were discharged under the category of desertion/services no longer required.[42]

In my examination of discipline and morale in the NZEF, I established a correlation between the exhaustion of the division after a major offensive and an increase in disciplinary problems and numbers reporting sick. Indeed, these measurements have been and remain a traditional and universal barometer of the morale of a unit, as any CO can gauge by talking to his RSM, RMO and chaplain. A counter to this in the NZEF was the insertion of new blood in the form of trained reinforcements. The AIF did not have this, and the disciplinary statistics are but one indication of a force being pushed to its limits and beyond.

Drunkenness and absenteeism soared after the destruction of I ANZAC at Pozières. Wahlert's study details the increase in courts martial convictions for desertion from 21 in 1915 to 288 in 1916, 1283 in 1917 and 1807 in 1918. The Fourth Army figures for December 1916 list 184 convictions for absence, 130 of which were Australians. In the first six months of 1917 the 62 divisions of the British Expeditionary Force had 677 convictions for desertion, 171 of which came from the five Australian divisions.[43] This was not the larrikinism of fearless Anzacs who would pick and choose what instructions to obey out of the line then revert to fearless fighters in battle, as the Australian public and some national historians would like to believe. It was but one of the symptoms of exhaustion, which was mirrored by the increasing sickness rates.

What is of concern is that when one contrasts the New Zealand and the Australian figures, the New Zealand statistics show a decline in late 1917 and in 1918 while the AIF figures continue to escalate. One would have thought that in an egalitarian force such as the AIF, officered by men who had come from the ranks and who knew their men, the reverse would be true. However, as studies show, the commissioning of officers from the ranks was the pattern throughout the British armies on the Western Front and not limited to the AIF.[44] Once commissioned an officer had to do his job, and the need to take hard decisions in hard times was reflected in the disciplinary statistics of the AIF. Tired, fearful men pushed beyond their limits do not always respond to reasonable requests or stay within the bounds, regardless of an officer's background and understanding. The business of war still had to be done and if necessary the men driven to do it, and punished if they did not.

In early 1917, when still part of Gough's army, I ANZAC was involved in the follow-up of the German withdrawal and the two attacks on the Hindenburg Line at Bullecourt in April–May. Gough's impetuosity overrode Birdwood and his staff, despite their objections, and the cost was borne by the attacking troops. The first attack by the 4th Division at 4.45 a.m. on 11 April was a fiasco. It was originally planned for the morning of 10 April, but the tanks lost their way and the attack was cancelled. It was resurrected at short notice for the next day, and resulted in the loss of 1000 Australian prisoners among the 3000 casualties.[45] Nothing more could have been asked of the soldiers, 'who went forward unaided against a strongly wired line and captured it and held it for seven hours' until forced to withdraw.[46] However, Australian tactics at division and corps level showed that little had been learnt since the Somme, and I ANZAC artillery in particular failed to support the Australian attack despite repeated requests for assistance.[47]

A second attack by the 2nd Division was planned and carefully practised, and in a repeat attack on 3 May a section of the line was seized by Gellibrand's 6th Brigade, and held against counterattacks, despite the failure of the 5th Brigade on its flank. The 5th Division replaced the 2nd and the village was held at a cost of 7000 Australian casualties. Here again the attack was launched over the same ground as the first, little attempt was made at division or corps to read the ground and assess the dangers of the German defence, with the result that the artillery fire plan ignored the dangers presented by German enfilade positions on the right flank.[48] It was not a mistake the Canadians would make before Vimy or in Currie's careful appreciation before Lens.

The individual courage and initiative of the Australian soldier, still not yet 'diggers' in their own parlance, was not matched by the tactical skills of their commanders. Bean speaks of an open distrust of British High Command, but it is naive to believe that this distrust was directed only at the British. Gellibrand, whose 6th Brigade had seized the line, resigned his command in disgust at the performances of Major-General N.M. Smyth, the 2nd Division's British commander, and Smith, the Australian commander of the 5th Brigade.[49] In 1917 Birdwood's I ANZAC Corps was torn by jealousies amongst its brigade and divisional commanders. Birdwood himself lacked the strength of character and tactical skills to impose the standards of discipline and skill exhibited by the Canadian Corps, first under its British commander Lieutenant-General Sir Julian Byng, and then under his successor, the Canadian citizen soldier Lieutenant-General Arthur Currie.

It was in Godley's II ANZAC Corps that more positive signs were shown. The 7 June attack on Messines was the first major action by Monash's 3rd Division, and showed a tactical skill not demonstrated by any other Australian division except perhaps Walker's 1st Australians. It was a product of the division's training in England, and the weeks of careful preparation before battle, with Monash himself being given the latitude to assess how best to employ his formations within his divisional area.

The same skill and leadership was not shown by Major-General W. Holmes' 4th Australian Division, which arrived before Messines with the men exhausted from Bullecourt and without time for preparation and training; consequently its gaining of the corps' depth objective was a shambles. A brigade-major in the 25th Division observed after watching them pass through, 'The latter did not get to their final objectives but spent their time in the first [objective] looking for souvenirs. Though fine men individually they have no cohesion, discipline or organization, and are in these respects far behind the New Zealanders.'[50]

The situation simply reflected the reality of an exhausted division shaken by its experience at Bullecourt, which was then transferred to another corps, given the most difficult of tasks with insufficient time to plan and prepare, and without the assistance that should have come from Godley's corps headquarters. Holmes as divisional commander was held in the spotlight's glare, and Haig noted that he 'does not seem to have the same qualities of character as Russell and others'.[51] Holmes was a citizen soldier with a breadth of experience that encompassed the Boer War, command of the Australian Naval and Military Expeditionary Force that occupied German New Guinea on the outbreak of war, Gallipoli and the Western Front.[52] He was another who had a reputation for being a 'stern disciplinarian' but, taking command of the 4th Australian

Division after the Somme, he had little time to stamp his personality on the formation before Bullecourt and Messines. He was mortally wounded while conducting a group of visiting Australian politicians to the battlefield on 2 July 1917.

In August the 4th Division, now commanded by Major-General E.G. Sinclair-MacLagan, was transferred back to I ANZAC and again committed to battle without the opportunity to rest, regroup and retrain for the four months given to the other Australian divisions of the corps. The disaster at Bullecourt and even more casualties at Messines saw it reinforced with a total of 9400 men, but this still left it below strength. Absence without leave was becoming a problem in all of the Australian divisions and, as Bean notes, especially so in the 4th.[53] As Bean records, while the 4th had the reputation of being 'the toughest of all the Australian divisions', it returned to I ANZAC before Third Ypres 'at its lowest ebb'.[54] The division resented not being given the same opportunities to rest as its counterparts. 'The apparent unfairness of throwing it into the fight along with the three rested divisions of 1 Anzac aroused audible protests at the parade of at least one battalion when the news was announced.'[55]

The details of this rest and retraining of I ANZAC are inevitably glossed over in the battalion histories. However, this was the first time that three of the Australian divisions collectively had a sustained period to assess the lessons of the Somme and adapt to the changes in battalion organisation and tactics that had been introduced in the British armies from February 1917.

Bean briefly details the elements of 'the long rest' in his official history. The progressive training was from 'company exercises to those of battalion, brigade and division'. Competitions were held in all divisions 'for the best trained platoon or the best turned-out transport, culminating in divisional tournaments — that of the 5th Division being held in a field at Henencourt on July 12th in presence of the King'. There were frequent demonstrations in the latest techniques: 'of barrages by the 1st Division's artillery and trench mortars ... of contact between aeroplanes and infantry by the 1st Brigade and the 3rd Squadron R.F.C.; of "a platoon in attack" by 28th Battalion and by a model platoon at the corps school'. We see the battalions of Gellibrand's brigade attacking a village, each in turn, 'while the others looked on and criticised'. The 2nd Division's final exercise took place on the old Somme battlefield where conditions matched those they would face in the Ypres Salient, with two brigades attacking a series of objectives in depth, before the third brigade passed through them and attacked.

The climax to all of this was a series of brigade attacks in the Lumbres training area, where techniques were practised on how to overcome the newly introduced German defensive tactics based on mutually supporting pillboxes in depth. Bean records that this involved changes to the supporting artillery barrage, 'with long halts at the main stages, so that, if at any point organised opposition survived, the platoons on the spot should have time to fight it down with the diverse arms now allotted to them'.[56]

In the 5th Division, commanded by Major-General J.J. Talbot Hobbs, the 'new defensive and offensive tactics ... coloured the entire training of the Division'. The divisional history records Hobbs' keen interest in the new offensive methods, and at his insistence 'scores of lectures and demonstrations were given until all ranks were perfectly familiar with even the details of the new warfare ... The men became keenly interested in the tactical considerations involved. Many of them became anxious to "have a go" at a pill-box.'[57]

These improvements were achieved throughout I ANZAC, and as the official historian noted, this allowed the Australian divisions to become 'very efficient instruments indeed'.[58] The period also saw the return of the 4th Division, and Haig and Plumer's approval for I ANZAC to remain entirely Australian with four Australian divisions, while Godley's II ANZAC would consist of the 3rd Australian and the New Zealand divisions plus two British divisions. 'In this way he [Birdwood] urged, Anzac divisions could be put into battle in pairs, and advantage thus taken of the longing of these troops to have other "Anzacs" beside them in action.' A letter from the Australian Government backed this decision, asking that Australians be kept in purely Australian formations.[59]

Despite the 4th Division's dismay at again being committed to preparations for a major offensive as part of I ANZAC Corps, the benefits of this were obvious. Haig inspected the 2nd and 5th Australian Divisions on 29 August 1917 and noted in his diary:

> I complimented Birdwood, his G.O.C.'s divisions and brigades on the splendid appearance of the troops to-day [sic]. The Australians have never looked better since they came to France than they did this morning. I was greatly pleased with their bearing and evident desire of each one to do his very best to show well at my inspection. These divisions have been out of the line for three months and have benefited from the training which they have undergone.[60]

After this extended period of rest and retraining it was in the series of battles before Passchendaele in September–October 1917 that Birdwood's I ANZAC Corps finally started to put it together. Working as part of Plumer's Second Army the Australian divisions achieved a series of successes: in the battles of Menin Road by the 1st and 2nd Divisions on 20 September; the 4th and 5th Divisions at Polygon Wood on 26

King George V accompanied by Lieutenant-General Sir William Birdwood, GOC I ANZAC Corps, views and is viewed in turn by soldiers of the AIF. Lieutenant-General Sir Alexander Godley is in the rear of Birdwood, three back. *(Royal Military Academy Sandhurst Collection).*

September, and at Broodseinde on 4 October. The Battle of Menin Road was the first time on the Western Front that two Australian divisions had attacked side by side. This was repeated at Polygon Wood, and seen again at the Battle of Broodseinde on 4 October when for the first and only time both I and II ANZAC Corps attacked together, involving the 1st, 2nd and 3rd Divisions as well as the New Zealanders.

The experience of I ANZAC Corps as part of Plumer's Second Army mirrored the detailed preparation, planning and rehearsals that had taken place in II ANZAC before Messines; one can also see the influence of the Canadian success at Vimy. It is important to stress the degree to which all of the corps attached to the Second Army benefited from the way the planning and preparation evolved in the build-up to the Passchendaele Campaign. Under Plumer's careful direction, and with the detailed and explicit outlines and directives of his Major-General General Staff, Major-General Tim Harington, an army plan evolved that ensured that each corps and its component divisions had time to assess, plan and train for the battles to come.

What we would like to believe are initiatives at divisional level by commanders such as Russell or Monash invariably grew out of the pool of ideas coming from Second Army conferences, visits to rehearsals, requests for suggestions and finally the clear directives that provided an army-level framework for the attack. A study of the Second Army war diary and conference notes shows that the integration of the artillery plan to the infantry attack, and a detailed understanding of the nature and importance of infantry platoon tactics, is evident within the Second Army in August. This confirms what was seen at Messines. The spread of this doctrine was not due to isolated enthusiasts working alone within their divisions or brigades, but a coherent attempt at army level to overcome the deficiencies of tactical doctrine so evident on the Somme.[61] It is also evident that the Second Army conference notes were based on studying the experience of Fifth Army formations in their August attacks in the Ypres Salient. The infantry revolution was not limited to one particular army, but was one that was being grappled with in all of Haig's armies.[62] What is more, as this extract shows, they were not dealing in general platitudes, but addressing specific problems faced at platoon and section level to ensure the tactics worked.

> The formation for advance adopted by most units was section columns in file or single file. This was probably the only way in which the broken ground could be traversed. The formation tends, however, to scatter units and throws great responsibility on subordinate commanders. In two Brigades the fighting was by platoons and sections. Platoon commanders who were questioned said that it was very difficult to keep control of sections so advancing. It is noteworthy, too, that evidence shows the men quite ready to advance in file or single file behind a platoon or section leader, especially an officer. On the other hand men apparently hesitate to deploy into line from such formations and this fact is noteworthy.[63]

This is hands-on practicalities being discussed at army level. The series of interchanges between army, corps and division, and then within each division itself, gave each level of command ownership of the process. It was this that allowed the Anzac divisional commanders — Hobbs, Monash, Russell, Sinclair-MacLagan, Smyth and Walker — to give it their personal touch, and in turn their refinements were fed back into the corps and army plan.

These touches lifted the practice and performance of I ANZAC Corps in the Third Ypres Campaign. They included a huge model of the terrain over which the corps would advance, which was studied by officers and NCOs as well as selected other ranks. This aided the rehearsals where techniques and timings were fine-tuned, with the critical artillery fire plan being adjusted accordingly. A study of the Second Army artillery fire plan makes it clear that this was not a template to which the infantry had to conform, but rather a considered pattern of covering fire worked out after a careful ground study and discussions with the infantry on how fast they could fight their way forward on that particular piece of ground. It was all arms cooperation at its finest, as the following extract shows.

(iii)   The barrage will be put down 150 yards in front of our jumping off line at ZERO.

(iv)   The barrage will advance after three minutes.

(v)   The barrage will cover the first 200 yards at the rate of 100 yards in four minutes.

(vi)   The barrage will then advance to the RED LINE at the rate of 100 yards in six minutes.

(vii)   There will be a halt of 45 minutes on the RED LINE.

(viii)   The barrage will advance from the RED LINE to the BLUE LINE at the rate of 100 yards in 8 minutes.

(ix)   There will be a halt of two hours on the BLUE LINE.

(x)   The barrage will advance from the BLUE LINE to the GREEN LINE at the rate of 100 yards in 8 minutes.

(xi)   The protective barrages on the RED, BLUE and GREEN LINES respectively will contain a proportion of smoke shell to indicate to the infantry that these lines have been gained.[64]

For the Battle of Polygon Wood on 26 September Hobbs' 5th Division attacked on a two-brigade frontage to seize two objectives, the farthest of which was 1000 yards from the front line. The creeping barrage covering the advance was carefully timed to allow the infantry to fight their way forward through the broken maze of shattered stumps in the dustbowl that was Polygon Wood. The task was made even more difficult by the successful German counterattack on 25 September, which meant that Brigadier-General 'Pompey' Elliot's 15th Brigade both had to stabilise the situation to his flank in the day before the attack and then ensure it was secured as his brigade fought its way forward.[65] It was a brilliant piece of work by one of the most colourful and effective fighting brigadiers in the AIF, whose critical failing was an explosive temper and an impulsiveness that matched his massive frame. It was this intemperateness that held him back from the divisional command that he believed he deserved. After the war this perceived lack of recognition would eat away at his soul and, a soured, embittered man, he committed suicide in March 1931.[66]

All that was to come, but at Polygon Wood we see examples of how no matter how detailed and careful the planning may be, thinking commanders of the likes of 'Pompey' Elliot and well-trained troops still needed to have the skills and initiative to respond to the unexpected. Artillery alone could not achieve this, nor could infantry; it relied on staff work and coordination to allow both to work in combination. There was, as Currie pointed out, the need for infantry to 'manoeuvre'. As we see in the Second Army attacks before Passchendaele, the artillery plan did not limit infantry initiative — a skilled German defence presented more than enough problems — but it did limit infantry objectives to ensure the artillery could provide cover and destroy the inevitable counterattacks.

These battles incorporated best practice at the cutting edge of technology. The use of creeping machine-gun barrages from the Vickers machine guns grouped under the divisional machinegun officer (DMGO) supplemented the creeping artillery barrage. Engineering and communication details were equally precise, with 'a series of visual stations ... sited at suitable places' plus a 'forward wireless set ... and, in addition, a wireless tank was to be utilised in the forward zone'. Royal Flying Corps contact aircraft flew overhead to keep in touch with the advancing infantry, who would keep in touch with red flares.[67]

At Menin Road and Polygon Wood Birdwood's I ANZAC mounted two sophisticated

Australian transport and soldiers move through the devastation astride the Menin Road during the September battles when dust, not mud, was the enemy. (*C-3260-1/2, Alexander Turnbull Library, Wellington, NZ*)

attacks that wanted for nothing in preparation and planning, but still required thinking, trained infantry to meet an equally sophisticated defensive plan. Many of the pillbox garrisons surrendered without a fight, while others:

> … perhaps better led or less severely shaken in the barrage, managed to get their machine guns into action. It was then that the … training proved its value. Instantly a couple of Lewis guns would open on the defenders and rifle bombers would drop their volleys of grenades all around them. Under cover of this fire a couple of parties would work round the flanks of the obstruction and in a few moments further resistance was impossible. It would all happen so quickly that the check to the general advance was imperceptible and touch with the barrage was never lost.[68]

These were hard-fought battles that achieved Plumer's limited 'bite and hold' objectives at a cost: 3750 in the 1st and 2nd Divisions at Menin Road and 4500 in the 4th and 5th Divisions at Polygon Wood. This was followed by the Battle of Broodseinde, which was another in the series of 'periodical battles', as Russell called them.

The successful attack on 4 October was notable for the fact that it was the first time four Anzac divisions had attacked side by side. It pre-empted a German spoiling attack by ten minutes, and the success of the artillery barrage left the forward shell-holes crowded with German dead. While the same tactical skills were extended to a greater or lesser degree army-wide, they were particularly evident in the two ANZAC corps. However, the conditions and the nature of the salient that Plumer's success created meant that more time was needed to achieve the detailed planning and preparation at corps and army level that underpinned each successful attack. The coming of the rains turned the powdered, pulverised earth into a muddy waste, making the positioning of guns forward more difficult. The ground gained meant that the attacking troops faced advancing into a pronounced salient into which German artillery could pour their fire from three sides. These problems meant that more time was needed between each attack to ensure that the artillery was in position to cut the wire, win the counter-battery battle, and cover the advance of the infantry forward.

Birdwood considered that I ANZAC had done enough and needed rest. He too had grown in the job, and after 4 October became increasingly assertive in demanding that his corps be rested. He provided support to II ANZAC on 9 October, but when it was suggested that I ANZAC take part in the 12 October attack after an interval of only three days Birdwood told Plumer that the objectives 'were far beyond the capacity of my troops in their now exhausted condition. I insisted that my action must be limited to safeguarding the flank of the II Anzac Corps on my left, whose commander, Godley, shared the optimism of Plumer and Haig.'[69] Godley ignored the conditions and showed that, unlike Birdwood, he and his staff had learnt nothing from Messines or Broodseinde. He was well aware of Haig's grand design for the Ypres offensive and he knew that Plumer, his Army commander, agreed with this plan. Godley, being Godley, told them both what they wanted to hear. He said that his divisional commanders, who do not appear to have been consulted, would brook no delay in the timetable and were confident that they could achieve success. He told Plumer that II ANZAC could continue in five days with his two British divisions. This action failed, and as we know, after reporting it as successful Godley was stung into trying again on 12 October. This too failed, and it was left to Currie's Canadians to do what Godley could not.

The difficulties faced by II ANZAC at Passchendaele on 9 and 12 October defy the imagination. The II ANZAC War Diary acknowledges that Haig's desire for a breakthrough had complicated the planning for the 9 October attack. The onset of rain also had a major impact: 'The assembling troops had had but little time to reconnoitre the ground, and were faced with the task of taking up their positions on a tape line in pitch darkness, across some 4 miles of country that can only be described as a quagmire.'[70]

A feature of the Second Army's preparatory conferences had been Plumer's insistence that:

> … care is necessary to make it fully understood that the preparation of barrage plans by higher authority does not absolve divisional commanders from full responsibility to obtain a barrage meeting all their requirements. The division is bound to see that preliminary bombardment and projected barrages deal with all 'sore places' on their front; of those places they have more definite knowledge than any higher authority.[71]

As we know the New Zealand Division had raised concerns about artillery support with Godley's Headquarters, and had been assured that it would be dealt with. It had been a major problem on 9 October and the situation remained unchanged on 12 October. Plumer's MGGS, Harington, had gone forward himself to see conditions on II ANZAC's front and could not have been blind to the problems, but Godley's enthusiasm carried the day. Messines was Godley's moment, but failure in front of Passchendaele suggests that the II ANZAC success at Messines was due more to Second

Diggers of the AIF occupying a trench on the objective during the attack on 4 October 1917, the first and only time that the divisions of both ANZAC corps attacked together in what was one of the most successful battles of the Ypres offensive. The success of this offensive convinced Haig that the German Armies were close to breaking point. (*Royal Military Academy Sandhurst Collection*)

Army planning and Russell and Monash's execution at divisional level. Certainly if one compares the performance of the two ANZAC corps headquarters during the battles of Third Ypres, I ANZAC was demonstrably superior.

Despite the image we have of Passchendaele, the battles of September and October 1917 saw the Australians in I ANZAC employ a level of command and tactical skills equal to those of the Canadian Corps. One could say that at last Birdwood's I ANZAC Corps matched the Anzac mythology. However, rather than native talent coming to the fore, the higher level of performance was the result of careful planning and preparation, detailed training and rehearsals at every level of command in what was now a professional and homogeneous national corps that had been encouraged to flower in the conducive atmosphere of Plumer's Second Army. This was confirmed with the formation of the Australian Corps on 1 January 1918, which grouped the 1st, 2nd, 3rd and 5th Divisions together.[72] The 4th Division was designated a depot division and tasked with retraining sick and wounded returning from convalescence. Once built back up to strength it would in turn relieve the weakest of the other four divisions, which in turn would become the depot division.

Haig's response to the manpower crisis affecting the British armies in France was to reduce divisional infantry strength from 12 to nine battalions. The Australians, Canadians and New Zealanders resisted this, but the parlous Australian reinforcement position made it impossible to sustain five effective divisions. This was the reason for the 4th becoming a depot division, and the 6th Division being raised in England was disbanded.[73] Scraping the bottom of the barrel and combing out the camps and depots in England built up the Australian Corps to strength. It was now a skilled professional organisation that had proved its staff and tactical efficiency in the battles before Passchendaele. The prolonged period of rest and retraining in the Messines sector over winter confirmed this proficiency, but it would have benefited if 4th Division had also been disbanded. As it stood there was nothing left to back up and sustain corps strength in the year ahead, casualties could not be replaced, and the corps' strength and efficiency would inevitably decline.

Australian professionalism at brigade and divisional level was again confirmed during the German March offensive of 1918, when at short notice elements of the Australian Corps were dispatched to shore up the line wherever necessary. The counterattack at Villers-Bretonneux by Elliot's 15th Brigade and Glasgow's 13th Brigade is notable both for being the first tank-to-tank battle in the history of war, but also for the ferocious skill the Australians demonstrated in ejecting the German defenders from the town.

The Australians played an important role in consolidating the British defensive line on the Somme, and once the line stabilised they demonstrated their superiority over the now exhausted Germans opposite. Ludendorff's gamble had failed at the cost of destroying his *Stosstruppen*. With the best having been used and destroyed, what was left lacked both the skill and the training of their equally tired opponents. The series of day and night raids along the Australian front, which Bean has termed 'peaceful penetration', saw small raiding parties from Australian units ambush German outposts at will in seeking both German unit identification and prisoners for interrogation. It was this almost total domination of the increasingly demoralised German opponent on their front that prompted General Rawlinson to mount what became the decisive Battle of Amiens on 8 August 1918.

On 4 May 1918 Birdwood was promoted to command the reformed Fifth Army and Monash became his replacement as Corps Commander. Monash's appointment was intensely resented in some circles, and became the focus of a barely covert campaign to replace him with Major-General C. Brudenell White, the Australian Corps Chief of Staff who accompanied Birdwood to Fifth Army as his Major-General General Staff (MGGS). The critical factor debarring White was that he had never commanded a division on operations, although he rebuffed Haig's suggestion in July 1917 that he should be commanding I ANZAC and professed his willingness to serve Birdwood.[74] To his credit White refused to be a party to the machinations led by Bean, the Australian official war correspondent, and the Australian journalist Keith Murdock.[75] The only other Australian contender was Hobbs, who commanded the 5th Division. Walker, Sinclair-MacLagan and Smyth were all out of contention because they were British, although in any other circumstances Walker would have been a front-runner.[76] Monash's performance in 1917 had brought him to Haig's attention and he was the outstanding candidate.[77]

Monash's appointment as Corps Commander also saw the Australians replace all the existing British divisional commanders with the exception of Sinclair-MacLagan, commanding the 4th Division. His long association with the Australian Military Forces, having served in Australia from 1901 to 1904 and again from 1910, led him to be one of the very few British officers to remain with the AIF until the end of the war. Glasgow replaced Walker in the 1st Division; Rosenthal replaced Smyth in the 2nd Division; and Gellibrand succeeded Monash in the 3rd Division.

Monash's approach to command was very different from Birdwood's laissez-faire style, and he immediately set about putting his imprint on the Australian Corps. The attack by Sinclair-MacLagan's 4th Division in the Battle of Hamel on 4 July 1918 demonstrated the Monash approach to perfection. It involved a coordinated attack by infantry, including four companies of attached US infantry, and the latest Mark V tanks of Vth Tank Brigade under an artillery barrage. The tight coordination between infantry, tanks, artillery and aircraft came closest to Monash's much-quoted description of a modern battle as 'nothing so much as a score for an orchestral composition, where the various arms and units are the instruments, and the tasks they perform are their respective musical phrases'. Once again, success was built around detailed planning and rehearsals at every level.

Every aspect was thrashed out in a series of conferences, the last of which involved 250 officers for four and half hours working through an agenda that covered 133 separate items. Once decided, there would be no changes; Monash had been frustrated by Godley's constant last-minute changes in II ANZAC and he was determined that at his Australian Corps conferences everyone would explain their plans in detail and, 'where there was any conflict or doubt or difference of opinion, a final and unalterable decision was given, there and then, and no subsequent "fiddling" with the plan was permitted'.[78] Here again Monash got involved in detail more properly left to his brigadiers and battalion commanders, but close supervision and detailed direction was his wont, and despite commanding five divisions and corps troops numbering an additional 50,000 personnel and vast material resources this continued to be his approach.

Hamel succeeded in 93 minutes. The tanks that crushed the German machine-gun posts when they showed resistance, as well as carrying reserves of water and ammunition for the attacking troops, ably supported the infantry. Aircraft reported progress and dropped machine-gun ammunition to the consolidating troops. It was a perfect battle in miniature, which confirmed the tactical skills of the units of the Australian Corps and gave them confidence in the command and staff skills of their new Corps Commander.

This was not a revolutionary battle that heralded something new and untried, as has often been claimed, but rather a consolidation of all that had been learnt in the evolution of Australian tactical and command proficiency since the Somme in 1916. It reflected the best in current tactical thinking and procedures in the British armies, and in particular the influence during 1917 of the staff and planning process employed by Plumer's Second British Army.[79] It showed that the Australian Corps under its new commander was evolving a tactical doctrine that fitted the Australian organisation and procedures in the same way that Currie's Canadians had evolved a doctrine that suited the structure and procedures practised in the Canadian Corps. Both were seen to effect in the Battle of Amiens that started on 8 August 1918.

Amiens was not Monash's brainchild, as he and others have suggested. As with most major plans, it was one that was influenced by a number of concurrent assessments in General Rawlinson's Fourth Army on how to take advantage of what seemed to be low German morale on the Somme front. Rawlinson and his staff, with considerable input from Monash and Currie, planned for a battle with limited objectives to push the Germans back from Amiens. The thrust would be conducted by the combined strength of the Australian and Canadian Corps, supported by the entire Tank Corps of 552 tanks. The range of covering artillery fire dictated the depth of the assault, but after assessing the strength of the defences this was set at between five and eight miles. This was impressive for its day but carefully planned for, incorporating both British experience at Cambrai and German performance in March–April. While III British Corps supported the two-corps central thrust on the left flank, XXXI French Corps of the French First Army provided support on the right.[80]

The assault on Amiens was spectacularly successful, with the Canadians advancing eight miles and the Australians seven to their depth objectives. The Australians attacked with two divisions up, Gellibrand's 3rd on the left and Rosenthal's 2nd Division on its right, with the 4th and 5th in the rear. The nature of the ground and the German front line made the Canadian Corps' task significantly more complex and difficult. In a series of phases the 2nd, 1st and 3rd Canadian Divisions attacked from left to right with 4th Division in depth.[81] There was no preliminary bombardment. The artillery fire plan had silently registered German artillery battery positions and the principal defensive positions. This opened up on the German Second Army with some 2000 guns at 4.20 a.m. on 8 August, largely silencing the German guns, and a creeping barrage kept the German defenders' heads down while the files of infantry and tanks moved forward in what was a thick, clinging morning mist.

It was a tribute to staff planning at army and corps that involved the covert move of the Canadian Corps from the Ypres Salient into position south of the Australian Corps.[82] The artillery fire plan, infantry-tank cooperation and aerial support were all closely coordinated and rehearsed. Monash believed that in a well-planned battle, 'nothing happens, nothing can happen, except the regular progress of the advance according to the plan arranged'. In broad terms Amiens fitted this description, but it is more than that; once again it was not simply a question of massive materiel and technical superiority against a demoralised enemy beaten by artillery fire that won the day, but rather the combined skills and careful coordination of the arms involved. On the left flank the 4th Australian Division had to react and compensate for the failure of Butler's III Corps to capture Chipilly Spur. Across its front the Australian advance outran its supporting fire, and even before the guns had redeployed forward overran the second objective, capturing German artillery before it could withdraw, taking large numbers of prisoners, principally by tanks and infantry working together to winkle out by fire and movement each centre of opposition.[83]

It was the same in the Canadian Corps' sector, with Brutinel's Canadian Independent Force of combined cavalry and Motor Machine Gun Battalions providing flank protection with the First French Army.

> The surprise was complete and overwhelming. The prisoners stated that they had no idea that an attack was impending, and captured documents did not indicate that any of our preparations had been detected. The noise of our Tanks going to the final position of assembly had been heard by some men and reported, but no deduction appears to have been made regarding this.[84]

This crushing victory totally changed the situation on the Western Front. It was convincing not just in terms of the ground gained but also in the 400 guns captured — 161 of them by the Canadians, 173 by the Australians — and the 27,000 casualties inflicted, 12,000 of whom were prisoners, at a cost of 9000 casualties.[85] It shattered Ludendorff's psyche and convinced him that the unthinkable was true, that this was a war that Germany could not win. 'August 8th was the black day of the German Army in this war … The 8th August put the decline of that fighting power beyond all doubt … The war must be ended.'[86]

An attack with limited tactical objectives was now translated into a bolder offensive, which, as on previous occasions, quickly ran out of steam in the subsequent days. Tank numbers decreased markedly as mechanical failure occurred, guns and ammunition had to be moved forward, and success exhausted the attacking infantry who still had to fight their way through determined pockets of skilful German machine guns contesting the advance. As we have seen in a previous chapter, it was at Currie's insistence that the Battle of Amiens was closed down on 11 August.

It was now that Haig translated local success into the series of dispersed hammer blows across the front of the British armies. Byng's Third Army attacked in the north on 21 August, with the Fourth Army involving the Australian Corps supporting it with attacks to the south on 23 August. Monash drove his corps on in a series of bold strokes that saw successive advances by each of his divisions, crowned by the capture of Mont St Quentin, north of Peronne, by the 2nd Australian Division on 31 August. Monash's handling of his corps in the series of attacks before Peronne shows a boldness and flexibility that, as Bean, Pedersen and Coates concur, shows Monash to be more than 'merely a composer of set pieces'.[87]

However, while in tactical terms Monash demonstrated a skill equal to Currie at corps level, there was increasing evidence during the Australian advance after 8 August that his unswerving determination to push on was having an impact on the fighting efficiency of his corps that he was not aware of, or chose to ignore. Lack of reinforcements had forced the disbandment of three infantry battalions in May. The cost of August also had its impact because the Australians had no reserves available. The gravity of the German March offensive had brought the 4th Division back into the line, and thoughts of using a 'depot division' were discarded. All five Australian divisions took an active part in the offensive, and by the end of August the 5th Brigade that captured Mont St Quentin was 1320 strong, an average of 330 a battalion. This was increasingly mirrored throughout the Australian divisions; depleted battalions were now reduced to three companies each with only two small platoons.[88] In contrast, Currie carefully assessed the staying power of his divisions, and while not afraid to commit them to hard fighting, ensured they had the strength to do the job.

Monash refused to face the implications of this decline in strength. As far as he was concerned it was nothing that a little rest would not cure. As he told Bean, 'Six days rest and a bath … restore the elasticity of a division and make it quite ready to fight again. The troops are not tired, [but] a little footsore.'[89] This reflects an increasingly tired corps commander who had not willingly visited his troops in the front line in his 18 months as a divisional commander in France and was now even more remote.

It is clear that, unlike Currie or Russell, Monash saw battalions as battalions regardless of their strength. As we have seen, Currie strongly believed that infantry battalions had

The guns moving forward during the Battle of Amiens. *(Royal Military Academy Sandhurst Collection)*

to be kept at full strength if they were to be effective, and that 'sending an under-strength unit into battle almost always resulted in greater losses than if that unit fought under the same conditions but at full strength'.[90] Monash did not; he believed that as long as a battalion had '30 Lewis guns it doesn't very much matter what else they have'.[91] However, the gradual attrition of under-strength battalions was as destructive in success as it was in failure. Indeed, failure would have seen Australian battalions pulled out of the line and rested; success meant that Monash asked them to do more again with less. Currie was prepared to drive under-strength battalions forward during battle to achieve a goal as ruthlessly as Monash, but he was aware that they were under-strength and knew that rest and reinforcement was essential before committing them again to battle; in contrast Monash just pushed on with an increasingly diminishing resource.

Both the Australian and the Canadian Corps were tasked with breaking the Hindenburg Line, which in 1918 had been converted into a defensive maze of wire and pillboxes some 6000 yards deep. In the Fourth Army, Monash's Australian Corps was given the major task of breaking in on 18 September and then breaking through on 26 September in what was a combined Australian/American Corps operation. Sadler's biography of Gellibrand indicates that Monash and his staff were out of touch both with the tactical situation and with the strength of the battalions, with Monash insisting the battalions were stronger than they were.[92] The men had reached breaking point, and to them winning was no longer enough if it destroyed the handful of infantry left in each battalion. This accounts for the mutiny and refusal to go into the attack in D Company of the 1st Battalion on 21 September, which Blair examines in detail in *Dinkum Diggers*.[93] Monash wanted more than his men could give, and commanders who told him that, such as Gellibrand before the Hindenburg Line, were ignored. Indeed, the breaking of the Hindenburg Line was a British success shared between the now-exhausted Australian Corps and the two British corps on each flank. It showed that despite the Australians' impressive achievements the torch had now passed to British divisions to carry on the offensive, which the Australian Corps was now incapable of doing.

By the end of September the Australian Corps was a spent force verging on total collapse. The 5th Division's historian describes it as 'utterly worn out', with its brigade fighting strength down to 1926 in the 8th Brigade, 1584 in the 15th Brigade and 1131 in the 14th Brigade.[94] W.H. Downing wrote of the 'tragic weakness of all our battalions', which were so reduced in strength that on 1 October his 57th Battalion went forward in two lines of skirmishers and on hitting the main German defences, 'for the third time in three days we were caught in the German barrage, for the third time caught in unsubdued machine-gun fire. By now there were so few of us left that a further advance was out of the question.'[95]

Monash's insistence that Montebehain be taken by the 2nd Division on 5 October 1918, which became the last act of the Australian Corps in battle, seems to have been driven by a determination to have another trophy on the wall, rather than any thought

Breaking the Hindenburg Line: prisoners assemble among the reserve wave of the Australian Corps as they prepare to move forward with the tanks near Bellicourt on 29 September 1918. *(Royal Military Academy Sandhurst Collection)*

for the state of the division itself or for any tactical implications. It was a brilliant tactical feat by the 6th Brigade, but it cost the 2nd Division some 30 officers and 400 men, including some of the best they had. Bean's vivid account finishes with a sober assessment of its worth: 'Yet — as with many local attacks — it is difficult to feel that it was wisely undertaken; it seemed, rather, devised to make some use of troops before withdrawing them in accordance with the Prime Minister's demand.'[96]

On 5 October 1918 the Australian Corps was withdrawn from the line at the insistence of William Morris Hughes, the Australian Prime Minister. Hughes took a measure of the state of the Australian Corps from his soundings of soldiers on leave.[97] He believed that the corps' survival as an effective force depended on their being adequately rested, and told Monash that he would sack him if the corps was not withdrawn.[98]

Gammage quotes from H.R. Williams in painting this picture of the battalions:

> … battle-worn and weary. Their faces were drawn and pallid, their eyes had the fixed stare common in men who had endured heavy bombardments, and they had the jerky mannerisms of human beings whose nervous systems had been shocked to an alarming degree. So tired, so dead beat were they that many of them, when opportunity offered, slept the heavy drugged sleep of utter exhaustion for twenty-four hours on end. Their faded earth-stained uniforms hung loosely from bodies which had lost as much as two stone in as many months. Sheer determination and wonderful esprit de corps had enabled these gallant fellows to work … when physically they were done.[99]

Monash was one of the outstanding corps commanders on the Western Front, but his limitations as a commander were also evident in these final battles. The entry in *The Oxford Companion to Australian Military History* is critical but fair:

> The most controversial aspect of the campaign was Monash's conduct of operations after Amiens and before the attack on the Hindenburg Line. Since Amiens, casualties had mounted. Most divisions were well under-strength and in need of rest. Rawlinson was quite prepared in these circumstances to slacken the offensive. Monash ignored him. With Haig-like tenacity he relentlessly drove the Australian Corps forward against an enemy that he rightly judged was losing even defensive capability. Monash might have judged the enemy correctly but in some cases he drove his own men beyond endurance.[100]

Monash had the 'determination and ruthlessness to obtain the maximum effort from his troops'. This is an essential strength provided the commander knows what their breaking point is. I suspect that by 1918 Monash had lost sight of that, and in doing so he destroyed the instrument that had given him his victories — the Australian Corps.[101] Because of this I rate him below Currie, ranking second of the two outstanding corps commanders in the British armies in France.

In 1918 the Australian Corps was tactically proficient and well led by its officers, most of whom had been commissioned from the ranks. It was comprised totally of volunteers, but this in itself gave no special military distinction. Indeed, one could argue that this was a critical weakness, in that at the time of its greatest efforts and greatest achievement, when the need for reinforcements was at its height, Australia could not meet its promise and sustain its men at the front.

It was an enormous effort to enlist 416,809 men out of a population of five million, but this achievement was done unthinkingly and in the end too much was asked of the soldiers. An example of this was when wounded men who should have been returned to Australia after convalescence were through necessity sent back to under-strength units at the front. Australia had the highest casualty rate in the Empire in proportion to numbers of soldiers at the front, and only New Zealand had a higher casualty rate in proportion to population.

The symptoms of the strain on the troops were seen in the soaring disciplinary and sickness rates that were typical of every Australian unit in 1918. Today this ill discipline is seen as an illustration of those egalitarian larrikins who were irrepressible out of the line and fearless in battle, but as I have argued it is more an indication of the destruction of a superb fighting machine that had overcome the inevitable weaknesses of a citizen army to forge itself into a professional force. When the war began the larrikin battalions were indicative of inexperienced command and ill-trained troops as the AIF grew from one to five divisions, plus all the associated units connected with sustaining a corps in the field. That changed as commanding officers learnt their trade. Review the divisional, brigade and battalion commanders of 1917 and 1918 and you will see citizen soldiers who understood their men, but were prepared to drive them when they needed to be driven.[102] They were commanders who knew you had to forge an instrument that was harder and more proficient than the opposition. Whatever else they were in terms of character and idiosyncrasy they were invariably regarded as 'strict disciplinarians'. Nothing else works in any army.

The exhaustion of late 1917 and 1918 saw a resurgence of larrikinism that today is indelibly associated with the AIF. It is paraded with unthinking pride as characteristic of the unique egalitarianism of the Australian soldier. This is myth, not a reflection of the true nature of the force. Rather, it is more a sad illustration of what overuse, lack of trained reinforcements, and a corps commander who had lost touch can do to an outstanding corps.

ELEVEN

THE 'DIGGERS' IN 1918

The Australian Corps was formed on 1 January 1918 and the New Zealand Division became part of Lieutenant-General Sir Alexander Godley's XXII British Corps and wintered in the Ypres Salient.[1] The defeat before Passchendaele on 12 October 1917 had shaken the division's confidence in itself, which the salient did little to restore. Major-General Sir Andrew Russell worked to build his division back to health, both in numbers and morale. In 1917 the division had four infantry brigades each of four battalions. In early 1918 British divisions were reduced in strength from 12 to nine infantry battalions, and on 7 February the 4th New Zealand Infantry Brigade was also disbanded.[2] Contrary to Russell's wishes, it was formed into an entrenching group of three so-called entrenching battalions, to be used as a corps and divisional labour force until its numbers were absorbed into the division.[3] Russell was unhappy with this as his experience with his brigades doing navvy work led him to believe that both 'discipline and efficiency have suffered considerably', and 'how much more so will it be the case in the Labour Group'.[4] However, while he was unhappy with their employment, Russell valued the experienced officers, NCOs and soldiers that were available to him as reinforcements.

The New Zealanders, like the divisions of the Canadian Corps, retained 12 battalions in the division in 1918. This was possible because of the effectiveness of the New Zealand reinforcement system. By late 1917 conscription was the norm. Intakes were called up each month and received basic and corps training in New Zealand. Soldiers who did not meet the standard were put back to the next intake, while those who showed the benefits of previous Territorial training were advanced. They were shipped as reinforcements to England and went through the training cycles at Sling and in the various corps schools before going as a draft to France. At the New Zealand Infantry and General Depot at Etaples they went through a further cycle of training before being called forward to the Divisional Reinforcement Unit. Reinforcements could spend six to ten months in training before they reached their units in the front line. By that time they knew the vagaries of the military system, had fired the musketry course at least three times, and were familiar with the rifle and bayonet, grenade and Lewis gun. In many ways they were far better trained in the use of their weapons and equipment than their Second World War counterparts.[5]

The standard of reinforcements was rigorously monitored and reported on as they progressed through the system. While this may have been over-insurance it was to good effect. By 1918 the New Zealand Government was determined to resist any increased commitment of personnel to the war effort; its priority was to keep its existing forces in the field fully manned. This comprised a Mounted Rifles Brigade in Palestine, the New Zealand Division in France, together with additional corps units including an artillery brigade, a tunnelling company, a cyclist battalion and a squadron of the Otago Mounted Rifles. New Zealand calculated that it could sustain these forces until late 1920. At the beginning of 1918 the New Zealand Expeditionary Force had 7000 reinforcements in Great Britain. Reinforcement rates were increased in March to meet the expected casualty bill of the German offensive, and by October 1918 the New Zealand depots in Great Britain and France reached 15,000.[6] The Canadian Corps of four divisions in France was considered to be fortunate to have 10,000 reinforcements to draw upon in August 1918, while the Australian Corps of five divisions faced a manpower shortage.[7]

The guarantee of trained reinforcements was of enormous importance to the operational efficiency of the New Zealand Division. For most of 1918 reinforcements were drawn from the entrenching group and:

> … comprised a large percentage of men who had previous military service in the field. They were of the utmost value, and among them were a large number of NCOs who readily filled the places of those who had become casualties. The small proportion of new men received were well trained and quite up to the standard of previous reinforcements.[8]

By October when the entrenching group's strength had been exhausted, reinforcements were still classified as being well-trained but 'there are fewer prospective NCOs although a small percentage are bright men of good morale, a large percentage are dull and slow'.[9] Nevertheless, the division was able to retain its relative edge because the calibre of the British and German armies was far worse. Russell noted:

> There is not much to choose between the two Armies; both being, I take it, pretty bad. It could not well be otherwise when you think of the combings

out on both sides which have been stuffed into the ranks of the opposing Armies to fill them out and give them at any rate a semblance of military strength.[10]

The strain of war was telling both on Russell and on his division. Russell suffered from increasingly protracted bouts of sickness each winter. His unit inspections confirmed the price his division paid in front of Passchendaele during the Third Battle of Ypres. The 3rd (Rifle) Brigade was 'a sorry sight … wants looking after'.[11] Everywhere he looked he saw an organisation that had been pushed to the limit and was breaking down. He was also concerned about the 2nd Infantry Brigade, which was as exhausted as its brigade commander, Brigadier-General W.G. Braithwaite, who 'is not well'[12] and whose brigade was 'temporarily a bit out of gear'.[13] This was reflected both in the standard of the units in the front line, where Russell was 'disappointed with the general trench discipline', and also in the training schools behind the line.[14] 'Visited 2 Infy Bde training school … it is not well organised, and the instructors [are] past [it]'.[15] Russell was equally concerned about the standard of reinforcement training conducted in the reserve battalions at Sling Camp in the United Kingdom: 'interior economy and discipline weak … it only requires good and careful inspection and good battn. and coy comdrs'.[16] He recognised that officers

Russell inspecting a platoon in 2nd NZ Infantry Brigade with Brigadier-General R. Young watching on the far left. Russell insisted that each platoon commander know the name of every man in his platoon and that every item of kit laid down be in each man's pack and equipment. (*National Army Museum, Waiouru Collection*)

exhausted from their experiences in France, his 'empties' as he termed them, were not the right men to ensure reinforcements reached the standards needed. Russell had hoped to escape Flanders' mud and take his division to Italy with Plumer in late 1917.[17] Despite the experiences before Passchendaele this was an indication of the trust Russell retained in Plumer and Harington, Plumer's MGGS, both of whom had been a strong influence on the professional development of the division during 1917. This did not happen, however, and in 1918 Russell's goal was to restore his division to operational efficiency with his characteristic attention to the care and welfare of the men, training and sound administration.

Tactical efficiency was built upon the calibre of the officers and NCOs. By 1918 these were almost exclusively drawn from men with trench experience. All of the original New Zealand brigade commanders had gone. Brigadiers-General Brown and Johnston were killed in 1917, Braithwaite's health broke down and he was returned to England unfit for active service, while Fulton, the last of the originals, was killed in March 1918.[18] By April 1918 the brigade commanders were Hart and Young, who had been majors in the Territorials on the outbreak of war, and Melvill, who had been a captain in the New Zealand Staff Corps on his first posting to the NZEF in November 1915.[19] The attrition rate for commanding officers was equally high, and it was the generation of subalterns and, in some cases, sergeants, of 1914 who were the battalion commanders of 1918. These were men like Hugh Stewart of the Canterbury Battalion and Leonard Jardine of the New Zealand Rifle Brigade, both of whom had been platoon commanders on Gallipoli and whose priorities were set by four years of combat.[20] A newly arrived young officer wrote of Jardine in 1918 that he was 'not overly fussy about unimportant details, though he is a stickler for having arms and ammunition kept clean'.[21]

Russell constantly monitored officer efficiency and rested or removed those commanders who could no longer cope with the strain of war. He demanded the same of his commanding officers in their monitoring of subordinates. 'To put it bluntly, there is a job to be done. Either a man can and will do it, or he must be got rid of.'[22] The division had enough satisfactory commanding officers with replacements always coming through, but efficient staff officers were far more difficult to find. Russell saw an effective staff as the key to an efficient division, and believed that the requirements of the division outweighed the need to allow the person in the appointment to move on once he had completed a tour. 'I made a mistake, I think, now two years old, in recommending Melvill for a command instead of keeping him for staff work. On the other hand he has turned out a very good Battalion and Brigade Commander.'[23] In the same way, while Russell preferred to find New Zealanders to fill the key staff appointments, he insisted that the best man get the job and that some positions had to

Training for war: The excellence of the New Zealand Division was founded on its preparation and training for each campaign. Here a New Zealand brigade carries out rehearsals in May 1917 that would be repeated before each major operation until the end of the war. *(G-12750-1/2, Henry Armitage Sanders, NZ Offi cial Photographer, Alexander Turnbull Library, Wellington, NZ)*

be filled by experienced and highly capable British staff officers. It was for this reason that while most of the appointments were filled by members of the NZSC, the primary staff appointment of GSO1 of the division (essentially the principal operations officer responsible for the coordination and dissemination of divisional planning and overseeing its effective execution) remained one that was filled by a British Regular officer. During 1918 this post was filled by Lieutenant-Colonel H.M. Wilson DSO, later Field Marshal 'Jumbo' Wilson.[24]

All staff officers in the New Zealand Division had to have served in the trenches. As a guide Russell stipulated:

> ... that they should have been with a unit in the field for not less than three months, that they should follow this by a period of attachment to a Brigade or a Divisional Staff and then go to a recognised Staff Course where their duties would be properly taught. Then, if they obtain a good report on all three occasions, they should be considered eligible for staff appointments.[25]

Russell's philosophy of command was built around anticipatory planning, thorough training and careful administration. The German offensive had been expected, and Haig's General Headquarters had sent out anticipatory instructions and training notes through the five armies to all corps and divisions. The inevitable inertia in time out of the line, particularly as there was an emphasis on defensive preparations based on the German philosophy of defence in depth, meant that in many divisions little effective training was done. Change parades, close order drill and corps working parties ate up much of the available time. As we have seen, this was not the case in either the Canadian or the Australian Corps, and it was not the case in the New Zealand Division. It came out of the line on the Ypres Salient in late February 1918 and met its quota of corps' labour tasks in preparing the defensive lines, but Russell insisted that it be fit to fight. Out of the line he instituted a programme that was a mix of open warfare training, inspections and sports, which was designed to absorb reinforcements into the division and to build up fitness.[26] It followed the pattern of training laid down in Army instructions and paralleled in detail that described by Rawling in his study of the Canadian Corps.[27]

A series of tactical exercises were conducted for commanders at all levels from brigade commander down, based on the anticipated scenario presented by a major German offensive. This forecast a situation where 'in the case of a breakthrough on either side that the Division might be hurried into action at short notice, and events might move so rapidly that quick decisions, followed by prompt action would be necessary'. Russell believed it was necessary to shake off the mental and physical cobwebs engendered by the more deliberate fashion of the past two years of trench warfare and, 'if we have learnt to do things quickly, we shall be able, all the better, to deal with them [than] in the more deliberate fashion with which we have become familiar during the last two years.'[28]

Emphasis was on physical training, bayonet fighting, range work and live firing platoon and company attacks 'embracing principles of mutual support and the use of rifle, Lewis Gun and Rifle Grenades'. Platoon commanders were given tactical problems at their level, such as, 'Taking over a section of a position where the situation is obscure and garrisoned by a mixture of many Units in a disorganised condition.' The aim was to develop 'initiative and power of leadership of the Platoon and Section Leaders, especially as regards use of ground, control and direction of fire and quick decision in dealing with situations', and to instil in everyone in the division 'the marked superiority of the New Zealand soldier over the enemy in any kind of fighting'.[29]

In March 1918 the division was at full strength and trained in open warfare tactics. This paid immediate dividends when the New Zealanders were committed to the Somme. On 20 March word was received that the German offensive had started against the British Third and Fifth Armies. The New Zealand Division was placed in General

Russell ensured that the training and rehearsals were as close as possible to the real thing and, as this photo shows, it looks and feels realistic. *(G-12752-1/2, Henry Armitage Sanders, NZ Official Photographer, Alexander Turnbull Library, Wellington, NZ)*

Headquarters' Reserve and was to be prepared to move at any hour after midnight on 22/23 March.[30] It moved on 23 March, and was ordered to close the gap between IV and V British Corps east of Amiens.[31] Russell wrote:

> The Division came in on the nick of time. There was a big gap, and by dint of hard marching we managed to fill it just in time. We had been despatched to a different destination. The railway communications were upset by a damaged bridge and the motor lorry service broke down, as one would expect, just when it was not convenient. After spending the night in getting from one headquarters to another, making plans, getting out orders, etc, I remarked to the GSO1 that I was not sure that we were not in for a catastrophe. However it turned out otherwise, and a miss is as good as a mile.[32]

Packs and blankets were left behind and each man was issued with 220 rounds and as much Lewis and Vickers machine-gun ammunition as the teams could carry. The New Zealanders went into line with ad hoc brigades between Colincamps and Mailly-Maillet.[33] The Hebuterne-Serre ridge was seized and held against a series of German attacks on 27–28 March, and the division consolidated and strengthened the line in the last days of the month. It was a successful operation in a situation that demanded initiative at platoon and company level, but it was not to Russell's satisfaction. He told his subordinate commanders about this in no uncertain terms, and it is worth quoting him in detail for the insight it gives into perhaps the most outstanding divisional commander in the British armies on the Western Front.

> The results obtained on Monday and Tuesday I look on as extraordinarily disappointing … Briefly I am of the opinion that we are altogether too slow in thought and movement. The failure to get forward on schedule time on Monday morning has led, in my opinion, to the failure to establish ourselves at Serre northwards to Hebuterne. This failure has already cost us a good many lives and casualties.
>
> A Battalion marches through the night and arrives comparatively tired at dawn. It gets orders to march again within a very short time. It gets what food and sleep it can — none at all if the case is, in my opinion, so urgent as to make it necessary to forego them.
>
> I put it to you in this way — that if we are justified in expending men's lives in putting them over the top in regulation fashion, we are still better justified in saving their lives at the expense of 20 per cent of our men falling by the wayside through extreme exhaustion. These latter will recover; those who are killed are lost.
>
> I shall make my plans on the assumption that troops will move forward at the exact time given them on starting, irrespective of hot meals or otherwise, irrespective of rest or weariness. I believe that you, all of you, have sufficient confidence in me to believe that I shall not ask exertions on the part of the troops which are unnecessary or beyond their physical endurance, but I must have it clearly understood — for the safety of us all — that punctuality in movement is observed … We must learn to think quickly and act boldly.
>
> I remember when I first took over the Division that General Johnston complained that I wanted to treat Infantry as if they were Mounted Rifles. I accept the criticism. I certainly do expect New Zealand Infantry, both in thought and action, to be at least 50 per cent quicker than the New Armies.[34]

This is classic Russell, a man not happy with second best, despite the confusion and the ad hoc nature of the groupings, but always wanting something better from his men and knowing they had the capacity to give it. It was this standard of performance that was his goal for the division throughout 1918. It was on the defensive from April to August, defeating a series of German attacks and then in turn mounting a series of raids. This was the so-called 'peaceful penetration' that Bean details in the Australian official histories.[35] For both the Australians and the New Zealanders it was anything but peaceful, nor for the Germans in the trench lines opposite. 'We get no sleep at nights and are on sentry for six to eight hours on end. You have to look out like a watch-dog here. Otherwise Tommy comes over and snatches you out of your trench.'[36]

During this period each New Zealand infantry battalion took turns at being relieved to spend a period in combined arms training behind the line, working with field artillery batteries practising attacks while the battery leapfrogged troop by troop to give support. Most of June was spent in corps reserve with tactical training and range practices in the mornings and sports in the afternoons.[37] This coincided with the first wave of the influenza epidemic that affected large numbers of troops: 'although severe for a few days, [it] left the men fit for duty again in 7 to 10 days time, and the large majority of cases were retained with their units'.[38] The epidemic had a similar impact in the German armies.[39]

The New Zealanders had little to do in the early days of the August offensive during the Battle of Amiens, which saw the initiative swing decisively towards the Allies. As part of IV Corps in Byng's Third Army the New Zealanders maintained contact as the Germans carefully withdrew opposite them. The division was first committed to

'The Division came in the nick of time. There was a big gap, and by dint of hard marching we managed to fill it just in time.' The New Zealand Division on trek to the Somme in August 1916, scenes that would be repeated in March 1918. (*Wilson and Horton Collection*)

the offensive on 21 August during the Battle of Albert, with the IV Corps' advance on Bapaume.[40] A pattern was established in the corps that saw under-strength British divisions committed to each initial set-piece attack, and once this stalled or reached the limits of artillery support the much stronger New Zealand Division was able to maintain the offensive and exploit success. Brigadier-General Herbert Hart commanded the 3rd New Zealand (Rifle) Brigade.

> The weather is fine and for once is kind towards us. The battle is entirely different to all earlier battles in France. Troops are not so densely packed, there is greater scope for initiative and leadership. Advances are deeper and on much wider frontages. Roads are good, the country is not blasted with shell craters, one can ridge across country anywhere and owing to the rolling billow nature of the spurs, horses and wagons go up within a mile of the battle line.[41]

In the attacks before Bapaume in late August the New Zealanders were inevitably ahead of flanking divisions. Russell and his reserve brigade commander would move each day to the forward brigade headquarters, 'keeping in touch with the situation and reconnoitring'.[42] Russell gave his brigadiers free rein and anticipated the support they needed to keep going, as well as continually urging the corps to keep the divisions on the flanks moving forward. Professionalism and a sense of well-practised drills was evident in every aspect of the advance, and the divisional orders detailing operations were down to two pages and a map overlay.

It was good country for movement against an enemy that could now be winkled out machine-gun post by machine-gun post and destroyed. The New Zealanders advanced, bypassing villages and strong points to be mopped up by those who followed, in accordance with Russell's strictures that 'villages are only obstacles — not ends in themselves'.[43] Bapaume was treated in this way and bypassed. Hart's 3rd New Zealand (Rifle) Brigade advanced with three of its four battalions in line and flank guards posted. Machine-gun platoons of the New Zealand Machine Gun Battalion, trench mortar batteries and batteries of field artillery kept close up behind each advancing battalion, ready to bring down fire on any counterattacks as well as providing support to each battalion attack. In this way the brigades leapfrogged forward, each close in numbers to the bayonet strength of some depleted British divisions. Russell's headquarters moved forward to occupy the vacated forward brigade headquarters once it moved.

The New Zealanders were skilled in the use of darkness and generally attacked

Whippet tanks of the 3rd Battalion at Mailly-Maillet, 26 March 1918; Tank A279 nearest camera. Some of these tanks were in action earlier that day and were the first of this make to be in action. Marching by them on the way through the town are 'diggers' of the 1st Canterbury Battalion hurrying to reinforce the 1st Battalion NZ Rifle Brigade, who are already in action, closing a critical gap in the line. *(Q.9821 Imperial War Museum, London)*

two hours before first light so as to defeat German counterattacks in daylight. On 9 September Hart's 3rd New Zealand (Rifle) Brigade 'attacked with 2nd Battalion at 4 a.m. in pitch darkness. Our objective was part of Trescault Spur ... The attack was a complete success owing to the surprise.' In Hart's assessment, had 'it not been dark it would have been impossible to have taken it this way', but it was and as predicted the Germans counterattacked in daylight 'but were beaten off'.[44]

By mid-September Haig's armies had punched their way forward to the Hindenburg Line. The evolution of infantry platoon tactics matched with superb artillery support meant the German defences were no longer the obstacles they would have been in 1916 or 1917. On 12 September the New Zealand Division attacked as part of Byng's Third Army in the Battle of Havrincourt.[45] Hart's was the leading brigade.

> We attacked on a three thousand yard frontage with three battalions in line, each only two-thirds normal strength. The attack commenced very well and we took our first objectives easily ... The enemy stoutly opposed our advance to the second or support trench. Some places we got in and some places we did not. Heavy fighting continued all day and until long after dark.

A section post of the 2nd Canterbury Battalion sheltering near the derelict tank, Jumping Jenny, in front of Rossignol Wood near Gommecourt on 25 July 1918. The nearest man at right is loading ammunition into a Lewis gun drum-magazine. The entrance to a dugout can be seen on the left. *(G-13484-1/2, Henry Armitage Sanders, NZ Offical Photographer, Alexander Turnbull Library, Wellington, NZ)*

> At intervals we turned on artillery and trench mortars to clear up enemy points of resistance, bombing parties and Lewis gunners were constantly engaged in close combat — he counter-attacked and we re-attacked, and so the battle line swayed to and fro all day. There was more close fighting of this kind than our Division has experienced since Gallipoli.[46]

One can read into this account the story of a professional brigade doing a job that it has learnt to do very well — able and continuing to fight after the opposition stiffens, calling up support from its mortars and artillery to subdue strong points and then using its infantry skills to fight on through. It is by now a citizen force that is indistinguishable from a Regular formation, skilled and professional at every level. Despite strong defences and determined resistance, it was something the Germans could no longer match and defeat, as Hart noted in his diary.

> Prisoners came forward steadily until the total reached 502 ... the trenches were crowded with enemy dead, a careful estimate put the numbers at 250 to

300. Our casualties were only 269 of which one half will return to the Field later, the results being that at least five enemy were put permanently out of action to every one of ours, quite apart from the casualties they must have suffered from shell fire.[47]

In these battles the calibre of the German opposition was high.

The enemy has been retiring, but retiring deliberately in good order with his rearguards offering fight on selected positions, carefully chosen to give the greatest scope to well placed Machine Guns supported by Field guns. He has fought cleverly and has always had another independently organised screen ready when the first has been broken through.[48]

The assessment of divisional intelligence was that the German 113th Division was 'probably as good and as determined a Division as any we have yet encountered on this front'.[49] The Jaeger Division, which was the enemy the New Zealanders faced on 12 September, was classed as a 'good assault division' but suffered because 'company strength is not high and averages 60 men'.[50] It was declining numbers that broke down German resistance.[51]

The best units had been siphoned off to become storm-trooper formations in the March offensive where they were used to destruction. This inevitably impacted on the average standard of the remaining divisions, which now bore the brunt of the Allied offensive. The best and most experienced soldiers were placed in the rearguard machine-gun detachments to cover the withdrawal, and these rarely escaped death or capture. This meant that as the numbers declined, soldiers who previously would never have been considered for this role now became machine gunners, less skilled and less determined. The careful matrix that was central to German defensive strength was being eaten away by the tactical skills of their opponent. If any proof is needed that the German armies were being beaten in the field in 1918 then a study of the New Zealand advance as a microcosm of British Army and Allied success offers that proof.

This success was bought at cost. In the New Zealand Division it was the section commanders, platoon sergeants and platoon commanders who featured in the casualty lists because it was these junior commanders who had to take the initiative when things bogged down. The New Zealand Division could make good these losses, but few other divisions, on either side, had that luxury.

On 12 September the New Zealand Division carried the brunt of the attack in IV Corps. Russell noted that the 38th (Welsh) Division on the right flank 'did nothing which hampers matters'.[52] Increasingly the New Zealand losses were caused by a failure by flanking divisions to keep pace with the New Zealanders' progress. This was a reflection on divisional strengths, the quality of reinforcements and the inevitable impact this had on the standards of tactical training. A common tactical doctrine was in place, but numbers on the ground dictated how effectively British divisions could employ it. By September most British divisions, other than the Guards, were down to 7000–8000 men. This was also true for the Australian Corps. In contrast the Canadians averaged 10,000 and the New Zealand Division numbered 12,243 with replacements at hand.[53] It was a factor Russell was very conscious of, and was determined to use carefully but to best effect. He assessed the situation and described the state of the division to Allen, his Minister of Defence:

> The fact is, so far as I can judge, the war is now going to be determined in the first place by the weight of numbers and in the second by morale and staying power. If I am right, we hold both the trump cards. I have no hesitation in saying the men of this Division are as fit and eager as in the past, and they really have done extraordinarily well during the last month, which has given, I think, scope for their innate qualities such as they have not had before. Operating on a comparatively small front, with only one brigade in line, the work has been carried out almost entirely by Brigadiers and Commanding Officers; the Divisional Staff having very little to do beyond helping and advising from a safe distance in rear. All three Brigadiers and their subordinates have shown plenty of go and initiative, and I am happy and proud to think that this Division is anything but a one-man show. There is no one but, if he was lost tomorrow, could not be suitably replaced at a moment's notice. In this lies a good deal of our strength.[54]

It was in this letter that Russell confessed to increased tiredness and a belief that it was time for a change. He and Godley had discussed the prospect of his taking over command of NZEF. Haig had offered Russell command of a British corps in July, but at that time he had turned it down. Now, in September, regardless of whether a second offer eventuated, he wrote to Allen:

> I have quite made up my mind that it is time for the benefit of the Division and whoever succeeds me, and myself that there should be a change in

command. I have now held the position for three years during which time I have been remarkably well served by all the commanders and my Staff. The men have always played their part faithfully and honestly. I cannot say too much for their fighting qualities. Consequently it is not astonishing that the Division has earned a pretty good reputation, though I say it myself. At the same time I have noticed in almost every line of life that a change is sometimes good.[55]

It was not to be. Events progressed too quickly to effect any change in command, and Russell remained with his division until the Armistice.

On 14 September the New Zealand Division was relieved and pulled back to Bapaume to regroup. Russell told Melvill, who was in the lead with his 1st New Zealand Infantry Brigade, 'to do nothing, but get out with as few casualties as possible'.[56]

In the break brigade commanders 'met one man or NCO from every section which took part in the last battle, and by cross examination, learnt first hand their experiences and views upon all matters they did and saw in action'.[57] These views were shared at a divisional conference chaired by Russell, which was attended by a cross-section of NCO section commanders, and the lessons from the discussions were disseminated.[58]

Each brigade submitted its lessons learnt. The New Zealand Division had brigade strengths that equated to the total infantry strength available in the British divisions on each flank. Russell's tactic was to advance with one brigade as advance guard, one following behind in support and ready to leapfrog through and take over the advance, with the third in reserve. The depth of advances that formations were exploiting now far exceeded the range of field artillery positioned to fire the covering barrage for the set-piece attack.

Artillery was still critical to success and it had to be as far forward as possible with the leading infantry advance guard:

> ... where the utility of having a section of 18-pounders was proved again and again. They were especially useful in putting isolated machine gun posts out of action ... Machine guns in depth can hold up any attack unsupported by Artillery. When the attack is held up it is far better to await artillery support than to go forward with the certainty of getting heavy casualties and probably not gaining the objective.[59]

The creeping barrage was no longer central to artillery tactics in open warfare. To guarantee support the tendency had become to group artillery under the command of the leading infantry brigadier. It was found that grouping a field artillery brigade with the leading infantry brigade was sound, but attempting to group any more simply overloaded both the artillery brigade commander and the infantry brigadier, as brigades lacked the communications necessary to link with the heavy artillery and with flanking formations.

It was decided that the most effective system was to keep artillery brigades under divisional control and move them forward in bounds to reconnoitred positions so that they could go into action as soon as strong opposition was met. Johnston, the New Zealand CRA, also noted that it was necessary for divisional artillery to train as an entity. Until now artillery had tended to stay on in the line when infantry were relieved for training, with no more than one artillery brigade being relieved from the line at any point. But as Johnston argued, after 'months of trench warfare Artillery cannot reasonably be expected to break into open warfare and develop the full use of their weapons without previous training in all the necessary adjuncts to a war of movement'.[60] He recommended that divisional artillery training be carried out in the coming winter months, anticipating at this stage an offensive that would continue into 1919.

All this was thrashed out in discussions while around them the division gathered breath. The rule was to keep it simple. Infantry brigadiers were reminded to bring in their artillery group commanders at the start of their planning, not once it was finished, so that fire could be properly coordinated and details worked out in time. It was also evident that for a quick attack 'the simpler the Barrage the better', and concentrations of fire on likely strong points, with batteries leapfrogging forward to give covering fire, were more effective than the delay imposed by the time required to arrange a creeping barrage.[61]

Adapting the role of the NZ Machine Gun Battalion to mobile warfare presented similar problems with communications difficulties and questions of coordination. Lieutenant-Colonel D.B. Blair argued against the easy system of delegating control to the infantry brigades and instead argued that it should be his job as commanding officer, who 'should be the most active fighting commander in the Division: his work should be well forward with the Brigade Commander where he can establish continuity of action between his companies'.[62]

During the break, reinforcements were absorbed and training conducted. This involved each rifle platoon and company carrying out 'one tactical exercise' for four hours each morning and one hour's sport in the afternoon.[63] Russell inspected all his units during the break and critiqued the exercises. On 24 September he assessed an attack exercise on Hart's 3rd New Zealand (Rifle) Brigade; it was obvious the attack formations came under scrutiny, with Russell's cryptic diary noting, 'Usual discussion re "worm" formation — I am gradually hardening in favour of them. A successful show.'[64] Russell inspected all 12 of his infantry battalions and was highly critical of the state of two of Hart's battalions. Nothing was left to chance, as Hart noted of Russell's inspection: 'Much scrutiny of scabbards, rifle swivels, packs, etc, seeking for rust, shortages or other signs of carelessness or neglect.'[65] Nevertheless, Russell was pleased with the standard of the division. 'Men wonderfully fit and cheery — the turnout far ahead of what one [could] have got 2 years ago.'[66]

In the opening attack of the Battle of the Canal du Nord on 27 September the New Zealand Division was in IV Corps reserve, ready to be sent forward to exploit initial success. On 29 September the 1st and 2nd Brigades attacked the Hindenburg Line and in moonlight advanced 5000–6000 yards through a barrier of wire and trenches. 'Our casualties, 200; prisoners taken, 1450.'[67] Hundreds of machine guns and about 44 artillery pieces were also captured. On 2 October a bridgehead was gained across the St Quentin Canal at Crevecour with 500 casualties to the 1st NZ Brigade, 350 of these being in the 1st Auckland Battalion.[68] These were heavy losses but the New Zealanders were again leading the divisions on either flank, and as Russell noted it was the failure of the flanking division that led to little gain with heavy loss. This was a fact of life, however, and it was 'useless to depend on British Divisions — they may succeed or they may not'.[69]

On 8 October the Battle of Cambrai started at 4.30 a.m.[70] In the New Zealand Division, Hart's 3rd (Rifle) Brigade:

> ... attacked on a three thousand yard frontage, three battalions [each] functioning on a frontage of 1000 yards. We advanced a distance of 4500, the longest distance we have ever made behind a barrage. The 4th Battalion had to capture Lesdain — a task it completed by 7 o'clock having killed 60 Huns and taken an additional 244 prisoner. The 2nd Brigade then passed through them to take the village of Esnes so the 4th Battalion was able to withdraw across the canal out of the battle entirely, wash, shave and take breakfast in peace and comfort. After lunch their Band came up and rendered a programme in the open.[71]

It was a superb set-piece attack, which then saw the battalions withdrawn to freshen up to a background of band music, while ahead of them the battle continued.

A German tank counterattack was defeated by supporting British tanks and at midday aircraft reported large bodies of enemy approaching from the northeast.

> At 4 p.m. the Hun attacked the 9th Brigade [2nd British Division] on our
> left in full view of our MGs and 18-pdrs as we had pushed on rather ahead
> of that Brigade. Everything we had was turned onto the Hun and in ten
> minutes not one live Hun could be seen.[72]

The day's fighting showed how sophisticated the war had become, with tanks supporting
infantry to defeat an extremely rare German tank attack, and RAF aircraft giving early
warning of a German infantry counterattack on a flanking brigade, which is then broken
up by New Zealand machine guns and supporting artillery. It is a level of cooperation
and coordination between different arms that was increasingly the norm throughout the
British armies in France. It would not be seen again to this degree in a British army until
the closing stages of the Second World War. What was succeeding now was less the fixed
template of the set-piece attack than the skilled coordination of infantry and supporting
artillery that were capitalising on a weakened and disorganised enemy with increased
boldness and initiative in their tactical conduct within brigades and battalions.

Russell was critical of what the British armies were not doing right. There was a
tendency to want to capture each town in turn, almost as a trophy to be hung on the
wall. Lieutenant-General Sir John Monash was as guilty of this as any British corps
commander, while Russell believed they were obstacles to be bypassed and encircled.
He was also critical of the unwillingness of British divisions to attack by night, 'though
the advantages are obvious and great in reducing casualties'.[73] He complained of the
lack of anticipatory planning in Lieutenant-General 'Uncle' Harper's IV Corps: 'After
shilly-shallying all day, word came finally that we attack again tomorrow morning at
5.20 a.m. — and this after a Corps conference at which it was stated that it would be 24
hours later — the Higher Command is oblivious of the difficulties of the lower ranks.'[74]
Russell's was the cry of an increasingly tired front-line commander.

Despite the short notice this attack was successful, and it broke through the last of
the Hindenburg defences into the green fields beyond, open country untouched by
war. The Germans withdrew stubbornly, demolishing roads and railways and leaving
plenty of booby traps to entice and wound the unwary. There was increasing evidence
of declining morale and transport difficulties in the German ranks. 'Everywhere along
the road one comes across horses killed by harassing fire and bombs and there are many
signs that the Hun eats all eatable parts of the horses.'[75]

The New Zealand Division was pulled out to regroup on 12 October. Russell's preoccupations were training, reinforcements, and the divisional farms that he had organised to provide fresh vegetables for the men. The entrenching group dissolved to provide reinforcements for the 1st and 2nd Infantry Brigades, but Hart's 3rd NZ Rifle Brigade was still only at three-quarters strength in its four battalions after receiving its reinforcements, and so the 2nd Brigade was warned that it would lead the next advance as Russell thought 'Hart's may be too weak for a long run'.[76]

The New Zealanders were committed again on 23 October. It was 'a beautiful day for attack. A thick ground mist following a bright moonlight night.' The leading brigade advanced 8000 yards, with the field artillery batteries leapfrogging through each other to maintain the barrage in front of the advancing infantry. The German resistance was becoming increasingly fragile, and it was commonly believed that the 'only obstacles in the way of a complete breakthrough to the Rhine are communications, supplies and the weather'.[77] The division secured three bridgeheads across the Ecaillon River, and Russell noted that this was due to 'exceptionally good performances' on the part of two of the commanding officers of the 2nd Brigade, Lieutenant-Colonel A.D. Stitt of the 2nd Canterbury Battalion and Lieutenant-Colonel J. Hargest of the 2nd Otago Battalion. Both had been second lieutenants on Gallipoli in 1915, Hargest having enlisted as a sergeant in the Otago Mounted Rifles in 1914.[78]

At the end of October the division paused and went onto the defensive while corps

A New Zealand 4.5-inch Howitzer Battery in an orchard supporting the attack on Le Quesnoy. Gunner A.C. Hall is the soldier nearest the gun, with sleeves rolled up, loading the shell into the breech. *(G-13684-1/2, Alexander Turnbull Library, Wellington, NZ)*

and army regrouped for the next thrust. On 4 November the advance resumed towards the River Sambre, with the New Zealand objective including the walled former fortress town of Le Quesnoy. Russell determined that the town should be bypassed and encircled, with his soldiers being 'ordered to move North and South of it in order to form a flank and encircle the ramparts'.[79] Once again the attack was to be launched before first light at 5.30 a.m. with the 3rd NZ (Rifle) Brigade encircling the town, while the 1st and 2nd Brigades bypassed the town and pushed on through the Forêt de Mormal. Hart recorded the work of his brigade:

> The attack was launched half an hour before dawn on a beautiful autumn morning … The 1st Battalion is on my right, the 4th in the centre, and the 2nd on the left. The 3rd Battalion had to leap-frog the 1st Battalion on the blue line, two hours before zero and advance 2000 yards, completing the investment of the town. Although we were 976 men below strength, each battalion attacked on a 1000 yard frontage. The enemy was holding strong positions in front of the town, mainly on the railway line which crossed our whole frontage. We had first to storm and capture these positions before we reached the town. The first effort yielded several hundred prisoners as the enemy was holding out in considerable strength. Each Battalion then proceeded steadily and surely to invest the town. It was completely surrounded by 8 a.m. and then our men manoeuvred forward from position to position, behind trees, mounds, outbuildings, anything that would give concealment from which fire could be brought to bear upon the garrison.[80]

The move into position was covered by artillery fire, and while the town itself was not bombarded, mortars fired smoke and burning oil onto the ramparts to prevent the German defenders interfering with the encirclement of the town. Once Le Quesnoy was invested the rifle battalions encircling the town saw it as a race to be first to get in. Lieutenant-Colonel Harold Barrowclough's 4th Battalion won the race, his men scaling the walls near the water gate using a borrowed ladder. Later the other battalions complained that they had been held up by citizens of the town, who delayed the soldiers with gifts of wine, cognac and cigars and insisted they be sampled on the spot.

The advance continued on 5 November and the leading elements of the division cleared their way through the Forêt de Mormal. This was the last active day of the war for the New Zealand Division, and already Russell's concern was the educational scheme to prepare his men to return to civilian life, with many of them knowing of no occupation other than the business of soldiering in war. It was the next challenge that his division faced and its commander was preparing for it in his typical methodical way.

In the final offensive between 21 August and 6 November 1918 the New Zealand Division captured 8756 prisoners, 145 guns, three tanks, and 1263 machine guns. Between 1 July and 6 November it had been a leading division for 49 of the 56 miles advanced on IV Corps' front as part of the Third Army. It had fought as the only dominion division in the Third Army from March through to the Armistice, and lacked the advantages of working within a national corps, as the Australians and Canadians did. Nevertheless, in the words of C.E.W. Bean, 'the New Zealand Division shone out wherever it went'.[81] This had a cost: divisional casualties from 29 September to 6 November numbered 3556 including 519 dead. When it stopped fighting on 6 November 1918 the New Zealand Division numbered 11,566 infantry out of an infantry establishment of 14,371.[82]

On 12 November 1918 the New Zealand Division's strength of 18,293 out of its establishment of 18,958 made it the strongest division in the British armies on the Western Front.[83] This strength had been sustained throughout 1918, enabling the

Riflemen of the 4th Battalion, NZ Rifle Brigade wait on the start line on 4 November 1918 for what will be their final attack of the war, one where they will be part of the encircling force around the walled fortress town of Le Quesnoy. Later that day it would be these men who would be first into the town, scaling the walls by ladder at the sluice gate bridge. *(F-1996-1/2 MNZ, Alexander Turnbull Library, Wellington, NZ)*

From left to right: Brigadier-General H. Hart, CB, CMG, DSO, (d[5]), GOC 3rd NZ Rifle Brigade; Lieutenant-Colonel F. Symon, RNZA, CMG, DSO, (d[2]), CO 1st NZ Field Artillery Brigade; Major-General Sir Andrew H. Russell, KCB, KCMG, ADC, (d[9]), GOC NZ Division; Brigadier-General R. Young, CB, CMG, DSO, (d[5]), GOC 2nd NZ Infantry Brigade; Brigadier-General C.W. Melvill, NZSC, CB, CMG, (d[4]), GOC 1st NZ Infantry Brigade. Both Symon and Melvill were regular soldiers with Hart and Young being Territorial officers, both of whom served under Lieutenant-Colonel W.G. Malone in the Wellington Battalion on Gallipoli. They, together with the 'lemon-squeezer' hat that was also introduced by him, represent Malone's legacy to the New Zealand Division. The photo was taken in Cologne in late 1918. (*G-2119-1/1, Henry Armitage Sanders, NZ Official Photographer, Alexander Turnbull Library, Wellington, NZ*)

division to maintain its tactical skills and operational efficiency. Like its Australian and Canadian counterparts, it had become a highly professional formation that was kept in fighting shape by its commander, Sir Andrew Russell. In November 1918 there were 852 New Zealand reinforcements in France, 11,526 reinforcements in England, 1052 reinforcements en route from New Zealand, and 9924 reinforcements under training in New Zealand.[84] Had the war continued past November 1918, the New Zealand Division had the organisation and administration to sustain its strength and tactical efficiency into 1919 and beyond. Indeed, the 'diggers' of 1918 had a staying power to match their tactical standards, which their Australian counterparts could not equal, and the Canadians could only match.

Epilogue

Poorly trained and cared for, often very poorly led, he was unmilitary but exceedingly warlike. A citizen in arms, incurably individualistic even under the rod of discipline, combined frontier irreverence with the devout piety of an unsophisticated society; he was an arrant sentimentalist with an inner core as tough as the heart of a hickory stump. And when the faint hearts and the weaklings had been winnowed out he became one of the stoutest fighting men the world has ever seen.[1]

'Unmilitary but exceedingly warlike'

These words by Bruce Catton in his centennial trilogy on the Civil War reflect an image of the American soldier that encompasses both the Blue and the Grey. It is an image that transcends the battle lines and, in the same way as the individual and regimental memorials raised by citizens on the Civil War battlefields throughout the United States, it was an important part of the healing process; a focus for both sorrow and pride, not Blue or Grey but integral to the sense of national identity. It is part of an American national mythology that we outside the United States have become aware of most vividly in the movies. For someone of my generation it is the individual exploits of Gary Cooper as the reticent Sergeant Alvin York in the film *Sergeant York* (1941), and Audie Murphy playing himself in *To Hell and Back* (1955).

This image of a nation's fighting man as the best in the world because of innate qualities that Americans see as uniquely American, this 'cult of the superior soldier',[2] is not confined to the US alone. I have read Catton's quotation to university classes and military audiences in both Australia and New Zealand, and if it was not for the allusion to the 'hickory stump' it would be accepted in both countries as representing the unique image of that country's fighting men. Indeed, what it shows us is that the Anzac experience that I have delved into in these chapters is universal to every nation's experience of war.

It was an image that matched public expectation in both New Zealand and Australia in August 1914 on the outbreak of the First World War. The editorial in a major New Zealand daily on 1 August 1914 read:

> The average young New Zealander ... especially the young New Zealander who lives in the country is half a soldier before he is enrolled. He is physically strong, intellectually keen, anxious to be led though being what he is, he will not brook being driven a single inch. Quick to learn his drill, easily adapting to the conditions of life in camp since camping usually is his pastime and very loyal to his leaders when those leaders know their job.[3]

Similar sentiments were aired in the Australian press, and became a primary theme in the writings of C.E.W. Bean, the official war correspondent and later official war historian of the AIF. Bean described Australian recruits in words that Catton would identify with: 'half-wild colts, many with an almost complete disrespect for custom and authority'; warlike but unmilitary, 'incorrigibly civilian' with '[an] individualism ... so strongly implanted as to stand out after years of subordination ... He was the easiest man in the world to interest and lead, but was intolerant of incompetent or uninteresting leaders.'[4] One finds the same image in Canadian writing. Indeed, every nation has a similar 'unique' image that personalises a sense of national identity, moulded by the land they live in, and including within it an expectation of how bravely their young men will fight in battle.[5]

A principal theme in this study is the concept of the 'Anzac'. ANZAC is the acronym for Australian and New Zealand Army Corps, the exploits of which are commemorated each Anzac Day, when we remember 25 April 1915 and the landing of the ANZAC Corps on the Gallipoli Peninsula of Turkey. In New Zealand and Australian eyes, their two countries' manhood was first put to the test in battle at these landings where they formed part of the combined Allied force of British, French and Imperial troops in what was the first major amphibious operation of the twentieth century in invading Turkey.

Every year on 25 April thousands of people gather at local war memorials in every district and community throughout New Zealand and Australia. Overseas, expatriates do the same. On the Gallipoli Peninsula of Turkey thousands of Australians and New Zealanders converge on Anzac Cove, almost as many as on the day itself. All this for a battle that is small and insignificant in world terms, but important to Australians and New Zealanders because it fixed national images that confirmed public expectations.

Before dawn on 25 April 1915 Australians of the 1st Australian Division landed on the wrong beach, one mile north of the intended landing place, against minor opposition and started to advance inland. The New Zealand Infantry Brigade of the New Zealand and Australian Division, which together made up the ANZAC Corps, followed them. The British official war correspondent at the landing, Ellis Ashmead-Bartlett, wrote of the Anzacs as 'the finest lot of men I have ever seen in any part of the world', commenting that these 'raw Colonial troops in those desperate hours proved themselves worthy to fight side by side with the heroes of Mons and the Aisne, Ypres, and Neuve Chapelle', the principal battles fought by the British Army in France to that time.[6]

The public of Australia and New Zealand eagerly devoured these words, written from a battleship offshore. They had an authority because they were the words of the official war correspondent, and they were important because it was a British reporter and not an Australian or a New Zealander giving this praise. That we had proved to be worthy members of the Empire was confirmed with the congratulations received from King George V on the 'splendid conduct and bravery' of the New Zealand troops as reported in New Zealand and of the Australian troops as reported in Australia. For both countries the altar of nationhood had 'been stained with crimson as every rallying centre of a nation should be'.[7]

As well as meeting the public expectation this imperial praise enabled the sorrow of the growing casualty lists to be balanced against a pride in being seen to be playing a part in the Empire's struggle. It was pride in Empire but also pride in self, a consciousness of young nations playing their part on the world stage. It led to a surge in recruiting numbers in both countries, and saw the spontaneous adoption of the day of the landing, 25 April 1915, as the 'Landing' or 'Anzac Day'. It was a day when New Zealand and Australia mourned their dead, but also celebrated a coming of age, a confirmation of their place as nations within the British Empire.

'POORLY TRAINED AND CARED FOR, OFTEN VERY POORLY LED ... A CITIZEN IN ARMS'

The reality on the ground at Anzac was somewhat different from the glorious achievement portrayed in Ashmead-Bartlett's words. The ANZAC Corps was not a homogeneous army but two separate citizen armies from two quite different countries, with both having but a token of military experience. They were enthusiastic, fit, but as Catton was to write of that generation of American soldiers 50 years earlier, 'Poorly trained and cared for, often very poorly led'.[8] Nineteen years after the landing, one of

George Edmund Butler, *The Digger in Ordinary*
(Walking out uniform), oil on board. *(National*
Collection of War Art, Archives New Zealand)

the Australians who got farthest inland on 25 April wrote that his 'most outstanding impression' was of 'a boy sent to do a man's job'.[9]

History is rewritten for each generation, and ours is a visual age, profoundly influenced by the films we see. I have mentioned two films that have shaped my image of the American fighting man. A pivotal film in shaping Australian and New Zealand perceptions of the Gallipoli campaign is Peter Weir's *Gallipoli*, which was released in 1981.[10] In this film one sees Australian youth sacrificed for British blunders and British inaction. As always, however, it was never that simple, and in looking for a villain the British high command is too easy a target, and a misleading one.

Anzac Day has become a symbol of Anzac achievement but the reality on the ground was one of 16,000 disorganised and inexperienced amateur soldiers being held at bay for most of the day by five weak and widely spread Turkish battalions. Mustafa Kemal, better known today as Kemal Ataturk — later the founding president of the Turkish Republic, then an unknown colonel — seized the moment and laid the foundation of Turkey's principal victory of the First World War. The untried and untrained Anzacs met the best of the Turkish Army who, although initially outnumbered, were grimly prepared to defend their homeland against the invader.

By nightfall on 25 April all was chaos and confusion ashore. General Sir Ian Hamilton, Commander of the Mediterranean Expeditionary Force, stiffened the wavering spirits of his Anzac commanders with the message that there was no prospect of evacuation so they had to dig in and hold on.

Given their lack of experience and rudimentary training one could expect little else. As First Manassas and the opening battles of the Civil War demonstrated to Americans in brutal relief, enthusiasm is no substitute for training and leadership. The eight-month Gallipoli experience was a hard, brutal lesson in war paid for with the lives of good men. Battalions with strong commanding officers survived, while battalions without that leadership fell apart. Leadership, not men, was the prerequisite for survival, and learning to survive and function as an organised body became the measure of Anzac success.

In the same way as the men, the potential leaders within these citizen armies had to learn their trade. Contrary to the mythology, the most outstanding commander within the Anzac perimeter was a British officer, Brigadier-General Harold 'Hooky' Walker. He commanded the New Zealand Brigade on the first day and would command the 1st Australian Division during the August offensive. It was he who forged the Australians into a professional formation. In each national force there were a handful of professionals, some Regular soldiers, some from the citizen army, who made the difference. Many did not survive the campaign, but their example and the standards they demanded brought through others to replace them. Gradually rank amateurism was replaced by bitterly won professionalism.

This process would be repeated on the Western Front where the two ANZAC corps fought in France and Flanders from 1916 to 1918. The rapid expansion of the AIF to five divisions and of the NZEF to one full-strength division was beyond their ability to sustain with the available leadership and administrative skills that this growth demanded. The lessons from Gallipoli were relearned the hard way in France and Flanders.

Once again the Anzacs were praised for their natural prowess and skills, the products of colonial life, but as I have argued it was not until mid to late 1917 that the tactical skills of the Anzac formations matched the reputation the forces had had bestowed upon them by the public at home at the news of that first Anzac Day. The basis for success on the Western Front was the evolution of a sound system of trained reinforcements, careful selection and training of junior officers and NCOs, care and attention to the details of administration in the care and welfare of the men, and equally careful tactical preparation, planning and rehearsals before each campaign. This was the process that forged two citizen armies into professional forces. It was happening throughout the British armies, with the Anzacs benefiting particularly because of the concentration of their two forces within the ANZAC Corps, and similarly the Canadians, being grouped into the Canadian Corps.

While improvements in the British armies in general were fostered at army level, it also depended a great deal on leadership and initiative at divisional level. Except for selected formations such as the Guards Division, British divisions were unable to conserve talent, with the best of their officers being posted to meet the needs of any one of the five British armies. They lacked the benefit of the guaranteed regular reinforcement by trained soldiers that followed from the national reinforcement systems supporting the Australian, Canadian and New Zealand forces.

What made the AIF and the NZEF uniquely Australian or New Zealand was the umbilical cord linking each to the country from which it came. Ostensibly an integral part of the British armies, they represented and were sustained by the hopes and fears of their populations at home, with the political fortunes of the governments that sent them riding on their achievements.

By 1918 the two ANZAC corps had ceased to exist. The Australian Corps had formed its own distinct identity apart from the New Zealand Division, which became part of a British corps. Both were veteran bodies, exhausted but professional, who together with the Canadian Corps were regarded as the key assault formations within the British armies on the Western Front. In late 1917–1918 the Anzacs could be said to match Catton's words when he spoke of 'the faint hearts and the weaklings [having been] winnowed out he became one of the stoutest fighting men the world has ever seen'.[11]

It was in early 1918 that the Australians and New Zealanders received units of the American Expeditionary Force (AEF) that were attached to them for training and front-line experience. One New Zealander wrote this somewhat patronising description of his first impression of the United States 80th Division, but one must read it in the context of any hardened professional assessing a new arrival:

> They were Virginians — the grandsons of the men who had fought under
> Lee and Jackson and indeed one of their captains was a grandson of the great
> Confederate commander-in-chief. They were very anxious to learn and were

not obsessed with any idea of teaching veteran troops how things should be done. They were very likeable folk; and with their quaint sayings, strange manoeuvres, their faculty for getting lost, and their remarkable simplicity, they provided much amusement and made many friends.[12]

More perceptively, an Australian viewing the calibre of the AEF noted in February 1918: 'We felt today as though we had been walking amongst ghosts … It was the old 1st Aust. Divn. over again to the life … the swing of them, and the make-up of the men, and the colour of them, and the independent look upon their faces …'[13] The AEF of 1918 were men who personified the image of Bruce Catton's Civil War soldier — young, keen, fit and as yet amateur. In the words of the New Zealand official historian, 'their temperament and enthusiasm recalled the fervour of 1914–15, yet undulled by habitude and vicissitude'.[14] The New Zealanders and Australians looked at these new arrivals and saw themselves as they had been.

A 'Digger' and two 'Doughboys' of the American Expeditionary Force on attachment to the New Zealand Division at Bertrancourt in France on 19 May 1918. *(G-13741-1/2, Henry Armitage Sanders, NZ Official Photographer, Alexander Turnbull Library, Wellington, NZ)*

A dispassionate assessment of the AEF in 1918 would say it was at the same level as the newly raised Australian and New Zealand divisions of 1916, full of potential but as yet lacking the leadership and organisational skills by which this fighting potential would be realised. This was an army that was at the beginning of the process of evolving from amateur to professional. It was a process that was far from completed by the time of the Armistice in November 1918, but one which, as the small-town memorials throughout the United States show, took its toll.

THE PRICE OF AMATEURISM

The public in Australia and New Zealand did not comprehend this inevitable and costly transformation from amateur to professionalism. The newspaper reports of high achievement on Gallipoli were accepted at face value, as were those from the Western Front.

What people had not expected was the cost of this achievement. A total of 8556 New Zealanders landed on Gallipoli in the eight-month campaign. Of these 2721 died; 1669 have no known graves and 252 are buried at sea. There are just 344 known graves of New Zealand's Gallipoli dead in Turkey — roughly one grave for every eight dead. Add to that the 4752 wounded and not counting those evacuated with dysentery and paratyphoid, which reached epidemic proportions in the summer months, one could say that in crude terms nine out of ten New Zealanders became a battle casualty on Gallipoli. Almost all of a small country's first offering of enthusiastic young men, the cream of its available officers and men from its citizen volunteers who sailed for war, in a sense vanished from the earth, without their families even having the prospect of at some point visiting a lonely grave on a Turkish coast.[15]

Australian figures among the original 1st Division reached similar proportions. The AIF suffered 26,111 casualties including 8141 dead.[16] British and Turkish casualties dwarfed those of the two British dominions, but the Australian and New Zealand response to that cost was the spontaneous adoption of the day of the landing, 25 April 1915, as Anzac Day. With the exception of 1917, when it was held on the nearest Sunday, it has been commemorated on 25 April ever since.

Anzac Day is a day of both sorrow and pride — pride in what was achieved, sorrow at the cost of that achievement. By the end of the war in 1918 New Zealand, with a population of just over one million and an estimated 243,376 men of military age, had raised 128,525 for service overseas, of whom 100,444 sailed for war. Casualties numbered 18,166 deaths and 41,317 wounded. The nation at the farthest point from the centre of the fighting had sent 9 percent of its total population, 40 percent of its eligible male population, with six out of ten becoming casualties.[17] This situation was paralleled in Australia, where almost half the eligible male population enlisted and 330,000 served overseas. Two-thirds of those who served overseas became casualties, the highest percentage in the Empire, with 60,000 dead, one in five of those who sailed for war.[18]

This sorrow and pride parallels the experience of the United States, but what distinguishes the US entry into the First World War was that it was a carefully considered political act; one resulting from President Woodrow Wilson's judgement that it was only by military involvement could a political settlement be imposed. This was matched by General Pershing's insistence that the American Expeditionary Force not be committed piecemeal, but fight, once it was ready, as a national army. Such national considerations were never articulated by Australia and New Zealand. In 1914 there were no doubts in the dominions about the righteousness of the cause. Britain declared war on their behalf and they were content to play a preordained role. National concerns grew with experience, not in terms of the worth of the fight but rather how it was being fought and their men employed.

I have used the word 'Anzac' in the way the term was originally intended, an Australian or a New Zealander serving within the Australian and New Zealand Army Corps. The bond between our two countries is self-evident, but the Anzac experience not only showed how much we have in common, it also demonstrated the differences. By 1918, with the exception of the ANZAC Mounted Division in Palestine, the Anzac linkage had been broken between the two national forces in France and Flanders.

The Anzac experience of 1914–18 confirmed that we are two different countries with very different approaches to how we see the world and how we assess matters of individual national interest. Today New Zealand, with four million people, is dwarfed in every respect by Australia. In the same way we are both dwarfed by the US. Then and now, there was and is an intense rivalry, a love-hate relationship between our countries. As Shelby Foote wrote of the American Civil War, it was a fight between brothers, and in one sense the relationship between Australia and New Zealand is one of an older, bigger brother and a smaller younger brother. New Zealand, being the smaller, is often considered best ignored, unless he is needed to do something.

The Anzac relationship forged on Gallipoli was one of grudging recognition of each other's strengths, and an ability to work together despite our differences. However, the Anzac experience was much more a discovery of self, a confirmation of the fact that we each are different. We have a different make-up in peoples and culture, and a different perspective of the world because of our respective geographical positions. Australia looks north while New Zealand, shielded by the Australian landmass, looks to the South Pacific. This is even more evident today in New Zealand's multiracial society, with so many of its citizens of Maori and Polynesian descent. New Zealand is a very different ethnic mix from the largely Anglo-Saxon force of 1914 when many New Zealanders, particularly those from the South Island, had to journey to Egypt, Gallipoli and France to meet Maori for the first time. At that time Maori were grouped in a separate Maori Contingent, which became the Pioneer Battalion of the New Zealand Division on the Western Front.[19]

This difference between the two countries is reflected in our commemoration of Anzac Day. Australia sees it as a national day, and indeed in Australia the term 'Anzac' is synonymous with 'Australian'. The need in 1916 to ensure sufficient volunteer reinforcements in a population that would not accept conscription as an option saw Anzac Day become a parade of heroes; of young men prepared to go and fight for their country. These parades through cheering crowds continue today, and this heroic image is reflected on war memorials throughout Australia. The names on the memorials are not just of the dead, but of everyone who went to war, because the personal decision to go marked them out as heroes. Anzac Day in Australia is a commemoration of both the heroes who went and those among them who died. It is a celebration of nationhood.

In New Zealand Anzac Day is different; the crowds are there, but the emphasis is not on the parade because, unlike Australia, conscription in New Zealand removed the element of choice. Because of this most memorials are inscribed with the names of the dead only. Anzac Day is a day where the national consciousness is one of cost. It is a commemoration of the price New Zealand has paid on its journey to nationhood, and the price it may be asked to pay again if it commits itself while as unprepared as it was in two world wars.

Australia and New Zealand share a common experience that has forged a unique relationship that still has relevance. But it should not disguise the fact that 'Wars are instruments of policy, and cannot be assessed just as the collective sum of personal experience.'[20] Britain has been the silent partner in this study, but our relationship with Britain in 1914–18 was taken for granted, a comfortable cloak of a relationship that only came into question under the strains of war.

The Second World War raised that question again. Both New Zealand and Australia paid the price of a lack of preparedness with the lives of its men and women. There was the same bitter passage from amateur to professional, but now both were more conscious of national concerns, and were prepared to question Britain's judgements.

We learnt that our interests were subordinate to the two major powers, first Britain and then, as the war progressed, the United States. Being junior members New Zealand and Australia could voice concerns, but had to fit in as best we could within the dictates of Allied strategy imposed upon us. We did not necessarily agree with each other either, and there were tensions between Australia and New Zealand over New Zealand's decision to keep its division in the Mediterranean instead of redeploying it into the Pacific theatre as Australia had done with the AIF.

By now the word 'Anzac' reflected national self-interests. External advice was scrutinised and there was no longer an unthinking acceptance of the cost. As the New Zealand Prime Minister Peter Fraser said at the time of the Crete campaign in May 1941, when Britain was undecided about attempting further evacuations in the face of German air power:

> I stated that while the United Kingdom with its 45,000,000 people could sustain a heavy loss of men without very disastrous effects, and that even Australia could sustain a large loss much better than New Zealand, it would be a crushing disaster for our country and its war effort if such a large number of our men fell into the enemy's hands without every effort being made to rescue them.[21]

Patriotism and professionalism

Those men and women whose names are inscribed on our memorials did not make the decision to fight; that, quite properly, was the government's role. They went to war in the belief that they had the leadership, training and enthusiasm to win through. In two world wars that was not initially the case, and the cost of learning to be professional was measured in thousands of lives. The US has been on parallel journeys, as any walk through Arlington or along the Vietnam Memorial Wall reveals.

In March 2002 the American film critic Robert Ebert, reviewing the film *We Were Soldiers*, commented that it and another recent release, *Black Hawk Down*, 'both seem to replace patriotism with professionalism'.[22] I believe that what Ebert was commenting upon reflects a change in public perception that is evident in New Zealand, Australia and the United States. It is the growing consciousness that patriotic enthusiasm is no longer enough, and the expectation that patriotism must be harnessed by professionalism if national and individual interests are to be properly served. The image of our soldiers as

Cenotaphs and cemeteries in every town and district carry their memories of war. *(Ross Giblin, Evening Post, Wellington, NZ)*

characterised by Catton's words is no longer acceptable in 'sophisticated' societies. This is because the 'winnowing' in war of untrained enthusiastic amateurs is more than any country can or should be asked to bear.

When watching Steven Spielberg's *Saving Private Ryan*, I was conscious of how the quiet professionalism of those by now veteran citizen soldiers, who had served in North Africa and Italy before landing in France, was portrayed on the first day at Omaha Beach in the Normandy landings. I was equally conscious of the image of that mother slumping to the porch in expectant agony at the arrival of an army staff car to a lonely farm. Today we must still face and accept that individual agony as an inevitable cost of war, and be prepared to justify it in national terms.

This consciousness of individual cost has led to the criticism that Western nations such as the US have become soft. Risk-aversion, 'the body bag syndrome', an unwilling-ness to accept casualties, is seen as a sign of weakness. It is wrongly interpreted as unwillingness to fight for what we believe in, and a questioning of our resolve to see it through. The concerted actions in Afghanistan since the events of 11 September 2001 and the international support the US has received in its determination to strike at terrorist groups give the lie to this. However, as events leading up to the invasion of Iraq have shown, such support is not given unthinkingly. War is a political act, the consequences of which have to be measured in national terms. Being threatened and feeling obliged to strike out must still quite properly be done within the context and legitimacy of actions approved by world bodies such as the United Nations, or if independently with the conscious determination that national security leaves no other option. Pre-emptive should not mean predetermined, and in this New Zealand chose a different path over Iraq from Australia, Britain and the United States.

In questioning the possible casualty bill I would argue that such questioning of cost is a proof of maturity. It is the inevitable consequence of the lessons that we each have learned in war in the twentieth century and that we face again in the twenty-first; an understanding that as nations we must be willing to marry the political act to the individual cost, and also display a willingness to re-evaluate those decisions against each life that is lost. Not easy, but the right thing to do. Not softness, but an understanding that in achieving a political end through military means there is no room for enthusiasm and amateurism, but only total professionalism at every level of government decision-making.

Today we as citizens expect professionalism from our military institutions; in the decision-making of the government that sends them, matched by professionalism in the selection, training, organisation and equipping of the services; in the preparation, planning and conduct by those services; in the sustaining of that effort on combat operations; and in the provision of professional support on their return home. This is the measure of any society that values its citizens.

As much as we would wish for a 'war to end all wars', which was the dream of 1918, relatively young nations such as Australia and New Zealand have found that with maturity comes uncertainty. The Second World War's end in 1945 brought no comforting guarantee of security, but a consciousness that our national defence was bound up in Western alliances. This resulted in a willing but measured and professional involvement in Korea, the Malayan Emergency, the confrontation in Borneo, Vietnam, the Gulf War, Somalia, East Timor and myriad multinational and United Nations-initiated peace support operations.

The dead of these campaigns have been added to the memorials, and their names make us conscious of the ongoing cost of being responsible members of the world community, a world in which we as members of the United Nations strive for peace, but one where we are prepared to fight when peace can only be achieved in this way.

Because of this, New Zealand and Australia fought in Afghanistan and, subject to national considerations, will continue to fight alongside the US and other multinational forces when we consider it justified. New Zealand did not join the coalition forces in their attack on Iraq in March 2003, but contributes to the rebuilding process in both Iraq and Afghanistan: measured national commitments in an uncertain world. Our contributions may be small beside those of the US and of other nations, but these elements are now fully trained and equipped, and capable of doing the job asked of them. They are the best we have — professional forces. To deploy anything of a lesser calibre would be to deny our experience in war and its impact upon our two nations.

For New Zealand and Australia, Anzac Day has become the day when we commemorate our dead in all wars. It is the day when we gather as citizens to read the names, picture the faces, and ponder not just on the nature of heroic sacrifice but more importantly to stand in judgement of ourselves — and in assessing why we fought and why we fight, we measure our progress as nations.

'Lest We Forget.'

NOTES

AJHR   *Appendices to the Journals of the House of Representatives*
AT   Alexander Turnbull Library, Wellington
AWM   Australian War Memorial
LHCMH   Liddell Hart Centre for Military History
KCL   King's College London
NA   Archives New Zealand
NAC   National Archives of Canada
NLA   National Library of Australia
NLS   National Library of Scotland
NZDQ   *New Zealand Defence Quarterly*
NZPD   New Zealand Parliamentary Debates
PRO   National Archives including Public Record Office
QEII   National Army Museum, Waiouru

Chapter One
New Zealand, Australia and ANZAC

1. C.E.W. Bean, ed., *The Official History of Australia in the War of 1914–1918*, vol. *1: The Story of ANZAC from the Outbreak of the War to the End of the First Phase of the Gallipoli Campaign, May 4, 1915*: 124–25.

2. Godley to Allen dated 17 January 1915, Godley to Allen dated 15 February 1915, Godley Papers, WA 252, NA.

3. W.H. Downing, *Digger Dialects: A Collection of Slang Phrases Used by the Australian Soldiers on Active Service*: 8.

4. This is examined in Jane Ross, *The Myth of the Digger: The Australian Soldier in Two World Wars*; Alistair Thomson, *Anzac Memories: Living with the Legend*; and John F. Williams, *ANZACs, the Media and the Great War*. See also 'Anzac Legend', in Peter Dennis, Jeffrey Grey, Ewan Morris and Robin Prior, eds, *The Oxford Companion to Australian Military History*: 42–49.

5. Christopher Pugsley, 'Putting the N.Z. back in ANZAC', *NZDQ*, 4, Winter 1994: 35–37.

6. For the different perspectives on the incident see 'Good Friday April 2', in C.E.W. Bean, *Gallipoli Correspondent: The Frontline Diary of C.E.W. Bean*: 46–48; Godley to Allen dated 2 April 1915, Godley Papers, WA 252; Christopher Pugsley, *Gallipoli: The New Zealand Story*: 95; Glen Wahlert, *The Other Enemy?: Australian Soldiers and the Military Police*: 28.

7. Tpr C. Pocock, CMR, Diary, 25 March 1915, RV1298, Kippenberger Archive, QEII.

8. Lt C.S. Algie, Auckland Infantry Regiment, Diary, Sunday 27 December 1914, MS Papers 1374, AT.

9. James Bodell, *A Soldier's View of Empire*: 132.

10. Trooper R. McCandlish, WMR, Letters, QEII.

11. 16 November 1914, Bean, *Gallipoli Correspondent*: 29.

12. 9–30 January 1915, ibid.: 39.

13. Godley to Allen, 10 January 1915, WA 252, NA; Wahlert, *The Other Enemy*: 26–33; Jeffrey Grey, *The Australian Army*: 41–42.

14. 29 April 1915, but more likely a reflective piece added some months or even years after, Bean, *Gallipoli Correspondent*: 83.

15. Ibid.

16. Ibid.

17. Pugsley, *Gallipoli: The New Zealand Story*: 155.

18. C.D. Coulthard-Clark, *A Heritage of Spirit*: 128.

19. Captain R.W. Campbell, *The Kangaroo Marines*: 110.

20. Chris Roberts, 'The Landing at Anzac: A Reassessment', *Journal of the Australian War Memorial*, 22, 1993; this is disputed by Denis Winter, *25 April 1915: The Inevitable Tragedy*: 192–97.

21. As Bean notes, 'Turkish officers afterwards referred to Lone Pine simply as "The Demonstration"'. Bean, ed., *The Official History of Australia in the War of 1914–1918*, vol. *2, The Story of ANZAC from 4 May 1915 to the Evacuation of the Gallipoli Peninsula*: 566.

22. Winter, *25 April 1915: The Inevitable Tragedy*: 165–67, 268; Pugsley, *Gallipoli: The New Zealand Story*: 131–34; Christopher Pugsley, *On the Fringe of Hell*:

New Zealanders and Military Discipline in the First World War: 34.

23. 'Lieutenant-General Harold Bridgewood Walker', in Dennis et al., eds, *The Oxford Companion to Australian Military History*: 627. An assessment of his ability as a 'fighting general' is given in Robert Rhodes James, *Gallipoli*: 242, and Les Carlyon, *Gallipoli*: 285–86.

24. Notes on Draft of Letter C.R. 22/10 from C in C M.E.F. to War Office — and on C in C's Memorandum to General Birdwood of March the 16th [1916], Godley Papers, WA 252, NA.

25. Ibid.

26. Field-Marshal Sir John French, Despatch dated 15th June 1915, published in the Supplement to the *London Gazette*, No. 29225, 10 July 1915: 263.

27. C.E.W. Bean, ed., *The Official History of Australia in the War of 1914–1918*, vol. *4, The AIF in France 1917*: 732-33. See also Pugsley, 'Putting the N.Z. back in ANZAC', *NZDQ*, 4: 35–37.

28. 'Digger', H.W. Orsman, ed., *The Dictionary of New Zealand English*: 206–7.

29. Pugsley, *On the Fringe of Hell*: 65.

30. Ibid.: 122–35, 206–13.

31. Lt Col C. Guy Powles, *The New Zealanders in Sinai and Palestine*; A.J. Hill, *Chauvel of the Light Horse*; H.S. Gullett, *Official History of Australia in the War of 1914–1918*, vol. *7, The Australian Imperial Force in Sinai and Palestine, 1914–1918*.

32. Mary Boyd, 'Australia-New Zealand Relations', in William S. Livingston & Wm Roger Louis, *Australia, New Zealand and the Pacific Islands Since the First World War*: 47.

33. John A. Moses, 'The Struggle for Anzac Day 1916–1930 and the Role of the Brisbane Anzac Day Commemoration Committee', *Journal of the Royal Australian Historical Society*, 88, Part 1, June 2002: 54–74; John A. Moses, 'Canon David John Garland (1864–1939) as Architect of Anzac Day', *Royal Historical Society of Queensland Journal*, 17, 2, May 1999: 49–64; John A. Moses, 'Canon David John Garland and the ANZAC tradition', *St Mark's Review*, Winter 1993: 12–21.

34. Massey to Allen dated 2 January 1917, Allen Papers, Box 9, NA.

35. Dale J. Blair, '"Those Miserable Tommies": Anti-British Sentiment in the Australian Imperial Force 1915–1918', *War and Society*, 19, 1, May 2001: 71–91. Dale Blair has come in for criticism for his conclusions in *Dinkum Diggers: An Australian Battalion at War*. It remains to be seen if the studies into Australian discipline and morale being conducted by Ashley Ekins also support Blair's findings, which from my research seem logical and better related to the universal experiences of battalions in combat than many current Australian perceptions. See also Jane Ross, *The Myth of the Digger: The Australian Soldier in Two World Wars*: 47, 49, 97, 101.

Chapter Two
The Empire at War in South Africa, 1899–1902

1. J.H.M. Abbott, *Tommy Cornstalk*: 11–13. 'Cornstalk' was the Australian nickname for a man from New South Wales, and was used by New Zealanders as a general term for an Australian during the First World War and less commonly during the Second. See 'cornstalk', in H.W. Orsman, ed., *The Dictionary of New Zealand English*: 171.

2. Abbott, ibid.

3. Ibid.

4. For a cross-section of current historical thinking from the various participants on both sides, see Peter Dennis and Jeffrey Grey, *The Boer War: Army, Nation and Empire*.

5. Carmen Miller, *Painting the Map Red: Canada and the South African War 1899–1902*: xi. See also Carmen Miller, 'The Crucible of War: Canadian and British Troops During the Boer War', in Dennis and Grey, eds, *The Boer War*: 84–98; and David J. Bercuson and J.L. Granatstein, *Dictionary of Canadian Military History*.

6. L.S. Amery, ed., *The Times History of the War in South Africa 1899–1902*, vol. VI: 276–78. For the detail of the Australian contribution, see Lieut-Colonel P.L. Murray, ed., *Official Records of the Australian Military Contingents to the War in South Africa*; and 'Second Boer War' in Dennis et al., *The Oxford Companion to Australian Military History*: 104–9. For New Zealand see D.O.W. Hall, *The New Zealanders in South Africa, 1899–1902*; J. Crawford with E. Ellis, *To Fight for Empire: An Illustrated History of New Zealand and the South African War 1899–1902*; and 'Boer War', in Ian McGibbon, ed., *The Oxford Companion to New Zealand Military History*: 59–63. In the case of all colonial contingents it is unusual if the figures in one source correspond to another.

7. Miller, *Painting the Map Red*: 16–30.

8. Ibid.: 48.

9. G.C. Dunstall, 'Public Attitudes and Responses in New Zealand to the Beginning of the Boer War 1899', *University of Auckland Historical Society Annual*: 8–22.

10. General Sir Redvers Buller quoted in *Report of His Majesty's Commissioners Appointed to Enquire into the Military Preparations and Other Matters Connected with the War in South Africa*: 78.

11. Erskine Childers, ed., *The Times History of the War in South Africa 1899–1902*, vol. V: 71.

12. Corporal F. Twistleton, *With the New Zealanders at the Front*: 5.

13. Miller, 'The Crucible of War: Canadian and British Troops During the Boer War'; Dennis and Grey, eds, *The Boer War*: 84–98.

14. Appendix B, 'Memorandum on the Colonial Forces employed in South Africa, 1899–1902, by

Lieut-Colonel John Adye CB, RA, Late Assistant Adjutant-General for Colonial Forces, South Africa', *Report of His Majesty's Commissioners Appointed to Enquire into the Military Preparations and Other Matters Connected with the War in South Africa*.

15. J. Bryant Haigh and Alan J. Polaschek, *New Zealand and the Distinguished Service Order*: 127. For the history of the New Zealand contribution to the war in South Africa see D.O.W. Hall, *The New Zealanders in South Africa 1899–1902*; and J. Crawford with E. Ellis, *To Fight for Empire: An Illustrated History of New Zealand and the South African War, 1899–1902*.

16. Childers, *The Times History of the War in South Africa 1899–1902*, vol. V: 67.

17. Major-General Sir Alfred C. Robin KCMG (1860– 1935), born Victoria, settled Dunedin 1864, coachbuilder, CO First NZ Contingent South Africa 1899, joined NZ Militia, CGS 1906, Dominion Representative IGS London 1912, GOC NZ Defence Forces 1914–19, Administrator Trustee of Samoa 1920. See *The New Zealand Dictionary of Biography*, vol. *3, 1901–1920*: 437–38.

18. Appendix B, 'Memorandum on the Colonial Forces employed in South Africa, 1899–1902, by Lieut-Colonel John Adye', *Report of His Majesty's Commissioners*.

19. Joseph Linklater, *On Active Service in South Africa with the Silent Sixth*: 35.

20. New Zealand, *General Orders* 33/01, HQ NZ Defence Force Library, Wellington.

21. Abbott, *Tommy Cornstalk*: 11–13.

22. Twistleton, *With the New Zealanders at the Front*, quoted in Unknown, 'A History of the New Zealand Army', unpublished manuscript, nd, HQ NZ Defence Force Library, Wellington.

23. Crawford with Ellis, *To Fight for the Empire*: 40, 60; 'Major William James Hardham', in Ian McGibbon, ed., *The Oxford Companion to New Zealand Military History*: 214–15. Lord Roberts' Despatch dated 1 March 1902, *London Gazette* No. 27443 of 17th June, 1902.

24. Appendix B, 'Memorandum on the Colonial Forces employed in South Africa, 1899–1902, by Lieut-Colonel John Adye', *Report of His Majesty's Commissioners*.

25. Ian McGibbon, *The Path to Gallipoli: Defending New Zealand 1840–1915*: 130–36.

Chapter Three
At the Empire's Call: New Zealand
Expeditionary Force Planning 1901–1918

1. As noted in the introduction, the first version of this paper was published in John A. Moses and Christopher Pugsley, eds, *The German Empire and Britain's Pacific Dominions 1871–1919: Essays on the Role of Australia and New Zealand in World Politics in the Age of Imperialism*: 239–50.

2. Extract from Report of Defence Minister to Prime Minister, June 1913, 'Defence Scheme — Expeditionary Action by Territorial Force', AD1 10 16/6, NA.

3. Jeffrey Grey, *The Australian Centenary History of Defence*, vol. *1, The Australian Army*: 37–40; Stephen J. Harris, *Canadian Brass: The Making of a Professional Army, 1860–1939*: 94–100.

4. John Mordike, *An Army for a Nation: A History of Australian Military Developments, 1880–1914*; Grey, *The Australian Army*: 5–35.

5. NZPD, 10 December 1909: 913–17; 12 Dec 1909: 1000–1029; 21 Dec 1909: 1412–26; 23 July 1913: 107–108, 741–42.

6. Major-General Richard Hutton Davies (1861– 1918), born London, emigrated New Zealand, surveyor Taranaki, active Volunteers, joined NZ Militia as Regular Officer 1899, member of First NZ Contingent, and later commanded Third and Fourth Contingents. Commanded Eighth Contingent. Seen as logical successor to Godley as GOC NZ Forces, sent to England attached to 2nd Cavalry Brigade then appointed Comd 6th Infantry Brigade, Aldershot. First dominion officer to command a British Regular formation. Mobilised in August 1914 and fought at Mons, transferred with NZ Government permission in February 1915 to command 20th (Light) Division until 1916 when he was relieved from command. Commanded training bases in Britain until his health broke down, committed suicide in 1918. See 'Major-General Richard Hutton Davies', in Ian McGibbon, ed., *Oxford Companion to New Zealand Military History*: 133–34.

7. Colonel Arthur Bauchop (1871–1915), sawmiller, Port Chalmers, served South Africa, CMG, MID (2), joined NZ Militia on return from South Africa in 1904, Regular Officer NZSC, reverted Lt Col to command Otago Mounted Rifles, NZEF. WIA Gallipoli, 4.7.15, 7.8.15, DOW, 8.8.15. See Pugsley, *Gallipoli: The New Zealand Story*: 49–50, 269, 274, 346.

8. This is a constant theme in the annual reports of the Commandant New Zealand Defence Forces contained in the *Appendices to the Journals of the House of Representatives* from 1887 on.

9. 'The composition of the Force and the details of establishment, arms and equipment etc to be worked out and kept up-to-date, and when the time arrives the Territorials or Reserves to be invited to volunteer.' Extract from Report of Defence Minister to Prime Minister, June 1913, 'Defence Scheme — Expeditionary Action by Territorial Force', AD 10 16/6, NA.

10. Secret Appendix A to 'Scheme for the Reorganization of the Military Forces of New Zealand', prepared and submitted by the Chief of

General Staff, War Office, August 1909. (B246), AD 10/16/6, NA.

11. 'Scheme for the Reorganization of the Military Forces of New Zealand': 4.

12. Ibid.

13. Ibid.

14. Secret Appendix B to 'Scheme for the Reorganization of the Military Forces of New Zealand'.

15. 'Scheme for the Reorganization of the Military Forces of New Zealand': 5.

16. Ibid.: 6.

17. Ibid.

18. Secret Appendix F, 'Scheme for the Reorganization of the Military Forces of New Zealand': 6.

19. Ibid.

20. Ibid.

21. GOC to Minister of Defence, Secret Memo dated 2 August 1912, AD10/16/6, NA.

22. GOC to Minister of Defence, Secret Memo dated 9 October 1912, AD10/16/6, NA.

23. Ibid.

24. Ibid.

25. Ibid.

26. Ibid.

27. Grey, *The Australian Army*: 33–34.

28. Appendix I, Secret Notes for Conference 18:11: 1912, Cablegram 31 October 1912, AD10/16/6, NA.

29. Secret Notes for Conference 18:11:1912, AD10/16/6, NA.

30. GOC to Minister of Defence, Secret Memo dated 10 December 1912, AD10/16/6, NA.

31. Secret Notes for Conference 18:11:1912, AD10/16/6, NA.

32. Grey, *The Australian Army*: 34–35.

33. General Sir Ian Hamilton, 'Report by the Inspector General of Overseas Forces on the Military Forces of New Zealand', in *The Times Documentary History of the War*, vol. *X Overseas, Part 2*: 472, quoted in Pugsley, *Gallipoli: The New Zealand Story*: 45.

34. *The New Zealand Official Year Book 1915*: 292.

35. Pugsley, *Gallipoli: The New Zealand Story*: 63, 364–65; New Zealand Military Forces, *New Zealand Expeditionary Force, Its Provision and Maintenance*; New Zealand Expeditionary Force (Europe), *1914 War Diary*.

36. Harris, *Canadian Brass*: 94–121; Desmond Morton and J.L. Granatstein, *Marching to Armageddon: Canadians and the Great War 1914–1918*: 9–12, 29–34, 106–110.

37. Pugsley, *Gallipoli: The New Zealand Story*: 363–64.

38. War Office, *Statistics of the Military Effort of the British Empire 1914–1920*, quoted in Cathryn Corns and John Hughes-Wilson, *Blindfold and Alone: British Military Executions in the Great War*: 37.

39. In September the New Zealand Infantry Brigade of 4500 and the New Zealand Mounted Rifles Brigade of some 2000, totalling some 6500 ashore on Gallipoli, were 4980 under-strength. Godley to Allen dated 3 September 1915, Godley Papers, WA 252, NA.

40. Pugsley, *Gallipoli: The New Zealand Story*: 151–53, 327.

41. Godley to Allen dated 10 October 1915, WA 252, NA.

42. L.L. Robson, *The First A.I.F.: A Study of Its Recruitment 1914–1918*: 60–61; Grey, *The Australian Army*: 44–45.

43. Harris, *Canadian Brass*: 108–109.

44. Lt Col W.S. Austin, *The Official History of the New Zealand Rifle Brigade*.

45. Godley to Allen letter dated 20 January 1916, Allen Papers, M1/15, NA.

46. Chief of General Staff, *War 1914–1918: New Zealand Expeditionary Force: Its Provision and Maintenance*: 6–9.

47. Min of Defence to PM dated 30 January 1916, 'Establishment of the New Zealand Division', D1/6/3 Box 7, Allen Papers, NA.

48. Minister of Defence to Secretary Army Council, 3 February 1916, 'Establishment of the New Zealand Division', D1/6/3 Box 7, Allen Papers, NA.

49. Allen to Godley dated 15 February 1916, M 1/15, Allen Papers, NA.

50. Lt-Col J.L. Sleeman, 'The Supply of Reinforcements During the War', in H.T.B. Drew, *The War Effort of New Zealand*: 1–21; Chief of General Staff, *War 1914–1918: New Zealand Expeditionary Force: Its Provision and Maintenance*.

51. Paul Baker, *King and Country Call*: 95.

52. See correspondence, Allen, Liverpool and Long, Secretary of State for Colonies, August–September 1917, WA 230/16, NA.

53. Telegram, Liverpool, Governor of New Zealand to Long, Secretary of State for the Colonies, 15 February 1917 and following correspondence, WA 230/16, NA.

54. Allen to Brigadier-General G.S. Richardson dated 23 September 1918, Allen Papers, NA.

55. Major-General Sir Andrew Russell to Colonel Sir James Allen, Minister for Defence, 7 November 1917, Allen Papers, NA.

56. A.M.J. Hyatt, *General Sir Arthur Currie: A Military Biography*: 93, 97–102.

57. 'General John Monash', Dennis et al.,eds, *The Oxford Companion to Australian Military History*: 404–406. For the case study of an individual battalion of the AIF see Blair, *Dinkum Diggers*.

Chapter Four
The Inevitable Gallipoli Campaign

1. Jenny Macleod, 'General Sir Ian Hamilton and the Dardanelles Commission,' *War in History*, 8, 4, November 2001: 418–41.

2. By far the best single-volume general history of the campaign in what is a still growing library of studies is Robert Rhodes James' *Gallipoli*; although not footnoted it is still the most balanced and accessible study. One that is a little more episodic but has equal merit is Tim Travers' *Gallipoli 1915*, while other recent works include Michael Hickey's *Gallipoli* and Nigel Steel and Peter Hart's *Defeat at Gallipoli*.

3. David French, *British Strategy and War Aims, 1914–1916*: 66–86; Paul G. Halpern, *A Naval History of World War One*: 109–124; James, *Gallipoli*: 14–38; Travers, *Gallipoli 1915*: 20–36; Geoffrey Till, 'Brothers in Arms: The British Army and Navy at The Dardanelles', in Hugh Cecil and Peter H. Liddle, eds, *Facing Armageddon: The First World War Experienced*: 160–79; Geoffrey Till, 'The Gallipoli Campaign: Command Performances', in Gary Sheffield and Geoffrey Till, eds, *The Challenges of High Command: The British Experience*: 34–56; Winter, *25 April 1915: The Inevitable Tragedy*: 3–13.

4. Godley to Lady Godley dated 22 April 1915, Godley Papers, WA252, NA.

5. The evolution of the Turkish defence of the Gallipoli Peninsula is described in Edward J. Erickson, *Ordered to Die: A History of the Ottoman Army in the First World War*: 76–79; and Travers, *Gallipoli 1915*: 38–44.

6. Admiralty, CB1550. *Report of the Committee Appointed to Investigate the Attacks Delivered on and the Enemy Defences of the Dardanelles Straits, 1919*: 70.

7. Naval Orders: 'Orders for Combined Operations, Issued by Vice-Admiral J.M. de Robeck, Commanding Eastern Mediterranean Squadron', Appendix A to *Report*: 108; Travers, *Gallipoli 1915*: 32–34.

8. *Report*: 71.

9. Michael and Eleanor Brook, eds, *H.H. Asquith Letters to Venetia Stanley*: 257, quoted in Pugsley, *Gallipoli: The New Zealand Story*: 93.

10. Ashley Ekins, 'A Ridge Too Far: Military Objectives and the Dominance of Terrain in the Gallipoli Campaign', in Kenan Celik and Cehan Koc, eds, *The Gallipoli Campaign: International Perspectives 85 Years On*: 1–36.

11. 'To the General Commanding, French Expeditionary Force, dated 18 April 1915', *Report*: 138.

12. Erickson, *Ordered to Die*: 81–82.

13. 'Instructions for G.O.C. Australian and New Zealand Army Corps, dated 13 April 1915, *Report*: 137.

14. Quoted in Pugsley, *Gallipoli: The New Zealand Story*.

15. This was the favourite saying of Major J. Young when Chief Instructor, Tactical School, New Zealand Army Schools, Waiouru, 1980–81. See

Martin van Creveld, *Supplying War: Logistics from Wallenstein to Patton*; and Ian Malcolm Brown, *British Logistics on the Western Front 1914–1918*.

16. Quoted in Pugsley, *Gallipoli: The New Zealand Story*: 87.

17. 'Turkish Narrative at ANZAC up to 28th April, *Report*: 167.

18. Ibid.

19. Erickson, *Ordered to Die*: 83.

20. Travers, *Gallipoli 1915*: 46–64.

21. For an assessment of staff training at divisional level see Brian Bond, *The Victorian Army and the Staff College 1854–1914*: 306–309.

22. A far more positive assessment of Limon von Sanders' reaction in deploying his forces is given in Erickson, *Ordered to Die*: 84–85.

23. *Report*: 182.

24. Erickson, *Ordered to Die*: 88–89.

25. Tim Travers, 'The Ottoman Crisis of May 1915 at Gallipoli', *War in History*, 8, 1, January 2001: 72–86.

26. *Report*: 249.

27. Ibid. The evolution of the August offensive and its purpose is detailed in Bean, *The Story of ANZAC*, vol. 2: 430–72; Travers, *Gallipoli 1915*: 138–40.

28. Bean, *The Story of ANZAC*, vol. 2: 452–53.

29. Ibid.: 466–67; Travers, *Gallipoli 1915*: 140–42.

Chapter Five
The New Zealanders at Anzac

1. The major New Zealand sources on the campaign are Major Fred Waite, *The New Zealanders at Gallipoli*, and Christopher Pugsley, *Gallipoli: The New Zealand Story*. See also O.E. Burton, *The Silent Division: New Zealanders at the Front*; Cecil Malthus, *Anzac: A Retrospect*; Malcolm Ross, 'The New Zealand Forces in the War', in Sir Charles Lucas, ed., *The Empire at War*, vol. III: 267–318.

2. Bean, *The Story of ANZAC*, vol. 1, devotes the bulk of its 662 pages to a detailed account of the day. The considerable numbers of Turkish official studies of the campaign and of Turkey's involvement in the First World War have not been translated into English, although extracts of Turkish accounts may be found in Brig-General C.F. Aspinall-Oglander, *Military Operations Gallipoli*, vols 1 & 2. There is a detailed part-chapter on the campaign in Edward J. Erickson, *Ordered to Die: A History of the Ottoman Army in the First World War*: 76–95, and its bibliography lists relevant Turkish sources.

3. The most vivid and detailed account of the day from a New Zealand perspective is Lieutenant H. Spencer Westmacott's Diaries Vols 12 and 13 (Micro MS 847), ATL, Wellington, which may be accessed with family permission. It forms the basis of much of my chapter in *Gallipoli: The New Zealand Story*: 105–155.

4. Ibid.: 136–40.
5. Godley to Lady Godley dated 29 April 1915, WA 252, NA.
6. Lt J.R. Byrne, *New Zealand Artillery in the Field 1914–1918*: 61–66.
7. Godley to Lady Godley dated 29 April 1915, WA 252, NA.
8. Godley to Allen dated 5 May 1915, WA 252, NA.
9. Lt-Col W.G. Malone, Diaries, letters and papers including his son D.G.W. Malone's correspondence with Aspinall-Oglander, Rhodes James and John North, ATL, Wellington. A typescript copy of the Diary is in the Kippenberger Archive, QEII; Chris Pugsley, 'William George Malone', in Claudia Orange, ed., *The Dictionary of New Zealand Biography*, Vol. *3, 1901–1920*: 326–28.
10. Major J. Wallingford MC, NZSC, papers, Wallingford family.
11. Pugsley, *Gallipoli: The New Zealand Story*: 192–206; Waite, *Gallipoli*: 119–31.
12. Malone to Hart dated 20 June 1915, quoted in Pugsley, ibid.: 202.
13. Bean, *The Story of ANZAC*, vol. 2: 251.
14. Excellent medical histories have been produced that cover the Gallipoli Campaign. The New Zealand contribution is A.D. Carbery, *The New Zealand Medical Service in the Great War 1914–1918*: 30–134. For the failure of RMOs to evacuate sick men, see 2 Lt C.W. Saunders DCM, Diary, QEII, quoted in Pugsley, *Gallipoli: The New Zealand Story*: 263.
15. Malone diary; Pugsley, ibid.: 250–54.
16. Travers, *Gallipoli 1915*: 118–23, 138–40; Michael Evans, *From Legend to Learning: Gallipoli and the Military Revolution of World War I.*
17. 'Diary of Major H. Hart from 5th August 1915 to 19 Feby 1916', 13 September 1915, QEII.
18. Malone diary, 14 May 1915.
19. Brig.-General C.F. Aspinall-Oglander, *Military Operations Gallipoli*, vol. *II, May 1915 to the Evacuation*: 23–27.
20. James, *Gallipoli*: 255.
21. Bean, *The Story of ANZAC*, vol. 2: 439–40.
22. Aspinall-Oglander, *Military Operations Gallipoli*, vol. II: 133–34.
23. James, *Gallipoli*: 245.
24. Aspinall-Oglander, *Military Operations Gallipoli*, vol. II: 139–40; Bean, *The Story of ANZAC*, vol. 2: 440, 466–72; James, *Gallipoli*: 257.
25. C.G. Nicol, *The Story of Two Campaigns: Official War History of the Auckland Mounted Rifles Regiment, 1914–1919*: 68.
26. Bean, Interview Major Chapman AMR, AWM 38, 3 DRL 1722.
27. Bean, *The Story of ANZAC*, vol. 2: 576.
28. Operation Order No. 7 by Brigadier F.E. Johnston Commanding New Zealand Infantry Brigade dated 6 August 1915, NZ Infantry Brigade War Diary, August 1915, WA 70/1, NA.
29. 4 August 1915, Malone diary, AT.
30. Private James W. Swan WIB, DCM, MID, Personal Account of Gallipoli, RV 3498, QEII.
31. C.E.W. Bean, Review, AWM 38, 3 DRL 1722.
32. K.M. Stevens, *Maungatapere, A History and Reminiscence*: 106.
33. Swan, RV3498, QEII.
34. Bean, Review, AWM 38, 3 DRL 1722.
35. Report of Fighting on 8/8/15 on CHUNUK BAIR, Wellington Battalion War Diary, August 1915, WA 73/1, NA.
36. Bean, Review, AWM 38, 3 DRL 1722. A section of No. 4 Howitzer Battery, NZFA, three 5" Howitzer batteries of 69th Brigade and a scratch battery of four 18-pounders firing at Chunuk Bair over open sights provided artillery support. Byrne, *New Zealand Artillery in the Field, 1914–18*: 75–86.
37. NZ Infantry Brigade War Diary, August 1915, WA 70/1, NA.
38. Hart diary, 6 September, QEII.
39. Hart to Mrs Malone dated 20 September 1915, Malone Papers, AT.
40. NZ Infantry Brigade War Diary, August 1915, WA 70/1, NA.
41. 'Despatch dated 11th December 1915 from General Sir Ian Hamilton, C.C.B, Describing the Operations in the Gallipoli Peninsula, including the landing at Suvla Bay', Supplement to *London Gazette*, No. 29429, 6 January 1916: 25.
42. Major W.H. Cunningham letter dated 23 February 1916, J.V. Macfarlane Collection.
43. Bean, Review, AWM 38, 3 DRL 1722.
44. Michael Hickey, *Gallipoli*: 282–85. Field-Marshal Lord Birdwood also assumed that Allanson's companies were the only troops to see the Narrows in the August offensive; Field-Marshal Lord Birdwood, *Khaki and Gown: An Autobiography*: 275.
45. The letters of H.D. Skinner, published in 'Anthropologist at War' by Roger Fyfe, author's collection.
46. Bean, Review, AWM 38, 3 DRL 1722.
47. Ibid.
48. Ibid.
49. Ibid.
50. Ibid.
51. Temperley Memoirs, Braithwaite Collection, QEII.
52. Bean, *The Story of ANZAC*, vol. 2: 714.
53. For an assessment of the ANZAC Corps' operations see Travers, *Gallipoli 1915*: 114–36.
54. General Sir Alexander Godley, *Life of an Irish Soldier*: 187–88.
55. Ibid.: 185.
56. Godley to Allen dated 9 December 1916, WA 252, NA.
57. Godley letter dated 20 December 1915, WA 252, NA.
58. Pugsley, *Gallipoli: The New Zealand Story*: 363–64.
59. Erickson, *Ordered to Die*: 94; Travers, *Gallipoli 1915*: 229.

Chapter Six
The New Zealand Mounted Rifles Brigade in Sinai and Palestine 1916–18

1. Nicol, *The Story of Two Campaigns*: 179.
2. Pugsley, *On the Fringe of Hell*: 34–56.
3. Ibid.: 36.
4. Chaytor as Commander NZEF (Egypt) was delegated powers from Godley. Although Chaytor remained the operational commander in the field, he had a separate small administrative headquarters attached to the British Headquarters in Egypt that handled postings, reinforcements, casualty notifications, pay and postal details. Lieutenant-General Sir Alex Godley, 2nd Anzac Headquarters to Brigadier-General E.W.C. Chaytor CB, dated 1 June 1916, WA 252, NA.
5. Major C.B. Brereton, *Tales of Three Campaigns*: 129–31.
6. Mike Wicksteed, 'Edward Walter Clervaux Chaytor (1868–1939)', in Orange, ed., *The Dictionary of New Zealand Biography*, vol. 3: 93–95.
7. Pugsley, *Gallipoli: The New Zealand Story*: 50.
8. Ion L. Idriess, *The Desert Column*: 173; Powles, *The New Zealanders in Sinai and Palestine*: 69.
9. Ray Grover, 'William Meldrum (1865–1964)', in Orange, ed., *The Dictionary of New Zealand Biography*, vol 3: 338–39; 'Brigader-General William Meldrum', in McGibbon, ed., *The Oxford Companion to New Zealand Military History*: 315–16.
10. Hill, *Chauvel of the Light Horse*: 67; Powles, *The New Zealanders in Sinai and Palestine*: 4.
11. Powles, ibid.: 3–4.
12. A. Briscoe Moore, *The Mounted Riflemen in Sinai and Palestine*: 16–17.
13. Hill, *Chauvel of the Light Horse*: xx.
14. Ibid.: xx.
15. Ibid.: 81.
16. Wicksteed, 'Edward Walter Clervaux Chaytor (1868–1939)', in Orange, ed., *The Dictionary of New Zealand Biography*, vol. 3: 93–95.
17. Powles, *The New Zealanders in Sinai and Palestine*: 8.
18. Ibid.
19. Major-General J. Spens, 'Report on the Training and Administration of the Australian and New Zealand Training Depot, for the First Six Months, 19 April–19 October 1915', under covering letter Heaton-Rhodes to Robin, NZ CGS, dated 22 December 1915, WA 206/2/19, NA.
20. Ibid.
21. Pugsley, *On the Fringe of Hell*: 259–60.
22. Hill, *Chauvel of the Light Horse*: 154.
23. Studholme, *Record of Personal Services During the War*: 10.
24. Powles, *The New Zealanders in Sinai and Palestine*: 2.
25. Ibid.: 7.

26. AD1, Box 846, File 22/30, NA.
27. The courts martial register for the NZEF (Egypt) starts in 1917 and lists 33 courts martial for 1917, 37 for 1918, and 24 for the seven months of 1919; a total of 97 (including 3 'unofficial' courts martial from 1916). Seventy of this number took place before the Armistice with Turkey on 30 October 1918, and of these, 50 arose from incidents during training in Egypt or when soldiers were convalescing or on leave from the front. The conviction rate was not as high as in France, but once again one's chances of escaping conviction were slim, 71 out of 94 being found guilty. Courts Martial Register NZEF (Egypt), WA 9/5/9, NA.
28. Pugsley, *On the Fringe of Hell*: 54; Hill, *Chauvel of the Light Horse*: 65.
29. Pugsley, ibid.: 214–18.
30. Wahlert, *The Other Enemy*: 45–46, 69; Pugsley, *On the Fringe of Hell*: 305–306, 315.
31. Courts Martial Register NZEF (Egypt), WA 9/5/9, NA.
32. Ibid.
33. Pugsley, *On the Fringe of Hell*: 46–47; Courts Martial Register NZEF (Egypt), WA 9/5/9, NA.
34. Courts Martial Register NZEF (Egypt), WA 9/5/9, NA.
35. John Robertson, *With the Cameliers in Palestine*: 197–98.
36. ANZAC Mounted Division, Circular Memo No 8 dated 4 Feb 1916, AWM 25/807/4/233. Wahlert, in *The Other Enemy*, questions this and states that the British Deputy Adjutant General, MEF Cairo regarded this as inappropriate and that the AIF detention barracks opened in Abbassia camp in February 1916. Wahlert, *The Other Enemy*: 73.
37. Pugsley, *On the Fringe of Hell*: 91–103, 349.
38. HQ Southern Section DA847 of 16 December 1916, AWM 25/807/4/233.
39. Courts Martial Register NZEF (Egypt), WA 9/5/9, NA.
40. Pugsley, *On the Fringe of Hell*: 56.
41. Moore, *The Mounted Riflemen in Sinai and Palestine*: 78.
42. Ibid.: 79–80.
43. Ibid.
44. Hill, *Chauvel of the Light Horse*: 71.
45. Carbery, *The New Zealand Medical Service in the Great War, 1914–1918*: 451.
46. 'Brigader-General William Meldrum', in McGibbon, ed., *The Oxford Companion to New Zealand Military History*: 315–16.
47. Carbery, *The New Zealand Medical Service in the Great War, 1914–1918*: 453.
48. Ibid.: 456.
49. There were 20 courts martial of New Zealanders for incidents on operations during the campaign. Ten of these were in units of the New Zealand Mounted Rifles Brigade, five in the New Zealand companies of the Camel Corps and on their

disbandment two in No. 2 NZ Machine Gun Squadron that served as part of 5th Australian Light Horse Brigade in the Australian Mounted Division. Three Rarotongan soldiers were also court martialled in XXI British Corps. Pugsley, *On the Fringe of Hell*: 346–55; Courts Martial Register NZEF (Egypt), WA 9/5/9, NA.

50. Moore, *The Mounted Riflemen in Sinai and Palestine*: 85.

51. 'Sinai-Palestine', in McGibbon, ed., *The Oxford Companion to New Zealand Military History*: 491–94.

52. Wicksteed, 'Edward Walter Clervaux Chaytor (1868–1939)', in Orange, ed., *The Dictionary of New Zealand Biography*, vol. 3: 93–95.

53. Philip W. Chetwode to Godley dated 19 January 1917, Godley Papers, WA 252, NA.

54. Carbery, *The New Zealand Medical Service in the Great War, 1914–1918*: 463.

55. Matthew Hughes, *Allenby and British Strategy in the Middle East, 1917–1919*: 19.

56. Nicol, *The Story of Two Campaigns*: 137.

57. Ibid.: 139.

58. Hughes, *Allenby and British Strategy in the Middle East, 1917–1919*: 2.

59. Coates, *An Atlas of Australia's Wars*: 102–103.

60. Moore, *The Mounted Riflemen in Sinai and Palestine*: 71.

61. Ibid.: 71.

62. Nicol, *The Story of Two Campaigns*: 154.

63. Lieutenant-Colonel J.N. McCarroll CMG, DSO and Bar, (d³), OC 11th Squadron 5.8.1914, CO 23.4.1917, twice wounded. Studholme, *Record of Personal Services During the War*: 191.

64. Nicol, *The Story of Two Campaigns*: 158. Studholme, *Record of Personal Services During the War*: 40, 169.

65. Nicol, ibid.: 159–60.

66. Moore, *The Mounted Riflemen in Sinai and Palestine*: 90.

67. Nicol, *The Story of Two Campaigns*: 165.

68. Carbery, *The New Zealand Medical Service in the Great War, 1914–1918*: 471.

69. Ibid.: 477.

70. C.E.W. Bean et al., 'The Australian Forces in the War', in Lucas, ed., *The Empire at War*, vol. III: 199–202; Malcolm Ross, 'The New Zealand Forces in the War', in Lucas, ed., *The Empire at War*, vol. III: 376–77; Coates, *An Atlas of Australia's Wars*: 104.

71. Carbery, *The New Zealand Medical Service in the Great War, 1914–1918*: 479.

72. Coates, *An Atlas of Australia's Wars*: 104–107.

73. Hill, *Chauvel of the Light Horse*: 173.

74. Carbery, *The New Zealand Medical Service in the Great War, 1914–1918*: 481; Edith M. Lewis, *Joy in the Caring*: 69.

75. Nicol, *The Story of Two Campaigns*: 233–34.

76. Robertson, *With the Cameliers in Palestine*: 199.

77. File XFE 1024, WA 1/3/6, NA.

78. Moore quoted in Malcolm Ross, 'The New Zealand Forces in the War', in Lucas, ed., *The Empire at War*, vol. III: 380–81.

79. Pugsley, *On the Fringe of Hell*: 286–88; Gullett, *The AIF in Sinai and Palestine*, vol. VII: 787–91.

80. Pugsley, ibid.

81. Ibid.: 288.

82. Courts Martial Register NZEF (Egypt), WA 9/5/9, NA.

Chapter Seven
'Flotsam on the fringe of hell': Discipline and Morale in the NZEF

1. Quoted in Pugsley, *On the Fringe of Hell*: 7.

2. Corns & Hughes-Wilson, *Blindfold and Alone: British Military Executions in the Great War*: 450. See also Peter Scott, 'Law and Orders: Discipline and Morale in the British Armies in France, 1917', in Peter H. Liddle, ed., *Passchendaele in Perspective: The Third Battle of Ypres*: 349–68.

3. Gerard Oram, *Military Executions During World War I*: 130. Oram is highly critical of the Corns and Hughes-Wilson study but also concludes that 'we should dispense with the notion that capital punishments were carried out merely at some implicit insistence of Douglas Haig. The reality was far more complex than that.' The study evaluates the perceivable differences in the application of discipline between Regular, Territorial and New Army divisions, and highlights the importance of the divisional commander; however, as my study shows, Haig was more than willing to override even insistent recommendations of divisional commanders.

4. Anthony Babbington, *For the Sake of Example*; Nicholas Boyack, *Behind the Lines*; Putkowski & Sykes, *Shot at Dawn*.

5. Pugsley, *On the Fringe of Hell*: 22.

6. Russell to Allen, 17 September 1916, Allen Papers, NA.

7. Russell Diary, 21 October 1916, AT.

8. Russell to Allen, 25 December 1916, Allen Papers, NA.

9. Department of Justice, *Crime in New Zealand*: 220.

10. Corns & Hughes-Wilson, *Blindfold and Alone*.

11. A.B. Godefroy, *For Freedom and Honour?: The Story of the 25 Canadian Volunteers Executed in the Great War*: 21–40.

12. Ibid.: 59–67.

13. A study of the discipline and morale of the AIF has been a long-term project of the Australian historian Ashley Ekins. For aspects of this research see Ashley Ekins, 'The Australians at Passchendaele', in Liddle, ed., *Passchendaele in Perspective*: 227–54; Ashley Ekins, 'Australians at the End of the Great War', in Hugh Cecil & Peter

H. Liddle, eds, *At the Eleventh Hour: Reflections, Hopes and Anxieties at the Closing of the Great War, 1918*: 157–80; Grey, *The Australian Army*: 62–66.

14. Pugsley, *On the Fringe of Hell*: 131–35.
15. Grey, *The Australian Army*: 62–64.
16. Ibid.: 64; Pugsley, *On the Fringe of Hell*: 134.
17. Pugsley, ibid.: 73.
18. Ibid.: 65.
19. Ekins, 'The Australians at Passchendaele', in Liddle, ed., *Passchendaele in Perspective*: 227–54; Ashley Ekins, 'Australians at the End of the Great War', in Cecil & Liddle, eds, *At the Eleventh Hour*: 157–80.
20. Ekins, 'The Australians at Passchendaele', ibid.: 245.
21. Pugsley, *On the Fringe of Hell*: 354–55.
22. *Pardon for Soldiers of the Great War Act 2000*, Statutes of New Zealand, www.legislation.govt.nz.
23. 'Review of Deaths by Execution in the Great War of 1914–1918': a report by Sir Edward Somers, tabled by the Hon. Max Bradford, Minister of Defence, 15 October 1999.
24. Paul Fussell, *Thank God for the Atomic Bomb and other Essays*.

Chapter Eight
Learning from the Canadian Corps on the Western Front

1. Quoted in Stephen J. Harris, *Canadian Brass: The Making of a Professional Army, 1860–1939*: 121.
2. Ibid.: 98.
3. Ibid.
4. Jeffrey A. Keshen, *Propaganda and Censorship during Canada's Great War*: 215.
5. C.E.W. Bean, ed., *The Official History of Australia in the War of 1914–1918*, 12 vols.
6. Robin Hyde, *Passport to Hell: The Story of James Douglas Stark, Bomber, Fifth Reinforcement, New Zealand Expeditionary Forces*.
7. A.M.J. Hyatt, *General Sir Arthur Currie: A Military Biography*: 35–43; Bill Rawling, *Surviving Trench Warfare: Technology and the Canadian Corps, 1914–1918*: 29–36; Major A.F. Becke, *History of the Great War, Order of Battle: Part 4, The Army Council, G.H.Qs, Armies, and Corps, 1914–1918*: 163.
8. Morton & Granatstein, *Marching to Armageddon*: 39.
9. Ibid.: 107.
10. C.E.W. Bean, *The AIF in France 1916*, vol. III: 244–45.
11. Ibid.: 244.
12. 'Trench Raids. Based upon raids done by Canadian Corps.' WA 250/34, NA.
13. Report re 1st Canadian Divisional Field Punishment Station, Westhof Farm, 31 March 1916, AWM 4 783/2, quoted in Pugsley, *On the Fringe of Hell*: 93.
14. Hyatt, *General Sir Arthur Currie*: 90.

15. Morton & Granatstein, *Marching to Armageddon*: 107.
16. In the dominions the implication of the change from eight companies to four companies was still being debated among the Territorial Force into 1915; see for example *The Four Company Battalion in Battle*, Special District Order No. 5a/1915 by Lieut-Colonel J.E. Hume, Commanding Auckland Military District, Auckland 1st July, 1915.
17. Gary Sheffield, 'British High Command in the First World War: An Overview', in Gary Sheffield & Geoffrey Till, eds, *The Challenges of High Command: The British Experience*: 15–25.
18. Bill Rawling, *Surviving Trench Warfare: Technology and the Canadian Corps, 1914–1918*.
19. Hyatt, *General Sir Arthur Currie*: 54–57.
20. Morton & Granatstein, *Marching to Armageddon*: 112; Jeffery Williams, *Byng of Vimy: General and Governor General*: 115–70.
21. Canadian Corps G530. S109/1 dated 13 May 1917, Battalion Organization (Army and Corps Scheme) RG 9, III, C1, Vol. 3864, Folder 99, File 3, NAC.
22. Ibid.
23. Hyatt, *General Sir Arthur Currie*: 63–67; 'Translation of a Note by the French General Headquarters of the Armies of the East', dated 11 November 1915, RG 9, III, C I, Vol. 3867, Folder 107, File 6; 'Notes on Exercise carried out by 4th French Army to demonstrate the New Training of Infantry Units', Canadian Corps G.343 dated 27 November 1916, RG 9, III, CI, Vol. 3864, Folder 99, File 4; 'Notes on French Attacks, North-East of Verdun in October and December, 1916', Major-General A.W. Currie, 1st Canadian Division dated 23 January 1917, RG 9, III, C1, 3871, Folder 115, File 8; 'Notes on a Visit of a Party of British Officers to Verdun, January 5th–8th, 1917', RG 9, III C1, Vol. 3873, NAC; Shane B. Schreiber, *Shock Army of the British Empire: The Canadian Corps in the Last 100 Days of the Great War*: 9–14.
24. 'Notes on a Visit of a Party of British Officers to Verdun, January 5th–8th, 1917', RG 9, III C1, Vol. 3873, NAC.
25. John A. English & Bruce I. Gudmundsson, *On Infantry*: 18–31.
26. 'Notes on French Attacks, North-East of Verdun in October and December, 1916', Major-General A.W. Currie, 1st Canadian Division dated 23 January 1917, p. 5, RG 9, III, C1, 3871, Folder 115, File 8, NAC.
27. Canadian Corps G340 dated 27 December 1916, Battalion Organization (Army and Corps Scheme) RG 9, III, C1, Vol. 3864, Folder 99, File 3, NAC.
28. Ibid.
29. Ibid.
30. Canadian Corps G499, S109/1 10 January 1917, Battalion Organization (Army and Corps Scheme) RG 9, III, C1, Vol. 3864, Folder 99, File 3, NAC.
31. GHQ to First Army OB 1919, dated 7 February

1917, Canadian Corps to First Army G519, S.109/1 dated 13 February 1917, Battalion Organization (Army and Corps Scheme) RG 9, III, C1, Vol. 3864, Folder 99, File 3, NAC.

32. Harry Davies, *Allanson of the 6th*: 131.

33. David J. Bercuson & J.L. Granatstein, *Dictionary of Canadian Military History*: 219.

34. Jeffery Williams, *Byng of Vimy*: 144–47.

35. Robin Prior & Trevor Wilson, *Command on the Western Front: The Military Career of Sir Henry Rawlinson 1914–1918*; Robin Prior & Trevor Wilson, *Passchendaele: The Untold Story*.

36. Ashley Ekins, 'The Australians at Passchendaele', in Peter H. Liddle, ed., *Passchendaele in Perspective: The Third Battle of Ypres*: 227–54.

37. Robin Prior & Trevor Wilson, *Passchendaele*: 130; see also p. 175 and equally validly where conditions render 'fire and movement' impossible on pp. 176–77.

38. Ian M. Brown, '"Not Glamorous but Effective": The Canadian Corps and the Set-piece Attack, 1917–1918', *Journal of Military History*, 58, July 1994: 421–44; A.M.J. Hyatt, *General Sir Arthur Currie*; and Bill Rawling, *Surviving Trench Warfare*.

39. 2nd Army G.140, 'General Principles on which the Artillery Plan will be Drawn', included with 2nd Army G.140 to GHQ dated 29 August 1917, Second Army War Diary, August 1917, Vol. XXXII, WO 95/275, PRO.

40. 4th Canadian Division G.13-8 dated 9 May 1917, RG 9, III, C1, Vol. 3864, Folder 99, File 3, NAC.

41. 1st Canadian Division dated 9 May 1917, Battalion Organization (Army and Corps Scheme) RG 9, III, C1, Vol. 3864, Folder 99, File 3, NAC.

42. For a succinct overview of the Bullecourt battles see the excellent summary and maps in John Coates, *An Atlas of Australia's Wars, Vol. VII, Australian Centenary History of Defence*: 60–64.

43. Jonathan Walker, *The Blood Tub: General Gough and the Battle of Bullecourt, 1917*: 101–104.

44. Walker, *The Blood Tub*: xx, 107–110, 142–48, 189–91.

45. Daniel G. Dancocks, *Legacy of Valour: The Canadians at Passchendaele*: 90.

46. Hyatt, *General Sir Arthur Currie*: 76–77.

47. Rawling, *Surviving Trench Warfare*: 142.

48. Quoted in Hyatt, *General Sir Arthur Currie*: 79.

49. Ibid.: 81–84; Rawling, *Surviving Trench Warfare*: 147–52.

50. Dancocks, *Legacy of Valour*: 100–103.

51. Dean Oliver, 'The Canadians at Passchendaele', in Liddle, ed., *Passchendaele in Perspective: The Third Battle of Ypres*: 255–71.

52. Haig Diary, Monday 23 July 1917, WO 256/20, PRO.

53. Dancocks, *Legacy of Valour*: 223–25.

54. Interim Report on Operations of the Canadian Corps during the Year 1918, p.2, RG 9 III, C1, Canadian Corps HQ, GS Folders 120, File 10,

NAC. See also *Report of the Ministry, Overseas Military Forces of Canada, 1918*: 103.

55. Report of the Department of the General Staff for the month of February 1918 by Brig.-General H.F. McDonald CMG, DSO, 'Training of Reinforcements at the Base and Within the Corps', RG9, III, C1, Canadian Corps, HQ GS, Vol 3870, Folder 112, File 13, NAC.

56. Hyatt, *General Sir Arthur Currie*: 98–102.

57. Ibid.: 93.

58. Report of the Department of the General Staff for the month of February 1918 by Brig.-General H.F. McDonald CMG, DSO, 'Training of Reinforcements at the Base and Within the Corps', RG9, III, C1, Canadian Corps, HQ GS, Vol 3870, Folder 112, File 13, NAC.

59. Canadian infantry strengths as at 9 March 1918: 1st Can Div 12,085 2nd Can Div 11,673 3rd Can Div 12,027 4th Can Div 11,924 Total infantry: 47,709. Canadian Corps Strength Returns: 7 January 1917 – 9 March 1918, RG9, III, C1, Vol. 3867, Folder 107, File 7, NAC. The importance of having full-strength infantry units is emphasised in S.F. Wise, 'The Black Day of the German Army: Australians and Canadians at Amiens, August 1918', in Peter Dennis & Jeffrey Grey, eds, *1918 Defining Victory*: 1–32; and in Schreiber, *Shock Army of the British Empire*: 19–22.

60. Minister Overseas Military Forces of Canada, *Report of the Ministry, Overseas Military Forces of Canada, 1918*: 198–99, 244–50, 276; Rawling, *Surviving Trench Warfare*: 176–77; Schreiber, ibid.: 17–32; Wise, ibid.

61. Rawling, ibid.: 177–78; Schreiber, ibid.

62. *Report of the Ministry*: 231–38.

63. 2nd Canadian Division Training Instructions dated 10 March 1918, RG 9, III C1 Canadian Corps HQ GS, Folder 109, File 3, Memoranda on Training Issued by Divisions, NAC.

64. Ibid.

65. *Report of the Ministry*: 124.

66. Interim Report on Operations of the Canadian Corps during the year 1918, p. 11, RG 9 III, C1, Canadian Corps HQ, GS Folders 120, File 10, NAC. See also *Report of the Ministry, Overseas Military Forces of Canada, 1918*: 109–110.

67. *Report of the Ministry*: 112.

68. Quoted in Hyatt, *General Sir Arthur Currie*: 105.

69. *Report of the Ministry*: 124.

70. Ibid.: 123.

71. Wise, 'The Black Day of the German Army: Australians and Canadians at Amiens, August 1918'; Bill Rawling, 'A Resource Not to Be Squandered: The Canadian Corps on the 1918 Battlefield', in Dennis & Grey, eds, *1918 Defining Victory*: 1–32, 43–71; Schreiber, *Shock Army of the British Empire*: 33–69.

72. Morton & Granatstein, *Marching to Armageddon*: 203.
73. Michael Howard, *The First World War*: 128.
74. *Report of the Ministry*: 140.
75. J.P. Harris with Niall Barr, *Amiens to the Armistice: The BEF in the Hundred Days' Campaign, 8 August–11 November 1918*: 119–20.
76. Quoted in Harris, *Amiens to the Armistice*: 145–46.
77. Bercuson & Granatstein, *Dictionary of Canadian Military History*: 69.
78. Morton & Granatstein, *Marching to Armageddon*: 222.
79. Bill Rawling, 'A Resource Not to Be Squandered: The Canadian Corps on the 1918 Battlefield', in Dennis & Grey, eds, *1918 Defining Victory*: 43–71; Schreiber, *Shock Army of the British Empire*: 71–86.
80. Harris, *Amiens to the Armistice*: 153–55.
81. *Report of the Ministry*: 168.
82. *Report of the Ministry*: 184.
83. Hyatt, *General Sir Arthur Currie*: 129–30.

Chapter Nine
Russell and Monash: Two ANZAC Divisional Commanders on the Western Front

1. Haig Papers, Diary, Volume XIII Jan–Feb 1917, 28 January 1917, discussions with Allenby, newly appointed commander 3rd Army, NLS.
2. P.A. Pedersen, *Monash As Military Commander*; Geoffrey Serle, *John Monash: A Biography*; John Monash, *The Australian Victories in France in 1918*; F.M. Cutlack, ed., *War Letters of General Monash*; see also 'General John Monash', in Dennis et al., eds, *The Oxford Companion to Australian Military History*: 404–408.
3. Christopher Pugsley, 'Andrew Hamilton Russell', in Claudia Orange, ed., *The Dictionary of New Zealand Biography*, vol. 3: 449–51.
4. 'General John Monash', in Dennis et al., eds, *The Oxford Companion to Australian Military History*: 404–408.
5. A.H. Russell, 'The Russell Saga', Volume III, World War I: 3, extracted and compiled by R.F. Gambrill, Russell Family/AT.
6. Ibid.: 4.
7. Ibid.: 9.
8. Major-General Sir Andrew Hamilton Russell, personal file, Base Records, Wellington.
9. Bean, *The Story of ANZAC*, vol. 2: 576.
10. Serle, *John Monash*: 236–37, 534–35; Pedersen, *Monash as Military Commander*: 93–113; James, *Gallipoli*: 272–73; 'General John Monash', in Dennis et al., eds, *The Oxford Companion to Australian Military History*: 404–408.
11. Aspinall-Oglander, *Military Operations Gallipoli*, vol. II: 192–95.
12. Serle, *John Monash*: 236–37, 534–35; Pedersen, *Monash as Military Commander*: 93–113.
13. 'General John Monash', in Dennis et al., eds, *The Oxford Companion to Australian Military History*: 404–408.
14. Brigadier-General G.N. Johnston to Russell in a post-war note, Russell Papers. Major Walter Guinness MP, who was a Brigade Major of 74th Brigade in the 25th Division at Messines, and had served on the peninsula at Anzac, wrote on 23 March 1917, 'He was not much thought of as a Brigadier at Gallipoli and was given a Division because the Australians don't like being commanded by British professional soldiers.' Brian Bond, ed., *Staff Officer: The Diaries of Lord Moyne, 1914–1918*: 149.
15. Monash to Steward dated 12 November 1915, 3DRL/2316—MONASH 3/31, AWM.
16. Pedersen, *Monash as Military Commander*: 128.
17. Ibid.: 130.
18. Ibid.: 131–34.
19. Ibid.: 199.
20. Ibid.: 141.
21. *Report of the Ministry, Overseas Military Forces of Canada, 1918*: 123.
22. Pedersen, *Monash as Military Commander*: 142.
23. Ibid.: 158.
24. Quoted in Peter S. Sadler, *The Paladin: A Life of Major-General Sir John Gellibrand*: 159.
25. Russell Diary, 21 October 1916, AT.
26. Russell to Allen, 25 December 1916, Allen Papers, NA.
27. Russell Diary, 5 March 1917, AT.
28. Notes of Conference held by G.O.C., NZ Division, 30 November 1916, WA 20/2, NA.
29. 'Preparation of Field Rations', WA 78/3/27, NA.
30. NZ Division Routine Order No. 924A, WA 20/2, NA.
31. Russell to Allen dated 3 April 1917, Allen papers, NA.
32. See, for example, War Diaries APM 3rd Australian Division, WO 154/78, PRO.
33. 'Individual Assault Practice', O.B./1146 dated 22 March 1917, WA 78/3/7, NA.
34. 'Organisation of a Platoon', 3 NZ [Rifle] Brigade dated 4 May 1917, WA 22/6/17, NA.
35. 'Reorganisation of Battalions', 2nd New Zealand Infantry Brigade to HQ NZ Division dated 7 March 1917, WA 22/6/17, NA.
36. Major A.F. Becke, *Order of Battle, Part 4: The Army Council, G.H.Q.s, Armies, and Corps 1914–1918*: 12.
37. Shelford Bidwell & Dominick Graham, *Fire-Power: British Army Weapons and Theories of War 1904–1945*: 125.
38. Paddy Griffith, *Battle Tactics of the Western Front: The British Army's Art of Attack, 1916–1918*.
39. Griffith, *Battle Tactics of the Western Front*: 110.
40. C.S. Forester, *The General*: 86.
41. Bidwell & Graham, *Fire-Power*: 125–26.
42. Quoted in Coates, *An Atlas of Australia's Wars*: 64.
43. Pedersen, *Monash as Military Commander*: 160.

44. Russell Diary, 25 March 1917, AT.
45. Russell Diary, 2 April 1917, AT.
46. Russell to Allen dated 19 June 1917, Allen papers, NA.
47. 'Outline Plan for the Offensive against Messines', HQ New Zealand Division, S.G.241/53, WA 20/3/13, NA.
48. Ibid.; Lieutenant J.R. Byrne, *New Zealand Artillery in the Field 1914–1918*: 167–70.
49. Report on the Capture of Messines by 4th Battalion 3rd N.Z.Rifle Brigade, WA 20/3/13, NA.
50. Ibid.
51. Haig Diaries, 24 May 1917, WO 256/18, PRO.
52. Russell Diary, 24 May 1917, AT.
53. Pedersen, *Monash as Military Commander*: 169.
54. Ibid.: 168.
55. Ibid: 164.
56. Haig Papers, Diary, 24 May 1917, Vol. XVI May 1917, NLS.
57. Ashley Ekins, 'The Australians at Passchendaele', in Liddle, ed., *Passchendaele in Perspective*: 231–32.
58. 2 NZ Inf Brigade, Report on Messines Operation, WA 76/3/99, NA.
59. Ibid.
60. Russell to Allen dated 19 June 1917, Allen papers, NA.
61. Pedersen, *Monash as Military Commander*: 169.
62. NZ Division, Lessons of the Messines Offensive compiled from Reports of Brigades, Battalions, and in some cases of Company Officers and NCOs, WA 20/3/8, NA.
63. Haig Diaries, 9 June 1917. Haig would later meet with Brigadier-General John Baird, one of Bainbridge's brigade commanders, who also 'was much down upon the 4th Australian Division for their conduct on the night of the 7th and the morning of the 8th'. Haig Diaries, 11 June 1917, WO 256/19, PRO.
64. Russell to Allen dated 19 June 1917, Allen papers, NA.
65. Ibid.
66. Haig Papers, Diary, Volume XVII June 1917, 7 June 1917, NLS.
67. Ibid.
68. Brown was not killed by a sniper, as stated in his entry, 'Brigadier-General Charles Henry Jeffries Brown', in McGibbon, ed., *The Oxford Companion to New Zealand Military History*: 73. See Stewart, *The New Zealand Division 1916–1919*: 207. It may be that Brown's death has been confused with that of his successor, Brigadier-General F.E. Johnston, who was sniped and killed on 7 August 1917. Stewart, ibid.: 242–43; 'Brigadier-General Francis Earl Johnston', McGibbon, ibid.: 260. Brigadier-General R. Young, Johnston's successor, almost shared the same fate when he was sniped and seriously wounded near the same spot on 9 August 1917. 'Major-General Sir Robert Young', McGibbon, ibid.: 625.
69. Russell Diary, 12 June 1917, AT.
70. Haig Diaries, 15 July 1917, WO 256/20, PRO.
71. Ibid.
72. Douglas Haig, Diary entry, 29 July 1918, quoted in Justin Wintle, ed., *The Dictionary of War Quotations*: 298.
73. Bruce I. Gudmundsson, *Storm Troop Tactics: Innovation in the German Army, 1914–1918*; Martin Samuels, *Doctrine and Dogma, German and British Infantry Tactics in the First World War*; John A. English & Bruce I. Gudmundsson, *On Infantry*.
74. Russell Diaries, 20 August 1917, AT.
75. Operations of the New Zealand Division, Period September 1st to October 31st 1917, WA 50/4/32, NA.
76. Russell Diaries, 5 September 1917, AT.
77. Russell Diaries, 21 and 24 August 1917, AT.
78. Russell Diaries, 5–11 September 1917, AT.
79. Haig Papers, Friday 14 September 1917, Vol. XX, NLS.
80. Russell Diaries, 20 September 1917, AT.
81. Russell Diaries, 25 September 1917, AT.
82. Russell Diaries, 27 September 1917, AT.
83. Russell Diaries, 28 September 1917, AT.
84. John Baynes, *Far From a Donkey*: 209–218; Griffith, *Battle Tactics of the Western Front*: 95–100; Peter Simkins, 'The War Experience of a Typical Kitchener Division — the 18th Division', in Cecil & Liddle, eds, *Facing Armageddon: The First World War Experienced*: 297–313.
85. Russell Diaries, 30 September 1917, AT.
86. Pedersen, *Monash as Military Commander*: 183–89.
87. Haig Diaries, Saturday, 22 September 1917, WO 256/22, PRO.
88. Haig Diary, 1 October 1917, WO 256/23, PRO.
89. A.H. Russell Diary, 2 Oct 1917, AT.
90. Russell to Allen dated 4 October 1917, Allen Papers, NA.
91. Pedersen, *Monash as Military Commander*: 192.
92. Ibid.
93. Gough's recommendation to do this is now questioned by many historians; however, Harington, Plumer's MGGS, recounts Gough ringing Plumer recommending postponement because of the weather. This Plumer refused after sounding out his corps commanders; General Sir Charles Harington, *Tim Harington Looks Back*: 62–63.
94. Russell Diary, 5 October 1917, AT.
95. Narrative of Operations of New Zealand Divisional Artillery. From 1st to 20th October, 1917, WA 50/4/32, NA.
96. Ibid.
97. Comments on Operations — 4th to 12th October, 1917, included in Narrative of Operations of New Zealand Divisional Artillery. From 1st to 20th October, 1917, WA 50/4/32, NA.
98. Ibid.
99. Russell Diary, 9 October 1917, AT.

100. Haig Diary, 8 October 1917, WO 256/23, PRO.
101. Haig Papers, 9 October 1917, Vol. XXI, NLS.
102. Haig Papers, 10 October 1917, Vol. XXI, NLS.
103. Ibid.
104. This confidence is reflected in Godley's report to Harington on the day of the attack when it was evident that the New Zealanders were in trouble. 'They are both determined to do the job and I think they will.' Pencilled note in Harington's hand, 11.45, 12 October 1917, Second Army Operations, 29 August–12 October 1917, WO 158/208, PRO.
105. II ANZAC Headquarters General Staff War Diary, 11/10/17, WO 95/1032, PRO.
106. Russell Diaries, 11 October 1917, AT.
107. 'Western Front', in McGibbon, ed., The Oxford Companion to New Zealand Military History: 598–610.
108. Pedersen, Monash as Military Commander: 199.
109. Russell Diaries, 12 October 1917, AT.
110. 'GOC New Zealand Division states that the BELLEVUE defences must be rebombarded heavily before another attack is launched.' This was initially planned for following day but then postponed. MGGS 2nd Army to Advanced GHQ, G699 dated 12 October 1917, 2nd Army Operations, 29 Aug–12 Oct 1917, WO 158/208, PRO.
111. NZ Division, Narrative of Operations for Passchendaele Attack, October 12th 1917, S.G. 151/24 dated 3 Nov 1917, WA 50/4/32, NA.
112. Russell Diary, 15–16 October 1917, AT.
113. Russell Diary, 31 October 1917, AT.
114. Russell Diary, 24 October 1917, AT.
115. Russell to Allen dated 7 November 1917, Allen Papers, NA.
116. II ANZAC Headquarters General Staff War Diary, 31/10/17, WO 95/1032, PRO.
117. Christopher Pugsley, 'The New Zealand Division at Passchendaele', in Liddle, ed., Passchendaele in Perspective: The Third Battle of Ypres: 272–91.
118. Pedersen, Monash as Military Commander: 204.
119. Becke, Order of Battle, Part 4, The Army Council, G.H.Q.s, Armies, and Corps 1914–1918: 257–58.
120. Russell Diary, 24 June 1918, AT.

Chapter Ten
The First AIF: More than larrikins but less than perfect?

1. Stuart Macintyre, The Oxford History of Australia, Vol. 4, 1901–1942: 176–77.
2. Ibid.: 176.
3. Ibid.
4. Ibid.
5. Peter Dennis, 'Introduction', in Peter Dennis, Jeffrey Grey & John McCarthy, Revue Internationale d'Histoire Militaire, 72: viii.
6. E.M. Andrews, 'Bean and Bullecourt: Weaknesses and Strengths of the Official History of Australia in the First World War', in Dennis et al., Revue Internationale d'Histoire Militaire, 72: 25–47.
7. Les Carlyon, Gallipoli; Bill Gammage, The Broken Years: Australian Soldiers in the Great War; John Robertson, ANZAC and Empire: The Tragedy and Glory of Gallipoli.
8. Dale Blair, Dinkum Diggers: An Australian Battalion at War: 194.
9. Jeffrey Grey, A Military History of Australia: 94.
10. Blair, Dinkum Diggers: 23–29, 37–68.
11. To be 'hooked' was to be punched. See 'Hook', in H.W. Orsman, ed., The Dictionary of New Zealand English: 357.
12. Lt C.S. Algie, Diary 1914–1915, Tuesday 16 February 1915, MS Papers 1374, AT.
13. Chris Roberts, 'The Landing at Anzac: A Reassessment', Journal of the Australian War Memorial, 22, April 1993: 25–34.
14. Alistair Thomson, '"The Vilest Libel of the War"? Imperial Politics and the Official Histories of Gallipoli', Australian Historical Studies, 25, 101, October 1993: 628–36.
15. Peter Burness, The Nek: The Tragic Charge of the Light Horse at Gallipoli.
16. C.D. Coulthard-Clark, No Australian Need Apply: The Troubled Career of Lieutenant General Gordon Legge.
17. Godley to Allen dated 20 Jan 1916, 19 Feb 1916 and 4 March 1916, Allen Papers, NA.
18. 'Lieutenant-General James Whiteside McCay', in Dennis et al., eds, The Oxford Companion to Australian Military History: 369–70.
19. Bean, The AIF in France 1916, vol. 3: 328–447.
20. Godley to Lady Godley, dated 22 July 1916, Godley 3/183, LHCMH, KCL.
21. Colonel W.E.H. Cass, CO 58th Battalion, broke down and was invalided home. Colonel Pope of the 14th Brigade was sacked after he was found asleep from exhaustion, in the belief that he was drunk. Both were Gallipoli veterans, with Pope being the fighting backbone of the 4th Australian Brigade on the peninsula. Bean, The AIF in France 1916, vol. 3: 447.
22. Lieutenant-Colonel H. Sloan, The Purple and Gold: A History of the 30th Battalion: 106–107.
23. 'Lieutenant-General (James) Gordon Legge', in Dennis et al., eds, The Oxford Companion to Australian Military History: 344–45; Rosemary Derham, The Silence Ruse: Escape from Gallipoli: A Record and Memory of the Life of General Sir Brudenell White KCB, KCMG,KCVO, DSO: 48.
24. G.D. Sheffield, 'The Australians at Pozières: Command and Control on the Somme, 1916', in David French & Brian Holden Reid, eds, The British General Staff: Reform and Innovation, 1890–1939: 112–26; David Horner, Blamey: The Commander-in-Chief: 42–45.
25. Derham, The Silence Ruse: 52–53.

26. See weekly summary of operations, I ANZAC GS War Diary 1–31 August 1916, WO 95/981, and the Reserve Army Operation Orders in late July and August directing I ANZAC to 'press on' in a series of repeated attacks. Reserve Army Operations April–September 1916, WO 158/245. Gough's approach is exemplified by his memorandum of 3 August 1916, issued again on 3 October 1916 to his corps commanders. 'Relentless pressure must be exercised everywhere and always.' Memorandum by Army Commander, Reserve Army dated 3 August 1916, 5th Army, 'Notes and Lessons on 1916 Operations', WO158/344, PRO.

27. Ivan Chapman, *Iven G. Mackay: Citizen and Soldier*: 78.

28. Bean, *The AIF in France 1916*, vol. 3: 869–77.

29. Ekins, 'The Australians at Passchendaele', in Liddle, *Passchendaele in Perspective*: 227–54; Ekins, 'Australians at the End of the Great War', in Cecil and Liddle, *At the Eleventh Hour: Reflections, Hopes and Anxieties at the Closing of the Great War, 1918*: 157–80.

30. Chapman, *Iven G. Mackay: Citizen and Soldier*: 79.

31. Ibid.: 83.

32. Norman K. Harvey, *From Anzac to the Hindenburg Line: The History of the 9th Battalion A.I.F.*: 137, 183–84.

33. Eric Wren, *Randwick to Hargicourt: The History of the 3rd Battalion A.I.F.*: 194–96.

34. David Coombes, *Morshead: Hero of Tobruk and El Alamein*: 40–65.

35. Ross McMullin, *Pompey Elliot*: 82–83, 177–90, 212, 240, 296–99, 371–74.

36. 'Major-General (Thomas) William Glasgow', in Dennis et al., eds, *The Oxford Companion to Australian Military History*: 269; Wren, *Randwick to Hargicourt*: 299.

37. Sadler, *The Paladin*: 85–89.

38. J.M. Bourne, 'The BEF's Generals on 29 September 1918: An Empirical Portrait with Some British and Australian Comparisons', in Dennis & Grey, eds, *1918 Defining Victory*: 96–113.

39. Blair, *Dinkum Diggers*: 189–90.

40. Chapman, *Iven G. Mackay: Citizen and Soldier*: 79–82.

41. Joan Beaumont, *The Australian Centenary History of Defence*, vol. VI, *Australian Defence Sources and Statistics*: 108–111.

42. Ibid.

43. Wahlert, *The Other Enemy?*: 58–61.

44. By November 1918 nearly 50 percent of the officers of the NZEF had been commissioned from the ranks. These selections were based on recommendations from their commanding officers, and in the case of candidates from non-combative units, this required a soldier to be transferred to a combative unit at the front and, 'having served at least three months with such unit, had been favourably reported on by the officer commanding such unit as regards behaviour under fire'. Lt-Colonel John Studholme, *Record of Personal Services During the War of Officers, Nurses, and First-Class Warrant Officers; and Other Facts Relating to the NZEF*: 10.

45. First ANZAC Corps Order No. 124 dated 10th April 1917 detailed the role of the 12 tanks placed in support of the 4th Australian Division but given the time available left the coordination of the fire plan to the GOC 4th Australian Division. I ANZAC Corps GS, War Diaries, 1–30 April 1917, WO 95/982. See also Fifth Army Instructions, Fifth Army Operations 1 April–12 May 1917, WO 158/248, PRO.

46. 'Report on Attack against the HINDENBURG LINE by the 4th Australian Division — 11th April 1917', I ANZAC Corps GS, War Diaries, 1–30 April 1917, WO 95/982, PRO.

47. Walker, *The Blood Tub*: 91–113.

48. Ibid.: 143.

49. Sadler, *The Paladin*: 137–42.

50. Bond, ed., *Staff Officer*: 157.

51. Haig Diaries, 9 June 1917, WO256/19, PRO.

52. 'Major-General William Holmes', in Dennis et al., eds, *The Oxford Companion to Australian Military History*: 295.

53. Quoted in Ekins, 'The Australians at Passchendaele', in Liddle, *Passchendaele in Perspective*: 231–32.

54. C.E.W. Bean, *The AIF in France 1917*, vol. IV: 733–34.

55. Ibid.

56. Ibid.: 730–32.

57. Capt. A.D. Ellis MC, *The Story of the Fifth Australian Division: Being an Authoritative Account of the Division's Doings in Egypt, France and Belgium*: 218–19.

58. Ibid.: 732.

59. Birdwood to Plumer dated 29 August 1917, Godley's concurrence to Plumer dated 30 August 1917, Second Army Operations, 29 August–12 October 1917, WO 158/208, PRO.

60. Haig Diary, Wednesday 29 August 1917, WO 256/21, PRO.

61. [Conference Notes] 2nd Army G503 dated 4 September 1917, Second Army Vol. XXXIII, September 1917, WO 95/275, PRO.

62. 5th Army, 'Notes and Lessons on 1916 Operations', WO158/344, PRO; however, it is interesting to read the views of Major Walter Guinness, later Lord Moyne, when Brigade Major in the 25th Division when the Division was transferred from II ANZAC in Plumer's Second Army to II Corps in Gough's Fifth Army. 'After the wonderful organization and devotion to detail which one found in 2nd Army, the 5th Army struck one as very haphazard in its methods … None of the lessons taught by Plumer's success seemed to have been learnt.' Bond & Robbins, eds, *Staff Officer*: 162.

63. [Conference Notes] 2nd Army G503 dated 4 September 1917, Second Army Vol. XXXIII, September 1917, WO 95/275, PRO.

64. First ANZAC Corps Order No. 172 dated 18 September 1917, First ANZAC Corps, GS May– September 1917, WO 95/ 983, PRO.

65. McMullin, *Pompey Elliot*: 305–46.

66. Ibid.: 630–55.

67. Ellis, *The Story of the Fifth Australian Division*: 235. See for example First ANZAC Corps Order No. 172 dated 18 September 1917, First ANZAC Corps GS War Diaries, 1–30 September 1917, WO 95/ 983, PRO.

68. Ellis, ibid.: 246.

69. Birdwood, *Khaki and Gown*: 316–17.

70. 2nd ANZAC Corps General Staff War Diary, 8 October 1917, WO 95/1032, PRO.

71. [Conference Notes] 2nd Army G503 dated 4 September 1917, Second Army Vol. XXXIII, September 1917, WO 95/275, PRO.

72. Confusion sometimes arises between Haig's approval of the Australian Corps in November 1917, and the formal change in nomenclature of I ANZAC to the Australian Corps and II ANZAC to XXII Corps at midnight, 31 December 1917.

73. Strength of divisions as at 30 November 1917, WO 95/276, PRO.

1 Aust	573	11,358
2 Aust	485	10,960
3 Aust	510	9192
5 Aust	497	11,841
NZ Div	517	14,671
1 Can	491	11,045 all strength of leaving army on 12 and 19 November 1917.
2 Can	499	10,228
3 Can	468	10,360
4 Can	493	10,484

74. Pedersen, *Monash as Military Commander*: 216.

75. Ibid.: 215–18, 255–56.

76. Walker was transferred to a divisional command in Italy, and after the Armistice commanded all British forces in that theatre. He retired in 1928 in the rank of Lieutenant-General. 'Lieutenant-General Harold Bridgewood Walker', in Dennis et al., eds, *The Oxford Companion to Australian Military History*: 627; James, *Gallipoli*: 242.

77. Haig Diaries, 24 May 1917, WO 256/18; 9 June 1917, WO 256/19; 19 July 1917, WO 256/20; 22 September 1917, WO 256/22; 10 October 1917, 23 October 1917, WO 256/23, PRO; Monash Correspondence, letter to wife 19 July 1917, MS1884/4/5102; letter to wife, 23 September 1917, MS1884/4/5154, NLA; Monash Correspondence, 19 May 1917, 19 July 1917, 3 August 1917, 24 September 1917, 3DRL 2316/1/2, AWM.

78. Pedersen, *Monash as Military Commander*: 223–33.

79. This view is shared by Coates, *An Atlas of Australia's Wars*: 78–80.

80. Pedersen, *Monash as Military Commander*: 233–45;

Wise, 'The Black Day of the German Army: Australians and Canadians at Amiens, August 1918', in Dennis & Grey, *1918 Defining Victory*: 1–32.

81. Schreiber, *Shock Army of the British Empire*: 41.

82. Hyatt, *General Sir Arthur Currie*: 115.

83. J.P. Harris, *Amiens to the Armistice: The BEF in the Hundred Days Campaign, 8 August–11 November 1918*: 89–92.

84. Minister of Overseas Military Forces of Canada, *Report of the Ministry, Overseas Military Forces of Canada, 1918*: 138.

85. Harris suggests 18,000 prisoners; Harris, *Amiens to the Armistice*: 104–107.

86. General Ludendorff, *My War Memories, 1914– 1918*, vol. II: 679–84.

87. Bean, *The AIF in France May 1918 to the Armistice*, vol. 6: 873; Pedersen, *Monash as Military Commander*: 265–68; Coates, *An Atlas of Australia's Wars*: 84.

88. Sadler, *The Paladin*: 173.

89. Pedersen, *Monash as Military Commander*: 276.

90. Hyatt, *General Sir Arthur Currie*: 93.

91. Pedersen, *Monash as Military Commander*: 277.

92. Sadler, *The Paladin*: 179–80.

93. Blair, *Dinkum Diggers*: 157–64.

94. Ellis, *The Story of the Fifth Australian Division*: 380–81.

95. W.H. Downing, *To The Last Ridge: The First World War Memoirs of W.H. Downing*: 175–83.

96. Bean, *The AIF in France May 1918 to the Armistice*, vol. 6: 1043.

97. Ibid.: 878–79; there is a rich if anecdotal version of the conversation between Hughes and Monash in W. Farmer Whyte, *William Morris Hughes: His Life and Times*: 368–71.

98. L.F. Fitzhardinge, *The Little Digger, 1914–1952: William Morris Hughes: A Political Biography*, vol. II: 346.

99. Bill Gammage, *The Broken Years*: 203.

100. 'General John Monash', in Dennis et al., eds, *The Oxford Companion to Australian Military History*: 404–406.

101. Horner, *Blamey*: 50–53.

102. J.M. Bourne, 'The BEF's Generals on 29 September 1918: An Empirical Portrait with Some British and Australian Comparisons', in Dennis & Grey, eds, *1918 Defining Victory*: 96–113.

Chapter Eleven
The 'Diggers' in 1918

1. Bean, *The AIF in France December 1917 to May 1918*, vol. 5: 18.

2. Stewart, *The New Zealand Division 1916–1919*: 328; Pugsley, *On the Fringe of Hell*: 236–38.

3. The entrenching group was gradually absorbed into the division as individual reinforcements and disbanded in 1918; Stewart, ibid.: 329.

4. Russell to Allen dated 7 November 1917, Allen Papers, NA.
5. Pugsley, 'The Second New Zealand Division of 1945: A Comparison with its 1918 Predecessor', in John Crawford, ed., *Kia Kaha: New Zealand in the Second World War*: 94–106; Pugsley, 'New Zealand: "From the uttermost ends of the earth"', in John Bourne, Peter Liddle & Ian Whitehead, eds, *The Great World War 1914–1945, vol. 2, Who Won? Who Lost? The People's Experience*: 211–32.
6. Russell to Allen dated 12 August 1918, Allen Papers, NA.
7. *Report of the Ministry*: 57–67; Beaumont, *Australian Defence: Sources and Statistics*: 108–111.
8. HQ NZ Division, Report on Operations, July 1 to August 31, 1918, WA 20/3/8, NA.
9. HQ NZ Division, Summary of Operations, May 1 to June 30, 1918, WA 20/3/8, NA.
10. Russell to Allen dated 16 September 1918, Allen Papers, NA.
11. Russell Diary, 9 November 1917, AT.
12. Ibid., 22 December 1917, AT.
13. Ibid., 15 and 18 December 1917, AT.
14. Ibid., 15 December 1917, AT.
15. Ibid., 12 December 1917, AT.
16. Ibid., 19 November 1917, AT.
17. Ibid., 20 November 1917, AT.
18. Lieutenant-Colonel, Temporary Brigadier-General C.H.J. Brown DSO, NZSC, born NZ 1872, CO 1 Cant 1915, WIA 5 June 15, CO 2nd Auck, Comd 1 NZ Brigade, KIA 8 June 1917. Brigadier-General F.E. Johnston CB, born NZ 1872, Regular Soldier (North Staffordshire Regt) Comd 1st NZ Bde 1914–1916, Comd A Group Sling 1917, Comd 1 NZ Bde 1917, KIA 7 August 1917. Lieutenant-Colonel, Brevet Colonel, Temporary Brigadier-General H.T. Fulton CMG, DSO, Indian Army, Comd 3rd NZ (Rifle) Brigade, DOW 29 March 1918. Colonel, Temporary Brigadier-General W.G. Braithwaite, Regular Soldier (Royal Welsh Fusiliers), GSO 1 NZ & A Division, Comd 2 NZ Brigade 1916–1918. Rejoined British Army. See entries in Studholme, *Record of Personal Services During the War*.
19. Lieutenant-Colonel, Temporary Brigadier-General H. Hart CB, CMG, DSO, Major, 2IC Wellington Battalion 1914, CO 1st Wellington 1915–1916, Comd 4 NZ Brigade 1917, Comd A Group Sling Camp 1918, Comd 3 NZ (Rifle) Brigade 1918, twice wounded. Lieutenant-Colonel, Temporary Brigadier-General R. Young CB, CMG, DSO, Major, Coy Comd, Wellington Battalion 1914, CO 1st Cant 1915–1916, Comd 1st NZ Brigade 1917, Comd 2nd NZ Brigade 1918, twice wounded. Lieutenant-Colonel, Temporary Brigadier-General C.W. Melvill, Regular Soldier, NZSC, Captain, Wellington Battalion 1915, CO 4th Battalion NZ Rifle Brigade, Comd 1st NZ Brigade 1918. See entries in Studholme, *Record of Personal Services During the War*.
20. Lieutenant-Colonel, Temporary Colonel H.

Stewart CMG, DSO and Bar, MC, Lieutenant Canterbury Battalion 1914, CO 2nd Cant, 1916, Temporary Commander 2nd Infantry Brigade, Director Education NZEF, author *The New Zealand Division 1916–1919*. Lieutenant-Colonel L.H. Jardine DSO and Bar, MC, Lieutenant, Wellington Battalion 1914, Attended Senior Officer's School Aldershot, CO 3rd Battalion Wellington Regt, and Co 2nd Battalion NZ Rifle Brigade 1918. See entries in Studholme, *Record of Personal Services During the War*.
21. R.J. Richards letter dated 23 May 1918, Richards Collection, Christ's College, Christchurch, NZ, quoted in Pugsley, *On the Fringe of Hell*: 278.
22. Russell to All Commanding Officers dated 12 January 1918, Russell Papers, Russell Family.
23. Russell to Allen dated 3 April 1918, Allen Papers, NA.
24. Lieutenant-Colonel H.M. Wilson DSO, Rifle Brigade, GSO1 NZ Division, 28 October 1917 – 1 April 1919. See entry in Studholme, *Record of Personal Services During the War*.
25. Russell to Allen dated 12 August 1918, Allen Papers, NA.
26. William J. McKeon, *Fruitful Years*: 176–78.
27. Rawling, *Surviving Trench Warfare*: 175; Rawling, 'A Resource Not to Be Squandered: The Canadian Corps on the 1918 Battlefield'; Dennis & Grey, *1918 Defining Victory*: 43–52.
28. 'Tactical Exercises for Brigadiers and Commanding Officers', HQ NZ Division, dated 3 March 1918, Russell Papers, Russell Family.
29. New Zealand Division Training Instruction No. 1 dated 4 February 1918, WA 20/1, NA.
30. New Zealand Division War Diary, March 1918, WA 20/1, NA.
31. Brigadier-General Sir James Edmonds, *Military Operations, France and Belgium 1918: The German March Offensive and its Preliminaries*: 4, 8, 31.
32. Russell to Allen dated 3 April 1918, Allen Papers, NA.
33. New Zealand Division War Diary, March 1918, WA 20/1, NA.
34. Russell to Brigadiers and COs dated 30 March 1918, Russell Papers, Russell Family.
35. Bean, *The AIF in France May 1918 to the Armistice*, vol. 6: 32–60.
36. Prisoner Report, 73 Fusilier Regt, New Zealand Divisional Intelligence Summary No. 19 of 11 July 1918, WA 21/2/6, NA.
37. New Zealand Division Summary of Operations, May 1 to June 30, 1918, WA 20/3/8, NA.
38. Ibid.
39. New Zealand Division Intelligence Supplement of 27 July 1918, WA 21/2/6, NA; Ernst Jünger, *Storm of Steel*: 263.
40. Harris, *Amiens to the Armistice*: 121–33.
41. Brigadier-General H. Hart Diary, 24 August 1918, QEII.
42. Ibid.
43. Russell Diary, 30 August 1918, AT.

44. Hart Diary, 8–9 September 1918, QEII.
45. Harris, *Amiens to the Armistice*: 174–80
46. Hart Diary, 12 September 1918, QEII.
47. Ibid.
48. 1st NZ Infantry Brigade 8/155/353 — Memo on Recent Operations, dated 20 September 1918, WA 10/3/7/11, NA.
49. New Zealand Division Intelligence Summary, No. 4 dated 10 September 1918, WA 21/2/6, NA.
50. This is a more favourable assessment of this division than found in AEF, *Histories of Two Hundred and Fifty-One Divisions of the German Army which Participated in the War (1914–1918)*.
51. Jünger, *Storm of Steel*: 272–73, 275–82.
52. Russell Diary, 12 September 1918, AT.
53. GHQ Adjutant General's Files 1918, WO 25/96, PRO.
54. Russell to Allen, dated 16 September 1918, Allen Papers, NA.
55. Ibid.
56. Russell Diary, 14 September 1918, AT.
57. Hart Diary, 17 September 1918, QEII.
58. Russell Diary, 18 September 1918, AT.
59. Second New Zealand Infantry Brigade to New Zealand Division dated 13 September 1918, WA 20/3/8, NA.
60. New Zealand Divisional Artillery to New Zealand Division dated 19 September 1918, WA 20/3/8, NA.
61. Ibid. See also Major R.A. Wilson, *A Two Years Interlude: France 1916–1918*: 101–114.
62. 'Lessons Technical and Tactical', New Zealand Machine Gun Battalion to New Zealand Division dated 26 September 1918, WA 20/3/8, NA.
63. Hart Diary, 19 September 1918, QEII.
64. Russell Diary, 23 September 1918, AT.
65. Ibid.
66. Ibid., 24 September 1918.
67. Ibid., 29 September 1918.
68. Ibid., 2 October 1918.
69. Ibid., 1 October 1918.
70. Harris, *Amiens to the Armistice*: 237–40.
71. Hart Diary, 8 October 1918, QEII.
72. Ibid.
73. Russell Diary, 8 October 1918, AT.
74. Ibid.
75. Hart Diary, 8 October 1918, QEII.
76. Russell Diary, 21 October 1918, AT.
77. Hart Diary, 2 November 1918, QEII.
78. Russell Diary, 21 October 1918, AT. Lieutenant-Colonel A.D. Stitt DSO, MC, 2 Lt, Canterbury Battalion 1914, CO 2nd Canterbury Battalion; Lieutenant-Colonel J. Hargest DSO, MC, Sergeant Otago Mounted Rifles 1914, CO 2nd Otago Battalion; see entries in Studholme, *Record of Personal Services During the War*.
79. New Zealand Division Report on Operations for November and December 1918, WA 20/3/8, NA.
80. Hart Diary, 4 November 1918, QEII.
81. Bean, *The AIF in France May 1918 to the Armistice*, vol. 6: 1080.
82. This reflects the bayonet strength of the battalion and is based on the three infantry brigades, their six Light Trench Mortar Batteries, which were manned by infantry, the Pioneer Battalion and the New Zealand Machine Gun Battalion whose establishment strength numbered 14,371 out of a total divisional strength of 18,958. Chief of General Staff, *War 1914–1918: New Zealand Expeditionary Force: Its Provision and Maintenance*: 15.
83. Ibid.: 15, 49.
84. Ibid.: 45, 49.

Epilogue

1. Bruce Catton, *The Civil War*: 142.
2. Jeffrey A. Keshen, *Propaganda and Censorship During Canada's Great War*: 215.
3. A.A. Grace, 'Our Little Army', *NZ Herald*, 1 Aug 1914.
4. Bean, *The AIF in France May 1918 to the Armistice*, vol. 6: 4–7.
5. This is a major theme in Jonathan F. Vance, *Death So Noble: Memory, Meaning, and the First World War*.
6. E. Ashmead-Bartlett, *Ashmead-Bartlett's Despatches from the Dardanelles*: 49, 77–78.
7. Quoting from Alfred Buchanan, *The Real Australia*, in K.S. Inglis, 'ANZAC and the Australian Military Tradition', *Current Affairs Bulletin*, 64, 11, 1988.
8. Catton, *The Civil War*: 142.
9. Lieutenant Loutit quoted in Roberts, 'The Landing at Anzac: A Reassessment', *Journal of the Australian War Memorial*, 22, April 1993: 25–32.
10. Peter Weir, director, *Gallipoli*, Australia, 1981.
11. Bruce Catton, *The Civil War*: 142.
12. O.E. Burton, *The Silent Division: New Zealanders at the Front: 1914–1919*: 296.
13. Bean, *The AIF in France May 1918 to the Armistice*, vol. 6: 260–61.
14. Stewart, *The New Zealand Division 1916–1919*: 406.
15. Pugsley, *Gallipoli: The New Zealand Story*: 363–64.
16. 'Gallipoli', in Dennis et al., eds, *The Oxford Companion to Australian Military History*: 252–62.
17. Pugsley, 'New Zealand: "The Heroes Lie in France"', in Cecil & Liddle, *At the Eleventh Hour*: 208.
18. Ekins, 'Australia at the End of the Great War', in Cecil & Liddle, *At the Eleventh Hour*: 171–72.
19. The major work on the Maori in the First World War is James Cowan's *The Maoris in the Great War*. Also of value are P.S. O'Connor, 'The Recruitment of Maori Soldiers 1914–1918', *Political Science*, XIX, 2, 1967: 48–83; and Christopher Pugsley, *Te Hokowhitu A Tu: The Maori Pioneer Battalion in the First World War*.
20. Brian Holden Reid, 'The Influence of the Vietnam Syndrome on the Writing of Civil War History', *Journal of the RUSI*, February 2002: 44–52.
21. James Thorn, *Peter Fraser*: 195.
22. Robert Ebert, 'We Were Soldiers', *Chicago Sun-Times*, 1 March 2002.

BIBLIOGRAPHY

A Brief Record of the Advance of the Egyptian Expeditionary Force under the command of General Sir Edmund H.H. Allenby GCB, GCMG, July 1917–October 1918. Compiled from Official Sources, HMSO, London, 1919.

Abbott, J.H.M., *Tommy Cornstalk*. London, 1902.

Adam-Smith, Patsy, *The ANZACs*. Hamish Hamilton, London, 1978.

Admiralty, CB1550. *Report of the Committee Appointed to Investigate the Attacks Delivered on and the Enemy Defences of the Dardanelles Straits, 1919*. Admiralty, Naval Staff, Gunnery Division, April 1921.

AEF, *Histories of Two Hundred and Fifty-One Divisions of the German Army which Participated in the War (1914–1918)*. AEF 1919, London Stamp Exchange, London, 1989.

Aitken, Alexander, *Gallipoli to the Somme: Recollections of a New Zealand Infantryman*. Oxford University Press, London, 1963.

Allen, Hervey, *Towards the Flame: A War Diary*. University of Pittsburgh Press, Pittsburgh, 1968.

Amery, L.S., ed., *The Times History of the War in South Africa 1899–1902*, vol. VI. London, 1909.

Andrews, E.M., *The Anzac Illusion: Anglo-Australian Relations During World War I*. Cambridge University Press, Melbourne, 1993.

'Bean and Bullecourt: Weaknesses and Strengths of the Official History of Australia in the First World War'. In Dennis et al., *Revue Internationale d'Histoire Militaire* 72: 25–47. Canberra, 1990.

Annabell, N., *Official History of the New Zealand Engineers During the Great War 1914–1919*. Evans, Cobb & Sharpe, Wanganui, 1927.

Arnold, Rollo, *Settler Kaponga 1881–1914: A Frontier Fragment of the Western World*. Victoria University Press, Wellington, 1997.

Ashmead-Bartlett, E., *Ashmead-Bartlett's Despatches from the Dardanelles*. George Newnes, London, 1915. *The Uncensored Dardanelles*. Hutchinson, London, nd.

Aspinall-Oglander, Brig.-General C.F., *Military Operations Gallipoli*, vols 1–2, maps and appendices. HMSO, London, 1924–1930.

Asprey, Robert B., *The German High Command at War: Hindenburg and Ludendorff and the First World War*. Warner Books, London, 1994.

Austin DSO, Lt-Col W.S., *The Official History of the New Zealand Rifle Brigade (The Earl of Liverpool's Own)*. L.T. Watkins, Wellington, 1924.

Babbington, Anthony, *For the Sake of Example*. Leo Cooper, London, 1983.

Baker, Paul, *King and Country Call*. Auckland University Press, Auckland, 1988.

Barclay, Brigadier C.N., *Armistice 1918*. J.M. Dent & Sons, London, 1968.

Barclay, Glen St J., *The Empire Is Marching: A Study of the Military Effort of the British Empire, 1800–1945*. Weidenfeld and Nicolson, London, 1976.

Barrett, John, 'C.E.W. Bean and Some Critics', *Australian Historical Studies*, 23, 90, April 1988.

Baynes, John, *Far From a Donkey: The Life of General Sir Ivor Maxse, KCB, CVO, DSO*. Brasseys, London, 1995.

Bean, C.E.W., *The ANZAC Book*. London, 1916.
ed., *The Official History of Australia in the War of 1914–1918*, vol. 1: *The Story of ANZAC from the Outbreak of War to the End of the First Phase of the Gallipoli Campaign, May 4, 1915*; vol. 2: *The Story of ANZAC from 4 May 1915 to the Evacuation of the Gallipoli Peninsula*; vol. 3: *The AIF in France 1916*; vol. 4: *The AIF in France 1917*; vol. 5: *The AIF in France December 1917 to May 1918*; vol. 6: *The AIF in France May 1918 to the Armistice*. Angus & Robertson, Sydney, 1921–1942.
Two Men I Knew: William Bridges and Brudenell White, Founders of the A.I.F. Angus & Robertson, Sydney, 1957.
Anzac to Amiens. Australian War Memorial, Canberra, 1961.
Gallipoli Correspondent: The Frontline Diary of C.E.W. Bean (K. Fewster, ed.). George Allen & Unwin, St Leonards, 1983.
et al., 'The Australian Forces in the War'. In Lucas, ed., *The Empire at War*, vol. III: pp. 199–202. Oxford University Press, London, 1924.

Beaumont, Joan, ed., *Australia's War, 1914–18*. Allen & Unwin, Sydney, 1995.
ed., *Australian Defence Sources and Statistics*, vol. VI, *The Australian Centenary History of Defence*. Oxford University Press, Melbourne, 2001.
'Australia'. In John Bourne, Peter Liddle and Ian Whitehead, eds, *The Great World War 1914–1945*, vol. 2, *Who Won? Who Lost? The People's Experience*: pp.197–210. HarperCollins, London, 2001.

Becke, Major A.F., *History of the Great War, Order of Battle: Part 4, The Army Council, G.H.Q.s, Armies, and Corps, 1914–1918*. HMSO, London, 1945.

Beckett, Ian F.W., *The Great War, 1914–1918*. Longmans, London, 2001.

The First World War: The Essential Guide to Sources in the UK National Archives. PRO, London, 2002.

& Keith Simpson, eds, *A Nation in Arms: A Social Study of the British Army in the First World War*. Tom Donovan, London, 1990.

Belford, Captain Walter C., *"Legs-Eleven" Being the Story of the 11th Battalion (A.I.F.) in the Great War of 1914–1918*. Facsimile of Imperial Printing Company, Perth, WA, 1940 edn. John Burridge Military Antiques, Swanbourne, WA, 1992.

Bercuson, David J., & J.L. Granatstein, *Dictionary of Canadian Military History*. Oxford University Press, Toronto, 1992.

Berton, Pierre, *Vimy*. McClelland and Stewart, Toronto, 1986.

Bidwell, Shelford, & Dominick Graham, *Fire-Power: British Army Weapons and Theories of War 1904–1945*. George Allen & Unwin, London, 1982.

Birdwood, Field-Marshal Lord, *Khaki and Gown: An Autobiography*. Ward Lock, London, 1941.

Blair, Dale J., *Dinkum Diggers: An Australian Battalion at War*. Melbourne University Press, Melbourne, 2001.

'"Those Miserable Tommies": Anti-British Sentiment in the Australian Imperial Force 1915–1918'. *War and Society*, 19, 1, May 2001: 71–91.

Blake, Robert, *The Private Papers of Douglas Haig, 1914–1919*. Eyre & Spottiswoode, London, 1952.

Bodell, James, *A Soldier's View of Empire* (Keith Sinclair, ed.). The Bodley Head, London, 1982.

Bond, Brian, *The Victorian Army and the Staff College 1854–1914*. Eyre Methuen, London, 1972.

ed., *The First World War and British Military History*. Clarendon Press, Oxford, 1991.

& Nigel Cave, eds, *Haig: A Reappraisal 70 Years On*. Pen and Sword, London, 1999.

& Simon Robbins, eds, *Staff Officer: The Diaries of Lord Moyne, 1914–1918*. Leo Cooper, London, 1987.

Boraston CB, OBE, J.H., *Sir Douglas Haig's Despatches*. J.M. Dent & Sons, London, 1920.

Bourne, J.M., 'The BEF's Generals on 29 September 1918: An Empirical Portrait with Some British and Australian Comparisons'. In P. Dennis and J. Grey, eds, *1918 Defining Victory*, pp. 96–113. Army History Unit, Department of Defence, Canberra, 1999.

Bourne, John, Peter Liddle & Ian Whitehead, eds, *The Great World War 1914–1945*, vol. *2, Who Won? Who Lost? The People's Experience*. HarperCollins, London, 2001.

Boyack, Nicholas, *Behind the Lines: The Lives of New Zealand Soldiers in the First World War*. Allen & Unwin, Wellington, 1989.

Bowers, Peter, *ANZAC: The Pain and the Glory of Gallipoli*. Australia Post, 2000.

Boyd, Mary, 'Australia-New Zealand Relations'. In William S. Livingston & Wm Roger Louis, eds, *Australia, New Zealand and the Pacific Islands Since the First World War*. Australian National University, Canberra, 1979.

Bray, R. Matthew, '"Fighting as an Ally": The English-Canadian Patriotic Response to the Great War'. *Canadian Historical Review*, LXI, 2, 1980: 141–68.

Brereton, Major C.B., *Tales of Three Campaigns*. Selwyn & Blount, London, 1926.

Brook, Michael and Eleanor, eds, *H.H. Asquith Letters to Venetia Stanley*. OUP, Oxford, 1982.

Brown, Craig, & Desmond Morton, 'The Embarrassing Apotheosis of a "Great Canadian": Sir Arthur Currie's Personal Crisis in 1917'. *Canadian Historical Review*, LX,1, 1979: 41–63.

Brown, Ian Malcolm, '"Not Glamorous but Effective": The Canadian Corps and the Set-piece Attack, 1917–1918'. *Journal of Military History*, 58, July 1994: 421–44.

British Logistics on the Western Front 1914–1918. Praeger, Westport, CT, 1998.

Brown, R.C., & D. Loveridge, 'Unrequited Faith: Recruiting the C.E.F., 1914–1918'. In Dennis et al., *Revue Internationale d'Histoire Militaire*, 51, 1982: 53–79. Canberra, 1990.

Bruce, Anthony, *The Last Crusade: The Palestine Campaign in the First World War*. John Murray, London, 2002.

Brugger, Suzanne, *Australia and Egypt 1914–1919*. Melbourne University Press, Melbourne, 1980.

Burness, Peter, *The Nek: The Tragic Charge of the Light Horse at Gallipoli*. Kangaroo Press, NSW, 1996.

Burton MM, 2/Lt O.E., *The Auckland Regiment*. Whitcombe & Tombs, Auckland, 1922.

Burton, O.E., *The Silent Division: New Zealanders at the Front*. Angus & Robertson, Sydney, 1935.

Byrne MC, Lt A.E., *Official History of the Otago Regiment, NZEF, in the Great War 1914–1918*. J. Wilkie, Dunedin, nd.

Byrne, Lt J.R., *New Zealand Artillery in the Field 1914–1918*. Whitcombe & Tombs, Wellington, 1922.

Callwell, Major-General Sir C.E., *The Dardanelles*. Constable, London, 1924.

Campbell, Captain R.W., *The Kangaroo Marines*. Cassell, London, nd.

Carbery, A.D., *The New Zealand Medical Service in the Great War 1914–1918*. Whitcombe & Tombs, Wellington, 1924.

Carlyon, Les, *Gallipoli*. Macmillan, Sydney, 2001.

Catton, Bruce, *The Civil War*. Fairfax Press, New York, 1984.

Cecil, Hugh & Peter H. Liddle, eds, *Facing Armageddon: The First World War Experienced*. Leo Cooper, London, 1996.

At the Eleventh Hour: Reflections, Hopes and Anxieties at the Closing of the Great War, 1918. Leo Cooper, Barnsley, 1998.

Celik, K., & Cehan Koc, eds, *The Gallipoli Campaign: International Perspectives 85 Years On*. Conference Proceedings, 24–25 April 2000. Ataturk and Gallipoli

Campaign Research Centre, Canakkale Osekiz Mart University, Canakkale, Turkey, 2002.

Chandler, David, & Ian F.W. Beckett, eds, *The Oxford Illustrated History of the British Army*. Oxford University Press, Oxford, 1994.

Chapman, Ivan, *Iven G. Mackay: Citizen and Soldier*. Melway Publishing, Melbourne, 1975.

Charlton, Peter, *Pozières: Australians on the Somme*. Methuen Haynes, Sydney, 1986.

Chickering, Roger, *Imperial Germany and the Great War, 1914–1918*. Cambridge University Press, Cambridge, 1998.

Childers, Erskine, ed., *The Times History of the War in South Africa 1899–1902*, vol. V. London, 1909.

Coates, John, *An Atlas of Australia's Wars. Vol. VII, Australian Centenary History of Defence*. Oxford University Press, Melbourne, 2001.

Cochrane, Peter, *Simpson and the Donkey: The Making of a Legend*. Melbourne University Press, Melbourne, 1992.

Coffman, Edward M., *The War to End All Wars: The American Military Experience in World War I*. University Press of Kentucky, Lexington, (1968), 1998.

Coombes, David, *Morshead: Hero of Tobruk and El Alamein*. Oxford University Press, Melbourne, 2001.

Corns, Cathryn, & John Hughes-Wilson, *Blindfold and Alone: British Military Executions in the Great War*. Cassell, London, 2001.

Coulthard-Clark, C.D., *A Heritage of Spirit: A Biography of Major-General Sir William Throsby Bridges, KCB, CMG*. Melbourne University Press, Melbourne, 1979.
No Australian Need Apply: The Troubled Career of Lieutenant General Gordon Legge. Allen & Unwin, Sydney, 1988.

Cowan, James, *The Maoris in the Great War*. Whitcombe and Tombs, Auckland, 1926.

Crawford, John, ed., *Kia Kaha: New Zealand in the Second World War*. Oxford University Press, Auckland, 2000.
with E. Ellis, *To Fight for Empire: An Illustrated History of New Zealand and the South African War, 1899–1902*, Reed, Auckland, 1999.

Creveld, Martin van, *Supplying War: Logistics from Wallenstein to Patton*. Cambridge University Press, Cambridge, 1977.

Cruttwell, C.R.M.F., *A History of the Great War, 1914–1918*. Clarendon Press, Oxford, 1934.

Cunningham DSO, W.H., C.A.L. Treadwell OBE, & J.S. Hanna, *The Wellington Regiment, NZEF, 1914–1919*. Ferguson and Osborn, Wellington, 1928.

Cutlack, F.M., ed., *War Letters of General Monash*. Angus & Robertson, Sydney, 1935.

Damousi, Joy, *The Labour of Loss: Mourning, Memory and Wartime Bereavement in Australia*. Cambridge University Press, Cambridge, 1999.

Davies, Harry, *Allanson of the 6th*. Square One Publications, Worcester, 1990.

Dawes, J.N.I., & L.L. Robson, *Citizen to Soldier:*

Australia Before the Great War. Recollections of Members of the First A.I.F. Melbourne University Press, 1977.

Dennis, Peter, Jeffrey Grey, & John McCarthy, *Revue Internationale d'Histoire Militaire*, 72, Canberra, 1990.

Dennis, Peter, Jeffrey Grey, Ewan Morris, & Robin Prior, eds, *The Oxford Companion to Australian Military History*. Melbourne, 1995.
& Jeffrey Grey, eds, *1918 Defining Victory*. Army History Unit, Department of Defence, Canberra, 1999.
& Jeffrey Grey, eds, *The Boer War: Army, Nation and Empire*. 1999 Chief of Army/Australian War Memorial Military History Conference. Army History Unit, Canberra, 2000.

Department of Justice, *Crime in New Zealand*. Government Printer, Wellington, 1968.

Derham, Rosemary, *The Silence Ruse: Escape from Gallipoli: A Record and Memory of the Life of General Sir Brudenell White KCB, KCMG, KCVO, DSO*. Cliffe Books, Armadale, Vic, 1998.

Dewar, G.A.B., assisted by Lt-Col. J.H. Boraston CB, *Sir Douglas Haig's Command, December 19, 1915 – November 11, 1918*. Constable & Co, London, 1922.

Downing, W.H., *Digger Dialects: A Collection of Slang Phrases Used by the Australian Soldiers on Active Service*. Lothian Book Publishing, Melbourne, 1919.
To The Last Ridge: The First World War Memoirs of W.H. Downing. Duffy and Snellgrove, Sydney, 1998.

Drew, H.T.B., *The War Effort of New Zealand*. Whitcombe & Tombs, Wellington, 1923.

Dunmore, John, ed., *New Zealand and the French: Two Centuries of Contact*. Heritage Press, Waikanae, 1990.
The French and the Maori. Heritage Press, Waikanae, 1992.

Dunstall, G.C., 'Public Attitudes and Responses in New Zealand to the Beginning of the Boer War 1899'. *University of Auckland Historical Society Annual*, vol. 1, 1967: 8–22.

Dyer, Geoff, *The Missing of the Somme*. Hamish Hamilton, London, 1994.

Ebert, Robert, 'We Were Soldiers'. *Chicago Sun-Times*, 1 March 2002.

Edmonds, Brig.-General Sir James E., *Military Operations: France and Belgium 1918*, vols 1, 2, 4, & 5. HMSO, London, 1935–47. *Military Operations: France and Belgium 1917*, vol. 2. HMSO, 1948.
A Short History of World War I. Oxford University Press, London, 1951.

Ekins, Ashley, 'The Australians at Passchendaele'. In Peter H. Liddle, ed., *Passchendaele in Perspective: The Third Battle of Ypres*, pp. 227–54. Leo Cooper, London, 1997.
'Australians at the End of the Great War'. In Hugh Cecil & Peter H. Liddle, eds, *At the Eleventh Hour: Reflections, Hopes and Anxieties at the Closing of the Great War, 1918*: 157–80. Leo Cooper, London, 1998.
'A Ridge Too Far: Military Objectives and the

Dominance of Terrain in the Gallipoli Campaign'. In Kenan Celik and Cehan Koc, eds, *The Gallipoli Campaign: International Perspectives 85 Years On*. Conference Proceedings, 24–25 April 2000: 1–36. Ataturk and Gallipoli Campaign Research Centre, Canakkale Osekiz Mart University, Canakkale, Turkey, 2002.

Ellis MC, Capt. A.D., *The Story of the Fifth Australian Division: Being an Authoritative Account of the Division's Doings in Egypt, France and Belgium*. Hodder & Stoughton, London. Facsimile edition, Naval and Military Press, Uckfield, nd.

Ellis, John, & Michael Cox, *The World War I Databook: The Essential Facts and Figures for All the Combatants*. Aurum Press, London, 2001.

English, John A., & Bruce I. Gudmundsson, *On Infantry*. Praeger, Westport, CT, 1994.

Erickson, Edward J., *Ordered to Die: A History of the Ottoman Army in the First World War*. Greenwood Press, Westport, CT, 2001.

Evans, Michael, *From Legend to Learning: Gallipoli and the Military Revolution of World War I*. Working Paper No. 110, Land Warfare Studies Centre, Duntroon, ACT, April 2000.

Falls, Cyril, *Military Operations: France and Belgium 1917*, vol.1. HMSO, London, 1940.

Farrar-Hockley, Anthony H., *Goughie: The Life of Sir Hubert Gough, GCB, GCMG, KCVO*. Hart-Davis, McGibbon, London, 1975.

Ferguson MC, Capt. David, *The History of the Canterbury Regiment, NZEF, 1914–1919*. Whitcombe & Tombs, Wellington, 1921.

Fewster, Kevin, 'Ellis Ashmead-Bartlett and the Making of the Anzac Legend'. *Journal of Australian Studies*: no.10, June 1982: 17–30.

Fitzhardinge, L.F., *The Little Digger, 1914–1952: William Morris Hughes, A Political Biography*, vol. II. Angus & Robertson, Sydney, 1979.

Fletcher, David, ed., *Tanks and Trenches: First Hand Accounts of Tank Warfare in the First World War*. Budding Books, Stroud, 2001.

Forester, C.S., *The General*. Michael Joseph, London, 1958.

Fraser, David, *Alanbrooke*. Collins, London, 1982.

French, David, *British Strategy and War Aims, 1914–1916*. Allen & Unwin, London, 1986.

The Strategy of the Lloyd George Coalition, 1916–1918. Oxford University Press, Oxford, 1995.

& Brian Holden Reid, eds, *The British General Staff: Reform and Innovation, 1890–1939*. Frank Cass, London, 2002.

'The Dardanelles, Mecca and Kut: Prestige as a Factor in British Eastern Strategy, 1914–1916'. *War & Society*, 5, 1, May 1987: 45–62.

Freyberg, Paul, *Bernard Freyberg, VC: Soldier of Two Nations*. Hodder & Stoughton, London, 1991.

Fussell, Paul, *The Great War and Modern Memory*. Oxford University Press, Oxford, 1975.

Thank God for the Atomic Bomb and other Essays. Summit Books (Simon and Schuster), 1988.

Gammage, Bill, *The Broken Years: Australian Soldiers in the Great War*. Penguin, Ringwood, 1975.

Gardner, Brian, *The Big Push: The Somme 1916*. Sphere, London, 1968.

Gasson, James, *Travis VC: Man in No Man's Land*. Reed, Wellington, 1966.

General Staff, War Office, *Infantry Training, 1911*. HMSO, London, 1911.

Field Service Regulations, Part I, Operations, 1909. (Reprinted with Amendments, 1914). HMSO, London, 1914.

Notes for Infantry Officers on Trench Warfare. Compiled by the General Staff, War Office, March 1916. HMSO, London.

Impressions and Reflections of a French Company Commander Regarding the Attack. HMSO, 1916.

SS 143, Instructions for the Training of Platoons for Offensive Action, 1917. GHQ, BEF, February 1917.

SS 143, Instructions for the Training of Platoons for Offensive Action, 1917. GHQ, BEF, amended August 1917.

SS 185, Assault Training. Issued by the General Staff, September 1917. HMSO, London, 1917.

The Organization of an Infantry Battalion and The Normal Formation for the Attack. Issued by the General Staff, BEF, April, 1917.

Gerster, Robin, *Big-Noting: The Heroic Theme in Australian War Writing*. Melbourne University Press, Melbourne, 1987.

Gibbs, Philip, *Now It Can Be Told*. Garden City Publishing, New York, 1920.

Godefroy, A.B., *For Freedom and Honour? The Story of the 25 Canadian Volunteers Executed in the Great War*. CEF Books, Nepean, 1998.

Godley, General Sir Alexander, *Life of an Irish Soldier*. John Murray, London, 1939.

Gooch, John, *The Plans of War: The General Staff and British Military Strategy c1900–1916*. Routledge & Kegan Paul, London, 1974.

Gough, Sir Hubert, *The Fifth Army*. Hodder & Stoughton, London, 1931.

Greenhalgh, Elizabeth, 'Why the British Were on the Somme in 1916'. *War in History*, 6, 2, April 1999: 147–73.

Gregory, Adrian, *The Silence of Memory: Armistice Day 1919–1946*. Berg, Oxford, 1994.

Grey, Jeffrey, *A Military History of Australia*. Cambridge University Press, Melbourne, 1990.

The Australian Army; vol. 1, Australian Centenary History of Defence. Oxford University Press, Melbourne, 2001.

Griffith, Paddy, *Forward into Battle: Fighting Tactics from Waterloo to the Near Future*. Crowood Press, Swindon, 1990.

Battle Tactics of the Western Front: The British Army's Art of Attack, 1916–1918. Yale University Press, New Haven, 1994.

ed., *British Fighting Methods of the Great War*. Frank Cass, London, 1996.

Guderian, Maj.-General Heinz, *Achtung-Panzer! The Development of Armoured Forces, Their Tactics and Operational Potential*. Brockhampton Press, London, 1992.

Gudmundsson, Bruce I., *Storm Troop Tactics: Innovation in the German Army, 1914–1918*. Praeger, New York, 1989.

Gullett, H.S., *Official History of Australia in the War of 1914–1918*, vol. 7: *The Australian Imperial Force in Sinai and Palestine, 1914–1918*. Angus & Robertson, Sydney, 1939.

Gwyn, Sandra, *Tapestry of War: A Private View of Canadians in the Great War*. HarperCollins, Toronto, 1992.

Haigh, J. Bryant, & Alan J. Polaschek, *New Zealand and the Distinguished Service Order*. John D. Wills, Christchurch, 1993.

Hall, D.O.W., *The New Zealanders in South Africa 1899–1902*. War History Branch, Department of Internal Affairs, Wellington, 1949.

Halpern, Paul G., *The Naval War in the Mediterranean, 1914–1918*. Allen & Unwin, London, 1986.
A Naval History of World War One. UCL Press, London, 1994.

Hamilton, Ian B.M., *The Happy Warrior: A Life of General Sir Ian Hamilton, GCB, GCMG, DSO*. Cassell, London, 1966.

Harington, General Sir Charles, *Plumer of Messines*. John Murray, London, 1935.
Tim Harington Looks Back. John Murray, London, 1940.

Harris, J.P., with Niall Barr, *Amiens to the Armistice: The BEF in the Hundred Days' Campaign, 8 August– 11 November 1918*. Brasseys, London, 1998.

Harris, Stephen J., 'From Subordinate to Ally: The Canadian Corps and National Autonomy, 1914–1918'. In Dennis et al., *Revue Internationale d'Histoire Militaire*, 51, 1982: 109–130.
Canadian Brass: The Making of a Professional Army, 1860–1939. University of Toronto Press, Toronto, 1988.

Harvey, Norman K., *From Anzac to the Hindenburg Line: The History of the 9th Battalion A.I.F.* William Brooks, Brisbane, 1941.

Haste, Cate, *Keep the Home Fires Burning: Propaganda in the First World War*. Allen Lane, London, 1977.

Hay, Ian, *The Ship of Remembrance: Gallipoli-Salonika*. Hodder & Stoughton, London, nd.

Hickey, Michael, *Gallipoli*. John Murray, London, 1995.

Hiley, Nicholas, '"Enough Glory For All": Ellis Ashmead-Bartlett and Sir Ian Hamilton at the Dardanelles'. *Journal of Strategic Studies*, 16, 2, June 1993: 240–64.

Hill, A.J., *Chauvel of the Light Horse*. Melbourne University Press, Melbourne, 1978.

Holmes, Richard, *Acts of War: The Behaviour of Men in Battle*. Free Press, New York, 1986.

Horner, David, *Blamey: The Commander-in-Chief*. Allen & Unwin, St Leonards, NSW, 1998.

ed., *The Commanders: Australian Military Leadership in the Twentieth Century*. Allen & Unwin, Sydney, 1984.

Howard, Michael, *The First World War*. Oxford University Press, Oxford, 2002.

Hughes, Matthew, *Allenby and British Strategy in the Middle East, 1917–1919*. Frank Cass, London, 1999.

Hyatt, A.M.J., *General Sir Arthur Currie: A Military Biography*. University of Toronto Press in association with Canadian War Museum, Toronto, 1987.

Hyde, Robin, *Passport to Hell: The Story of James Douglas Stark, Bomber, Fifth Reinforcement, New Zealand Expeditionary Forces*. Auckland University Press, Auckland (1937), 1986.
Nor the Years Condemn. New Women's Press, Auckland, 1986.

Hynes, Samuel, *A War Imagined: The First World War and English Culture*. The Bodley Head, London, 1990.
The Soldiers' Tale: Bearing Witness to Modern War. Allen Lane, New York, 1997.

Idriess, Ion L., *The Desert Column*. Angus and Robertson, Sydney, 1951.

Imperial War Graves Commission, *The Chunuk Bair Memorial Gallipoli: The Register of the Names of Soldiers of the New Zealand Expeditionary Force Who Fell in the Battle of Sari Bair and in Certain Subsequent Operations and Have No Known Graves*. London, 1925.

Inglis, Ken, *Sacred Places: War Memorials in the Australian Landscape*. Melbourne University Press, Melbourne, 1998.
'Men, women, and war memorials: Anzac Australia'. In Richard White and Penny Russell, *Memories and Dreams: Reflections on Twentieth-century Australia, Pastiche II*: 40–61. Allen & Unwin, St Leonards, NSW, 1997.
'ANZAC and the Australian Military Tradition'. *Current Affairs Bulletin*, 64, 11, 1988.
'The Australians at Gallipoli: I'. *Historical Studies*, 14, 54, April 1970: 219–30.
'The Australians at Gallipoli: II'. *Historical Studies*, 14, 55, October 1970: 361–75.

Jacques, Alain, ed., *La Bataille d'Arras, Avril–Mai 1917*. Documents d'Archéologie et d'Histoire du XXᵉ Siècle, 5, Arras, 1997.

James, Robert Rhodes, *Gallipoli*. Batsford, London, 1965.

Johnson, J.H., *1918: The Unexpected Victory*. Arms and Armour, London, 1997.

Jünger, Ernst, *Storm of Steel*, trans. Michael Hofman. Penguin, Allen Lane, London, 2003.
Copse 125: A Chronicle from the Trench Warfare of 1918. Chatto & Windus, London, 1930.

Keagan, John, *The Face of Battle*. Jonathan Cape, London, 1976.

Kempe, Humphrey, *Participation*. Hawthorn Press, Melbourne, 1973.

Kennedy, Brian, *Silver, Sin and Sixpenny Ale: A Social History of Broken Hill, 1883–1921*. Melbourne University Press, Melbourne, 1978.

Keshen, Jeffrey A., *Propaganda and Censorship During Canada's Great War*. University of Alberta Press, Alberta, 1996.

Lake, Marilyn, *A Divided Society: Tasmania During World War I*. Melbourne University Press, Melbourne, 1975.

Lawrence, Cyril, *Serjeant Lawrence Goes to France* (Peter Yule ed.). Melbourne University Press, Melbourne, 1987.

Lawson, Will, *Historic Trentham, 1914–1917*. Wellington Publishing Co, Wellington, 1917.
Featherston Military Training Camp: Soldiers in the Making. Brett, Auckland, nd.

Lee, John, *A Soldier's Life: General Sir Ian Hamilton 1853–1947*. Macmillan, London, 2000.

Lee, John A., *Civilian into Soldier*. T. Werner Laurie, London, 1937.

Lewis, Edith M., *Joy in the Caring*. N.M. Peryer, Christchurch, 1963.

Liddell Hart, B.H., *The Real War: 1914–1918*. Faber & Faber, London, 1930.

Liddle, Peter H., ed., *Passchendaele in Perspective: The Third Battle of Ypres*. Leo Cooper, London, 1997.

Linklater, Joseph, *On Active Service in South Africa with the Silent Sixth*. McKee, Wellington, nd.

Lodge, A.B., *Lavarack: Rival General*. Allen & Unwin, Sydney, 1998.

Longworth, Philip, *The Unending Vigil: A History of the Commonwealth War Graves Commission, 1917–1984*. Leo Cooper, London, 1985.

Lucas, Sir Charles, ed., *The Empire at War*, vols I–III. Oxford University Press, London, 1924.

Ludendorff, General, *My War Memories, 1914–1918*, vol. II. Hutchinson, London, nd.

McCarthy, Dudley, *Gallipoli to the Somme: The Story of C.E.W. Bean*. John Ferguson, Sydney, 1983.

Macfarlane, David, *Come From Away*. Abacus, London, 1992.

McGibbon, Ian, *The Path to Gallipoli: Defending New Zealand 1840–1915*. GP Books, Wellington, 1991.
ed., *The Oxford Companion to New Zealand Military History*. Oxford University Press, Auckland, 2001.
New Zealand Battlefields and Memorials of the Western Front. Oxford University Press, Auckland, 2000.

Macintyre, Stuart, *The Oxford History of Australia*, Vol. 4, 1901–1942. Oxford University Press, Melbourne, 1986.

Mackenzie, Clutha, ed., *Chronicles of the NZEF*, 1916–1918 (NZEF newspaper).

McKeon, William J., *The Fruitful Years*. William J. McKeon, Wellington, 1973.

McKernan, Michael, *The Australian People and the Great War*. Nelson, Melbourne, 1980.
& M. Browne, eds, *Australia: Two Centuries of War and Peace*. Australian War Memorial/Allen & Unwin, Canberra, 1988.

McKinlay, Ernest, *Ways and By-Ways of a Singing Kiwi: With the NZ Divisional Entertainers in France*. McKinlay, Dunedin, 1939.

McKinnon, Malcolm, ed., *New Zealand Historical Atlas: Visualising New Zealand*. David Bateman, Auckland, 1997.

Maclean, Chris, and Jock Phillips, *The Sorrow and the Pride: New Zealand War Memorials*. GP Books, Wellington, 1990.

Macleod, Jenny, 'General Sir Ian Hamilton and the Dardanelles Commission'. *War in History*, 8, 4, November 2001: 418–41.

McMullin, Ross, *Pompey Elliot*. Scribe, Melbourne, 2002.

Main, J.M., *Conscription: The Australian Debate, 1901–1970*. Cassell, Sydney, 1970.

Malthus, Cecil, *Anzac: A Retrospect*. Reed, Auckland, 2002.
Armentières and the Somme. Reed, Auckland, 2002.

Mann, Leonard, *Flesh in Armour: A Novel*. Robertson & Mullens, Melbourne, 1944.

Maroney, Paul, '"The Great Adventure": The Context and Idealogy of Recruiting in Ontario, 1914–1917'. *Canadian Historical Review*, 77, 1, March 1996: 62–98.

Marshall, S.L.A., *World War I*. American Heritage Press, New York, 1971.

Marshall-Cornwall, General Sir James, *Haig as Military Commander*. B.T. Batsford, London, 1973.

Martin, A.W., *Robert Menzies: A Life*. Vol. 1. 1894–1943. Melbourne University Press, Melbourne, 1993.

Maxwell, J., *Hell's Bells and Mademoiselles*. Angus & Robertson, Sydney, 1932.

Meaney, Neville, *A History of Australian Defence and Foreign Policy, 1901–1923: Vol. 1: The Search for Security in the Pacific, 1901–1914*. Sydney University Press, Sydney, 1976.

Miles, W., *Military Operations, France and Belgium 1916*, vol. 2. HMSO, London, 1938.

Miller, Carmen, *Painting the Map Red: Canada and the South African War 1899–1902*. Canadian War Museum, Montreal & Kingston, 1993.
'The Crucible of War: Canadian and British Troops During the Boer War'. In Peter Dennis and Jeffrey Grey, *The Boer War: Army, Nation and Empire*: 84–98. 1999 Chief of Army/Australian War Memorial Military History Conference. Army History Unit, Canberra, 2000.

Miller, Eric, *Camps, Tramps and Trenches: Diary of a New Zealand Sapper, 1917*. Reed, Wellington, 1939.

Millett, Allan R., & Murray Williamson, *Military Effectiveness, Vol. I The First World War*. Allen & Unwin, Winchester, Mass, 1988.

Mitchell MC, DCM, Captain G.D., *Backs to the Wall*. Angus & Robertson, Sydney, 1937.

Monash, John, *War Letters of General Monash* (F.M. Cutlack ed.). Angus & Robertson, Sydney, 1934.
The Australian Victories in France in 1918. Angus & Robertson, Sydney, 1936.

Moore, A. Briscoe, *The Mounted Riflemen in Sinai and Palestine*. Whitcombe & Tombs, Christchurch, 1920.

Moorhouse, Geoffrey, *Hell's Foundations: A Town, Its Myths and Gallipoli*. Hodder & Stoughton, London, 1992.

Mordike, John, *An Army for a Nation: A History of Australian Military Developments, 1880–1914*. Allen & Unwin, Sydney, 1992.

Morton, Desmond, '"Junior but Sovereign Allies": The Transformation of the Canadian Expeditionary Force, 1914–1918'. *Journal of Imperial and Commonwealth History*, VIII, 1, October 1979.

— *A Military History of Canada*. Hurtig, Edmonton, 1985.

— *When Your Number's Up: The Canadian Soldier in the First World War*. Random House, Toronto, 1993.

— & J.L. Granatstein, *Marching to Armageddon: Canadians and the Great War 1914–1918*. Lester and Orphen Dennys, Toronto, 1989.

Moses, John A., 'Canon David John Garland and the ANZAC Tradition'. *St Mark's Review*, Winter 1993: 12–21.

— 'Canon David John Garland (1864–1939) as Architect of Anzac Day'. *Royal Historical Society of Queensland Journal*, 17, 2, May 1999: 49–64.

— 'The Struggle for Anzac Day 1916–1930 and the Role of the Brisbane Anzac Day Commemoration Committee'. *Journal of the Royal Australian Historical Society*, 88, Part 1, June 2002: 54–74.

— & Christopher Pugsley, eds, *The German Empire and Britain's Pacific Dominions 1871–1919: Essays on the Role of Australia and New Zealand in World Politics in the Age of Imperialism*. Regina Press, Claremont, CA, 2000.

Mosse, George L., *Fallen Soldiers: Reshaping the Memory of the World Wars*. Oxford University Press, New York, 1990.

Mottram, R.H., *Through the Menin Gate*. Chatto & Windus, London, 1932.

Murray, James, *Larrikins: 19th Century Outrage*. Landsdowne Press, Melbourne, 1973.

Murray, Lieut-Colonel P.L., ed., *Official Records of the Australian Military Contingents to the War in South Africa*, Melbourne, 1911.

Neill, J.C., *The New Zealand Tunnelling Company 1915–1919*. Whitcombe & Tombs, Auckland, 1922.

Nevinson, Henry W., *The Dardanelles Campaign*. Nisbet, London, 1920 (rev. edn).

New Zealand at the Front 1917. Written and illustrated by men of the New Zealand Division. London, 1917.

New Zealand at the Front 1918. Written and illustrated by men of the New Zealand Division. London, 1918.

New Zealand Expeditionary Force (Europe), *1914 War Diary*. Government Printer, 1915.

— *Roll of Honour: The Great War 1914–1918*. Government Printer, Wellington, 1924.

New Zealand Government, *The New Zealand Official Year-Book 1915*. Government Printer, Wellington, 1916.

New Zealand Military Forces, *New Zealand Expeditionary Force, Its Provision and Maintenance*. Prepared in the branch of the Chief of General Staff, HQ New Zealand Military Forces. Government Printer, Wellington, 1919.

Nicholson, G.W.L., *Canadian Expeditionary Force: Official History of the Canadian Army in the First World War*. Canadian Department of National Defense, Ottawa, 1962.

Nicol, Sgt C.G., *The Story of Two Campaigns: Official War History of the Auckland Mounted Rifles Regiment, 1914–1919*. Wilson and Horton, Auckland, 1921.

Nicolson, W.N., *Behind the Lines: An Account of Administrative Staff Work in the British Army 1914–1918*. Jonathan Cape, London, 1939.

North, John, *Gallipoli: The Fading Vision*. Faber & Faber, 1936.

O'Connor, P.S., 'The Recruitment of Maori Soldiers 1914–1918'. *Political Science*, XIX, 2, 1967: 48–83.

Officers, *Regimental History of the New Zealand Cyclist Corps in the Great War of 1914–1918*. Whitcombe & Tombs, Auckland, 1922.

Oliver, Dean, 'The Canadians at Passchendaele'. In Peter H. Liddle, ed., *Passchendaele in Perspective: The Third Battle of Ypres*: 255–71. Leo Cooper, London, 1997.

— 'A Canadian Armistice'. In Hugh Cecil and Peter H. Liddle, eds, *At the Eleventh Hour: Reflections, Hopes and Anxieties at the Closing of the Great War, 1918*, pp. 181–88. Leo Cooper, Barnsley, 1998.

Oram, Gerard, *Military Executions During World War I*. Palgrave Macmillan, Basingstoke, 2003.

Orange, Claudia, ed., *The New Zealand Dictionary of Biography*, vol. *III, 1901–1920*. Auckland University Press and Department of Internal Affairs, Auckland, 1996.

Orsman, H.W., ed., *The Dictionary of New Zealand English*. Oxford University Press, Auckland, 1997.

Pakenham, Thomas, *The Boer War*. Weidenfeld & Nicolson, London, 1979.

Palazzo, Albert, *Seeking Victory on the Western Front: The British Army & Chemical Warfare in World War I*. University of Nebraska Press, Lincoln, 2000.

Panichas, George A., *Promise of Greatness: The War of 1914–1918*. Cassell, London, 1968.

Partridge, Eric, *Frank Honeywood, Private: A Personal Record of the 1914–1918 War*. Melbourne University Press, Melbourne, 1929, 1987.

Passingham, Ian, *Pillars of Fire: The Battle of Messines Ridge June 1917*. Sutton, Stroud, 1998.

Pedersen, P.A., *Monash as Military Commander*. Melbourne University Press, Melbourne, 1984.

Phillips, Jock, *A Man's Country: The Image of the Pakeha Male — A History*. Penguin, Auckland, 1987.

Phillips, Jock, Nicholas Boyack & E.P. Malone, *The Great Adventure: New Zealand Soldiers Describe the First World War*. Allen & Unwin/Port Nicholson Press, Wellington, 1988.

Piehler, G. Kurt, *Remembering War the American Way*. Smithsonian Institute, Washington, 1995.

Pitt, Barrie, *1918, The Last Act*. Papermac, London, 1984.

Polaschek, Alan J., *The Complete New Zealand Distinguished Conduct Medal*. Medals Research, Christchurch, 1983.

Powell, Geoffrey, *Plumer: The Soldier's General*. Leo Cooper, London, 1990.

Powles, Lt Col C. Guy, *The New Zealanders in Sinai and Palestine*. Whitcombe & Tombs, Wellington, 1922.

Prior, Robin, & Trevor Wilson, *Command on the Western Front: The Military Career of Sir Henry Rawlinson 1914–1918*. Blackwell, London, 1992.
Passchendaele: The Untold Story. Yale University Press, New Haven 1996.

Pryce, Henry Weston, *Your Old Battalion: War and Peace Verses*. Cornstalk Publishing Company, Sydney, 1926.

Pugsley, Christopher, 'World War I: New Zealanders in France'. In John Dunmore, ed., *New Zealand and the French: Two Centuries of Contact*: 116–26. Heritage Press, Waikanae, 1990.
'"The Honorary Rank of Captain": Artists of the Great War 1914–1918', National Archives, 1990.
On the Fringe of Hell: New Zealanders and Military Discipline in the First World War. Hodder & Stoughton, Auckland, 1991.
'The Maori Battalion in France in the First World War'. In John Dunmore, ed., *The French and the Maori*: 139–51. Heritage Press, Waikanae, 1992.
'Putting the N.Z. back in ANZAC'. *New Zealand Defence Quarterly*, 4, Winter 1994: 35–37.
Te Hokowhitu A Tu: The Maori Pioneer Battalion in the First World War. Reed, Auckland, 1995.
'William George Malone'. In Claudia Orange, ed., *The Dictionary of New Zealand Biography*, vol. III, 1901–1920, pp. 326–28. Auckland University Press and Department of Internal Affairs, Wellington, 1996.
'Andrew Hamilton Russell'. In Claudia Orange, ed., *The Dictionary of New Zealand Biography*, vol. III, 1901–1920: 449–51. Auckland University Press and Department of Internal Affairs, Wellington, 1996.
'The Moles of Arras'. *New Zealand Defence Quarterly*, 18, Spring 1997: 28–31.
'The New Zealand Tunnellers at Arras, 1916–1918'. In Alain Jacques, ed., *La Bataille d'Arras, Avril–Mai 1917*, pp. 15–19. Documents d'Archéologie et d'Histoire du XXᵉ Siècle, 5, Arras, 1997.
'The New Zealand Division at Passchendaele'. In Peter H. Liddle, ed., *Passchendaele in Perspective: The Third Battle of Ypres*: 272–91. Leo Cooper, London, 1997.
'New Zealand: "The Heroes Lie in France"'. In Hugh Cecil and Peter H. Liddle, eds, *At the Eleventh Hour: Reflections, Hopes and Anxieties at the Closing of the Great War, 1918*: 200–212. Leo Cooper, Barnsley, 1998.
'"Who Is Sanders?": New Zealand's Official Cameraman on the Western Front 1917–1919'. *Stout Centre Review*, 5, 1, March 1995: 19–22.
ANZAC: The New Zealanders at Gallipoli. Reed, Auckland, 2000.

'The Second New Zealand Division of 1945: A Comparison with Its 1918 Predecessor'. In John Crawford, ed., *Kia Kaha: New Zealand in the Second World War*: 94–106. Oxford University Press, Auckland, 2000.
'At the Empire's Call: New Zealand Expeditionary Force Planning, 1901–1918'. In John Moses and Christopher Pugsley, eds, *The German Empire and Britain's Pacific Dominions 1871–1919: Essays on the Role of Australia and New Zealand in World Politics in the Age of Imperialism*: 221–38. Regina Press, Claremont, CA, 2000.
'New Zealand: "From the Uttermost Ends of the Earth"'. In John Bourne, Peter Liddle and Ian Whitehead, eds, *The Great World War 1914–1945*, vol. 2, *Who Won? Who Lost? The People's Experience*: 211–32. HarperCollins, London, 2001.
Gallipoli: The New Zealand Story. Reed, Auckland, 2003.
with Laurie Barber, Buddy Mikaere, Nigel Prickett & Rose Young, *Scars on the Heart: Two Centuries of New Zealand at War*. David Bateman, Auckland, 1996.

Putkowski, J., & J. Sykes, *Shot at Dawn*. Wharncliffe Publishing, Barnsley, 1989.

Rawling, Bill, *Surviving Trench Warfare: Technology and the Canadian Corps, 1914–1918*. University of Toronto Press, Toronto, 1992.
'A Resource Not to Be Squandered: The Canadian Corps on the 1918 Battlefield'. In Peter Dennis and Jeffrey Grey, eds, *1918 Defining Victory*: 1–32. Army History Unit, Department of Defence, Canberra, 1999.

Reid, Brian Holden, 'The Influence of the Vietnam Syndrome on the Writing of Civil War History'. *Journal of the RUSI*, February 2002: 44–52.

Remarque, E.M., *All Quiet on the Western Front*. G.P. Putman's Sons, London, 1929.

Repington, Lt-Col C.A. à Court, *The First World War 1914–1918*, 2 vols., *Personal Experiences*. Constable, London, 1920.

Report of His Majesty's Commissioners Appointed to Enquire into the Military Preparations and Other Matters Connected with the War in South Africa. HMSO, London, 1903.

Roberts, Chris, 'The Landing at Anzac: A Reassessment'. *Journal of the Australian War Memorial*, 22, April 1993: 25–34.

Robertson, John, *With the Cameliers in Palestine*. Reed, Dunedin, 1938.

Robertson, John, *ANZAC and Empire: The Tragedy and Glory of Gallipoli*. Hamlyn, Melbourne, 1990.

Robson, L.L., *The First A.I.F.: A Study of Its Recruitment 1914–1918*. Melbourne University Press, Melbourne, 1970.

Ross, Jane, *The Myth of the Digger: The Australian Soldier in Two World Wars*. Hale and Iremonger, Sydney, 1985.

Ross, Malcolm, 'The New Zealand Forces in the War'. In Sir Charles Lucas, ed., *The Empire at War*, vol. III:

267–318. Oxford University Press, London, 1924.

Roy, Reginald H., *The Journal of Private Fraser, 1914–1918, Canadian Expeditionary Force*. CEF Books, Nepean, 1998.

Roze, Anne, *Les Lieux de la Grande Guerre*. Réunion des Musées Nationaux, Paris, 1996.

Sadler, Peter, 'Bean and Gellibrand: Some Implications of Their Friendship'. *Journal of the Australian War Memorial*, 23, October 1993: 36–44.

The Paladin: A Life of Major-General Sir John Gellibrand. Oxford University Press, Melbourne, 2000.

Samuels, Martin, *Doctrine and Dogma, German and British Infantry Tactics in the First World War*. Greenwood Press, Westport, CT, 1992.

Sanders, Liman von, *Five Years in Turkey*. Williams and Wilkins, Baltimore, 1928.

Scates, Bruce, & Raelene Frances, *Women and the Great War*. Cambridge University Press, Melbourne, 1997.

Schreiber, Shane B., *Shock Army of the British Empire: The Canadian Corps in the Last 100 Days of the Great War*. Praeger, Westport, CT, 1997.

Scott, Peter, 'Law and Orders: Discipline and Morale in the British Armies in France, 1917'. In Peter H. Liddle, ed., *Passchendaele in Perspective: The Third Battle of Ypres*: 349–68. Leo Cooper, London, 1997.

Serle, Geoffrey, *John Monash: A Biography*. Melbourne University Press, Melbourne, 1982.

Shadbolt, Maurice, *Voices of Gallipoli*. Hodder & Stoughton, Auckland, 1988.

Sheffield, G.D., *Leadership in the Trenches: Officer-Man Relations, Morale and Discipline in the British Army in the Era of the First World War*. Macmillan, Basingstoke, 2000.

Forgotten Victory: The First World War, Myths and Realities. Headline, London, 2001.

'The Australians at Pozières: Command and Control on the Somme, 1916'. In David French and Brian Holden Reid, eds, *The British General Staff: Reform and Innovation, 1890–1939*: 112–26. Frank Cass, London, 2002.

The Somme. Cassell, London, 2003.

'British High Command in the First World War: An Overview'. In Gary Sheffield and Geoffrey Till, eds, *The Challenges of High Command: The British Experience*: 15–25. Palgrave Macmillan, Basingstoke, 2003.

Simkins, Peter, *Kitchener's Army: The Raising of the New Armies, 1914–1916*. Manchester University Press, Manchester, 1988.

'The War Experience of a Typical Kitchener Division: The 18th Division'. In Hugh Cecil and Peter H. Liddle, eds, *Facing Armageddon: The First World War Experienced*: 297–313. Leo Cooper, London, 1996.

Sinclair, Keith, *A Destiny Apart: New Zealand's Search for National Identity*. Unwin, Wellington, 1986.

Sloan, Lt-Col H., *The Purple and Gold: A History of the 30th Battalion*. Facsimile of Sydney, 1938 edn.

Smart, Judith, & Tony Wood, eds, *An ANZAC Muster: War and Society in Australia and New Zealand, 1914–1918 and 1939–1945*. Monash Publications in History, Melbourne, 1991.

Smith, Lt the Hon. Staniforth, *Australian Campaigns in the Great War, Being a Concise History of the Australian Naval and Military Forces 1914–1918*. Macmillan & Co, Melbourne, 1919.

Smithers, A.J., *Sir John Monash: A Biography of Australia's Most Distinguished Soldier of the First World War*. Leo Cooper, London, 1973.

Solling, Max, & Peter Reynolds, *Leichhardt: On the Margins of the City*. Allen & Unwin, St Leonards, NSW, 1997.

Somers, Sir Edward, *Review of Deaths by Execution in the Great War of 1914–1918: A Report by Sir Edward Somers*. Tabled by the Hon. Max Bradford, Minister of Defence, House of Representatives, New Zealand, 15 October 1999.

Spagnoly, Tony, *The Anatomy of a Raid: Australia at Celtic Wood, 9th October 1917*. MultiDream Publications, London, 1991.

Steel, Nigel, & Peter Hart, *Defeat at Gallipoli*. Macmillan, London, 1994.

Stevens, K.M., 'Maungatapere, A History and Reminiscence'. *Whangarei Advocate*, Whangarei, nd.

Stewart, Col H., *The New Zealand Division 1916–1919: A Popular History Based on Official Records*. Whitcombe & Tombs, Auckland, 1921.

Strachan, Hew, *The First World War*, Vol. I: *To Arms*. Oxford University Press, Oxford, 2001.

Strawson, John, *Gentlemen in Khaki: The British Army, 1890–1990*. Secker & Warburg, London, 1989.

Studholme, Lt-Col John, *Record of Personal Services During the War of Officers, Nurses, and First-Class Warrant Officers; and Other Facts Relating to the NZEF*. Government Printer, Wellington, 1928.

Taylor F.W., & T.A. Cusack, *Nulli Secundus: A History of the Second Battalion, A.I.F. 1914–1919*. Facsimile 1942 edition. John Burridge Military Antiques, Swanbourne, WA, 1992.

Taylor, William, *The Twilight Hour: A Personal Account of World War 1*. Sutherland, Morrinsville, 1978.

Terraine, John, *Douglas Haig, the Educated Soldier*. Hutchinson, London, 1963.

The Road to Passchendaele: The Flanders Offensive of 1917: A Study in Inevitability. Leo Cooper, London, 1977.

The Smoke and the Fire: Myths and Anti-myths of War, 1861–1945. Sidgwick & Jackson, London, 1980.

To Win a War: 1918 The Year of Victory. Sidgwick & Jackson, London, 1978, 1981.

White Heat: The New Warfare 1914–1918. Sidgwick & Jackson, London, 1982.

The First World War 1914–1918. Leo Cooper, London, 1965, 1983.

Impacts of War 1914 & 1918. Leo Cooper, London, 1970, 1993.

Thomson, Alistair, '"Steadfast Until Death"? C.E.W. Bean and the Representation of Australian Military Manhood.' *Australian Historical Studies*, 23, 93, October 1989: 462–78.

'"The Vilest Libel of the War"? Imperial Politics and the Official Histories of Gallipoli'. *Australian Historical Studies*, 25, 101, October 1993: 628–36.

Anzac Memories: Living with the Legend. Oxford University Press, Melbourne, 1994.

Thorn, James, *Peter Fraser*. Odhams Press, London, 1952.

Till, Geoffrey, 'Brothers in Arms: The British Army and Navy at the Dardanelles'. In Hugh Cecil and Peter H. Liddle, eds, *Facing Armageddon: The First World War Experienced*: 160–79. Leo Cooper, London, 1996.

'The Gallipoli Campaign: Command Performances'. In Gary Sheffield and Geoffrey Till, eds, *The Challenges of High Command: The British Experience*: 34–56. Palgrave Macmillan, Basingstoke, 2003.

Tolerton, Jane, *Ettie: A Life of Ettie Rout*. Penguin, Auckland, 1992.

Travers, Timothy, *The Killing Ground: The British Army, the Western Front and the Emergence of Modern Warfare, 1900–1918*. Allen & Unwin, London, 1987.

Gallipoli 1915. Tempus, Stroud, 2001.

'The Ottoman Crisis of May 1915 at Gallipoli'. *War in History*, 8, 1, January 2001: 72–86.

Twistleton, Corp. F., *With the New Zealanders at the Front*. Whitcombe & Tombs, Christchurch, 1902.

Vance, Jonathan F., *Death So Noble: Memory, Meaning, and the First World War*. UBC Press, Vancouver, 1997.

Wahlert, Glenn, *The Other Enemy? Australian Soldiers and the Military Police*. Oxford University Press, Melbourne, 1999.

Waite, Major Fred, *The New Zealanders at Gallipoli*. Whitcombe & Tombs, Wellington, 1919.

Walker, James W. St G., 'Race and Recruitment in World War I: Enlistment of Visible Minorities in the Canadian Expeditionary Force. *Canadian Historical Review*, LXX, 1, 1989: 1–26.

Walker, Jonathan, *The Blood Tub: General Gough and the Battle of Bullecourt, 1917*. Spellmount, Staplehurst, 1998.

Wavell, Field-Marshal Earl, *The Palestine Campaigns*. Constable, London, 1968.

Weston, Lt-Col C.H., *Three Years with New Zealanders*. Skeffington & Son, London, nd.

White, Richard, 'The Soldier as Tourist: The Australian Experience of the Great War'. *War & Society*, 5, 1, May 1987: 63–78.

& Penny Russell, *Memories and Dreams: Reflections on Twentieth-century Australia, Pastiche II*. Allen & Unwin, St Leonards, NSW, 1997.

Whyte, W. Farmer, *William Morris Hughes: His Life and Times*. Angus & Robertson, Sydney, 1957.

Wilcox, Craig, assisted by Janice Aldridge, eds, *The Great War: Gains and Losses — ANZAC and Empire*. Australian War Memorial and Australian National University, 1995.

Australia's Boer War: The War in South Africa 1899–1902. Oxford University Press, Melbourne, 2002.

Williams, Jeffery, *Byng of Vimy: General and Governor General*. Leo Cooper, London, 1983.

Williams, John F., *ANZACs, the Media and the Great War*. University of New South Wales Press, Sydney, 1999.

Wilson DSO, RGA, Major R.A., *A Two Years Interlude: France 1916–1918*. Keeling & Mundy, Palmerston North, nd.

Wilson, Trevor, *The Myriad Faces of War: Britain and the Great War, 1914–1918*. Polity Press, Cambridge, 1986.

Winter, Denis, *Death's Men: Soldiers of the Great War*. Penguin, Harmondsworth, 1979.

Haig's Command: A Reassessment. Viking, London, 1991.

ed., *Making the Legend: The War Writings of C.E.W. Bean*. University of Queensland Press, St Lucia, 1992.

25 April 1915: The Inevitable Tragedy. University of Queensland Press, St Lucia, 1994.

Winter, Jay, *Sites of Memory, Sites of Mourning: The Great War in European Cultural History*. Cambridge University Press, Cambridge, 1995.

Wintle, Justin, ed., *The Dictionary of War Quotations*. John Curtis and Hodder & Stoughton, London, 1989.

Wise, H., *New Zealand Index, 1917: A Valuable Handbook to Every Place in New Zealand*. H. Wise & Co, Wellington, 1917.

Wise, S.F., 'The Black Day of the German Army: Australians and Canadians at Amiens, August 1918'. In Peter Dennis and Jeffrey Grey, eds, *1918 Defining Victory*: 1–32. Army History Unit, Department of Defence, Canberra, 1999.

Woodward, David R., *Lloyd George and the Generals*. University of Delaware Press, Newark, 1983.

Wren, Eric, *Randwick to Hargicourt: The History of the 3rd Battalion A.I.F.* Ronald G. McDonald, Sydney, 1935.

Wynne, Captain G.C., *If Germany Attacks: The Battle in Depth in the West*. Greenwood Press, Westport, CT, 1940, 1976.

INDEX